# Uprooted

Each year, millions of people are uprooted from their homes by wars, repression, and natural disasters. In *Uprooted*, Volha Charnysh presents a fresh perspective on the developmental consequences of mass displacement, arguing that accommodating the displaced population can strengthen receiving states and benefit local economies. Drawing on extensive research on post-WWII Poland and West Germany, Charnysh shows that the rupture of social ties and increased cultural diversity in affected communities not only decreased social cohesion but also shored up the demand for state-provided resources, which facilitated the accumulation of state capacity. Over time, areas that received a larger and more diverse influx of migrants achieved higher levels of entrepreneurship, education, and income. With its rich insights and compelling evidence, *Uprooted* challenges common assumptions about the costs of forced displacement and cultural diversity and proposes a novel mechanism linking wars to state-building.

Volha Charnysh is an associate professor of political science at the Massachusetts Institute of Technology. Her work has been published in journals including the *American Political Science Review, Annual Review of Political Science, British Journal of Political Science, Comparative Political Studies*, and *World Politics*. She holds a PhD from Harvard University.

## Cambridge Studies in Comparative Politics

*General Editor*

Kathleen Thelen, *Massachusetts Institute of Technology*

*Associate Editors*

Lisa Blaydes, *Stanford University*
Catherine Boone, *London School of Economics and Political Science*
Thad Dunning, *University of California, Berkeley*
Anna Grzymala-Busse, *Stanford University*
Torben Iversen, *Harvard University*
Stathis Kalyvas, *University of Oxford*
Melanie Manion, *Duke University*
Prerna Singh, *Brown University*
Dan Slater, *University of Michigan*
Susan Stokes, *Yale University*
Tariq Thachil, *University of Pennsylvania*
Erik Wibbels, *University of Pennsylvania*

*Series Founder*

Peter Lange, *Duke University*

*Editor Emeritus*

Margaret Levi, *Stanford University*

*Other Books in the Series*

Christopher Adolph, *Bankers, Bureaucrats, and Central Bank Politics: The Myth of Neutrality*
Michael Albertus, *Autocracy and Redistribution: The Politics of Land Reform*
Michael Albertus, *Property without Rights: Origins and Consequences of the Property Rights Gap*
Santiago Anria, *When Movements Become Parties: The Bolivian MAS in Comparative Perspective*
Ben W. Ansell, *From the Ballot to the Blackboard: The Redistributive Political Economy of Education*
Ben W. Ansell and Johannes Lindvall, *Inward Conquest: The Political Origins of Modern Public Services*
Ben W. Ansell and David J. Samuels, *Inequality and Democratization: An Elite-Competition Approach*
Ana Arjona, *Rebelocracy: Social Order in the Colombian Civil War*
Leonardo R. Arriola, *Multi-Ethnic Coalitions in Africa: Business Financing of Opposition Election Campaigns*

*(Continued after the index)*

# Uprooted

## How post-WWII Population Transfers Remade Europe

VOLHA CHARNYSH

*Massachusetts Institute of Technology*

CAMBRIDGE
UNIVERSITY PRESS

# CAMBRIDGE
## UNIVERSITY PRESS

Shaftesbury Road, Cambridge CB2 8EA, United Kingdom

One Liberty Plaza, 20th Floor, New York, NY 10006, USA

477 Williamstown Road, Port Melbourne, VIC 3207, Australia

314–321, 3rd Floor, Plot 3, Splendor Forum, Jasola District Centre,
New Delhi – 110025, India

103 Penang Road, #05–06/07, Visioncrest Commercial, Singapore 238467

Cambridge University Press is part of Cambridge University Press & Assessment,
a department of the University of Cambridge.

We share the University's mission to contribute to society through the pursuit of
education, learning and research at the highest international levels of excellence.

www.cambridge.org
Information on this title: www.cambridge.org/9781009442008

DOI: 10.1017/9781009441995

First published 2025

*A catalogue record for this publication is available from the British Library*

*Library of Congress Cataloging-in-Publication Data*
NAMES: Charnysh, Volha, author.
TITLE: Uprooted : how post-WWII population transfers remade Europe / Volha
Charnysh, Massachusetts Institute of Technology.
DESCRIPTION: Cambridge ; New York, NY : Cambridge University Press, 2025. |
Series: Cambridge studies in comparative politics |
Includes bibliographical references and index. |
IDENTIFIERS: LCCN 2024011990 | ISBN 9781009442008 (hardback) |
ISBN 9781009441995 (ebook)
SUBJECTS: LCSH: Population transfers – Germans – History – 20th century. |
Forced migration – Germany (West) – History. |
Forced migration – Poland – History – 20th century. | World War, 1939–1945 – Peace. |
Germany (West) – Politics and government. | Poland – Politics and
government – 1945–1980. | Europe – Ethnic relations.
CLASSIFICATION: LCC D820.P72 G394 2025 | DDC 940.53/1450943–dc23/eng/20240725
LC record available at https://lccn.loc.gov/2024011990

ISBN 978-1-009-44200-8 Hardback
ISBN 978-1-009-44197-1 Paperback

# Contents

# Figures

# Maps

# Tables

# Preface and Acknowledgments

This project is inspired by the history of my native region – a history at many turns tragic but also rich in human stories. My hometown Grodno was part of the Russian Empire on the eve of WWI, then part of Poland in the interwar period, and during WWII was incorporated into the Belarusian Soviet Republic, which became independent in 1991. It saw a dramatic turnover of its population during and after WWII: In the 1930s, Grodno was 42 percent Polish and 40 percent Jewish; today, it is predominantly Belarusian. When I was a teenager in the 2000s, I heard many wistful comments about how much better off Grodno would have been had Poland's border been drawn further to the east in 1945. Many in my community were rediscovering their Polish roots and seeking ways to emigrate west.

The research opportunities stemming from Eastern Europe's fluid borders and identities came into focus during my PhD work at Harvard. I jumped at the opportunity to use my rusty Polish and do fieldwork closer to my native region. During a year in Poland, I occasionally saw my parents and brother back in Grodno. It was a short trip – in theory – but could take many hours owing to lengthy inspections at the Polish–Belarusian border. Cramped into a small minibus on long nights, I had time to reflect on the waves of migrants who had passed through there in the wake of WWII, en route to a new life in western Poland.

Having the motivation to write a book is one thing – bringing it to fruition is another. This book would not have been possible without the enduring support of many kind and brilliant people. It started through long conversations with my PhD advisor, Grzegorz Ekiert, who also shared my deep attachment to Eastern Europe. Grzegorz, our many conversations about life in western Poland have left an indelible mark on this work!

I would also like to thank the other members of my dissertation committee – Bart Bonikowski, Timothy Colton, Ryan Enos, and Jeffry Frieden – for their unwavering encouragement and diligent reading of numerous drafts. Jeff, thank you for checking in with me throughout graduate school, asking incisive questions, and prodding me to improve my theory. Ryan, I am grateful for your guidance in introducing me to experiments and spatial analysis in political science and for providing level-headed advice on this book and related projects. Bart, I appreciate your invaluable insights on nationalism and ethnicity, as well as your contribution in incorporating sociological perspectives into my research. Tim, thank you for helping me decide to attend Harvard at the start of my graduate school experience and for remaining a supporting presence in my academic career ever since. I also benefited tremendously from insightful discussions with Daniel Ziblatt, whose work inspired me to work in the field of historical political economy.

I would like to thank the participants of my book conference – Anna Grzymala-Busse, Evan Lieberman, Prerna Singh, David Stasavage, Andreas Wimmer, and Daniel Ziblatt – who helped me soldier through a very difficult period during COVID-19. Your insightful feedback, scholarly wisdom, and intellectual rigor have been instrumental throughout the entire process. Evan Lieberman, who chaired my book workshop on Zoom during a long COVID winter, has been a source of tremendous intellectual and emotional support. Evan – I am so grateful for your mentorship and advice over the years.

I also benefited from exchanges with Michael Bernhard, Devin Caughey, Mark Dincecco, Eugene Finkel, Timothy Frye, Scott Gehlbach, Avner Greif, Peter Hall, Yossi Harpaz, Daniel Hidalgo, Jeffrey Kopstein, Chappell Lawson, Isabela Mares, Harris Mylonas, Gareth Nellis, Leonid Peisakhin, Didac Queralt, Grigore Pop-Eleches, Ben Schneider, Kathy Thelen, Lily Tsai, Andrzej Sakson, Jan Vogler, Yuhua Wang, Jason Wittenberg, and Christina Zuber who read drafts, attended my research presentations, and encouraged me along the way. Paul Staniland and Abbey Steele provided valuable suggestions at the tail end of the project, encouraging me to sharpen the introduction just as writer's fatigue was setting in. Max Schaub has helped vet ideas about the impact of forced displacement in Germany, navigate the inscrutable German bureaucracy, and successfully obtain census publications from a distance.

I owe so much to my Harvard grad school friends and MIT colleagues, who not only commented on multiple drafts of this book but also kept me motivated on this long journey. In particular, I'd like to thank Tomasz Blusiewicz, James Conran, Leslie Finger, Noam Gidron, Shelby Grossman, Alexander Hertel-Fernandez, Jeffrey Javed, Konstantin Kashin, John Marshall, Noah Nathan, Brendan McElroy, Agustina Paglayan, and George Yin for comments on the content and Charlotte Cavaillé, Mai Hassan, and Noah Nathan for advice about the publishing process. At MIT, Mariya Grinberg, In Song Kim, Erik Lin-Greenberg, Rich Nielsen, Ariel White, and Bernardo Zacka made their way through several messy chapters and somehow emerged with constructive criticism and words of encouragement.

I am indebted to participants at seminars and conferences at Harvard University, Princeton University, University of Montreal, Massachusetts Institute of Technology, London School of Economics, Stanford University, University of Michigan, Center for the Study of Governance and Society at King's College London, Higher School of Economics in Moscow, Brown University, Ohio State University, University of Konstanz, Duke University, University of Virginia, Columbia University, the Wissenschaftszentrum Berlin, and the Global Diversity Lab at MIT.

My fieldwork in Poland and Germany was made possible by many generous people. Tomasz Zarycki extended me a warm welcome at the University of Warsaw and shared shapefiles of Polish administrative units. Marek Okólski invited me to present at the Center for Migration Studies. Beata Halicka introduced me to historians and sociologists working on Poland's western and northern territories in Słubice, Poland. Marek and Asya Makola provided company, feedback, and invaluable research assistance. Ruud Koopmans welcomed me for a research stay at the Migration, Integration, Transnationalization unit at the Wissenschaftszentrum Berlin.

My special thanks go to Anna Weissman, BreAnne Fleer, and Esteban Dominguez-Lash, who helped produce the graphs, gather data, and proofread. Valentina Pugliano and Iacob Koch-Weser helped me edit the book from cover to cover; their meticulous attention to detail and dedication to refining the prose have greatly enhanced the overall quality of the book.

My research benefited from the financial support of the Social Studies Research Council, Harvard Center for European Studies, Princeton University, and the Harvard Weatherhead Center for International Studies. The Niehaus Fellowship at Princeton University and the Hoover National Fellowship at Stanford helped me see the book and related projects through to completion by providing an intellectual community and quiet time to write.

Finally, I owe a great debt of gratitude to my family. Thank you, Iacob, for helping me keep things in perspective, for taking such good care of our two cats, for putting up with my terrible work habits, for uprooting yourself from DC to Boston to support my career at MIT, and not least, for painstakingly editing numerous drafts of this manuscript and related work. I am also grateful to my husband's family in Germany for generously offering me a space to stay and work.

Last but not least, my parents. My mother has always been my biggest supporter. She offered to go to the archives and libraries herself! And she always brought me amazing food and words of encouragement. My father, along with my brother, helped enter data that I collected from the archives during my time as a graduate student. My parents cannot read this book in English, but they know the dedication it took. So I dedicate this book to them.

# Abbreviations

| | |
|---|---|
| BHE | *Block der Heimatvertriebenen und Entrechteten* (Bloc of Expellees and Dispossessed Persons) |
| BSOP | *Biuro Studiów Osadniczo-Przesiedleńczych* (Bureau for Resettlement Studies) |
| CDU | Christian Democratic Union of Germany |
| CSU | Christian Social Union |
| DiD | Difference-in-differences |
| DM | Deutsche Mark |
| DNVP | *Deutschnationale Volkspartei* (German National People's Party) |
| DP | Displaced Person |
| EAC | European Advisory Commission |
| EU | European Union |
| FDP | Free Democratic Party |
| FF | *Freiwillige Feuerwehr* (Volunteer Fire Brigade) |
| GDP | Gross Domestic Product |
| GNP | Gross National Product |
| GDR | German Democratic Republic |
| HASt | *Heimatauskunftstellen* (Homeland information centers) |
| IRO | International Refugee Organization |
| KfW | *Kreditanstalt für Wiederaufbau* (Reconstruction Loan Corporation) |
| KLD | *Kongres Liberalno-Demokratyczny* (Congress of Liberal Democrats) |
| KPD | *Kommunistische Partei Deutschlands* (Communist Party of Germany) |
| LAG | *Lastenausgleichsgesetz* (Equalization of Burdens Law) |
| LSO | Liaison and Security Office |
| LZS | *Ludowy Zespół Sportowy* (Sports Club) |
| MGR | Military Government Regulations |
| MO | *Milicja Obywatelska* (Citizens' Militia) |
| MZO | *Ministerstwo Ziem Odzyskanych* (Ministry for the Recovered Territories) |

| NGO | Non-Governmental Organization |
|---|---|
| NKVD | *Narodnyj Komissariat Vnutrennih Del* (People's Commissariat for Internal Affairs) |
| NSDAP | *Nationalsozialistische Deutsche Arbeiterpartei* (Nazi Party) |
| OLS | Ordinary least squares |
| OMGUS | Office of Military Government, United States |
| OSP | *Ochotnicza Straż Pożarna* (Volunteer Fire Brigade) |
| PGR | *Państwowe Gospodarstwo Rolne* (State Agricultural Farm) |
| PKWN | *Polski Komitet Wyzwolenia Narodowego* (Polish Committee of National Liberation) |
| PPR | *Polska Partia Robotnicza* (Polish Workers' Party) |
| PZPR | *Polska Zjednoczona Partia Robotnicza* (Polish United Workers' Party) |
| PSL | *Polskie Stronnictwo Ludowe* (Polish People's Party) |
| PUR | *Państwowy Urząd Repatriacyjny* (State Repatriation Office) |
| PZZ | *Polski Związek Zachodni* (Polish Western Union) |
| RDD | Regression discontinuity design |
| SLD | *Sojusz Lewicy Demokratycznej* (Democratic Left Alliance) |
| SPD | *Sozialdemokratische Partei Deutschlands* (Social Democratic Party) |
| SSR | Soviet Socialist Republic |
| TRZZ | *Towarzystwo Rozwoju Ziem Zachodnich* (Association for the Development of the Western Territories) |
| UB | *Urzędy Bezpieczeństwa* (Security Offices) |
| UD | *Unia Demokratyczna* (Democratic Union Party) |
| UPA | *Ukrayins'ka Povstans'ka Armiia* (Ukrainian Insurgent Army) |
| UNRRA | United Nations Relief and Rehabilitation Administration |
| USSR | Union of Soviet Socialist Republics |
| WWI | World War I |
| WWII | World War II |
| ZSCh | *Związek Samopomocy Chłopskiej* (Peasant Self-Help Association) |
| ZSL | *Zjednoczone Stronnictwo Ludowe* (United Peasant Party) |
| ZvD | *Zentralverband vertriebener Deutscher* (Central Association of Expelled Germans) |
| ZvF | *Zentralverband der Flieger- und Währungsgeschädigten* (Central Association of Bomb and Currency Damaged) |

PART I

# INTRODUCTION

# Understanding Forced Migration

Świebodzin, a town of about 22,000 inhabitants in western Poland, hosts two large monuments. One is more famous: At a height of 36 m, it once claimed the Guinness World Record as the tallest Jesus statue. The other is more remarkable: a large gray hexagon topped with three white crosses. Known as the Kresy Necropolis (*Pomnik Nekropolii Kresowych*), it lists some 400 cemeteries around the world where the ancestors of Świebodzin's current residents are buried. Inside the monument are urns with soil from those faraway cemeteries. The monument was installed in 2015, on the seventieth anniversary of WWII, to pay tribute to the town's migratory history.

Świebodzin's residents trace their origins to hundreds of localities in Poland and abroad. This is no coincidence: Świebodzin experienced a near-complete turnover of its population in the wake of WWII. The same holds true for most localities in western Poland (see Map 1.1). In 1945, Poland's borders shifted 200 km to the west – the country received a portion of German territory, in return for ceding its eastern borderlands to the USSR. The redrawing of the borders had massive human consequences. Some eight million ethnic Germans, including the inhabitants of Świebodzin (then called Schwiebus), were expelled from what became western Poland. They were replaced, in turn, by Poles displaced from the eastern borderlands and elsewhere.

This reconfiguration of territory and people resulted from a joint decision by the USSR, the United States, and Britain. Their ostensible goal was to reduce interstate conflict by creating ethnically homogeneous nation-states. Removing ethnic minorities was widely regarded as a legitimate approach to mitigating conflict; so much so that it received far less attention from the Allies than the positioning of the borders themselves (Frank 2017, 227).

These population "transfers," combined with the genocide and ethnic engineering perpetrated by Nazi Germany during the war, made Poland one of the most ethnically homogeneous states in postwar Europe. This was an

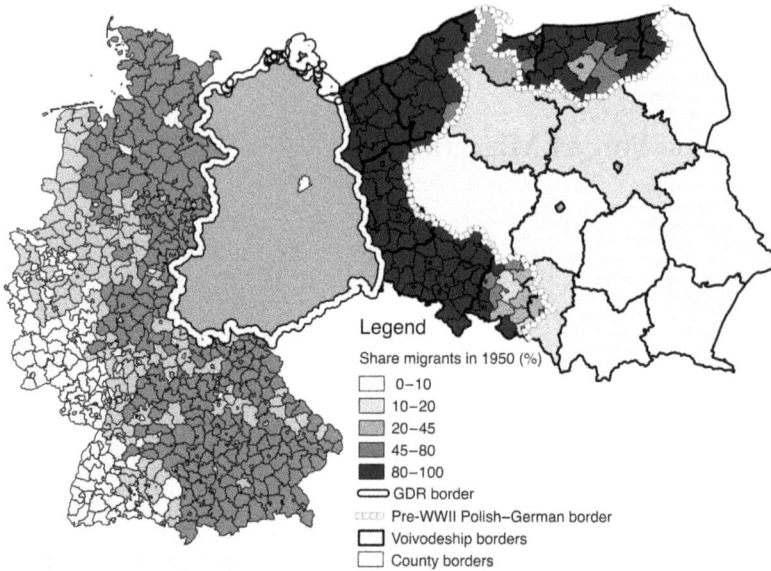

Map 1.1 Extent of uprooting in Germany (left) and Poland (right) after WWII. Data for the GDR (DDR) are at country level. Data for Polish territory east of the pre-WWII border are at the voivodeship level.

extraordinary outcome. In 1931, ethnic minorities had constituted nearly a third of the country's population.[1]

In parallel, West Germany received some 12.5 million migrants expelled from the territories annexed to Poland, in addition to ethnic Germans expelled from other countries in Eastern and Central Europe (see Map 1.1). In some localities, the German "expellees" came to outnumber the existing population. Reminiscent of the Kresy Necropolis in Świebodzin, monuments were erected in German towns to commemorate the expulsions, with soil taken from cemeteries in faraway places.

How did the uprooted populations form ties to their new states and societies? Did increased ethnic homogeneity reduce conflict and strengthen social solidarity? How did the influx of millions of displaced individuals affect the receiving states' ability to govern? What were the short- and long-term economic consequences of mass immigration for receiving communities?

---

[1] According to the 1931 Census, which undercounted ethnic minorities in the east of the country, only 68.9 percent of the population was Polish. Poland's three million Jews largely perished in the Holocaust. After WWII, most members of Poland's Ukrainian, Lithuanian, and Belarusian minorities were located east of the new Polish–Soviet border, in their ethnic republics. The fate of Poland's German minority as well as the *Volksdeutsche* settled in Poland during the war was similar to the fate of Germans who lived east of the Oder–Neisse line.

Answering these questions is critical in today's world. The number of forcibly displaced people has surpassed 100 million. The grim reality is also manifest in Europe, which is currently experiencing its largest refugee crisis since WWII. Fourteen million Ukrainians have fled their country following Russia's invasion in January 2022. Refugees crossing into the EU today are finding shelter in the same towns and villages emptied by bombing, deportation, and genocide eighty years prior; only now, Poles and Germans are on the other side, providing shelter to the displaced Ukrainians.

This book uses the cases of Poland and West Germany to reexamine existing theories about the consequences of mass migration and ethnic homogeneity for state building, public goods provision, and economic development. My contention is that although forced migration has very real negative impacts on societal cohesion and public goods provision in the short term, it ultimately creates opportunities for building stronger states and more prosperous economies.

I will make three related arguments. First, shared nationality does not guarantee acceptance of the uprooted population in receiving communities. Rearranging ethnically homogeneous populations in space is bound to create new cleavages based on migration status and place of origin. These cleavages are no less contentious than ethnic divisions and can undermine the cooperation required to provide collective goods. Second, because heterogeneous societies find it difficult to cooperate, they turn to the state as the main provider of collective and private goods. States that respond to this increased demand not only succeed in incorporating the uprooted population but also expand their capacity. Third, increased state capacity, fused with the skills and knowledge brought by migrants from different places of origin, improves long-run economic performance. Polish and West German communities that were on the receiving end of forced migration after WWII achieved superior levels of income and entrepreneurship. Moreover, communities that received migrants of more diverse origins outperformed those which received more homogeneous groups.

Altogether, postwar population movements diversified Polish and German societies in profound ways and, in so doing, contributed to the growth of each country's state capacity and improved economic performance.

## EXISTING RESEARCH ON FORCED MIGRATION AND ETHNIC DIVERSITY

In 1945, the Allies agreed to uproot millions of people in order to create ethnically homogeneous states and societies. They viewed ethnic minorities as "a constant source of grievances and friction," to quote the British foreign secretary Anthony Eden (Frank 2017, 233). Their decision-making was grounded in strong assumptions regarding *national* identities. Individuals' ties to abstract national communities were considered more important than their ties to the very real communities in which they lived (Long 2013, 47). In the parlance of modern political science, this was a primordialist – or essentialist – view of ethnicity. It held that ethnic identities derive from deeply ingrained biological or cultural attributes, remain stable over time, and produce deep "emotional" attachments. The Allies thus supported the elimination of ethnonational differences as a way to reduce conflict and facilitate democratization.

Scholarly confidence in the ingrained and unchanging features of ethnic attachments has dwindled over time. The view that separating populations can be a viable solution to conflict is now expressed rarely and with caveats (e.g., Kaufmann 1998). Ethnicity is now viewed as constructed and contingent, with individuals able to choose from and hold multiple identities. Institutions, economic resources, demography, and politics are all believed to shape individual identity at any given point (Laitin 1998). Not only has constructivism achieved hegemony in research on ethnicity across the social sciences (Wimmer 2013, 2), but scholars also no longer subscribe to the idea that the presence of multiple ethnic groups and strong ethnic attachments invariably produce conflict. Our theories of conflict and cooperation in ethnically heterogeneous societies have become more nuanced, with greater attention paid to the role of electoral incentives and political institutions, of social norms and networks, of resource scarcity, and of economic inequality.[2]

Despite this shift in our understanding of ethnic identity, ethnic homogeneity remains in high regard among researchers. The idea that ethnic divisions undermine economic development is "one of the most powerful hypotheses in political economy" today (Banerjee, Iyer, and Somanathan 2005, 636). A large body of research has found a negative relationship between ethnic heterogeneity and prosocial behavior, institutional quality, public goods, democratic governance, welfare spending, and economic performance.[3] Studies have shown that empathy and prosocial behavior stop at ethnic boundaries, and that people are less willing to contribute to the welfare of individuals from different cultures and backgrounds (Greenwald and Pettigrew 2014). Heterogeneous societies are believed to be at a disadvantage because their members

---

[2] On the role of electoral incentives and political competition see Wilkinson (2004); Wimmer, Cederman, and Min (2009); Kopstein and Wittenberg (2018). On the role of voluntary associations and economic interdependence see Varshney (2002); Jha (2013). Economic factors have been highlighted in Dancygier (2010); Fearon and Laitin (2011); Schaub, Gereke, and Baldassarri (2020).

[3] Studies on the costs of ethnic diversity include Alesina, Baqir, and Easterly (1999); Luttmer (2001); Knack (2002); Uslaner (2002); Stolle, Soroka, and Johnston (2008); Gershman and Rivera (2018). Some recent articles have challenged the universal nature of this relationship by demonstrating the endogeneity of contemporary levels of ethnic diversity to historical levels of state capacity and public goods provision (Darden and Mylonas 2016; Singh and vom Hau 2016; Wimmer 2016), or by highlighting the role of ethnic discrimination as an alternative mechanism for the "diversity detriment" finding (Lee 2017) Nonetheless, the notion that homogeneity is beneficial remains relatively unchallenged.

distrust one another and have a reduced capacity for collective action.[4] Ethnic diversity is seen to undermine the accumulation of social capital, defined as "the ability of actors to secure benefits by virtue of membership in social networks or other social structures" (Portes 1998, 6).

Yet, these conclusions about the costs of ethnic divisions contrast with the evidence from cognitive science, sociology, law, economics, political science, and other disciplines that cooperation without trust is common and that modern societies are already endowed with many alternative mechanisms designed to sanction free riding.[5] Throughout history, people successfully bridged their differences and deliberately formalized social ties, when informal trust was lacking, in order to pursue their economic objectives (Greif 2006; Alfani and Gourdon 2012; Jha 2013). Relatedly, a well-established consensus in the literature on economic development is that modern economic growth was made possible by the gradual expansion of formal law and public authority rather than by the accumulation of social capital.[6] Today, specialized state agencies, rather than tight-knit communities, monitor opportunistic behavior and curb free riding in collective action dilemmas. Individuals contribute to public goods by paying taxes. The state, not civil society, is in charge of enforcing fiscal rules.

In their quest for homogeneity at the end of WWII, European policymakers ended up creating a new problem – millions of uprooted people. "Resented and resentful, they crowd in on the overcrowded, always wanting to 'go home' and thus a constant stimulus to the 'irredentism' that has caused so many wars," read a *New York Times* description of West Germany in 1951. The fact that Poles and Germans were "repatriated" into their home states and settled next to their purported coethnics did not prevent conflict in the receiving communities or settle questions of nationality once and for all (Kossert 2008; Zaremba 2012). The challenge of housing and feeding these dispossessed and dispirited individuals strained the capabilities of already weak postwar governments. In West Germany, some openly argued that "only the death or emigration of 20 million" people could alleviate food shortages (Lemberg 1959, 31).

Contemporary political discourse about refugees and internally displaced persons echoes these sentiments. Forced migration is considered a developmental challenge. The recent influx of refugees, particularly from the Middle East, has given rise to xenophobic sentiment among Europeans who perceive the newcomers as a security threat and economic burden (Esipova, Ray, and Pugliese 2020). Across Europe, anti-immigration, populist parties have risen

---

[4] See, for example, Alesina and Ferrara (2002); Banerjee, Iyer, and Somanathan (2005); Putnam (2007); Habyarimana et al. (2009); Dinesen and Sønderskov (2015); Algan, Hémet, and Laitin (2016).

[5] See, for example, Williamson (1979); Knight (1998); Lazzarini, Miller, and Zenger (2004); Cook, Hardin, and Levi (2005); Stagnaro, Arechar, and Rand (2017).

[6] See North (1990); Greif (1993); Ogilvie and Carus (2014); Dincecco (2017).

to power by exploiting fears that forced and voluntary migrants will pose a burden on the welfare system and fail to assimilate (Dinas and Fouka 2018; Hangartner et al. 2019). These fears are not entirely unfounded: A large refugee inflow has been shown to reduce wages and increase unemployment among the native population in some contexts (Calderón-Mejía and Ibáñez 2016; Morales 2018).[7] Scholars further find that immigration-based diversity reduces support for redistributive policies (Burgoon, Koster, and van Egmond 2012; Alesina, Murard, and Rapoport 2021).

But for how long do these negative effects persist? Our knowledge of the consequences of large-scale uprooting is based predominantly on evidence from the last couple of decades, when most of the current refugees resettled. Scholars generally investigate the immediate electoral or labor market consequences of refugee inflows. They draw conclusions from observing migrant–native interactions at the height of the distributional conflict, when communities are still adjusting to the sudden demographic changes produced by internal and cross-border population movements.

While ongoing refugee crises are easier to study and generate more headlines, they limit the kinds of questions we can answer. As a result, the conclusions we can draw from these recent migration episodes may be provisional and incomplete. In fact, the consequences of migration typically unfold over a long time horizon, changing in magnitude and direction over time (Charnysh 2023). For instance, opposition to redistribution and intolerance among the receiving population generally declines as the natives become more accustomed to cultural diversity and as migrants assimilate (Christ et al. 2014; Ramos et al. 2019). Migrants' participation in politics and the labor market changes after they stay in the country long enough to naturalize and learn the language. The receiving economies recalibrate, adjusting to the expansion of the population and labor force over time. Migrants' children face lower adaptation barriers and typically achieve greater economic well-being than the migrants themselves. On a grander scale, large-scale population movements can alter the trajectory of socioeconomic development altogether – by changing how states and societies interact. Adopting a longer time horizon is thus necessary to gain a more comprehensive and accurate evaluation of the impact of forced migration on social and economic outcomes.

This book urges scholars to rethink both the benefits of ethnic homogeneity and the costs of hosting refugees. It shows that forced migration, a traumatic event, can strengthen states and benefit local economies in the long run by increasing social heterogeneity at the subnational level.

---

[7] However, a meta-analysis of fifty-nine empirical studies in economics concludes that most results on employment and wages are nonsignificant (Verme and Schuettler 2020).

## THE ARGUMENT

To gain a better understanding of the prospects of postmigration societies, I propose to trace their trajectory of social and economic development over a longer timeframe. To that end, I study the impact of mass displacement at a critical juncture – "time zero," the period of fundamental institutional and social transformation in Poland and West Germany in the 1940s – on outcomes measured at various points in time up to the present. I ask not only how migrants and natives learned to live together in their shared communities in the immediate postwar period, but also whether and how postwar migration matters for state–society relations and economic performance in these communities generations later.

### Migration and Social Cohesion

I argue that forced migration can create new social cleavages based on migration status and place of origin. This is the case even when the displaced population belongs to the same ethnic group as the native population. To develop this insight, I build on theoretical perspectives that emphasize the role of boundaries in the creation and dissolution of social groups (Barth 1969; Lamont and Molnár 2002; Wimmer 2013). This view privileges "self-ascription and the ascription of others" over "objective cultural traits" and emphasizes the role of contact in defining contrasting group identities (Barth 1969, 15). It does not treat ethnic groups as automatically endowed with distinct cultures, dense network ties, or ingroup solidarity (Wimmer 2013, 22). The adoption of a boundary-making perspective enables me to analyze the processes of group formation in a given setting without assuming that they will follow ethnic lines.

Mass uprooting creates new boundaries via two related processes. One is the accentuation of differences between individuals originating in different regions or countries through intergroup interaction and physical proximity. Most cultural traits, such as language, dialect, religion, dress, customs, and the strength of national attachment, vary across space. Cultural distance may be larger between individuals from different countries of origin, but it also exists between individuals from different regions of the same country as a function of historical, economic, or geographic factors (Kaasa, Vadi, and Varblane 2014). Geographic variability, in particular, has been linked to the production of location-specific human capital that can give rise to ethnolinguistic cleavages (Michaloupoulos 2012). As people from one region move to another, they stand out more starkly from the local population.

Another process leading to the creation of new boundaries is exposure to forced displacement itself. The sudden inflow of migrants, regardless of their ethnicity and cultural traits, is likely to provoke the native population to close its ranks. The larger the demographic shock, the greater the incentives for the locals to mobilize around their native status to protect their access to land, housing, and jobs. This is the dynamic highlighted by the literature on the "sons-of-the-soil" conflicts, conventionally understood as conflicts between members of a native ethnic group and recent immigrants from other ethnic groups within the same country (Fearon and Laitin 2011). Yet, as I show in this book, conflict between native and migrant populations need not follow ethnic lines.

At the same time, the experience of forced displacement is bound to generate mutual solidarity among the uprooted. Studies have shown that shared suffering produces a sense of common fate (Drury 2018) and "a pervasive and intense feeling of social interconnectedness in which people are aware of a common predicament and a common interest" (Baehr 2005, 182, 188). This shared group identity not only fosters cooperation among individuals who share the experience of displacement but also separates them from others.

Once the boundaries are in place, their salience will vary with the extent of competition over resources in receiving communities and with the way formal institutions regulate this competition. As argued by Dancygier (2010), the relationship between migrants and natives is more antagonistic in conditions of economic scarcity and when the state, rather than the market, allocates scarce resources. Relatedly, as highlighted by Schwartz (2019), migration-based identities increase in importance when access to state resources is tied to migration status. More generally, scholars have shown that boundaries between ingroups and outgroups harden when group membership enables the acquisition of material goods (Bates 1974; Caselli and Coleman 2012; Pengl, Roessler, and Rueda 2021). Paradoxically, this means that sharing nationality can actually increase intergroup tensions in the aftermath of forced displacement because it places migrants and natives in direct competition for state-provided resources, a competition that is less acute when migrants lack access to full citizenship rights.

Migration-based cleavages will have important implications for cooperation in affected communities. I expect them to operate in ways similar to ethnic cleavages, that is, to increase conflict and reduce investment in collective goods. Multiple studies have shown that salient group boundaries – regardless of whether they are based on ethnicity, language, religion, or region of origin – reduce agreement over which public goods should be provided and lower an individual's willingness to make sacrifices for the well-being of others.[8] Baldwin and Huber (2010) further demonstrate that the provision of public goods suffers when group boundaries overlap with economic status.

I expect forced migrants, voluntary migrants, and natives to have different economic and cultural needs. For instance, the loss of property and disruption of family networks may increase forced migrants' dependence on social

---

[8] See, for example, Habyarimana et al. (2009); Freier, Geys, and Holm (2013); Lieberman and McClendon (2013); Singh (2015); Rueda (2018); Enos and Gidron (2016).

welfare, relative to other groups. Migrants and natives often live in different neighborhoods and therefore disagree over how public goods should be allocated across space. Cultural differences may lead to disagreement over the content of school curricula, as each group prefers its language and history to be taught. These differences in preferences increase transaction costs associated with collaborative efforts. They may also reduce contributions to collective goods from which the other group cannot be easily excluded.

## Migration and State Capacity

Counter to the existing literature, I propose that mass displacement can actually *strengthen* state capacity. It does so precisely by creating new societal divisions and undermining the displaced individuals' ability to provide for themselves. State capacity is commonly understood as the ability of a state to perform its core functions, including the maintenance of internal order, the extraction of revenue, and the provision of basic services (Hanson and Sigman 2020). Scholars sometimes distinguish between infrastructural power, defined as the capacity "to actually penetrate civil society and to implement logistically political decisions throughout the realm," and despotic power, defined as "a range of actions which the elite is empowered to undertake without routine, institutionalized negotiation with civil society" (Mann 1984, 188–189). Discussion in this book pertains primarily to infrastructural power.

The expansion of infrastructural power constitutes a significant intervention into social life. It is bound to provoke resistance from different societal actors. Strong societies may resist third-party attempts to impose control because they have already developed effective social organizations for service provision (Migdal 1988) and do not want to bear the burden of taxation (Scott 1977; Bodea and LeBas 2016). Another source of resistance to the expansion of state infrastructural power comes from local and national elites. Elites may oppose the expansion of state capacity because it undermines their autonomy and curtails rent-seeking opportunities (Garfias 2018) or because it can be used to redistribute wealth in the future (Suryanarayan 2016; Hollenbach and Silva 2019). As Slater (2010, 11) argues, it is extremely challenging for rulers who seek to strengthen the state to "bring a wide range of elites into supportive relations with their regime, and prevent them from playing oppositional roles."

I argue that forced displacement can reduce these societal barriers to the expansion of state authority. First, communities formed by uprooted individuals from different places of origin are less successful at self-organizing. They lack effective collective action mechanisms to oppose state intervention and, at the same time, have more to gain from the expansion of state authority. As a result, the demand for state-provided public and private goods in such communities will be higher, relative to communities that are more cohesive and self-sufficient.[9] Second, individuals who are uprooted from their communities and lose their belongings have fewer outside options and are thus more likely to turn to the state and other formal organizations for credit, insurance, and welfare. Third, displacement deprives communal elites, who would otherwise oppose the expansion of state infrastructural power, of economic and organizational resources to do so. As a result, these elites may become more willing to endorse – or less able to resist – state-building projects in their communities.

Forced displacement thus creates a window of opportunity for strengthening the state by reducing resistance to revenue extraction and shoring up societal demand for state-provided public goods. The more resources a government can allocate to satisfy the increased demand for its services, the stronger the ties that develop between the migrant population and the incumbent regime. Even small initial investments in the expansion of state provision can go a long way: Positive experiences with the state increase future compliance with state policies. Furthermore, the transfer of state resources makes the recipients more legible: The information that the state acquires in the process may facilitate tax collection in subsequent periods.

It is not guaranteed that the governing elites will recognize the opportunity to expand state capabilities in the aftermath of displacement and step in to assist the uprooted communities. Elite disagreements over the desired size and the scope of the state are extremely common and have been shown to impede the accumulation of infrastructural capacity across different historical periods and geographic regions (e.g., Slater 2010; Soifer 2015; Beramendi and Rogers 2018; Wang 2022).

Investments in future capacity are more likely when the displacement is perceived as permanent and when the uprooted population has citizenship rights and is entitled to make claims on the state. I further expect the governing elites to be more supportive of mobilizing state resources to invest in integrating the uprooted population in the presence of internal or external threats. Elites may unite to bolster the state's power when they fear the outbreaks of contentious politics and perceive the provision of state services as an effective approach to containing social unrest (Slater 2010; Tajima 2014; Distelhorst and Hou 2017). Elites may also support investment in state capacity when they face the threat of territorial conquest or externally supported secession (Wimmer 2012; Darden and Mylonas 2016). Mass displacement often aggravates these threats by provoking intergroup competition over scarce resources and raising the risk of civil and international conflict (Salehyan and Gleditsch 2006; Salehyan 2008; Rüegger 2019).

---

[9] Arjona (2016) uses similar logic to explain variation in rebel governance in Colombia. She shows that armed groups are more likely to create governments that collect taxes, provide mechanisms for settling disputes, enforce laws, and deliver public services in places where prior local institutions are of low quality.

## Migration and Economic Development

I further argue that the mixing of people from different places of origin may foster private entrepreneurship and produce superior economic outcomes in the long run. Several related mechanisms contribute to this outcome. One is the greater reach of state institutions and increased supply of centrally provided public goods, which have been shown to increase the returns to productive economic activity and to lower the costs of economic exchange (North 1990; Besley and Persson 2014; Dincecco 2017). While many public goods can be provided endogenously through informal norms and networks, this solution is only "second-best." Informal norms and networks limit the gains from occupational specialization and economies of scale, and may also lower competition and segment markets (Fafchamps 2004; Robinson 2016).

Importantly, the accumulation of state capacity advances private economic activity only in states with "good" formal institutions. Such states are variously categorized as inclusive, common-interest, or open-access because they protect property rights and allow all citizens to use their skills and talents (North, Wallis, and Weingast 2006; Acemoglu and Robinson 2012; Besley and Persson 2014). Institutions matter because they regulate transaction costs and enforce cooperative behavior. Sustained economic growth is more likely when formal institutions encourage broad societal participation in economic activity by protecting property rights, enforcing contracts, and providing market-supporting public goods to all citizens (Acemoglu and Robinson 2012, 144). The alternative is extractive or limited-access institutions that benefit only some segments of society (such as the economic or political elites or the dominant ethnic group). Such institutions fail to protect property rights, create barriers to entry into specific occupations or industries, and reduce opportunities for entrepreneurship and human capital accumulation. An increase in the capacity of a state with extractive institutions lowers the returns to productive economic activity by raising the risk of expropriation and/or excessive taxation.

Another mechanism that leads from migration to superior economic outcomes is the diversity of skills and perspectives that migrants bring. People who have lived in different environments and were educated in different school systems can work together in a way that enhances their collective productivity. Correspondingly, researchers have found that the diversity of the immigrant population increases entrepreneurship, stimulates innovation, and generates economic prosperity (Peri 2012; Brunow, Trax, and Suedekum 2012; Alesina, Harnoss, and Rapoport 2016; Docquier et al. 2020). In contrast to existing work, which focuses on international migration and short-term outcomes, I examine the implications of diversity produced by migration within (historic) borders of the same country and extend my analysis to second- and third-generation migrants. I expect the benefits of a diverse workforce to pay off only in states with inclusive institutions, which enable all individuals to apply their skills and facilitate cooperation between people from different cultures by enforcing the rule of law (Acemoglu and Robinson 2012, 144).

To summarize, mass displacement creates new cleavages by rearranging the population in space and increasing competition for local resources. Migration-based cleavages operate in ways similar to ethnic cleavages, by increasing tensions and reducing cooperation for the provision of collective goods. At the same time, by weakening cooperation between individuals in the affected communities and undercutting resistance to state control, mass population movements can shore up the role of formal state institutions in the provision of public goods. An important scope condition for this first part of the argument is that the governing elites have sufficient resources and incentives to expand infrastructural power.

Higher state capacity, in turn, creates greater opportunities for predictable and enforceable arm's-length transactions and facilitates private economic activity. Migration and diversity may also increase economic productivity by diversifying skills, increasing competition, and encouraging occupational changes and entrepreneurship. Counterintuitively, mass uprooting in the aftermath of a destructive conflict can advance economic development in the long run. This second part of the argument requires that formal state institutions be inclusive; namely, that they protect private property rights and enforce contracts of all citizens.

## STUDYING THE EFFECTS OF DISPLACEMENT WITHIN AND ACROSS COUNTRIES

I support my argument with qualitative and quantitative evidence from Polish and German communities affected by postwar migration movements. I focus on subnational variation *within* each country to maximize internal validity. The combination of original micro-level data and quasi-experimental research designs enables me to measure key concepts more precisely as well as to estimate the causal effects of receiving migrants from different places of origin, thereby enhancing the reliability and accuracy of the findings.

The Polish case amounts to a natural experiment that produced new migrant communities in an area previously governed by Germany. The prewar German residents were expelled en masse, and both their place and property were taken over by forced and voluntary migrants from different regions. The structure of transportation networks, the duration of travel, and the availability of vacant housing at the time of arrival determined the composition of the migrant population in a given settlement. The nature of the resettlement process allows me to compare communities that vary in the composition of migrant population but share the experience of uprooting and of living in former German settlements. Importantly, in these analyses, I am able to hold constant the nature of national political and economic institutions as well as the starting levels of state capacity. Analysis *within* Poland also enables me to compare communities located on the opposite sides of the now-defunct pre-WWII border between Poland and Germany. Such communities differed in their migration histories but faced similar institutional environments and policies after the war.

The German case offers variation in the share of expellees to population, in addition to the heterogeneity in expellee origins. Expellees were assigned to specific communities based on the availability of housing, which itself was influenced by the level of wartime destruction and prewar population density. Ultimately, it was the timing of expulsions, the distance expellees had to cover, and arbitrary decisions of the occupation authorities that shaped the mix of expellees assigned to a specific community. As I show in the book's empirical chapters, the composition of the displaced population was unrelated to the socioeconomic characteristics of the receiving localities. This feature of the West German case allows me to estimate the causal effects of both the presence and diversity of expellees.

An additional benefit of within-country analysis is the opportunity to construct measures for evaluating intergroup cooperation, state capacity, and private economic activity that hold greater validity and are context-appropriate. For these key outcomes, comparing social and economic indicators in Poland and West Germany directly would be misleading because of the numerous differences in these countries' economic and political systems. By carefully selecting measures that align with the specific institutional context and historical period, I enhance the internal validity of the analysis and bolster the credibility of my conclusions.

Evaluating the argument requires explaining variation in social and economic outcomes across both time and space. Specifically, I need to account for the local-level variation in the provision of public and private goods and in state capacity across migrant communities as well as for the changes in economic performance over time. These objectives place demands on the kinds of evidence I use. Statistical evidence is most suitable for evaluating the short- and long-term economic effects of forced migration on the receiving communities. Narrative sources, instead, are more important for understanding how migration creates new group boundaries and undermines cooperation for the provision of collective goods.

Accordingly, I use a mixed-methods approach. My qualitative evidence comes from archival sources, memoirs, newspapers, and secondary literature in Polish and German, which I collected over fifteen months of field research. My quantitative analysis draws on four original datasets. For the analysis of the effects of mass migration in Poland, I collected and georeferenced original data for over a thousand historical municipalities (*Gmina*) from the unpublished Polish and German censuses, preserved on microfilm, as well as from historical maps and statistical yearbooks. In addition, I complemented these sources with village-level data on the population composition in Upper Silesia compiled by other scholars based on property documents (Dworzak and

TABLE 1.1 *Differences between cases and empirical implications.*

| Difference | Western and northern Poland | West Germany | Relevant outcomes and mechanisms |
|---|---|---|---|
| Native population | Mostly absent | Present, in majority | The capacity for self-help collective action, the demand for state-provided collective goods |
| Economic institutions | Extractive (1947–1989) Inclusive (1989–present) | Inclusive | Incentives for private economic activity |
| Political institutions | Extractive (1947–1989) Inclusive (1989–present) | Inclusive | State responsiveness to citizens' demands |
| Starting levels of state capacity | Low | Medium | State ability to provide collective goods |

Goc 2011). For the analysis of forced migration in West Germany, I compiled an original dataset at the commune level (*Gemeinde*) for the states of Bavaria and Schleswig-Holstein, using census material from 1939, 1946, 1950, 1961, 1970, and 1987. I also incorporated and extended two county-level (*Kreise*) datasets created by others (Schmitt, Rattinger, and Oberndörfer 1994; Braun and Franke 2021).

In addition to validating causal claims about each case of mass displacement using subnational analysis, this book compares outcomes between Poland and West Germany. Cross-national comparisons are helpful to assess the generalizability of the argument. If forced migration can be shown to have comparable consequences in both a socialist autocracy and a free-market democracy, in the context of a nearly complete population turnover and in the context where the displaced population is allocated into settled communities with intact social structures, then we can have greater certainty that the argument applies to a wider range of real-world situations. Conversely, if empirical patterns diverge across cases, then we can learn more about the background conditions under which the argument holds. I summarize the key differences between cases in Table 1.1.

One important difference between the two cases is the presence of the native population. Polish migrants typically settled in villages emptied of their original inhabitants, in a region where Polish society did not exist before the war. They started out in an institutional vacuum and had to come together to form self-defense units and fire brigades, rebuild schools and churches, and establish new norms and customs, overcoming mutual distrust. By contrast, German expellees were allocated to tight-knit communities where formal and informal institutions remained largely intact. The native residents outnumbered the expellees five to one. Native elites preserved their assets and influence. Most communal institutions survived the war and associational activity resumed several years before the establishment of state and federal governments. Therefore, I expect to see lower capacity for self-help collective action and greater demand for state-provided collective goods in Poland's newly acquired territories, where eight out of ten residents were migrants, than in West Germany, where four out of five residents were natives. In both cases, I expect the demand for state resources to be higher among the uprooted population than among the native population.

As far as formal institutions are concerned, postwar Poland and West Germany could not be more different. From 1947 to 1989, Poland was a communist autocracy with repressive secret police. Only the communist party and its satellites competed in elections, and the results were predetermined. The communist government sought to establish a socialist economy by nationalizing most of the industrial sector and pursued (but eventually abandoned) forced collectivization of agriculture. Although the government provided a broad range of social services, private economic activity was restricted, overtaxed, and at risk of expropriation. In other words, Poland's political and economic institutions from 1947 to 1989 were extractive, as the state limited societal participation in the economy and political power rested with the communist party. Conversely, West Germany became a multiparty democracy. Regular elections enabled the expellees and natives to organize and express their preferences for state-provided public goods and welfare through voting. The economic reforms of the Adenauer-Erhard administration established the institutions of a social market economy. Private entrepreneurship was encouraged; private property was protected, and state intervention was limited to the provision of social welfare and public services. West Germany thus enjoyed a combination of inclusive economic and political institutions, allowing its citizens a broad range of political and economic opportunities. The two political and economic systems began to converge only in the 1990s, as Poland democratized and transitioned to a market economy.

The differences in formal economic institutions between Poland and West Germany are central to my theory about the conditional effects of forced displacement on economic development. I argue that receiving migrants from different places of origin is more likely to benefit local economies under inclusive economic institutions, which incentivize productive economic activity and allow migrants to participate in the economy on equal terms with the native population. Under extractive institutions, the economic potential of migration is squandered as aspiring entrepreneurs are discouraged from pursuing economic initiatives. For these reasons, we should observe a positive relationship between the diversity of migrants and private entrepreneurship in West Germany but not in Poland in the pre-1989 period.

The variation in political institutions, on the other hand, may have influenced each state's responsiveness to the demand for collective and private goods in the aftermath of displacement. Scholars have shown that resource allocation in autocracies and democracies follows different logics, even though both regimes respond to pressure from below. Autocratic governments are concerned about managing social stability and appeasing their core supporters (Chen, Pan, and Xu 2016; Distelhorst and Hou 2017; Knutsen and Rasmussen 2018). Democratic governments are concerned about reelection; they are accountable to multiple constituencies and face greater institutional constraints (Tsebelis 1995; Powell 2000; Cleary 2007). We should be mindful of these distinctions when seeking to understand postwar state-building processes in Poland and West Germany. In line with existing literature, I expect the allocation of state resources in the newly acquired Polish provinces to reflect the priorities of the governing elites, which may or may not correspond to the needs of the migrant population. Conversely, the West German authorities may be more responsive to expellee demands, particularly in areas where the expellees are well organized and outnumber the native population. At the same time, I expect the West German government to be more constrained in the implementation of pro-expellee policies than the Polish government, which enjoyed a monopoly of power between 1947 and 1989 and thus had greater leeway in deciding how to allocate state resources.

Finally, the two cases differ in terms of their starting levels of state capacity. Postwar Poland started out as an extremely weak state. State organizations were gutted during the Nazi and Soviet occupations, and the establishment of civil administration was hampered by the interference of the Red Army and the ongoing civil war between the pro-Soviet government and the anticommunist underground. The state's ability to provide basic public goods was limited, particularly in the newly acquired territories, where it arrived relatively late. Poland thus presents a particularly hard test for the argument that mass displacement can strengthen states and economies over time. The state was much stronger in postwar West Germany, notwithstanding its complete military defeat and its territorial fragmentation under the occupation. State organizations were reinvented rather than rebuilt from scratch. Postwar recovery and reconstruction further benefited from the inflow of foreign aid under the Marshall Plan. Accordingly, the West German government was much more capable of providing collective goods and containing violence between expellees and the disgruntled native population.

## SUMMARY OF KEY FINDINGS

Let us now revisit the questions posed at the beginning of the chapter. First, how did the uprooted populations form ties to their communities? Did increased ethnic homogeneity reduce conflict and strengthen social solidarity? I find the opposite: Population transfers were followed by processes of cultural differentiation in both Poland and West Germany. Cultural markers, such as religious denomination or dialect, all contributed to the salience of new group boundaries, but what ultimately mattered most was opposing economic interests. Thus, the migrant–native cleavage was much more salient than cleavages between migrant groups from different regions of origin.

Using memoirs of migrants settled in Poland's newly acquired territories, I show that the fiction of shared Polish nationhood broke down once migrants came together in the newly acquired territories. If one were to go by the terminology settlers used in daily life, she would conclude that the region was populated not only by Poles but also by Germans, Ukrainians, Russians, and other ethnic groups. Minor cultural differences were amplified, leading to the formation of new group boundaries. Forced migrants were united by their collective experience of displacement, forming a separate identity from the native population and voluntary migrants alike. The native population turned inward in response to migrants' hostility and discrimination. Uprooted communities initially struggled to provide basic collective goods, because migrants coming from different regions viewed each other with suspicion and distrust. Accordingly, I show that villages that were populated by the native population, or by migrants originating from the same region, were more likely to have a volunteer fire brigade than villages populated by a heterogeneous migrant population. Mass migration therefore created new cleavages that reduced collective action capacity in the newly formed communities.

Similarly, in West Germany, the arrival of expellees led to the rise of nativist sentiments and the tightening of fiscal policy in receiving communities. Although "Germanness" was a key reason for their uprooting, the natives viewed expellees as foreigners, associating them with the population of the regions they had left. Expellees were framed as Poles, Russians, or Gypsies. Previously minor cultural differences became salient markers in the competition for scarce resources. The native population sought to exclude the expellees from preexisting voluntary associations and circumvent the laws on expellee assistance. In response to the hostile reception in their new settlements, many expellees themselves disavowed German identity and organized around their migration status and regional origins.

Second, how did the influx of millions of displaced individuals affect the receiving states' ability to govern? Counterintuitively, I find that dealing with a sudden inflow of migrants shored up the role of the state in the provision of collective goods and increased state capacity in the long run. In Poland's newly acquired territory, a near-complete turnover of the population facilitated state building by creating the demand for state-provided resources and undermining resistance to state authority. By the 1950s, the communist state accumulated higher administrative capacity and assumed a bigger role in the economy in the newly acquired territory than was the case in the parts of the country with a longer history of Polish control. Within the resettled region, counties that received a more heterogeneous migrant population came to have more state bureaucrats per capita than counties that received a more homogeneous population. In this region, moreover, the state was able to marginalize the Catholic Church, its main competitor for the hearts and minds of Polish migrants. The expansion of state infrastructural power was facilitated by the decimation of economic and political elites during WWII and ideological cohesion among the remaining elites, who supported state building in the formerly German territory.

In West Germany, on the other hand, the governing elites faced greater resistance from the native population, which did not experience uprooting. At the same time, once expellees overcame their differences and organized, they were able to exert considerable influence on government policy through electoral and extraparliamentary channels, which prompted large-scale state intervention on their behalf. In the 1940s, the expellees disproportionately endorsed the Social Democrats, in line with their preferences for a more active and redistributive state policy. They subsequently formed their own party, the Bloc of Expellees, and occupied key positions in the expellee ministries, which allowed them to directly influence state policy. The mobilization of administrative and fiscal resources in response to expellee pressure ultimately led to the expansion of state infrastructural power. New governmental agencies were set up to mediate conflicts between expellees and the native population and to compensate expellees for their financial losses. However, in seeking to integrate expellees, state and federal government officials also had to contend with entrenched local elites and insubordinate local governments, which constrained their policy.

It stands to reason that the increase in state capacity in the aftermath of mass displacement requires that the receiving state has sufficient baseline capacity to govern. However, my analysis indicates that the initial level of state capacity does not necessarily have to be high. Postwar Poland, in particular, started out as an extremely weak state, but accumulated considerable infrastructural power in a short period of time because the state did not have to compete for influence with strong societal organizations.[10]

Finally, what were the short- and long-run economic consequences of mass displacement? I find that receiving large numbers of forced migrants strained local resources in the short run, in line with other research. One to two generations later, however, communities that received a larger and more heterogeneous migrant population not only rebounded to their original levels of development but also economically outperformed communities with a smaller or more homogeneous migrant population. With an important caveat: The benefits of migration-based diversity appeared only under inclusive formal

---

[10] As Boone (2003) argues, states can offer fewer goods and services to gain access when societal actors are weak than when they are strong. Migdal (1989) similarly argues that the weakening of society's strategies of survival can help the state to gain social control and enforce its rules.

institutions. During the communist period in Poland, there were no significant differences in levels of wealth and private economic activity between
communities settled by homogeneous and by heterogeneous migrants. However, following the transition to a market economy, communities settled by
a more heterogeneous migrant population achieved higher rates of private
entrepreneurship and income levels than communities that were more homogeneous. Significantly, the descendants of postwar migrants today are generally
wealthier and better educated than their counterparts who still inhabit the
regions that forced and voluntary migrants had left after the war.

In West Germany, which started out with inclusive economic institutions,
the economic benefits of migration and cultural diversity appeared sooner. The
localities that had received larger and more heterogeneous expellee populations
outpaced those localities that had received fewer expellees and/or expellee populations that were more homogeneous by the 1980s. The size and diversity of
the expellee population at the county level predicted higher entrepreneurship
rates and education levels. In the 2000s, higher-inflow areas recorded higher
incomes as well as more enterprises per capita in the professional, scientific,
and technical sectors.

Altogether, my analysis of the impact of population transfers indicates that
although mass migration engenders new societal divisions, it can also facilitate
state building and generate superior economic outcomes in the long run. Both
the size and the composition of the migrant population matter for economic
performance in receiving communities. The divergence in short- and long-term
economic outcomes also suggests that it is crucial to adopt a longer temporal
framework in order to fully understand migration's impact.

In developing these insights, the book advances our understanding of
the impacts of forced migration and enriches our knowledge of post-WWII
population transfers. It makes four distinct contributions.

First, I challenge the dominant view that forced migration and resulting
heterogeneity are detrimental to the institutional development and economic
performance of receiving societies. I show, on the contrary, that the effects
of displacement and cultural divisions vary in direction and magnitude over
time and are also conditional on the nature of state institutions. Notwithstanding important short-term costs, the choice to accommodate refugees provides
states with an opportunity to strengthen their institutions and improve economic performance. Furthermore, the more diverse the incoming population
is, the greater the economic benefits for the receiving communities. It should
be noted, however, that it is only in states with inclusive formal institutions
that new skills and knowledge brought by refugees from different places
of origin translate into economic payoffs. In developing this conclusion, I
contribute to the growing literature on the mediating role of political and
economic institutions in the relationship between ethnic heterogeneity and
economic performance (Easterly 2001; Miguel 2004; Weldon 2006; Gao
2016).

My findings on the beneficial economic effects of forced migration and resulting diversity resonate with conclusions of recent work on the positive economic effects of voluntary immigrants from diverse countries of origin.[11] But refugees are not just another group of immigrants. They leave home against their will, lose most of their assets, and experience violence and discrimination. They end up in suboptimal locations where their occupational skills are less useful and where they lack social networks, which may slow down their economic and social integration into a host society. Given these additional costs of forced migration, it is remarkable that mass displacement in Poland and West Germany produced beneficial long-run effects on economic activity, incomes, and education levels.

Second, the book shows that migration-based cleavages do not simply lower the provision of public goods. Instead, they change the dominant *mode* of public goods provision: They shore up the importance of formal state institutions and reduce the role of informal networks. In doing so, the book corrects the perception that social capital is unambiguously favorable for economic performance and democratic governance (e.g., Putnam, Leonardi, and Nanetti 1993; Putnam 2007). While shared norms and networks may play a vital role when state institutions are absent or dysfunctional, they provide a poor substitute for formal institutions in developed market economies, such as post-1989 Poland and West Germany. Indeed, high levels of group-specific social capital can be detrimental: In West Germany, tight-knit native communities in the countryside were more likely to discriminate against expellees and deny them access to jobs and housing than larger, more loosely organized urban communities.

Third, the book contributes to research on state building by highlighting a novel theoretical mechanism through which wars can strengthen states. Whereas the canonical bellicist accounts emphasize that wars contribute to state building by incentivizing tax collection (Tilly 1990), the book shows that mass displacement in the aftermath of conflicts provides additional opportunities to strengthen the state. It highlights a mechanism that state capacity literature rarely considers: the increased demand for state presence that stems from the rupture of communal ties and the mixing of people from different places of origin.

Fourth, the book offers new empirical knowledge on postwar displacement in Europe, which has received little attention from social scientists until recently. Most studies on postwar migration have used cross-country comparisons and have treated refugees as internally homogeneous populations (Curp 2006; Douglas 2012; Urbatsch 2017). Through extensive fieldwork and archival research, I am able to explore the effects of forced migration at a much more granular level and over a longer timeframe than was previously

---

[11] See, for example, Rodríguez-Pose and von Berlepsch (2014); Ortega and Peri (2014); Alesina, Harnoss, and Rapoport (2016); Bove and Elia (2017); Sequeira, Nunn, and Qian (2020).

possible. More specifically, I depart from previous studies, which set their gaze at the level of county and region, by studying the community – a much smaller administrative unit. This was made possible by the careful compilation of historical data on the origins of migrants at the community level, whether *Gminy* in Poland or *Gemeinde* in Germany.

At this level of analysis, the assumption of homogeneity adopted by earlier research no longer holds. Instead, I find that rearranging people in space created new cleavages – based on migration status and place of origin – with enduring consequences for long-term political and economic development. If shared identity motivated the decision of policymakers to uproot millions of Germans and Poles after the change of international borders, their resettlement created new cleavages and conflicts that proved detrimental to communal cooperation and political stability in the short run. The ethnic homogeneity of contemporary Poland and Germany is thus a product of active state- and nation-building policies adopted by each country's government in response to the need to integrate populations that had been affected by the redrawing of borders and by population transfers.

WHERE THE ARGUMENT APPLIES

As shown in Figure 1.1, large-scale displacement of population has been historically common and remains front and center today. The dissolution of multiethnic states and empires dislocated millions; wars, famines, and natural disasters wrought displacement on an even greater scale.

The cases of forced migration can be arranged along a continuum of citizenship rights, from full citizenship to statelessness. My argument about the positive effects of migration and diversity on state capacity and economic development fits best in cases where the uprooted population enjoys full citizenship rights. Some of the largest instances of forced migration in the last century fit this description. Such cases include the exchange of some 1.5 million people between Greece and Turkey in 1919–1922, the uprooting of some 17.9 million people during the Partition of India and Pakistan in 1947–51, and the return migration of five to seven million Europeans during the independence wars in former colonies. I review evidence from these cases in the concluding chapter. Furthermore, the majority (60 percent) of forced migrants today are displaced within their own home countries and retain citizenship rights. In cases where internal displacement is permanent, we should observe similar dynamics to those in postwar Poland and Germany.

When refugees have no citizenship rights, their sudden inflow may still motivate the receiving states to mobilize resources in order to avoid political instability. As evident from the West German case, the governing elites supported the allocation of resources toward expellee needs not only because expellees could influence electoral outcomes but also because they perceived the expellees as a potentially dangerous group. However, when the receiving

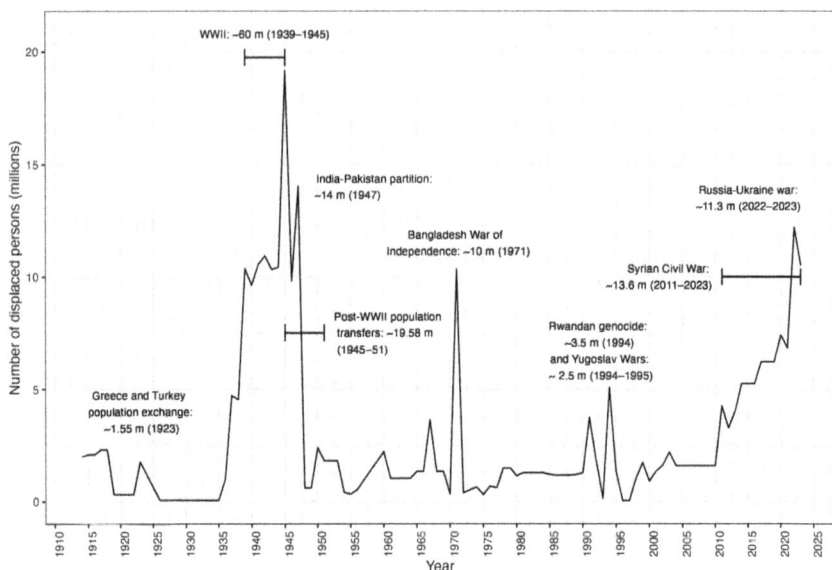

FIGURE I.I  Major episodes of forced displacement between 1900 and 2023. The graph includes episodes that affected at least 500,000 people and occurred between 1900 and 2023. For multiyear conflicts, the number of displaced persons is averaged across conflict years. The full list of displacement episodes is presented in Table A.I.

governments rely exclusively on international aid and NGOs to accommodate refugees, the expansion of state infrastructural power is unlikely.

The analysis in this book also tells us something about the economic consequences of voluntary migration. Voluntary migrants differ from forced migrants in that they have far more agency in deciding when and where to move and arrive with greater social and economic resources. They are thus less likely to make claims on the receiving states, even if they obtain citizenship. Nonetheless, large-scale immigration may also erode communal solidarity and reduce investment in the provision of collective goods by the native population. Furthermore, cultural diversity that results from large-scale voluntary immigration also increases economic productivity in receiving economies, as recent work has demonstrated (e.g., Brunow, Trax, and Suedekum 2012; Peri 2012; Alesina, Harnoss, and Rapoport 2016; Docquier et al. 2020). This beneficial effect of immigration is more likely in states with inclusive economic institutions.

ORGANIZATION OF THE BOOK

I begin the book with a historical account of how border changes and migration in the aftermath of WWII reshaped the ethnic landscape in Poland and Germany. **Chapter 2** discusses when and how decisions were made to uproot millions of Germans and Poles; provides background on the characteristics of the affected populations; and describes the resettlement process. I emphasize three points in this account. First, the population groups that were displaced after the war were extremely heterogeneous; the policymakers' assumption of singular ethnic attachments did not reflect the actual complexity and ambiguity of group identification on the ground. Second, the vast majority of migrants did not select into migration; their relocation was prompted by the revision of borders and/or exposure to violence and repression. Third, the allocation of migrants to specific settlements was shaped by the availability of housing at the time of the migrants' arrival, which, in turn, depended on the timing of the expulsions and the length of the journey from each place of origin. As a result, the mix of migrants in each receiving locality was uncorrelated with its socioeconomic characteristics.

The policymakers who sanctioned the population transfers sought to create homogeneous states by concentrating all Germans in Germany and all Poles in Poland. They believed that slotting Poles and Germans into their own states would reduce ethnic conflict. In Part II of the book, I instead show that by rearranging ethnically homogeneous populations in space, population transfers created new intergroup divisions. These new boundaries – based on migration status and regional origin – undermined the provision of collective goods at the community level.

In **Chapter 3**, I draw on migrants' memoirs and archival sources to trace the process of boundary-making in the newly formed communities in the territory Poland acquired from Germany. I find that common nationality did not prevent cultural differentiation between the native population, forced migrants from eastern borderlands, and voluntary migrants from Poland and abroad. The native–migrant cleavage was particularly salient, given the conflicting economic interests of these two groups. Next, I examine the consequences of these newly created boundaries by comparing communities settled by migrants from different regions to more homogeneous, resettled, and non-resettled communities. I find that volunteer fire brigades, which provide a local public good and have a long tradition in Poland, were less likely to form in heterogeneous migrant villages, relative to both homogeneous migrant villages and villages dominated by the native population.

**Chapter 4** examines how the arrival of expellees affected social cohesion in West German communities, where the native population remained in place. Using qualitative evidence, I show that notwithstanding shared ethnicity, the natives policed group boundaries between themselves and the expellees and excluded expellees from prestigious local organizations such as the volunteer fire brigades. The expellees likewise coordinated around their shared identity to gain access to local resources. I then analyze the effects of expellee presence on municipal taxes in over 7,000 Bavarian municipalities using an original historical dataset. I find that in 1950, municipalities with a larger expellee population taxed land and businesses at lower rates, a sign that the natives reduced investment in the provision of collective goods in response to the influx of expellees.

Part III asks whether receiving large numbers of forced and voluntary migrants helped or hindered postwar state building. Mass uprooting coincided with a critical juncture in state development in both Poland and Germany. The Polish state was dismantled during WWII and reconstructed under Soviet tutelage, with the communist party monopolizing political power and nationalizing much of the economy. Institutional continuity with the prewar period was greater in West Germany, where postwar reconstruction of state administration was managed by the four occupying governments. Divergent occupation policies led to the division of Germany into two states: West Germany became a multiparty democracy, and East Germany became a single-party autocracy like Poland.

In **Chapter 5**, I show that the deficit of informal cooperation in Poland's newly acquired territory, repopulated by migrants from different regions of origin, increased the demand for state presence and undercut resistance to collectivization and other unpopular economic reforms. Although the Polish state was extremely weak in the aftermath of WWII, it benefited from the nationalization of German property, which could be redistributed to the migrants, as well as from the expropriation of prewar economic elites during the occupation. To demonstrate that the state accumulated higher administrative capacity in the resettled region, I compare it to the Polish territory located just east of the pre-WWII border, which shared the legacy of German rule but did not experience mass displacement. I further show that after the democratic transition, the communist-successor party, the SLD, received greater support in the resettled region relative to the neighboring areas with a more stable population history.

**Chapter 6** examines the process of state building in West Germany. Whereas the Polish state suppressed political organization, West Germany held elections at the local, state, and federal levels. Expellees and natives could, therefore, channel their demands on the state through democratic institutions. I show that expellees depended on the government both for the enforcement of their rights vis-à-vis the native population and for the provision of social services. In the early elections, they were more likely to vote for the Social Democrats, a party that endorsed greater state planning and redistribution. The chapter shows that considerable administrative and fiscal resources were mobilized to facilitate expellee integration through measures such as one-off payments, business loans, and partial compensation for lost property, funded through a levy on capital. The governing elites were motivated not only by the expellee vote but also by the risk of expellee radicalization. Just as in Poland, the presence of expellees increased administrative capacity at the county level.

Part IV explores the long-run economic consequences of uprooting and resulting cultural heterogeneity. Within the context of communities that have been diversified by the inflow of forced and voluntary migrants, I consider several channels that may result in beneficial economic outcomes in the long run. One is greater state presence in places with a more heterogeneous population. Another is the diversity of skills, experiences, and ideas, brought by migrants from different places of origin. I also explore the change in occupation structure and human capital that may result from forced displacement.

**Chapter 7** compares the economic performance of Polish communities *within* the resettled region that vary in the share of migrants and in the composition of the migrant population. The transformation of Poland's formal institutions from extractive to inclusive in the late 1980s offers an opportunity to consider the importance of institutional characteristics in mediating the costs and benefits of cultural diversity. I start by showing that homogeneous and heterogeneous communities were economically similar during the communist period. I then show that the fortunes of heterogeneous and homogeneous migrant communities diverged after 1989, with heterogeneous communities contributing more in tax revenue and registering higher levels of private entrepreneurship and income than homogeneous communities.

In **Chapter 8**, I evaluate the economic consequences of forced migration in West Germany. To do so, I employ a community-level dataset for the state of Bavaria, which received the most heterogeneous mix of expellees, alongside county-level data for the entire country. I find that expellee presence initially increased unemployment and reduced entrepreneurship rates. Expellees left most of their property behind and had difficulties integrating into the local labor market, where their occupational skills were often irrelevant. At the same time, they were more likely to invest in human capital and create their own businesses. I show that by the 1980s, counties that received larger numbers of expellees, together with a more heterogeneous expellee population, achieved higher entrepreneurship and education levels than counties that had been less exposed to postwar migration. The effects of expellee presence have persisted over time.

**Chapter 9** concludes the book by reviewing the argument's applicability beyond the context of post-WWII Europe and by highlighting the implications of the findings for broader debates in the fields of comparative politics and political economy.

A NOTE ON TERMINOLOGY

This book deals with a complex period in human migration as well as Polish and West German history, so my choice of terminology merits clarification. The book is concerned primarily with *forced* migration (or forced displacement), understood as migration driven by force, compulsion, or coercion (IOM Global Migration Data Analysis Centre 2023). The Polish case is more complicated: The territories annexed from Germany were repopulated not only by forced migrants displaced from eastern borderlands but also by voluntary migrants from other parts of the country and from abroad. Still, the majority of migrants I study were forced to flee their homes and crossed an international border; what complicates matters is that among those Poles and Germans who crossed an international border, the vast majority originated in and arrived in the same country (Borutta and Jansen 2016, 9). Thus, neither the term "refugees" nor the term "internally displaced persons" is a perfect fit.[12]

To facilitate interpretation, the book uses a series of specific terms for migrants adopted by the Polish and West German governments during the historical period under analysis. They represent the actual categories used in the census data and migrants' memoirs and thus reflect historical context more accurately. I readily acknowledge that these terms may downplay the human toll of forced displacement and blur the differences in experiences of various population groups uprooted by the war.

Regarding migrants into Poland's resettled territories, I deploy three distinct terms. First, for migrants originating from Polish territories annexed to the USSR (Kresy), I use "repatriates" (*repatrianci*). The term was adopted in the 1940s by the Polish Communist government. It conceals the involuntary nature of the resettlement process by portraying the displaced population as returning home to Poland from abroad. The reader should bear in mind that these migrants did not consider themselves as returning home: They were uprooted from their homes after the Polish borders shifted and were placed in what they initially viewed as a foreign (German) territory. Some endured deportations to the USSR before they were repatriated to Poland. Nonetheless, setting aside its implicit bias, I prefer "repatriates" due to its regular use in Polish census data and other official documents, which facilitates transparency and interpretability. Second, for those who came from within post-1945 Polish borders, I use the term "resettlers" (*przesiedleńcy*) because their relocation was typically voluntary. Third, for voluntary migrants from other countries, including France, Yugoslavia, and Germany, who returned to Poland after several generations of living abroad, I use "re-emigrants" (*reemigranci*) where needed, to distinguish them from other population groups.[13]

As regards the population that remained in the territories annexed by Poland from Germany, I make some use of the term "natives" (native population). But I also use "autochthones" (*autochtoni*), which is commonly used in Polish historiography and is value-neutral. Some sources also refer to the native population as "locals" (*miejscowi*).

In my discussion of West Germany, I have made separate choices on how to refer to migrants. The standard term used in West Germany to describe

[12] According to the UNHCR, "[a] refugee is someone who has been forced to flee his or her country because of persecution, war or violence" while "[a]n internally displaced person, or IDP, is someone who has been forced to flee their home but never cross an international border." See UNHCR, "What Is a refugee?" www.unrefugees.org/refugee-facts/what-is-a-refugee.

[13] Some early Polish sources describe this group as *repatrianci*, that is, using the same term as for forced migrants from Kresy.

German citizens displaced from the German territories annexed to Poland and the USSR, as well as ethnic Germans displaced from various countries in Central and Eastern Europe, is "expellees" (*Vertriebene* or *Heimatvertriebene*). Before 1953, other terms were used, including *Aussiedler, Flüchtlinge, Ostvertriebene, Ausgewiesene,* and *Heimatverwiesene.* "Expellees" (*Vertriebene*) was first adopted in the US occupation zone to signal that the expulsion was final and the return was impossible. It was introduced into German in 1946 as a translation from the English term promoted by the American occupation government (Nachum and Schaefer 2018, 47). The expellees were defined in the 1953 Law on Expellees (*Bundesvertriebenengesetz*) as "Germans who, as citizens of the former German Reich or as ethnic Germans living in other lands, [...] had to leave their homes as a consequence of World War II" (Ther 1996, 782). The term became popular among Germans from the annexed territories and Eastern Europe because it portrayed them as victims of expulsion and signalled their special status. Nachum and Schaefer (2018, 48) argue that the leaders of expellee associations wanted to underscore the involuntary nature of expulsions by separating themselves from refugees from the Soviet zone, who made "a conscious decision to flee from danger."[14]

I use the term "expellees" throughout the book to help distinguish this population of displaced Germans from other categories of migrants who found themselves in West Germany after the war. One such category is the Displaced Persons (DPs), or foreign civilians – mostly former forced laborers and concentration camp inmates – who were expected to return to their home countries and qualified for assistance from the United Nations Relief and Rehabilitation Administration (UNRRA) and later the International Refugee Organization (IRO). Another category is that of refugees from East Germany (*Flüchtlinge*), as mentioned earlier. The boundary between *Flüchtlinge* and *Vertriebene* is somewhat blurry: In many cases, the refugees fleeing the Soviet zone were previously expelled from their homes in Central and Eastern Europe. Many official statements from the postwar period use the term "refugees" (*Flüchtlinge*) to refer to either group.

West German sources further distinguish expellees based on their places of origin: "National Germans" (*Reichsdeutsche*) designates those who came from areas that formed part of pre-1937 Germany, whereas Ethnic Germans (*Volksdeutsche*) refers to those who had for generations lived as ethnic minorities in various states in Central and Eastern Europe. The latter term was first introduced by the Nazi government to identify individuals who had German origins but not German citizenship. Despite these associations with the Nazi past, the term has often been employed in recent historical work on postwar population movements (e.g., Connor 2007), and I occasionally use it in this book for clarity.

[14] In the Soviet zone, the same category of forced migrants was named "resettlers" (*Umsiedler*) and later, even more euphemistically, "new citizens" (*Neubürger*) (Connor 2007, 8). By the 1950s, the entire subject became forbidden in the GDR (Nachum and Schaefer 2018, 47).

The German population that lived within post-1945 German borders and did not experience uprooting is typically designated as *Einheimische* in German sources, which translates into English as "natives" or "locals." I use the two terms interchangeably.

Furthermore, as regards the process of forced migration, I use the term "population transfers" to refer to the large-scale resettlement sanctioned at the Potsdam Conference in 1945. It is helpful for separating state-sponsored relocation programs from relocation forced by military action or voluntary migration. I also use the term "expulsion" to describe the forced removal of ethnic minorities either by the government or by the majority population, and "resettlement" to describe the distribution of forced – and voluntary – migrants in a new area. "Deportation" is reserved for the organized round-ups of Polish citizens by Hitler and Stalin during the occupation, which are outside the scope of this book. Some scholars have used the term "ethnic cleansing" to describe the same cases, but this designation is less precise and more politicized, so it is generally avoided in the book.[15]

Finally, various terms can describe the territories annexed by Poland from Germany after WWII. Between 1945 and 1949, the Polish government referred to them as the "Recovered Territories" (*Ziemie Odzyskane*), to emphasize that they had belonged to Poland in the medieval period and were now being taken back. By 1949, "Recovered Territories" was superseded by the less ideological "Western and Northern Territories" or simply "Western Territories," to remove all distinctions between the new and old parts of Poland (Thum 2011, 212). While I use both terms when describing communist policies and quoting sources, I have decided to make more frequent use of the term "resettled territories." It highlights that the region experienced mass migration after WWII and also avoids both the ideological bias of "Recovered Territories" and the ambiguity of "Western Territories" (as western Poland also encompasses the territory that was Polish before WWII and did not experience mass uprooting). I also occasionally use "newly acquired territories" when discussing the process of establishing Polish institutions in the region, to highlight that it had belonged to another state before 1945.

---

[15] For example, Bulutgil (2016) considers the expulsion of Germans from Central and Eastern Europe as a case of ethnic cleansing. See Rieber (2000, 3) for an alternative perspective.

## 2

# Europe's Zero Hour

## *Population Transfers in the Aftermath of WWII*

WWII was fought over race and ethnicity. Hitler planned to transform the amorphous ethnic quilt of Central and Eastern Europe into a homogeneous community of Germanic peoples. The Nazis invaded Czechoslovakia and Poland under the pretext of protecting ethnic Germans from persecution. They carried out genocide against Europe's Jews and Roma and forcibly displaced hundreds of thousands of Poles to make space for German settlers (Schechtman 1953, 152). Similarly, the Soviet Union used the pretext of protecting its "[Ukrainian and Belarusian] blood brothers" to occupy Poland's eastern borderlands in September 1939 (Frank 2017, 231). Stalin then ordered the deportation of ethnic groups suspected of disloyalty to the Soviet regime, including the Crimean Tatars, Russian Germans, Poles, Chechens, and Ingush, to remote regions in Siberia and Central Asia.

After Germany's defeat, demographic engineering in Central and Eastern Europe was continued by the Allied Powers. In 1945, they decided to resettle millions of people in order to align the ethnic composition of the population to the revised borders between Poland, Germany, and the Soviet Union. Population transfers were justified by the widespread belief that ethnic minorities were a source of political instability and that they could not be assimilated. The 'Big Three' – the Soviet Union, the United States, and Britain – agreed that the creation of ethnically homogeneous nation-states, achieved by "repatriating" ethnic outsiders, would safeguard European security. They considered forced resettlement "a legitimate tool of international as well as of domestic politics" (Frank 2017, 227).

The map of Europe changed dramatically as a result of these policies. Nearly twenty million people were uprooted from their homes, and at least two million died in the process. The share of ethnic minority groups within states decreased from 26 percent in 1930 to 7.2 percent in the 1960s due to a combination of genocide, border changes, and forced expulsions.[1]

---

[1] These proportions are estimated by Kosinski (1969, 393, 397). According to his analysis, of the ninety-four million people living in East-Central Europe in 1930, twenty-four million

In this chapter, I first review the decisions that led to postwar population transfers. This survey provides the historical background necessary for understanding the analyses presented in the rest of the book. I show that population transfers imposed a shared fate of expulsion on internally heterogeneous populations. I also show that the presumption that residents of Germany and Poland might share a singular attachment to the German or Polish nation did not reflect the complexity of identification on the ground.

Next, I explain why studying post-WWII population transfers can be useful for understanding the effects of mass displacement on political and economic development. The analysis of migration's economic and political consequences is challenging because much of the time, migrants sort into specific destinations on the basis of economic opportunities and the presence of other migrant communities. As a result, the size and composition of migrant population in a given locality is correlated with its economic potential and political openness to migration. Furthermore, individuals who choose to migrate differ from those who stay in terms of their economic profile, social capital, and political preferences. Immigrants who do not succeed economically, or fail to assimilate, often return home, introducing yet another form of selection. This selection could be positive, when individuals with above-average skill levels in their sending regions are more likely to emigrate or stay abroad, or negative, when the opposite occurs. This kind of selective in- and out-migration makes the effects of migration challenging to interpret.

In the case of Poland and Germany, these inferential problems are mitigated. The majority of Poles and Germans did not select into migration. It was the shift in borders that determined who was uprooted and who was not. Voluntary settlers from central and eastern Polish voivodeships (*wojewódtzwa*) were an exception; nonetheless, even this group included a significant proportion of individuals whose decision to migrate after 1945 was precipitated by forcible displacement during the Nazi occupation. Thus, most migrants represented a broad cross-section of society in their sending regions. Even more significantly, migrants had little agency in choosing where to settle at their destination. They were allocated to specific localities based on the availability of housing at their time of arrival. The assignment process was largely independent of the future economic prospects of destination communities and of migrants' characteristics and preexisting networks. Once the initial assignment had been made, sorting was limited: Forced migrants' former homes were now located in foreign states whose citizenship they did not possess; within their new borders, moreover, the communist authorities and Western occupation governments restricted relocation.

(26 percent) belonged to ethnic minority groups. By the 1960s, the number and proportion of ethnic minorities had declined to 7.1 million (7.2 percent). The biggest shifts resulted from the Holocaust and the expulsion of the German minority from Czechoslovakia.

These features of postwar population transfers in Poland and Germany – minimal selection into migration and little control over destination settlements – lie at the heart of my research design in this book. They allow me to estimate the causal effect of migration and resulting cultural diversity on community-level social and economic development after accounting for factors that influenced assignment of migrants. Below, I provide support for these claims using the historical record. Formal tests are presented in the relevant chapters.

## PEACE SETTLEMENT AT POTSDAM AND POPULATION TRANSFERS

Czechoslovak President Edvard Beneš was among the earliest advocates of the homogenization of European states by means of population transfers (Ahonen et al. 2008, 62). He began with moderate plans to reduce the size of German and Hungarian minorities in Czechoslovakia through compact settlement and territorial adjustments. After Germany invaded the Soviet Union, his aims grew more radical.[2] Beneš blamed the war on "Germany as a people and state" and alleged that national minorities, the German one especially, were "a real thorn in the side of individual nations" (Beneš 1942, 230, 235). He pushed for large-scale population transfers as a way to prevent future conflict. As the war dragged on, the Allied Powers became convinced that homogenizing the border areas was necessary for securing peace (Kittel and Möller 2006; Cattaruza 2010).

Mass resettlement of some ethnicities seemed all but inevitable after the Great Powers reached an agreement on redrawing Europe's borders. At the Tehran Conference (Nov. 28–Dec. 1, 1943), Joseph Stalin used the large proportion of Ukrainian, Lithuanian, and Belarusian populations in Poland's eastern territories occupied by the Red Army in September 1939 as a justification for the permanent annexation of Poland's prewar eastern territories, at 179,000 km² (69,000 mi²) and 45 percent of the country's prewar territory.[3] This shift of Poland's eastern border would precipitate the "voluntary" population exchanges between Poland and the Soviet republics of Belarus, Ukraine, and Lithuania in 1944–46.

The Polish government objected to the loss of its eastern borderlands, known as *Kresy*, which included the major cultural centers of Wilno (Vilnius) and Lwów (Lviv). The Western Allies also initially resisted the Soviet annexation, but they were unable to challenge Stalin over the issue (Lowe 2012, 220). Instead, they opted to extend Polish territory westward to the

---

[2] In September 1938, after learning that Neville Chamberlain was meeting Hitler in Munich, Beneš made a secret proposal to Hitler, hoping to prevent a deal between the British and the Germans. He offered 6,000 km² of Czechoslovak territory in exchange for the forced transfer of up to two million Sudeten Germans to the Third Reich, but Hitler did not respond. See Hauner (2009).

[3] Today, these territories are part of sovereign Belarus, Ukraine, and Lithuania.

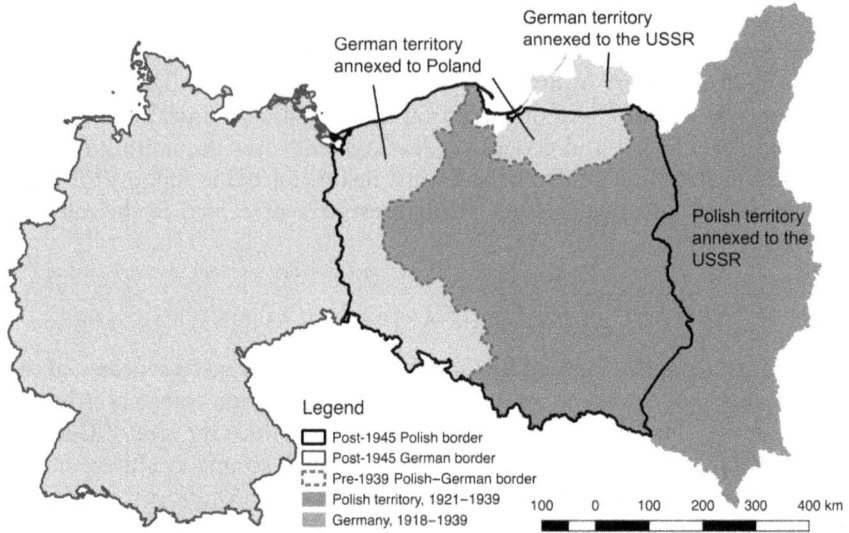

Map 2.1 Changes in the borders of Poland and Germany after WWII.

Oder and Neisse rivers. As Churchill explained on the first day of the Tehran conference, "Poland might move westwards, like soldiers taking two steps 'left close.' If Poland trod on some German toes, that could not be helped ..." (Churchill 1948, 733). The redrawing of the Polish–German border was justified on geopolitical grounds; by annexing the bedrock of Prussian militarism, the Allied Powers hoped to prevent future German aggression. It was also justified on moral grounds, to compensate Poland for its war damages (Blusiewicz 2015).

The status of Poland was discussed again at the Yalta Conference in February 1945. With the Red Army just 65 km (40 mi) from Berlin, the three leaders reaffirmed that the USSR would retain Poland's eastern borderlands and that Poland would receive parts of Germany in compensation (101,000 km², or 39,000 mi²), including the provinces of Pomerania, East Brandenburg, and Lower and Upper Silesia. Poland would also be awarded the former Free City of Danzig (Gdańsk) and most of East Prussia, as shown in Map 2.1. The Soviet Union kept for itself the northernmost territories around the port of Königsberg (now Kaliningrad). The Allies further agreed that eleven million Germans, who had lived in the annexed territories, would be "repatriated" to reconstituted Germany. The decision to transfer this population was reached with little deliberation and virtually no dissenting opinions (Frank 2017, 233).

The borders were confirmed at the 1945 Potsdam Conference (July 17–Aug. 2, 1945), where Stalin, Roosevelt's successor Harry Truman, and Churchill (succeeded on July 28 by Clement Attlee) convened for one last time. The Allies intended to finalize the borders by signing a peace treaty with Germany. However, due to the breakdown of relations between Moscow and the West, the signing of such a treaty was delayed until 1990. Article XIII of the Potsdam Agreement authorized the "orderly and humane" transfer of Germans from Poland, Czechoslovakia, and Hungary (Schechtman 1953). German minorities in Romania, Yugoslavia, the Baltic States, and other European countries were not included in the Potsdam settlement. Nonetheless, they met a similar fate.

The Allies further agreed to divide Germany and Austria into four occupation zones, administered by the Soviet, British, US, and French military administrations. A joint Allied Control Council was established to deal with matters affecting the country as a whole, with a focus on the "five Ds": demilitarization, denazification, democratization, decentralization, and deindustrialization. In addition, the Allies worked out a compromise on German reparations and created a Council of Foreign Ministers, which counted membership from the Big Three, plus China and France, and was tasked with drafting the peace treaties with Italy, Hungary, Romania, Finland, and Bulgaria.

The justification for mass population transfers derived, in part, from the unhappy experience with national minorities during the interwar period and from the widespread primordialist understanding of national identity among policymakers. As the British foreign secretary Anthony Eden explained in an off-the-record interview in 1943, "[Minorities] are a constant source of grievances and friction and they will always be used by some other Power to ferment trouble" (quoted in Frank (2017, 233)). In August 1944, the European Advisory Commission concluded that "German minorities became the advance guard of National Socialist penetration and the states which they helped to deliver to Hitler have a well-founded grievance against them. Their transfer to Germany would probably contribute to the tranquility of the countries concerned" (quoted in Schraut (2000, 116)). The removal of some groups justified the subsequent removal of others. In particular, the expulsion of the German minority from Hungary was premised on the need to make space for the Hungarian minority that had been expelled by the Czechoslovak government. Similarly, the need to accommodate Poles arriving from the territory annexed by the Soviet Union was invoked as a reason to expel the Germans living east of the Oder-Neisse line.

Moscow was well-acquainted with mass resettlement policy, having recently deported entire populations on the basis of nationality or for economic expediency (Lowe 2012, 221). The Soviet government exhibited little concern for the potential human toll. In Hungary, where the national government was reluctant to deport the German community, Soviet pressure was instrumental in starting the transfers (Kertesz 1953). When Beneš first mentioned the expulsion of then 3.5 million Germans from Poland in 1943, Russia's Foreign Minister Vyacheslav Molotov reacted with "That's nothing. That's easy" (quoted in Frank (2017, 261)). At pains to distinguish their approach to mass resettlement from that of the Soviet government (Frank 2017, 257), Western allies nevertheless agreed that population transfers were the only solution on the table.

There were multiple historical precedents for such policies. The British and US governments drew inspiration from the 1923 Treaty of Lausanne, which sanctioned the transfer of 1.5 million Orthodox peasants from Turkey to Greece and of over 350,000 Muslims from Greece to Turkey. This population exchange exemplified a technocratic approach to dealing with ethnic minorities that was buttressed by the primordialist conviction that ethno-nationalist attachments were innate and immutable (Özsu 2015).

For Churchill, the solution embodied by the Greco-Turkish population exchange held the promise of dealing with German aggression once and for all. In a speech to the British House of Commons on December 15, 1944, he proclaimed: "For expulsion is the method which, so far as we have been able to see, will be the most satisfactory and lasting. There will be no mixture of populations to cause endless trouble as in Alsace-Lorraine. A clean sweep will be made. I am not alarmed at the prospect of the disentanglement of population, nor am I alarmed by these large transferences, which are more possible than they were before through modern conditions" (quoted in Naimark (2001, 110)). Churchill put his thoughts in even more colorful terms at Yalta, claiming that "it would be a pity to stuff the Polish goose so full of German food that it got indigestion" (Lowe 2012, 231, ft. 4). US President Franklin Roosevelt drew similar lessons from the Greco-Turkish population exchange, though he avoided the issue in public.

Throughout this period, the Polish and Czechoslovak governments lobbied the US, the UK, and the USSR to authorize the removal of the German minority within their borders. From the perspective of both the Polish government in exile and the communist Lublin Committee, the German population presented a threat to Poland's territorial integrity and statehood (Naimark 2001, 136–37). A homogeneous Polish nation, by contrast, would be easier to manage. On September 1, 1945, the Polish Minister of Industry Hilary Minc, of the Polish Workers Party, expressed no qualms about the removal of millions of Germans as he discussed Poland's new territories:

We acquired territory with ready highroads, railway lines, and waterways, with towns waiting for settlers to come, with industry which can be put into service, with mines, and at the same time with remnants of a German population which we have the moral and international right to liquidate in such time and by such means that we shall deem proper. (Quoted in Bouscaren (1963, 49))

THE UPROOTING OF GERMANS

### Defining the German Community

But who counted as German, exactly? On the eve of WWII, many communities of German descent did not speak German; many German speakers were not German citizens either. From the twelfth century onward, multiple waves of emigration from the multiethnic Holy Roman Empire to the fertile and underpopulated regions of Central and Eastern Europe created pockets of Germandom across Central and Eastern Europe. Over the course of centuries, many of these German settlers intermarried with the native population, joined the ranks of native economic and political elites, and retained little but a memory of their Germanic origins. Even within the borders of the pre-1937 German state, ethnically mixed, multilingual, and nationally indifferent communities thrived in some regions, defying official census categories and nationalizing policies. This section briefly reviews the changing meaning of "Germanness" as an ethnic and political category.

The ethnocultural conception of German nationhood first appeared in the early nineteenth century, in response to the civic nationalism developing in France. In his address to the German nation, written in French-occupied Berlin in 1808, Johann Gottlieb Fichte envisioned the German nation as a living entity bound together through a shared language. Romantic Nationalists such as Fichte reimagined the speakers of various German dialects as one German *Volk* held together by shared language and history. The Romantic movement provided a blueprint for unifying populations divided by region, class, religion, and – not least – international borders, as one national community. However, Romantic ideas did not speak to the daily struggles of the average peasant, who in fact remained "nationally indifferent" and continued to have stronger local and religious allegiances (Zahra 2010). Nor did Romantic ideas influence early legislation establishing the boundaries of the German polity.

In the early 1800s, when modern state citizenship was introduced, descent was merely one of several avenues to citizenship rights, and there was no mention of ethnolinguistic traits whatsoever. In both the Germanic Confederation and the German Empire, citizenship laws lay within the jurisdiction of individual states (*Länder*). Each state sought to regulate the entry of foreigners, understood as citizens of another German state rather than as non-Germans, to regulate access to poor relief (Fahrmeir 1997, 728). A typical state constitution from the 1820s granted citizenship by birth (inherited from the father), by naturalization, by marriage to a male citizen, and by employment in civil service (Fahrmeir 1997, 732). Emigration entailed the loss of citizenship, even for those who preserved their native tongue and descended from eminent local families.[4]

After German unification in 1871, states remained in charge of regulating citizenship, thereby making citizenship in the Empire (*Reichsangehörigkeit*) dependent on citizenship in each constituent state (*Landesangehörigkeit*) (Brubaker 1992, 12). Citizens of one state within the empire could apply for a simplified form of naturalization in another state, but their passports still

---

[4] Citizenship received only a brief treatment in state constitutions, which instead focused on the political rights of *Staatsbürger*, a subcategory of citizens who were male, Christian, of independent means, and without a criminal record.

identified them as Prussian, Bavarian, Hessian, Saxon, and so on (Fahrmeir
1997, 751). National identity thus remained secondary to state or even
substate (regional) identities. In continuity with the earlier laws, citizenship
extended to all ethnic groups within state borders, including Poles in eastern
Prussia, Danes in North Schleswig, and newly emancipated Jews throughout
the empire. The population of German descent living abroad was not included
(Brubaker 1992, 13). As before, citizenship was lost following a decade of living abroad.[5] That is, even first-generation emigrants were no longer considered
German citizens.

To be sure, the descent-based and ethnic understanding of German identity
retained its appeal. As the German Empire confronted waves of Polish and
Jewish immigrants from the East, state authorities increasingly relied on ethnic
and descent-based attributes, discriminating against Poles and Jews in the provision of schooling, military service, and politics. The ethnocultural ideal of
Germanness found a powerful advocate in the Pan-German League, founded
in 1891. The League submitted several unsuccessful proposals to restrict the
naturalization of Slavs and Jews and to allow Germans living abroad to retain
citizenship status (Sammartino 2010, 23). Its initiatives finally bore fruit in
the imperialist and xenophobic climate that pervaded Germany on the eve of
WWI. The 1913 nationality law grounded German citizenship in the descent
(*jus sanguinis*) principle and removed the requirement of consular registration for Germans residing abroad. The law enabled fathers of German descent
to transmit citizenship to their offspring in perpetuity, no matter their ethnic heritage (Sammartino 2010, 24). Individuals of German descent who had
lost their citizenship acquired the opportunity to naturalize more easily. The
1913 law thus extended German nationhood beyond Germany's borders, in a
marked departure from earlier practice. As the German Empire went to war,
Germans living abroad were perceived as an opportunity to expand imperial
territory. The Interior Ministry drafted plans for supporting the "return migration" of German colonists into the expanded German lands and recognized
ethnic Germans inside Russia as in need of state support (Sammartino 2010,
37–44).

After Germany lost the war and its territory shrank, the promises made
to Germans living abroad became impossible to fulfill. Although the 1919
Weimar Constitution reaffirmed the principles of nationality delineated in the
1913 citizenship law, the return of German minorities from abroad as well as
of German citizens from the imperial territories returned to Poland under the
Versailles agreement was discouraged.

The possibilities open to individuals of German descent changed under
National Socialism. The Nazis sought to bring Germans from Eastern Europe

---

[5] After 1871, it was possible to register with a German consulate and retain one's citizenship for
a longer period.

"back into the Reich" as well as to extend the Reich's borders to incorporate Germans residing in Central and Eastern Europe. They coined the new term *Volksdeutsche* both to incorporate these heterogeneous populations into the new *Volksgemeinschaft* and to justify their military objectives. Following the Anschluss of Austria in 1938, Austrians were granted Reich citizenship. Sudeten Germans became Reich citizens following the annexation of Sudetenland in the same year. Germans living in Poland, and virtually all citizens of the Free City of Danzig (Gdańsk), became Reich citizens after September 1939.

No drop of "German blood" was to be lost. Nazi officials were willing to overlook considerable linguistic and cultural differences among the non-Jewish population in order to expand the size of the German community in the occupied territories and to fill the ranks of the Wehrmacht and the labor force, once manpower shortages began to intensify. They encouraged Czechs, Poles, and Slovenes with distant German ancestry to apply for Reich citizenship, provided they had no Jewish roots. These individuals were expected to assimilate over time. Speaking German was not required. For example, the Nazis classified Kashubians and Silesians, ethnic groups within postwar Poland, as *eigensprachige Kulturdeutsche*, or "non-German-speaking Germans united with the German nation through the shared German culture" (Kamusella 2004, 23).

To deal with the resulting ambiguity of what constituted "Germanness," the Nazis devised multiple categorizations. From 1940 onward, the German People's Lists (*Deutsche Volksliste*) divided the inhabitants of occupied territories into four categories: (1) *Volksdeutsche* at the top of the hierarchy; (2) *Deutschstämmige* (of German Descent); (3) *Eigendeutschte* (voluntarily Germanized); and (4) *Rückgedeutschte* ("forcibly Germanized"), applied to racially valuable individuals who resisted Germanization. Some individuals who could pass as German signed up for opportunistic reasons, because being classified as *Volksdeutsch* ensured privileged treatment during the occupation. Others signed up to avoid repression: Individuals who resisted being put on the *Volksliste* could be sent to concentration camps, while their children were taken away for forcible Germanization. Ethnic Poles from German-occupied Silesia were tacitly encouraged to register on the *Volksliste* by the Polish government-in-exile, keen to preserve the Polish population in that region. The total number of registrants on the German People's Lists reached 2.76 million people, with nearly two-thirds in categories 3 and 4 (Broszat 1961, 134).

In addition to relying on the *Volksdeutsche* to administer regions under military occupation, the Nazis encouraged their resettlement into the territories annexed into the Reich in 1939. By 1944, some 900,000 *Volksdeutsche* from the Baltic States, Yugoslavia, and Romania were resettled in this way. Resettlement policies were again applied broadly, producing linguistically mixed settlements. In reaction to this overly inclusive approach, the SS officers in the Warthegau complained that the incoming German settlers spoke Polish, Russian, and Ukrainian instead of German (Bergen 1994, 573).

## The Complexity of Identification on the Ground

It is this expansive, descent-based conception of the German nation that would guide postwar expulsions – not only from the German territory that had been transferred to Poland and the Soviet Union but also from Czechoslovakia, Hungary, Romania, Ukraine, Yugoslavia, and the USSR. Building on the Nazi Germanization policies, postwar transfers imposed a shared misfortune on communities that had little in common until the rise of Hitler and had until then identified with their locality, region, or confession.

Some of the largest "nationally indifferent" communities, to use the concept proposed by Zahra (2008) to describe individuals who resisted national identification, were located in the Sudetenland, Upper Silesia, and East Prussia.[6]

On the eve of WWII, the Sudetenland was home to three million Germans who settled in this mountainous region in medieval times. Until the end of the nineteenth century, the majority of the Sudetenland's population spoke both Czech and German. To encourage bilingualism, local families customarily exchanged their children for the summer or school year (*Kindertausch-handl*) (Glassheim 2016, Ch. 1). However, in the final years of the Habsburg empire, activists on both Czechoslovak and German sides worked hard to undercut such practices and establish linguistic separation. They marked the landscape with nationalist symbols and founded ethnic associations to conjure up national loyalties. Their efforts intensified following the creation of independent Czechoslovakia. To inflate the number of Czechoslovaks, the new government forcibly reclassified some Germans as Czechs and imposed fines for declaring a "false" nationality on the census (Zahra 2008). German speakers responded to such measures by rallying around the Sudeten German identity and seeking support from Germany. Their discontent with the Czechoslovak government peaked during the Great Depression, as they blamed their economic woes on the state and voted for the Sudeten German Party (*Sudetendeutsche Partei*), which campaigned for German annexation of the Sudetenland and was secretly funded by the Third Reich. After the war, the Sudeten Germans, alongside all those registered in the German National Lists, were subjected to expulsion.

Even the population that had lived within Germany's pre-1937 borders did not always identify with the German nation nor, indeed, speak German. National loyalties were particularly ambiguous in Upper Silesia, where confessional identity predominated (Jarząbek 2009, 17). Religion "provided both the ideological framework and the social space for Upper Silesia to navigate between German and Polish orientations" (Bjork 2008, 18). Most Silesians were bilingual in Polish and German or spoke the Silesian dialect. In the 1921 plebiscite, organized to determine the future of Silesia, in line with

---

[6] National indifference was also common in Poland's eastern borderlands, discussed in the next section.

the principle of national self-determination, 60 percent of Silesians supported remaining in Germany. Some 25 percent of Polish speakers identified with the German state, confounding ethnonationalist predictions. As pro-German Reverend Paul Nieborowski quipped, the "Polish-speaking population of Upper Silesia expressed many times that they wish to live in a Catholic way, speak Polish, and stay in the German fatherland" (quoted in Jarząbek (2009, 28)). In the end, the plebiscite failed to produce a clear mandate for the region's future, and the League of Nations proposed an alternative solution, namely, dividing the industrial region of Silesia in half. During the Nazi occupation, the Polish part of Upper Silesia was subjected to intensive Germanization. About 90 percent of its residents were put on the German People's Lists (*Volksliste*) and conscripted into the German army. After the war, Silesians placed on the *Volksliste* had to prove their Polish roots in order to avoid expulsion.

Ethnoreligious boundaries were similarly ambiguous in East Prussia. This region was home to some half a million Masurians, a Protestant community that spoke the Polish language. Commenting on the apparent contradiction, Richard Blanke (2001) described this group as "Polish-speaking Germans." In the 1920 plebiscite, 99 percent of Masurians voted to remain part of Germany rather than Catholic Poland, frustrating Polish Catholic nationalists who subsidized Polish newspapers, savings banks, and cultural activities in the region. In the 1930s, Masurians overwhelmingly supported the NSDAP. However, after the region was transferred to Poland, many Masurians applied for Polish citizenship, seeking to avoid expulsion.

In sum, Germans uprooted at the end of WWII held multiple identities and came from regions with complex histories of nation-building. Paradoxically, the decision to expel them into a territorially reduced Germany after 1945 "reinforced and powerfully legitimized" the conception of the German race promoted by the Nazis, which incorporated all individuals of German descent no matter their language, religion, and customs (Brubaker 1992, 168–69).

## The Process of Uprooting

Who left home and when, was largely determined by three factors: (1) the advance of the Red Army across Europe; (2) proximity to populations victimized by Nazi Germany during the war; and (3) the arbitrary decisions of local authorities, who were left in charge of deciding who counted as German.

The first wave of refugees from Central and Eastern Europe fled the advancing Red Army in late 1943 and early 1944. At that time, the Wehrmacht evacuated several hundred thousand civilians from the southern Soviet Union, Romania, Hungary, Yugoslavia, and Slovakia. By contrast, in the core German territories that belonged to the pre-1937 Reich, organized evacuations of civilians were rare because Nazi leaders did not want to admit military defeat. Many Germans residing in these areas, as in the territories of the pre-1937 Reich, fled independently, often in horse-drawn vehicles, at the start of the

Vistula–Oder offensive in January 1945. The years of Nazi propaganda about Soviet savagery and rumors of atrocities in localities occupied by the Red Army contributed to their flight (Ahonen et al. 2008, 135). It is estimated that some six million people left Germany's eastern provinces at this time, including 2.4 million who were evacuated by sea from the Baltic ports (Connor 2007, 13). Among them were around 9,600 refugees who boarded the *Wilhelm Gustloff*, the ship sunk by the USSR and immortalized by Günter Grass in his novel *Krebsgang*. All of these refugees intended to return home when hostilities subsided, unaware of the border changes planned by the Allied Powers.

Once Germany retreated, those Germans who had remained in the areas previously controlled by the Nazis were attacked by the victimized local population. Many were marched toward the German and Austrian borders and abandoned on the other side. The Polish and Czech governments supported these so-called "wild expulsions" and sent millions of settlers to expropriate German property in an attempt to force the Allies' hand at Potsdam. The army or paramilitary units would enter German villages and order the local population to vacate their homes in half an hour or less. Germans caught in the "wild expulsions" brought little with them and were often robbed of the few belongings they had along the way. Scholars estimate that 1.2 million Germans, including 400,000 from the territories incorporated into Poland and 800,000 from Sudetenland, were expelled in this way (Ahonen et al., 2008, 139; Glassheim, 2016, 43). "Wild expulsions" were prevented only in areas occupied by US troops, such as western Czechoslovakia.

Article XIII of the Potsdam Agreement, signed on August 2, 1945, called for the suspension of the expulsions until the appropriate infrastructure could be created to transport and settle the expellees. Nevertheless, little changed in areas controlled by the Red Army, where "wild expulsions" continued until December 1945. To evade accountability, the Polish and Czechoslovak governments outsourced the task to local authorities and military units.

In November 1945, the Allies released a plan for the "transfer" of the remaining six million Germans from Poland, Czechoslovakia, and Hungary into the Soviet, British, and American occupation zones.[7] Potsdam-sanctioned expulsions began between January and February of 1946. They did not look much different from the "wild expulsions" described earlier. As before, military and police units would round up Germans from either their homes or from the labor camps and detention centers where they were held. Eventually, the expellees would be marched to collection points and sent off to specific occupation zones located in Germany.

In Hungary, where no Germans had been expelled prior to the Potsdam provisions, transfers took place under somewhat better conditions. Still, the

---

[7] The French were not part of the Potsdam agreement and refused to admit expellees into their occupation zone.

procedures were similarly inhumane. As a rule, German settlements were encircled at night in order to prevent the residents from escaping; in the morning, the population was transported to an internment camp, where they were examined by medics and then sent off to the US occupation zone in Germany by train (Apor 2004, 40). On paper, the expulsions were limited to individuals who declared themselves to be German in the 1941 census, re-Germanized their Hungarian names, or joined the Nazi organizations. New exemptions were introduced over time as the logistical problems mounted. On June 1, 1946, the United States closed its occupation zone to arrivals from Hungary, creating backlogs. From 1947 until June 1948, German expellees were sent to the Russian occupation zone. In March 1950, the Hungarian government reversed its policies entirely, decreeing that expelled German inhabitants could return and would be guaranteed equal rights upon doing so.

How this final stage of expulsions proceeded depended on the local authorities, who were in charge of deciding not only who was German but also who was economically useful and to what degree. As a rule, the groups considered to be the least economically productive, including the old, the sick, and women and children, were expelled first. The able-bodied were sometimes held back until the end, as they could be employed to clear the rubble and perform other unpleasant tasks. Skilled workers in select occupations were retained, to facilitate the resumption of economic activity. Two exceptions to this rule are worthy of mention. In Czechoslovakia, Germans who had fought against the Nazis were permitted to stay (Kučera 1992). Conversely, the wealthy were forced out early from Hungary so that their property could be nationalized and redistributed (Kertesz 1953).

In Poland, approximately one million of the prewar inhabitants of the German provinces of East Prussia and Upper Silesia, subsumed under the term autochthones (*autochtoni*), remained in the country after signing declarations of loyalty. This autochthonous population was diverse and comprised several separate ethnic groups, including Catholic Kashubians in the northwest; Protestant Mazurians and Catholic Warmiaks in the north; and Catholic Silesians in the southwest. These were the same groups that the Nazi officials had viewed as German just a few years prior.

The Polish government viewed the autochthones as essential for replenishing population losses and as a justification for Polish claims on the historically German region. In 1946, in his position as minister of the newly acquired territory, Władysław Gomułka referred to the locals as "the living proof of the Polishness of the Recovered Lands." When discussing verification criteria in March 1946, he went so far as to argue that "even those who over the years succumbed to Germanization should be restored to Poland" (Kulczycki 2016, 170, 175). At the same time, Polish authorities feared German sabotage and suspected that the autochthones were staying for economic reasons. The resulting policy was inconsistent across localities and time periods: In numerous instances, autochthones of Polish descent were expelled, while many

German-speaking autochthones were prevented from leaving against their will (Stola 2010, 67).

The autochthones' ties to Poland were verified by a committee that typically included: a local governor or foreman (as chairman); two representatives of the People's Council; autochthones who had already proven their allegiance to Poland; representatives of the Polish Western Union (*Polski Związek Zachodni, PZZ*), an anti-German patriotic organization; a Catholic priest; a teacher; a head of the District Office of Public Safety (*Powiatowy Urząd Bezpieczeństwa Publicznego*); and a head of the district police station (*Milicja Obywatelska*) (Łach 1978, 64). As a rule, identification with the German nation as well as membership in the Nazi party or affiliated organizations was sufficient to disqualify one's claim to Polish citizenship. Beyond this, the criteria were vague. Language, religion, and self-identification were all considered. Yet, the various regional authorities often disagreed on what exactly constituted Polishness. For example, the new governor of Gdańsk emphasized self-identification as the most important criterion, citing the "insufficient clarity" of the 1946 directive on nationality issued by the Polish Ministry for the Recovered Territories (*Ministerstwo Ziem Odzyskanych, MZO*) (Kulczycki 2016, 176). By contrast, the governor of Szczecin argued that the majority of the population in his province "no longer felt any link with Polishness" and should, therefore, be removed to Germany (Kulczycki 2016, 178). Families were generally kept together; so, the German spouse of a Pole could remain in Poland after "commit[ting] in writing to maintain loyalty to the Polish nation and state and to raise the children in a Polish spirit" (Kulczycki 2016, 177).

The verification process, much like the population transfers, operated under the assumption that every individual held an enduring, well-defined national identity. Yet, as noted earlier, the majority of the locals who remained in the territories acquired from Germany were neither Polish nor German, and they preferred religious or regional identification, at least before they were forced to choose by the Nazi government. Upon learning about the hunger and discrimination faced by the expellees in defeated Germany, they made every effort to secure Polish citizenship for themselves (Sakson 1998, 214). A few years later, many autochthones would have a change of heart and seek to emigrate.

The transfers were largely concluded by 1948. Altogether, some 12.5 million ethnic Germans were uprooted from their homes between 1944 and 1951. At least 600,000, and possibly as many as 1.5 million, died en route (Connor 2007, 15). At the end of the 1940s, only 125,000 to 431,000 Germans still lived in Poland; 200,000 remained in Czechoslovakia, according to these countries' official statistics (Ahonen et al. 2008, 95). In Hungary, only 22,445 individuals declared German nationality in the 1949 census (Apor 2004, 43). If we are to go by the numbers, it is fair to say that the territories annexed from Germany, along with the Czechoslovak Sudetenland, experienced a near-complete population turnover.

## THE UPROOTING OF POLES

WWII and subsequent border changes also resulted in the forced and voluntary migration of approximately five million Polish citizens. This was a heterogeneous group, originating from three former imperial partitions of Poland and also from abroad.

In 1795, the multiethnic Polish-Lithuanian Commonwealth was divided between the German, Russian, and Austro-Hungarian empires. The empires pursued divergent policies toward the populations under their control. The Austro-Hungarian empire offered the most permissive environment for nurturing Polish nationalism. Poles living under Habsburg rule practiced Catholicism freely, had access to education in the Polish language, and enjoyed regional self-governance. The German and Russian empires suppressed Catholicism and Polish national identity. The brief period of nation-building following the creation of independent Poland in 1918 proved insufficient for erasing cultural differences between Poles from different imperial partitions. Indeed, the cultural imprint of different empires remains visible to this day, despite the massive population movements unleashed by WWII (Grosfeld and Zhuravskaya 2015; Zarycki 2015; Charnysh and Peisakhin 2022). Interwar Poland also failed to integrate its sizable ethnic minorities, which comprised 35 percent of the population in 1931 – a failure that would prove costly during the war when some of the ill-treated groups would collaborate with the Nazi and Soviet occupiers.

Divergent interpretations of Polish history under the control of foreign empires contributed to the development of two opposing conceptions of Polish national identity: as an ethnocultural community sharing one language and religion and as a political community sharing one state. These conceptions were articulated best by the prominent political thinkers Marshall Józef Piłsudski, on the left, and Roman Dmowski, on the right. Piłsudski glorified Poland's past as the multiethnic Polish-Lithuanian Commonwealth (1569–1795) and embraced ethnic minorities as part of the Polish nation. Dmowski, by contrast, perceived Poland's diversity as its Achilles' heel. He condemned the religious tolerance that attracted a large Jewish population to the Commonwealth and argued that the future belonged to the ethnically homogeneous Polish nation (Dabrowski 2011). The Piłsudski camp ruled independent Poland between 1926 and 1935, but many of its policies were adopted in reaction to the National Democrats, its main competitor. After the war, it was Dmowski's vision that triumphed. Formerly bitter enemies, Polish communists and surviving members of the interwar Endecja movement would collaborate in creating an ethnically homogeneous Polish state by expelling the remaining German and Ukrainian minorities and inventing the myth of Polish roots in the newly acquired German territories (Curp 2006).

## Repatriation from Kresy

After the westward shift of Polish borders, some 2.2 to 2.7 million prewar Polish citizens wound up outside of their home country. The resettlement of this population into the reconstituted Poland was governed by agreements signed between the Soviet-installed Polish Committee of National Liberation and the governments of the Ukrainian, Belarusian, and Lithuanian Soviet Socialist Republics (SSRs) in September 1944.[8] The agreements covered "all Poles and Jews who were Polish citizens until 17 September 1939 … and want[ed] to resettle in the territory of Poland," that is, they did not include Polish citizens of Ukrainian, Belarusian, or Lithuanian ethnicity. The agreements with Ukraine and Belarus restricted the "evacuation" to the territory that had belonged to Poland in 1939.

The deadlines set for repatriation were short and, as it turned out, unrealistic. It was determined that registration of potential migrants would take place from October 1 to December 31, 1944. The resettlement was to be completed during the period from December 1, 1944, to April 1, 1945 (Czerniakiewicz 1987, 33). This meant that Poles were supposed to leave before the status of German territory east of the Oder–Neisse line was finalized (Ther 1996, 789).

Determining who counted as Polish in the eastern borderlands was even more complicated than separating Germans from Poles in Upper Silesia and Eastern Prussia. One of the reasons for ethnic fluidity and "national indifference" in the borderlands was that this region had been part of independent Poland for just under two decades. Prior to 1918, the area had been split between the Habsburg and Russian empires, with opportunities for nation-building particularly limited in the Russian partition. As a result, the population outside major cities was ethnically mixed, and identities were ambiguous. The population "made up a continuum of cultures that stood literally and figuratively on the border between Poland, Ukraine, and Russia" (Brown 2005, 40).

Two imperfect heuristics have been used to distinguish Poles from other ethnic groups in the interwar period: language and religion. According to the 1931 Polish census, Polish speakers in the annexed region numbered 3.6 million, accounting for 34 percent of the population, while Catholics totaled 3.1 million, or 29 percent of the population. Neither indicator accurately mapped onto national loyalties, however. In the countryside, local residents often claimed that they belonged to the "Catholic nationality" or that they were simply peasants. In the Polesie region, annexed to the Belarusian SSR, some 60 percent of residents identified themselves in the 1931 Polish census as *tutejsi*, or "people from here." The ethnic divide sometimes overlapped with social class, with Polish-speaking Catholic landlords wielding authority over a Ukrainian and Belarusian Orthodox peasantry. Lamenting the difficulties in

---

[8] The Polish government-in-exile opposed the agreements and continued to advocate with the Allies against the annexation at this time.

TABLE 2.1 *Repatriation from the territory incorporated into the USSR.*

|  | Ukraine | Belarus | Lithuania | Other USSR |
|---|---|---|---|---|
| Eligible population | 854,809 | 520,355 | 379,498 | 800,000 |
| Registered for repatriation | 816,870 | 499,600 | 380,000 | – |
| Repatriated | 787,674 | 274,163 | 197,156 | 258,990 |
| Repatriated (%) | 92 | 53 | 52 | 32 |

*Note:* Eligible Polish population in other USSR republics was estimated based on the 1926 population census.
*Sources:* Czerniakiewicz 1987, Ciesielski 2000.

delineating nationalities in the region, the Secretary for the Ukrainian Commission for National Minority Affairs observed in 1925 that conversational language was a poor metric because the local Polish and Ukrainian dialects sounded nearly identical (Brown 2005, 32–33).

During the war, the Kresy region experienced not one but three occupations: first by the Soviet Union (1939–41), then by Nazi Germany (1941–44), and then again by the Soviet Union (1944–45). During the first occupation, the Soviets deported tens of thousands of Polish elites to Siberia and Kazakhstan and collectivized agriculture. The Nazis, then in alliance with the USSR, moved ethnic Germans from these territories into western Poland. During the second occupation, the Nazis murdered the Jewish population, with the help of the Ukrainian and Lithuanian police forces. From 1943 onward, anticipating the change of power, the Ukrainian Insurgent Army murdered 60,000 to 100,000 Polish civilians in Volhynia and Galicia (southern borderlands) to pave the way for the incorporation of these regions into postwar Ukraine (Snyder 2003, 168–170). The cleansings escalated into a full-scale civil war between Poles and Ukrainians. As the Red Army secured the area in 1944, Stalin was determined to separate Poles and Ukrainians once and for all, by removing the remaining Poles from the region annexed into the Ukrainian SSR and by removing all Ukrainians from the territory that would become postwar Poland in Operation Vistula (*Akcja Wisła*).

The emigration of "Poles and Jews" from Kresy was, on paper, "voluntary." Indeed, not all Polish nationals in the annexed regions registered for repatriation. Still, Poles leaving this area were doing so under duress: They fled communal violence, Soviet repression, and looming collectivization. Ultimately, the rates of emigration depended not so much on individuals' preferences, but on the corresponding policies toward Polish nationals in the newly created Ukrainian, Belarusian, and Lithuanian states (see Table 2.1).

The exodus of Poles was nearly universal from the territory of western Ukraine, which experienced ethnic cleansing in 1943–45. Fearing the Ukrainian nationalists, an estimated 100,000 civilians had fled across the new border by the time the organized resettlement process started (Czerniakiewicz 1987, 46). As the Polish plenipotentiary in Łuck reported in November 1944, "the rural population of Volhynia and other voivodeships, plagued by gang attacks, is literally begging to depart" (Ciesielski 2000, 22). Nevertheless, some dispute remained over the issue of nationality and, thus, over who had the right to leave. For example, the Polish plenipotentiary complained that whereas members of the Greek Catholic or Uniate Church were automatically considered Ukrainians, Roman Catholics listed as Ukrainians in their documents were not approved for departure on religious grounds (Kulczycki 2003). It is estimated that 95.6 percent of eligible residents of western Ukraine registered for repatriation, and of these, 96.4 percent left for Poland (Czerniakiewicz 1987, 47,131–132) (see Table 2.1).

In Belarus and Lithuania, intergroup relations tended to be less antagonistic. The key push factor for Poles seeking to leave these newly created Soviet republics was the traumatic experience of the Soviet occupation in 1939–1941. Convinced that staying in their homes meant collectivization and repression, many individuals with prewar Polish citizenship registered for repatriation (Kochanski 2012, 546). However, the Lithuanian and Belarusian authorities sought to retain Poles living in the countryside – at least until the fields were sown and harvested – even as they supported the emigration of urban residents, whom they viewed as difficult to assimilate (Kulczycki 2003). As a result, 80 percent of those who registered in the city of Vilnius (*Wilno*) were able to leave, compared to just 31.3 percent of the population in other parts of Lithuania. Additional factors complicating emigration from the countryside were poor access to transportation and attachment to the land (Czerniakiewicz 1987, 60–63). Altogether, it is estimated that only 54.8 percent (Belarus) and 51.8 percent (Lithuania) of the individuals who registered for departure were actually transported to Poland (Czerniakiewicz 1987, 228).

The occupational distribution of repatriates is shown in Table 2.2. Peasants made up the largest proportion of the population repatriated from the Ukrainian and Belarusian SSRs, at 38 percent and 35 percent of total migrants, respectively. Among those repatriated from Lithuania, craftsmen (31 percent) and white-collar workers (28 percent) predominated. These differences reflected varying levels of economic development in Kresy. Urbanization was much higher in the regions transferred to Ukraine and Lithuania – which included the cities of Lwów and Wilno – than in those transferred to Belarus (Czerniakiewicz 1987, 66). Czerniakiewicz estimates that approximately 60 percent of all Polish workers and about 50 percent of landowning farmers were repatriated. This is consistent with the greater obstacles for leaving rural areas, particularly from the Lithuanian SSR. Notably, an equal proportion of small landowners (5 ha or less) and large landowners (15 ha or more) repatriated. Each group comprised about a quarter of all repatriates. This suggests that economic resources were not the decisive factor behind leaving Kresy.

The experience of "Polish repatriates" was only marginally better than that of German expellees. Individuals registered for repatriation were exempt from

TABLE 2.2 *Repatriates' occupations by republic of origin.*

| Occupation | Ukraine (%) | Belarus (%) | Lithuania (%) | Other USSR (%) |
|---|---|---|---|---|
| Peasant | 38.22 | 35.28 | 18.37 | 28.46 |
| Worker | 16.23 | 4.85 | 10.36 | 36.75 |
| Craftsman | 10.10 | 4.56 | 31.18 | 9.74 |
| White-collar worker | 27.78 | 23.19 | 27.65 | 5.97 |
| Teacher | 0.41 | 0.85 | 1.30 | – |
| Share of urban population | 44.1 | 25.94 | 69.78 | 35.54 |
| Total | 100 | 100 | 100 | 100 |

*Source:* Czerniakiewicz (1987, 160).

paying taxes and entitled to receive property in Poland of comparable value to the property they were leaving behind. They were also allowed to take with them up to two tons of property, including livestock. In reality, few succeeded in transporting their possessions. Some departed in a hurry, fearing for their lives and lacking the necessary documentation. Others were denied ownership certificates by the local authorities (Ahonen et al. 2008, 132). Those who managed to bring their belongings were often robbed on the way, or forced to give up their assets in bribes to the multitude of officials responsible for transporting them. There were no schedules, and migrants would often spend 10–15 days in the open air at railway stations, waiting for transport (Kulczycki 2003; Sula 2002). Families coming from the same village were often split into several trains, which departed weeks or even months apart. Most migrants were transported in open carriages or cattle cars, and some died from overexposure, hunger, and disease. The passengers often had to bribe railway servicemen with alcohol – the only recognizable currency in 1945 (Blusiewicz 2015).

Most transports of "repatriates" were directed to the territories acquired from Germany following the Potsdam settlement. Only a small group was settled in the old Polish lands, numbering 250,000 in rural areas and 300,000 in urban areas by the end of 1947 (Banasiak 1965, 149). The repatriation from Kresy was completed within two years, with 98.8 percent of all repatriates relocated by 1946.

On July 6, 1945, an additional agreement was signed with the Soviet Union, allowing some 520,000 Poles and Jews to renounce their Soviet citizenship and return to Poland (Kochanski 2012, 545). Many of these migrants were deported to Siberia and Kazakhstan from Kresy during the Soviet occupation, that is, they originated from the same territories as the repatriates and had lived in the Soviet Union only during the war (Kulczycki 2003). These repatriates were relocated through 1948.[9]

---

[9] In 1955–59, an additional 250,000 migrants from the interior of the Soviet Union followed.

Polish–Soviet treaties also envisioned the repatriation of Lithuanians, Belarusians, and Ukrainians into the newly created Soviet republics. In late 1944, the Polish State Office for Repatriation estimated that some 546,000 people would be moved east. Ukrainians were the largest group, and their removal was prioritized owing to the history of ethnic cleansing in Volhynia and neighboring areas. In 1945, Ukrainians living near the border were ordered to move within fourteen days or face expulsion by force. Under pressure, most Ukrainians registered for relocation left Poland by the end of the year (Ahonen et al. 2008, 100–101).

Upon completion of the formal population exchange between Poland and Ukraine, some 140,000 ethnic Ukrainians and Lemkos still lived in southeastern Poland.[10] The Soviet authorities refused to accept more "repatriates." This decision led to the deportation of these remaining communities to the newly acquired German territories in Operation Vistula between April and September 1947 (Ahonen et al. 2008, 101).

## Settlers from within post-1945 Poland

The annexation of German territory also led to the voluntary migration of an estimated 2.2 million Poles from the territory that remained Polish after the war. Most originated from the overpopulated central and south-eastern voivodeships. Approximately 51.2 percent of voluntary migrants came from the former Russian partition, which had suffered the most destruction during WWII. Another 25.2 percent and 23.6 percent came from the Austrian and Prussian partitions, respectively (GUS 1950).

The first to move to the territories annexed from Germany were Poles who lived in proximate areas. They could simply walk or bike across the former border to occupy farms and houses abandoned by fleeing Germans. Later on, transports were organized from more distant areas to accommodate larger groups of settlers. These later migrants traveled with resettlement certificates from the local authorities in their places of origin, which enabled them to receive German farms and covered the costs of rail travel and food supplies (Gieszczyński 1999, 87–88).

Government marketing played no small part in driving resettlement. Advertisements and slogans were posted on city walls and hung on utility poles in villages, publicizing opportunities to obtain land and employment in the newly acquired territories (Dulczewski and Kwilecki 1963, 642). For example, a 1945 slogan by the Central Committee for Resettlement read:

Peasants! You no longer have to emigrate [from Poland]. You want bread – in the West there is bread. You want land – in the West there is land. Let's harvest the sown fields

[10] Lemkos originated in an ethnographic region of the Carpathian Mountains, shared among Ukraine, Slovakia, and Poland. In postwar Poland, they were viewed as a subgroup of ethnic Ukrainians and treated as such.

to fill our barns and granaries. The urban population will find factories and stores abandoned by the Germans in the West. The white-collar workers will find work in departments and offices. (Quoted in Blusiewicz (2015))

In April 1946, over 50,000 young Poles from all over the country attended "We Keep a Guard on the Oder" (*"Trzymamy Straż nad Odrą"*), a propaganda event held in the newly acquired port city of Szczecin (Stettin). The government facilitated attendance by paying for transportation and room and board. The authorities used such events not only to encourage resettlement but also to dispel rumors about insecurity and disorder in the west (McNamara 2012, 31).

To encourage migration, some areas were also designated to support specific localities in the newly acquired territories. For example, a coal mine in prewar Polish Upper Silesia was tasked with helping to revive its Lower Silesian counterpart by sending volunteer crews. The volunteers received monetary incentives (Jedruszczak 1967; Blusiewicz 2015). Under Circular No. 22 issued in March 1946, farmers from regions damaged during the war were given priority for resettlement.

To repopulate larger landed estates, prevalent in East Prussia and Pomerania, the Polish Ministry of Agriculture and Land Reform created a network of voivodeship and county-level councils tasked with propaganda and recruitment of potential settlers. They were also charged with maintaining economic and cultural connections between the sending communities and the settlers (Kersten 1962, 56). The success of this operation was mixed, given the poor state of large estates in the aftermath of war and looting. By the end of 1947, cooperative and parcel settlement covered 1,156 estates (254,280 ha) and 17,040 families throughout the country – approximately 16 percent of the planned number (Kersten 1962, 65).

Soldiers of the Polish People's Army were invited to settle in areas along the new international borders. They were given priority in farmland allocation and enjoyed free amenities such as agricultural tools, seeds, livestock, and furniture, along with tax incentives (Gieszczyński 1999, 112).

Surveys of sending villages shed some light on the socioeconomic characteristics and regional makeup of these migrants. A significant proportion were landless and poor and resettled in hopes of acquiring their own farms. For example, Żmiąca (Limanowa county), a large village in south-east Poland, saw 21 percent of its population ($N = 166$) migrate west between 1945 and 1952 (Wierzbicki 1960). Most emigrants (76 percent) were in their prime working years, between 15 and 45 years of age, and previously owned no land or only small plots. In the resettled regions, they could acquire larger farms (59 percent) or leave agriculture altogether (41 percent). Migration "resolved numerous longstanding conflicts, fulfilled many desires, and allowed the union of several marriages based on love by eliminating the need for a dowry" (Wierzbicki 1960, 100–101).

Sending regions were not limited to overpopulated rural areas. Settlers from Poznań region, which shared the longest stretch of border with the newly acquired territories, represented a cross-section of the population, including the intelligentsia, workers, and shop owners (Burszta 1995, 89). In large towns and cities destroyed by the war, such as Warsaw, Poznań, Białystok, and Grudziądz, inhabitants were enticed to resettle by the promise of finding better housing and simply by the opportunity to start anew. Kersten (1962, 48) observes that a typical settler from post-1945 Poland decided to settle in the newly acquired territories after already being separated from a native community during the war. Just like forced migrants from Kresy, many voluntary migrants had lost their property, experienced deportations, and spent time in forced labor camps. Thus, the boundary between forced and voluntary migrants in the aftermath of WWII was blurred.

### Settlers from Other Countries

An additional, smaller group of repatriates and re-emigrants (150,000) arrived from other European states (Germany, France, Belgium, Romania, Denmark, Netherlands, and Yugoslavia). Most came from working-class families that had first immigrated to the industrial centers of Western Europe in the late nineteenth and early twentieth centuries. The Polish government mobilized to facilitate their return, including by signing a series of agreements with states that had large Polish diasporas before WWII. Prior to the resettlement, the re-emigrants' real estate was surveyed to facilitate compensation for the items left behind upon their resettlement to Poland (Banasiak 1965). Warsaw was especially keen on attracting skilled workers in the mining industry to take the place of German miners in Lower and Upper Silesia, but the majority of re-emigrants were unskilled manual laborers. They returned to Poland in hopes of securing better career opportunities and for ideological reasons.

The largest number came from France, at 89,777 people between 1946 and 1949. The movement of these individuals was managed through repatriation offices in Międzylesie (Kłodzko County, Lower Silesian voivodeship) and Zebrzydowice (Cieszyn County in Silesian voivodeship) (Sula 2002, 155). Re-emigrants experienced in mining were directed to the coal-mining region of Wałbrzych and nearby areas (Sula 2002, 154).

Another large group of Polish re-emigrants was returning from German Westphalia, Rhineland, and Saxony, where they had settled in the 1870s. These Poles had spent WWII in concentration camps. The Polish government sought to bring them home, expecting their familiarity with German agriculture and industry to facilitate the appropriation of German farms and factories.

Yugoslav Poles, numbering about 30,000, comprised another distinctive group of re-emigrants. Under Habsburg imperial rule (1867–1914), many Poles were recruited to work in administrative positions in the empire's southern territories. They stayed put after the dissolution of the empire, finding protection under the 1919 Minorities Treaty. However, their status became more precarious once Yugoslavia entered the war on the German side in 1941.

This turn of events ultimately contributed to the diaspora's decision to return to Poland after the war (Sula 2002, 164). Most re-emigrants from Yugoslavia were farmers, though the group also included artisans, merchants, and laborers working in foundries and the textile and tanning industries.

## ALLOCATION OF MIGRANTS IN POLAND

In Poland, limited state capacity after a devastating war, coupled with time constraints, restricted the government's ability to regulate population flows. According to Thum, the resettlement process "serve[d] only the aim of territorial appropriation, with little regard to optimizing settlement patterns" (Thum 2011, 59). Where and how many people settled in a specific locality depended on factors largely orthogonal to the migrants' characteristics and preferences.

The Polish government did harbor ambitions to manage migration. In October 1944, it established the State Repatriation Office (*Państwowy Urząd Repatriacyjny, PUR*). PUR was organized territorially, with separate branches in each voivodeship. By August 1945, the organization had 259 regional offices, including input points (*punkty wlotowe*) that accepted migrants; through-points (*punkty przelotowe*) that provided food to people in trains and managed the trains' routes; transshipment points (*punkty przeładunkowe*) that switched trains from the broad to the standard gauge rail system; and destination points (*punkty docelowe*) tasked with delivering people from trains to their final destinations (on foot, by horse cart, or by car) (Ciesielski 2000). In 1945, PUR was incorporated into the newly created Ministry for the Recovered Territories (*Ministerstwo Ziem Odzyskanych, MZO*), which was responsible for repopulating the territory, providing material support and credit to settlers, managing the German property, and creating guidelines for economic development of the region.

A key concern of officials in charge of resettlement was to avoid conflict between migrants from different regions. The 1945 Regional Plan for the Resettlement of Agricultural Settlers to the Recovered Territories stipulated that migrants from the same region should be resettled as compact groups, avoiding intergroup mixing where possible. The authorities also sought to prevent economic grievances. The Plan recommended prioritizing forced migrants and ensuring that the conditions in the new settlements were not worse than in the ones left behind (Lewandowski 2013, 205).

The government coordinated migration from Kresy along three latitudinal railway routes: Southern (Rawa Ruska to Śląsk); Central (Baranowicze, Pinsk, Kowel to Pomorze Zachodnie, Zielona Góra); and Northern (from Vilnius to East Prussia). Thus, repatriates from western Ukraine – the largest group – were directed to Silesia; repatriates from the Lithuanian SSR to East Prussia and West Pomerania; and repatriates from Belarus to the Warta and Kostrzyn areas. Transportation networks were not the only factor considered; the government also sought to maximize agricultural productivity. According to the resettlement plan developed by the Council for Scientific Issues of the Recovered Territories (*Rada Naukowa dla Zagadnień Ziem Odzyskanych*), agricultural conditions in the settlers' destination regions were to resemble those in their regions of origin.

Orchestrating an orderly migration process, however, faced a number of challenges. For one, the government perceived an urgent need to rapidly repopulate the newly acquired territory to ensure the permanence of the new borders and prevent further looting of German property. In May 1945, the Polish Council of Ministers called for accelerating the resettlement process "without devoting too much attention to the mistakes and doubts" that might arise. In addition to moving migrants from the annexed eastern borderlands, the authorities encouraged spontaneous immigration from within post-1945 Poland (Banasiak 1965, 125). As Bolesław Rumiński, an official from the Ministry of Industry, said in a speech to the provisional parliament (*Krajowa Rada Narodowa*) at the time:

We have to take control, the faster the better. Don't wait for instructions or proclamations. The plan is simple. We have to take control by means of sending at least 10 percent of the population from just across the old border – without waiting for those who will come from behind the Bug River [i.e., from the eastern borderlands] to conduct the proper colonization. (Quoted in Blusiewicz (2015, 5))

A more fundamental challenge was limited state capacity. The task of carrying out an orderly resettlement turned out to be "more than the new administration could handle" (Kenney 1997, 158). Relocating millions of people in a state devastated by war and divided by internal political struggle, and doing so while the German population was leaving, was a logistical nightmare. The railway system, the central conduit for relocation, proved especially difficult to handle. Many train carriages were either destroyed in the war or expropriated by the Red Army. Important bridges and railway hubs had been blown up by retreating Germans.[11] Military priorities and the poor condition of trains made the length of the journey unpredictable. The trains frequently changed course, and migrants often failed to reach their destinations. For example, in March 1945, migrants were thrown out of the trains when Marshall Zhukov ordered that train carriages be immediately sent west (Ahonen et al. 2008, 131).

Once the resettlement process was set in motion, carefully deliberated policy objectives quickly gave way to an indiscriminate process, described by historians as "total chaos" (Kersten 2001, 83) and a "fail[ure of] coordination" (Kochanowski 2001, 143). PUR Director Władysław Wolski lamented that migrants were often offloaded midway to their destinations, in the middle of

---

[11] It was estimated that 50 percent of railway and road infrastructure was destroyed, including 2,465 locomotives, 6,250 passenger cars, and 83,636 freight cars as well as 5,948 km of railroads, 48 km of railway bridges and viaducts, 14,900 km of paved roads, and 15.5 km of road bridges (Kowalczyk et al. 1970, 1149).

an open field, because the train conductors lacked planned itineraries (Ciesiel-ski 2000, 23). Migrant Henryk Zaborowski describes the process at one of the PUR transfer stations as follows: "A PUR employee would write the name of a destination in chalk on the side of the railway car, and the cars would be uncoupled and shunted down the tracks" (quoted in Thum (2011, 69)). As a result, "sometimes where the transported ended up was a matter of pure chance" (Thum 2011, 68).

The rational management of housing for settlers also posed a challenge. A major drawback was that Polish officials relied on the outdated 1939 German census to estimate housing availability in specific settlements. This meant that they lacked data about the extent of war damages. Their job was also compli-cated by the fact that the population numbers were constantly changing. By the time some resettlers disembarked, other migrants had already taken their assigned places. As a result, migrants were frequently sent from one destination to another when officials overestimated housing capacity in a given area.

Silesia was repopulated first because Silesian settlements were easiest to reach for repatriates from western Ukraine, who comprised the largest group of forced migrants. Migration processes in East Prussia and Pomerania took longer; in these areas, voluntary migrants from central and western Poland were more numerous. Migrants from abroad traveled from west to east and were settled in larger numbers in areas closer to the post-1945 border between Poland and Germany (see Map A.1).

The haphazard nature of the assignment process, implemented by short-staffed administrators, produced considerable variation in the local distri-bution of various migrant populations. Despite the official policy to settle migrants as compact groups, many communities were broken up upon arrival because there was not enough housing available (Kersten 2001; Dworzak and Goc 2011). In a representative account, Marian Samulewski (n.d.) described the tribulations of his repatriated village in western Poland: "We were told our trip was over [...] but there were no more empty houses in Wierzchówo, so only three to four families were able to settle there."[12] Samulewski's family stayed put in Wierzchówo; others continued on their journey.

How many migrants from the same region settled together in one place was largely left to chance. For example, the entire village of Budki Nieznanowskie moved from western Ukraine largely intact to the village of Gierszowice, Opole voivodeship. For repatriates from Budki, only the material environment had changed following migration, as they now lived in brick rather than wooden houses and farmed larger plots of land with more sophisticated machinery. The inhabitants of nearby Busk, by contrast, were dispersed across nineteen villages and eight counties of Opole voivodeship and their neighbors were migrants from other parts of Poland (Dworzak and Goc 2011).

---

[12] Interview with Marian Samulewski, Centrum Historii Zajezdnia, www.zajezdnia.org/swiadek-historia/marian-samulewski (November 3, 2018). Translation by the author.

Conversely, there were many examples of groups mixing within a single settlement. For example, the population of Pszcew (Lubuskie region) consisted of migrants from central Poland, who came from ten different voivodeships, and repatriates from the USSR, who came from seven different voivodeships. Three villages in the Koszalin region were settled by migrants from eleven voivodeships in central Poland and six voivodeships from beyond the Bug River (Burszta 1995, 80).

While some migrants took advantage of the administrative chaos in order to move elsewhere after 1948, most remained in the settlements initially assigned to them. Not only did the Polish settlers lack knowledge about settlements in this historically German territory, but they viewed their assignments as temporary due to rumors that another war with Germany was imminent (Sakson 2011, 247). There was too much uncertainty as to whether accommodation would be available in some other settlement. In addition, the communist government restricted the sale and exchange of land. Migrants' ability to relocate was thus hampered by their incomplete property rights (Machałek 2005).

### Dataset on the Distribution of Population in Poland's Resettled Territories

To understand the resulting regional composition of the population in western and northern Poland, I digitized an unpublished survey of 1,217 historic municipalities conducted in December 1948 and located in the Polish Archive of Modern Records (*Archiwum Akt Nowych, AAN*). The survey recorded the size of the autochthonous population (*miejscowi*) as well as the number of repatriates from Kresy and USSR (*repatrianci z ZSSR*), settlers from within post-1945 Poland (*przesiedleńcy z Polski centralnej*), and returnees from abroad (*repatrianci i reemigranci z innych krajów*). It also collected information about the population temporarily present on the municipality's territory, which is not included in my analysis.[13]

I use these data to compute the total share of migrants as well as the diversity of the migrant population, measured as a fractionalization index based on the shares of these three migrant groups.[14] Map 2.2 confirms that Poland's newly acquired territories experienced a turnover of population. The share of migrants is low only in parts of Upper Silesia and East Prussia, populated by "nationally ambiguous" ethnic groups (Silesians, Warmiaks, and Mazurians) that received Polish citizenship. The map further illustrates that migrants from different regions were mixed unevenly across space, in line with the haphazard nature of the allocation process described earlier. In Chapter 7, I show that this

[13] The survey did not separate out the approximately 137,000 Ukrainians and Lemkos uprooted during the secret Operation Vistula in 1947. Because the Vistula deportees were deliberately dispersed in small groups and not allowed to exceed 10 percent of the population, their omission does not have a large impact on the population totals.

[14] The formula is as follows: Diversity $= 1 - \sum_{i=1}^{n} (s_i)^2$, where $s_i$ is the share of the population in each regional group and $n$ is the number of groups.

Legend
☐ International border
Share migrants in 1948
☐ 0.000–0.200
▨ 0.200–0.484
▨ 0.484–0.764
▨ 0.764–0.936
■ 0.936–1.000

100    0    100    200    300    400 km

Legend
☐ International border
Migrant diversity in 1948
☐ 0.000–0.173
▨ 0.173–0.324
▨ 0.324–0.445
▨ 0.445–0.542
■ 0.542–0.665

100    0    100    200    300    400 km

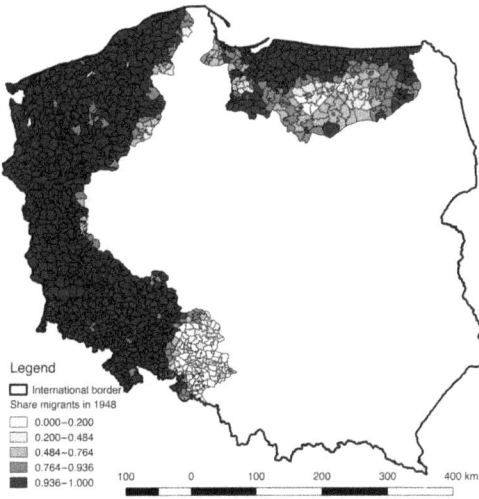

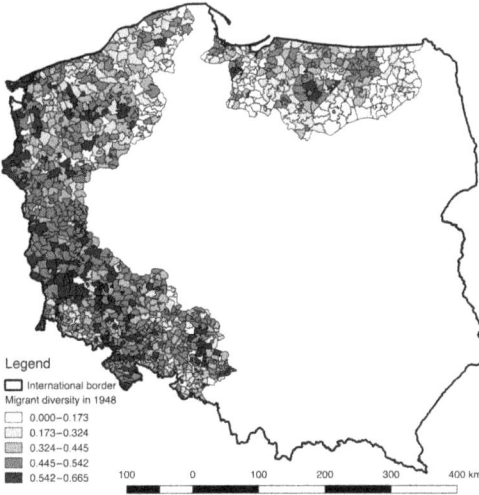

Map 2.2 Share and diversity of migrants in Polish municipalities in the territory annexed from Germany. Diversity is measured as an inverse Herfindahl index, with higher numbers signifying greater diversity. Municipality boundaries were reconstructed by the author based on a 1949 map from the Central Office for National Measurements (*Główny Urząd Pomiarów Kraju*).

local-level variation in the diversity of migrants within the resettled region was largely uncorrelated with the share of migrants, urbanization level, and population size, and only weakly correlated with distance to the German border and railway.

ALLOCATION OF EXPELLEES IN WEST GERMANY

Expellees arriving in West Germany similarly had little choice regarding where to go. During the "wild expulsions," they sought shelter in the regions that were closest to and most accessible from their former homelands (Müller and Simon 1959, 300–346). Accordingly, Germans from East Prussia and the Danzig region fled via the Baltic Sea to Schleswig-Holstein in the far north of Germany. Germans from the Sudetenland crossed over into neighboring Bavaria. As a rule, larger numbers of expellees arrived in the areas bordering Germany's former eastern provinces.

Once transport became more organized, expellees were first assembled in the distribution areas and then directed to a specific occupation zone. France did not view the Potsdam Agreement as binding and refused to accept expellees (Schulze 1989, 333). As a result, the share of expellees in proportion to the total population was much lower in the French occupation zone (6.6 percent) than in the American (18.7 percent) and British zones (17.2 percent).

The occupying governments insisted that expellees should be accommodated in private houses rather than placed in dedicated camps. They estimated that one room had to accommodate two people on average (Connor 2007, 31). The U.S. Military Government Regulations on refugees and expellees further stipulated that "expellees from any one community abroad will be distributed and resettled among several German communities," with the aim to "prevent minority cells from developing" (Schraut 2000, 117).

Expellees' first stop in West Germany was typically the district transit camp, where new arrivals were registered and subjected to medical examinations, vaccinations, and delousing. After the intake process was completed, expellees reboarded the trains and proceeded to other camps or their final destinations. Trains were often divided before departure.

The chief concern of the officials involved in the relocation of expellees was finding a spare room. In urban areas, acute housing shortages had existed even before the war and were now exacerbated by wartime bombing. For this reason, most expellees were directed to the countryside, with the number of refugees assigned to specific communities again based on the estimated availability of housing. The local mayor, in consultation with the housing boards, was tasked with "assigning the newcomers to individual householders at the parish level" (Connor 2007, 30–31). A small proportion of expellees was also temporarily housed in camps, although the occupation governments did not favor this practice.[15]

Like Polish migrants, German expellees were dispersed in small groups. Many receiving communities came to house newcomers from different places of origin, who shared little but the fate of losing their homes. The flight itself contributed to this outcome: Many communities were split apart, as they weaved their way across borders and into a territorially reduced Germany.

---

[15] Some camps were formerly used as forced labor camps.

The deliberate policy of breaking up large expellee groups from the same place of origin played an even bigger role. For instance, in 1947, expellees from a municipality of 2,000 residents in the Danube River valley (the so-called Danube Swabians, *Donauschwaben*) were dispersed across 158 localities in the occupation zones of West Germany (Kossert 2008, 55). As a result, "[i]n the vast majority of cases, the refugees were not able to settle in established groups with their social network still intact" (Schulze 1989, 334).

Once resettled, the expellees could not move at will. Until 1947, the occupying powers banned relocation altogether. In the next two years, relocation required permission from the military authorities and was limited primarily to family reunification. The freedom of movement was restored only following the creation of West Germany in 1949 (Müller and Simon 1959). Over time, there were a few shifts that aimed to equalize the burden of refugees across German states and to facilitate employment in urban centers. However, the initial distribution of expellees proved "sticky," as many expellees remained in the settlements to which they had originally been allocated (Connor 2007, 146).[16]

## Dataset on the Distribution of Expellees

My primary sources of data on the size and regional origin of the expellee population for West Germany at the county (*Kreis*) level are the 1946 and 1950 population censuses, digitized by Braun and Franke (2021). I supplement these sources with data from *Statistisches Taschenbuch über die Heimatvertriebenen* (1953). For analysis at the municipality (*Gemeinde*) level, I digitized results of the 1950 census from *Amtliches Gemeindeverzeichnis für Bayern* (1950) and *Gemeindestatistik von Schleswig-Holstein* (1951).

The 1950 census, conducted after the expulsions ended, defines the expellees (*Heimatvertriebene*) as the population which as of September 1, 1939, lived on lost eastern territories or in the Saarland, as well as people who lived abroad (using borders from December 1937) but spoke German as their native tongue. A child is counted as an expellee in this group (1) if his father was an expellee or (2) for children born out of wedlock, if the mother was an expellee. That is, the expellee group includes both Germans from the pre-1937 German territories and Germans from abroad.

The variation in the share of expellees to the population at the county level is presented in Map 2.3. According to the 1950 census, the state of Schleswig-Holstein (33 percent of expellees) followed by Lower Saxony (27.2 percent) and Bavaria (21.2 percent) were the most affected. These states had a larger agricultural sector and suffered less destruction during the war. As shown in Chapter 8, there is a strong positive correlation between wartime destruction,

---

[16] At the county level, expellee shares in 1950 and 1961 are highly correlated ($\rho = 0.83$, $p < 0.001$).

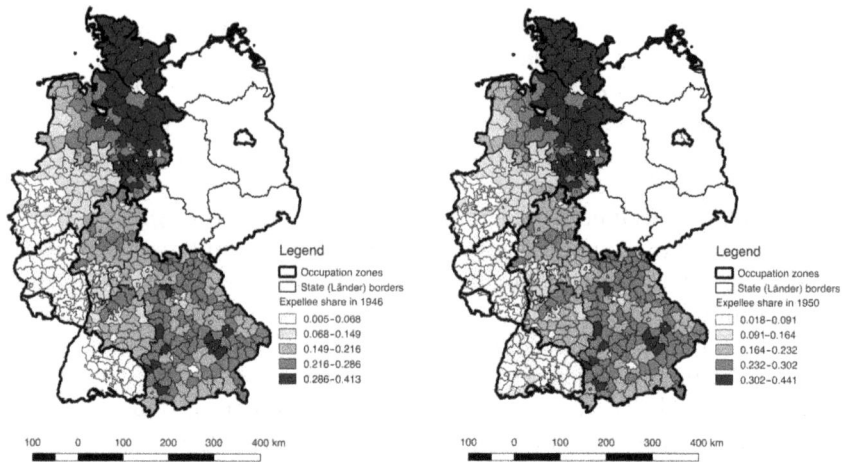

Map 2.3 Distribution of expellees in West German counties in 1946 and 1950. Data for the Soviet occupation zone are unavailable. Data from some parts of the French occupation zone exist only for 1950. Saarland joined West Germany in 1957. County boundaries are based on a shapefile from by MPIDR and CGG (2011).

reliance on agriculture, and the size of the expellee population. Distance to the eastern border is negatively correlated with the share of expellees. These factors are important to consider when studying the consequences of expellee presence for political and economic outcomes. The data further indicate that the heterogeneity of the expellee population, measured as a fractionalization index based on shares of expellees from different countries of origin, is higher in southern Germany, which was more accessible than northern Germany for expellees from Czechoslovakia, Hungary, Yugoslavia, Romania, and Silesia (see Map 2.4). Aside from the north–south pattern, the expellee diversity index is uncorrelated with the socioeconomic characteristics of receiving areas (see Chapter 8).

CONCLUSION

WWII and the revision of European borders upended the lives of millions of Poles and Germans, inflicting terrible human costs on people who had already endured six years of war.

The majority of postwar migrants had little choice on whether to move and where to settle. The allocation process in both Poland and West Germany was shaped by the availability of housing rather than by the economic potential of receiving localities. In Poland's newly acquired territories, migrants were allocated to settlements emptied of the German population. Only a small

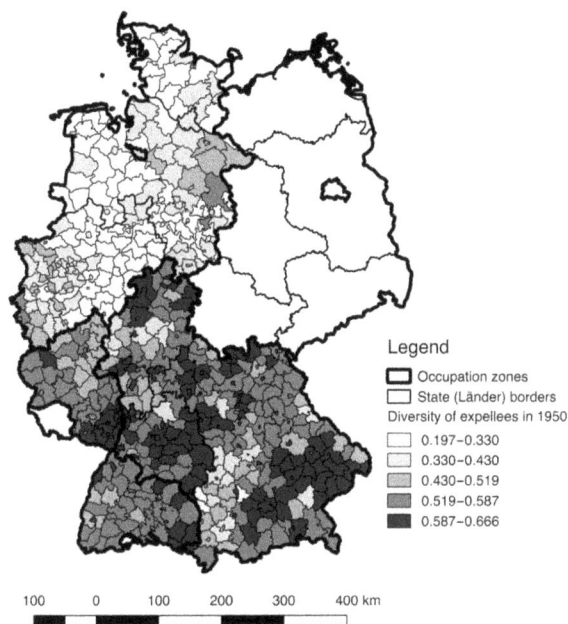

Map 2.4 Diversity of expellees in West Germany in 1950. Diversity is measured at the county level as an inverse Herfindahl index based on shares of expellees from different countries of origin, with higher numbers signifying greater diversity. Data for the Soviet occupation zone are unavailable. County boundaries are based on a shapefile from MPIDR and CGG (2011).

number of original inhabitants remained. In West Germany, expellees were distributed into private houses in settlements that had lower population density and suffered less destruction during the war.

While some localities received large groups of migrants from the same region or even village, other localities received migrants from multiple regions and countries of origin. Migrants that started their journeys together were often separated upon resettlement, by chance (Poland) or by design (West Germany). The timing of (forced) departure, the distance migrants had to cover, and the fast-changing availability of housing shaped the composition of the migrant population in each receiving settlement.

As noted earlier, the intent of population transfers was to harmonize ethnic and political boundaries. Yet, policymakers who expected population transfers to stabilize international and domestic politics were soon disappointed. While it is true that ethnic homogeneity within states increased, the resettlement process also triggered new boundary-making processes in receiving communities. As I show in Chapters 3 and 4, homogeneity in the regions most affected by population transfers was a myth. In both Poland and Germany, localities that received large migrant inflows ended up more diverse in the aftermath of the war than at any other point in their history. Even though migrants were considered "Poles" and "Germans" on paper, there were salient differences between them and the native populations in the immediate postwar period. Differences in dialect, customs, religion, and migration experience loomed large in the context of conflicting economic interests.

PART II

SOCIAL COHESION AND PUBLIC GOODS

3

# Cooperation in Homogeneous and Heterogeneous Polish Villages

The village of Pyrzany lies 30 km east of the Polish–German border in a flat open landscape of wheat fields. The houses lining the main street are painted neatly in white and yellow with steep, red-tiled roofs. At first blush, Pyrzany does not look or feel much different from a sleepy German hamlet. But then, a mural catches the eye. Painted on the outer wall of a shabby cement building, the first house built after WWII, it depicts a strikingly different landscape: rolling hills, small white huts with thatched roofs, and an eastern-style church surmounted by a tall, white bell tower. This is the village of Kozaki, now located in Ukraine, nearly a thousand kilometers to the east. It is a reminder that Pyrzany, as picturesque and timeless as it seems, is a product of tremendous upheaval and loss.

The artist who painted the mural, Bronisław Iśków, was just a teenager when the entire Polish population of Kozaki packed up its belongings and embarked on a four-week journey west. Iśków first painted the eastern landscape on the wall of his house from memory, but in 1998, more than half a century later, he and other Pyrzany residents made a pilgrimage to their native village in western Ukraine. With sadness, they stood in front of the old church building, run down after having served as a warehouse to Kozaki's postwar residents. Some of their old homes looked just as they remembered, while others had been demolished or were unrecognizable. A few of the visitors gathered handfuls of Kozaki soil to take back home with them. Iśków was busy making sketches – he would update the Kozaki panorama upon his return.[1]

Pyrzany's current inhabitants, like much of western Poland's population, descend from migrants who arrived from the east at the end of WWII. Yet, few other communities so diligently preserved the memory of their past. Few migrants were resettled in large enough groups to enable the preservation of

---

[1] The story about Pyrzany was sourced from materials published in Halicka (2011) and Witnica (n.d.).

communal bonds. Much more typical was the experience of the inhabitants of Kozłów, a village near Tarnopol (Ternopil). During resettlement, its 150 families were dispersed across 6 different counties in Upper Silesia. The largest wound up in Kuniów, a community that had a large native population and also received migrant families from other parts of western Ukraine, from Kielce voivodeship in central Poland and from Nowogródek voivodeship (now in Belarus). In the Opole region, where there is village-level data on migrants' places of origin, it is estimated that only 20 percent of migrants were settled as groups comprising at least twenty families from the same village (Dworzak and Goc 2011, 57).

This chapter examines how different settlement patterns affected intergroup relations and the capacity for collective action *within* Poland's resettled territories. It tests the first part of my argument: Mass migration can create new cleavages based on migration status and region of origin, with consequences for the bottom-up provision of collective goods.

It is commonly asserted that WWII made Poland one of the most homogeneous states in Europe. The vast majority of Poland's three million Jews perished in the Holocaust; the Ukrainian and Belarusian minorities shrank to single digits following the border's shift westward; and the German minority was eventually deported as well. Thus, many parts of the country that boasted a multiethnic population in the interwar period became exclusively Polish and Catholic by 1945.

What I will demonstrate is this chapter, however, is that by reconfiguring the remaining population within Poland, postwar resettlement created new forms of diversity in the newly reconstituted communities east of the Oder–Neisse line. In this area, the diversity of the population in terms of cultural norms, religious practices, dialect, and WWII experiences *increased* manifold. New cleavages developed within settlements that state officials viewed as ethnically homogeneous as migrants from different regions formed groups based on their places of origin and migration status (forced vs. voluntary) and emphasized their distinctiveness from the native population. Even in ethnic terms, western Poland came to be more heterogeneous than other parts of the country. This is where Poland's surviving Jewish population concentrated; where the remaining Ukrainians and Lemkos were resettled in Operation Vistula; and where other ethnic minorities – Silesians, Kaszubians, Mazurians, and Warmians – sought to preserve their distinctive culture in spite of the homogenizing policies of the communist government.

In the first part of this chapter, I analyze personal narratives and official documents to demonstrate that migrants relied on regional markers in order to structure social relationships in the new environment. My source materials highlight the role of three factors in the creation of socially relevant identities. First, migrants of different origins perceived differences in one another's language, customs, and value systems. Even individuals who shared language and religious denomination did not necessarily view one another as compatriots.

Second, divergent migration and wartime experiences, which often coincided with easily perceptible cultural markers, produced a sense of "shared fate" and "we-ness" among some, to the exclusion of others. This process of boundary-making was particularly relevant for forced migrants from Kresy, united by the loss of their homes in the east, Soviet repression during the occupation, and memories of violence at the hands of the Ukrainian Insurgent Army. It was also pervasive among the native population, united by the shared experience of discrimination under both German and Polish rule. Finally, cleavages rooted in regional origins and migration status were reinforced by conflicts over the distribution of farmland and housing, which varied in quality in the aftermath of the destructive war and the looting that followed. Eager to take over houses occupied by the autochthones, some migrants accused them of being German turncoats.

These boundary-making processes in the resettled territories not only mani-fested themselves in interpersonal relations but also impacted the communities' ability to provide public goods. In the second part of this chapter, I therefore assess the effect of cultural heterogeneity on the creation of the volunteer fire brigades, an indicator of a community's capacity for self-help collective action. I focus on the Opole voivodeship (Upper Silesia), which retained a significant number of its original inhabitants from before the war, while also receiving a sizeable, diverse migrant population.

I leverage an original fine-grained dataset on the origins of migrants in Opole villages. The dataset allows me to calculate the proportion of the pop-ulation that came from the same prewar *village* and that, therefore, preserved its social ties upon resettlement. It also allows me to measure the degree of cultural heterogeneity within the incoming group, on the basis of the shares of migrants from different *regions* of origin. I combine these data on the origins of new settlers with statistics on the distribution of the autochthonous popula-tion and on the occupational structure of the villages from the 1939 German census.

I find that the establishment of volunteer fire brigades was influenced both by the disruption of social ties and by cultural heterogeneity. Volunteer fire brigades are most prevalent in villages populated by the native population or by migrants who originated in the same village in the eastern borderlands. Such villages are 20 percent more likely to have a volunteer fire brigade than villages that experienced a greater degree of uprooting and cultural mixing. There are also differences based on the composition of the migrant popula-tion: Homogeneous villages settled by migrants from different localities in the same region of origin, which preserved shared norms but not networks, are 18 percent more likely to have a fire brigade than heterogeneous migrant villages, which preserved neither shared norms nor networks.

The analysis supports my argument that mass migration created new cleav-ages and weakened social cohesion in the affected communities, reducing their ability to act collectively. It corroborates the well-established finding in the literature that shared norms and social networks enable cooperation to supply public goods (e.g., Knack and Keefer 1997; Costa and Kahn 2003; Habyari-mana et al. 2007; Miguel and Gugerty 2005). Contrary to claims that western Poland's resettled territories became culturally homogeneous, in the immediate postwar period, many migrants did not recognize one another as compatriots and were reluctant to participate in shared endeavors. As I will further demonstrate in Chapter 5, weak intergroup ties in the resettled territories facilitated the expansion of the Communist state.

GROUP CONFLICT IN MIGRANTS' MEMOIRS

### Memoirs as a Source of Information

The Polish authorities classified the population in the resettled territories into four categories: native residents (*autochtoni* or *miejscowi*), resettlers from within post-1945 ("central") Poland (*osadniki* or *przesiedleńcy*), repatriates from the eastern borderlands and the USSR (*repatrianci*), and re-emigrants (*reemigranci*) from abroad. The terminology was politically motivated and intentionally overlooked the fact that the population within each category was heterogeneous.[2] As argued by Rogers Brubaker (2002), it is important to distinguish categories from groups: "Groupness" is an event that may not happen. In this chapter, I draw on memoirs written by migrants and natives in the resettled territories to examine whether these official categories had meaning in everyday life and, if so, how they manifested in relations among people.

Starting in the 1920s, Poland developed a tradition of organizing competitions to solicit diaries and memoirs (*pamiętniki*) from ordinary people. This practice continued into the communist period (Vickers 2014, 13–14). The Communist government and Polish social scientists viewed memoirs as an invaluable source of information on public sentiment. They were particularly interested in the experience of migrants repopulating western Poland. The Institute of Western Affairs (*Instytut Zachodni*) in Poznań announced the first competition at the beginning of the post-Stalinist thaw, at the end of 1956. Additional competitions were held in 1966 and 1970. In 1961–88, the Institute published several editions of select memoirs, archiving the rest. In the 2000s, there was renewed interest in the history of the eastern borderlands, leading to the publication of additional volumes. These later publications included essays that did not appear in communist-era publications and emphasized accounts that diverged from the official narratives.

How trustworthy are these sources? One advantage of relying on memoirs from the 1950s and 1960s is the incorporation of the migrants' own voices, despite the passage of time. Another reason to use these sources is that they

---

[2] The official count also entirely omits information about Ukrainians and Lemkos displaced by Operation Vistula and distributed in small groups across the resettled territory in 1947.

enable us to read history *forward*, thereby mitigating the presentist bias that occurs when past events are interpreted in light of their present-day consequences (Møller 2020). These two objectives are difficult to accomplish solely by interviewing the descendants of first-generation migrants today. Few of the original settlers are still alive, and even fewer are willing to recall past intergroup conflicts. During the four decades of communist rule, regional identities were suppressed and intergroup tensions were interpreted through the lens of class struggle. Over time, a national "Polish" identity evolved, encompassing most – though not all – residents of the newly acquired territories. Relying on memoirs therefore reduces the risk of misreading migrants' experiences in light of the political and economic transformations that followed.

At the same time, texts from the communist period cannot be taken at face value. Self-censorship was widespread, even after the political thaw in 1956. It is likely that few Poles were willing to challenge communist narratives about the successful "Polonization" of the "Recovered Territories," especially if they wanted to win the competitions to have their stories published. That is why it is important to supplement historical memoirs with post-1989 interviews and triangulate between different sources. I do so by drawing on oral interviews with first-generation immigrants recorded by the Centrum Historii Zajezdnia in Wrocław and the Historical Musem in Ełk.

It should also be noted that the authors of memoirs represent a self-selected group. They likely had higher than average education levels and possibly faced fewer integration challenges. Nonetheless, the analysis of writers' occupations suggests participation of a remarkably broad cross-section of society. For instance, the 205 participants of the first memoir competition included seventy-three farmers, forty-seven administrators, twenty-seven teachers, fifteen workers, twelve craftsmen, and twenty-eight people without permanent employment (including retirees and housewives) (Halicka 2016, 15).

### Group Divisions in Migrants' Own Words

The ostensible "Polishness" of the new residents of western Poland concealed salient cultural differences. As Thum (2011, 178) argues, migrants "may all have considered themselves Poles, but often they had little in common. They dressed differently, spoke different dialects, thought differently, and behaved differently." No less importantly, migrants from different regions experienced postwar territorial changes differently, and, as a result, several distinct communities of shared fate came into being. The population of *Kresy*, for instance, bonded over the loss of their homes and traumatic experiences during the Soviet occupation (Halicka 2013, 271). Conversely, migrants from central Poland regarded migration as an opportunity for social and material advancement; some genuinely believed in the communist vision of "Polonizing" the German lands that rightfully belonged to Poland. The native population experienced discrimination and continued to be harassed and distrusted, even after their Polish identity was "verified."

The official categories of autochthones, repatriates from Kresy, and reset-tlers from central Poland frequently appeared in the stories that postwar residents of the resettled region told about themselves and others.[3] In some cases, memoirs reference even narrower identities: It was especially common to group others by reference to the provincial city nearest to their place of origin, as *Poznaniacy, Wielunianie, Lubliniacy, Lwowiaki*, or *Złoczowcy* (Burszta 1995, 86). For example, a resident of a village settled by repatriates from the USSR and settlers from central Poland wrote in his 1961 memoir: "Besides the people from Poland, [emphasis added] there were also *lwowiaki* [people from Lwów] and *złoczowcy* [from Złóczow]" (Chałaciński 1965, 25). Both Lwów and Złóczow were Polish cities in the interwar period, but in the eyes of migrants from different regions their population looked foreign.

Shared regional origins, in turn, influenced social cohesion and coopera-tion in everyday life. Migrants from the same region were far more likely to come together for night watches, plowing and harvesting campaigns, and the rebuilding of damaged houses. Importantly, they were also reluctant to share public institutions, such as schools and churches, with the native population.

Regional origins were easy to identify because of differences in dialect, mate-rial culture, and even dress. One salient difference was linguistic: Owsińska (1987, 110) describes her surroundings as "a Tower of Babel of strange lan-guages [with] [d]ifferent accents, speech, different expressions." Kołodyńska (1976, 68–69) notes that, in her class, children from the east wore headscarves and felt boots, whereas children from Poznań "dressed more progressively." People also did not hesitate to inquire about one another's regional prove-nance. Kazimiera Jurkowa arrived from central Poland to Świdnica relatively late, in January 1950, but acknowledged that she knew "who's from where because they ask right away which part of Poland you are from" (Jurkowa in Kotlarska (1978, 131)).

Migrants from *Kresy* stood out because they had a strong bond with the Roman Catholic Church and spoke "archaic" Polish. Their culture was shaped by their living in a multiethnic and multilingual environment, side-by-side with speakers of Belarusian, Lithuanian, Ukrainian, and Yiddish. These migrants may have been forced to leave their native land because they were Polish in the eyes of Ukrainian nationalists or Lithuanian communists, but from the perspective of their new neighbors from central Poland, they spoke a strange language and may well have been foreigners (Halicka 2013, 271). To make matters worse, their identity cards stamped them as "born in the USSR" (McNamara 2012, 30), interfering with their memories of the borderlands as a Polish territory and suggesting to others that they were indeed foreigners.

---

[3] The re-emigrants from abroad made up the smallest group and were mentioned only rarely.

The "repatriates" had similar suspicions about migrants from central Poland, questioning their loyalty to the Polish state (Halicka 2013, 270–71).

The informal names given to different groups further highlight this process of boundary-making. Forced migrants from the east, for example, could be called *zabużanie* – a neutral term – but also *zabugole, zabugaje, zabugoży, ruski, ukrainioki, chadziaje*, or *ciubaryki*, which were unambiguously derogatory. Likewise, migrants from central Poland could be called *centralniacy* or *Mazurzy*, but also *kongresowiacy or galicjoki*, with reference to the imperial partition where they had previously lived, or *poznańskie pyry, (krakowskie) centusie*, or *(kieleckie) bose Antki*, with reference to their home voivodeship and poverty. It was common to lump forced migrants from the eastern borderlands together, regardless of whether they came from Vilnius or Lwów, because they arrived in larger groups and shared the experience of expulsion (Lewandowski 2013, 206–207).

Stanisława Sekowska, who moved from Uhnów (now in Ukraine), fondly recalls a sense of social harmony between forced migrants and the Germans slated for departure from Wleń, her new settlement in Lower Silesia. She empathized with the Germans because they shared the painful experience of being forced to leave their homes. She writes that the situation actually grew worse following the arrival of her fellow Poles from central Poland: "We 'easterners' stuck together, and some knew one another already from the east. We worked together, and we had fun together. We didn't hide anything from one another, we didn't lock our houses. We helped one another. Then everything changed because people from central Poland [z 'centrali'] started to arrive" (Sekowska in Maciorowski (2011, 75)). Sekowska's narrative suggests that at least in some cases, the experience of displacement produced a cleavage that trumped ethnic and national categories.

Even memoirs sanitized by Communist publishers speak to the suspicion and distrust between groups from different regions. Czesław Rajca, who had moved from a village in Western Ukraine to Święta Katarzyna near Wrocław, recalls: "Even though we lived in the same settlement, the old regional divisions prevailed. We from the east considered ourselves more important, and we lumped together all those who come from areas to the west of the regions now occupied by the Soviets as 'Masurians'" (Bömelburg and Traba 2000, 139). Józef Gałczyniak, who moved from southern Poland to the mixed village of Nososice, observes that migrants from the Poznań region were the first to find work, which fed jealousy and quarrels within the village. He also mentions "aversion, conflict, and frequent enmity" that for years characterized interaction between his mixed village and the neighboring Krzepów, settled by Poles from the eastern part of the country (Gałczyniak in Halicka (2013, 275)). In his memoir, Edward Morus notes that cultural differences "had a negative impact on the coexistence of the residents" and fueled "quarrels and mistrust among adults and young people and children alike" (Morus in Halicka (2013, 163)). Aleksander Pietraszko, from central Poland, wrote about migrants from the east: "A large proportion of the people who settled in the west came from beyond the Bug, where there was backwardness and ignorance, and therefore in most cases had no idea about technology and electricity." He recounted how he bought a vacuum cleaner cheaply from the parents of children who had been dragging it down the street, playing as if it were a dog (Pietraszko 1963, 189).

Helena Wróblewska, who arrived with her family in Drawsk Pomorski (northwest Poland) from territory in present-day Belarus, recalls that regional origins determined how social networks developed: "Migrants from each regional group stick to themselves. Friendships or closer acquaintances are based on the principle of originating from the same or neighboring towns. The search for compatriots is intense. People from the same locales are greeted like brothers" (Wróblewska in Isański (2017, 583–584)). Regional differences were no less important in large cities like Wrocław. In an interview conducted by historian Irena Turnau in the 1950s, one resident of Wrocław admits that he socialized only with people he knew back in the east: "My neighbors and I have nothing in common because they are from the central region and don't even go to church" (Turnau 1960, 277).

Local elites echo these sentiments as they discuss their struggles to bring people together. A Catholic priest in the Wrocław diocese writes that "the parishioners from the east looked with suspicion and distrust at the so-called "Centralists" [those from central Poland]." When it came to family events such as christenings and weddings, it was common to invite mostly "one's own folk" (Urban (1965, 65), quoted in Thum (2011, 178)). Jan Jakubek, a teacher in the Gdańsk region, writes that integrating "people from different parts of Poland [...] of different social and regional origins [...] into one harmonious community [...] was truly a difficult task" (Dulczewski and Kwilecki 1963, 620). Another teacher, Wiesław Sauter, recalls the reluctance of Polish migrants to send their children to the same schools as the native population, whom they viewed as "German turncoats." He writes that his Polish colleague "could not forgive [him for the fact] that on the first day of school, all children were led to church wearing white-red-white [Polish] flags" (Sauter 2016, 314). Not all elites were equally sensitive though, and even communist activists often blundered. Wróblewska recalls that one of them addressed the crowd as follows: "Dear comrades! Oh ... and you people from beyond the Bug River" (Wróblewska in Isański (2017, 583–584)).

The larger the population from the same region that settled in one place, the more likely it was to form a self-sufficient group and avoid contact with migrants from another region. For example, the repatriates from Yugoslavia retained their social organization after they moved, as a cohesive group, to Bolesław county (Wrocław voivodeship). They kept apart from the rest of the population and were belittled as "Gypsies" and "Godslavs" (*Bogoslowianie*) (Burszta 1995, 96–97).

The relations were particularly tense between migrants and the native population, concentrated in Silesia and East Prussia.[4] Although they were "verified" as Polish by the authorities, the autochthones were treated as foreigners and experienced discrimination. They stood out linguistically in their continued use of German, despite the official ban on its use. For instance, according to estimates run in 1949 by local authorities and organizations, only 37 percent of the 2,769 autochthones in Wrocław were fluent in Polish, and up to 20 percent of the 13,000 autochthones in the city of Gdańsk understood no Polish at all (see Kulczycki (2016, 250)). In Eastern Prussia, the Protestant religion of the autochthonous population served as an additional marker of Germanness that distinguished it from the Catholic Polish migrants.[5]

Linguistic and confessional differences were not the only reason for strained intergroup relations. The native presence in the region meant less farmland for the migrants. Sometimes the native residents returned from expulsion or forced labor to find their farms and houses occupied by the migrants (McNamara 2012, 25). Even when the settlers received alternative housing, bad blood between the two groups endured. Material incentives led migrants to harass the autochthones, accusing them of being Germans in disguise, in hopes of acquiring their houses (Kulczycki 2016, 275–280).

The mistreatment and exploitation of the autochthonous population was widespread. In one instance, a Polish immigrant stole the image of the Virgin Mary from a native resident (ethnic Mazurian) of Szczytno county in East Prussia, justifying it as follows: "I am a Pole and a Catholic. You are a German pig, and you believe in Luther. You do not deserve to have the Mother of God" (Plotek 2011, 194). Edward Zwingelberg, from a family of Mazurians who remained in Ełk after the war, recalls being bullied by children in school because of his German surname despite the fact that he spoke Polish at home (Zwingelberg 2021). Helena Kłos, a Kashubian living in Gdańsk, recounts her experience as follows: "Kashubians were treated very badly here. I could not speak Kashubian at home. I have worked in the city council in Gdańsk for 35 years but could [not] say that I am a Kashubian. People from the eastern parts of Poland who worked treated Kashubians as Germans" (quoted in Pryczkowski (2019)).

Unpleasant encounters with Polish settlers served to convince the native population that they were lazy and incompetent. One native Silesian described the newcomers as follows: "The repatriates came here devastated, but with food, bacon, and vodka. Initially, they did not work; Silesians did all the work while the repatriates were enjoying themselves" (quoted in Nowakowski (1957, 40)). Tensions between the two groups sometimes escalated into open violence. In January 1946, an extra militia unit was called up to break up

---

[4] A smaller group of autochthones, represented by Kashubians, was also present in Pomerania.
[5] The autochthones in Silesia were predominantly Catholic.

a fight between the migrant and native workers at the Groszowice cement factory.[6]

The experience of discrimination, by incoming settlers as well as by the new authorities, strengthened ingroup identification among the autochthones, who largely kept to themselves. Marek Zdzisław Zdziech, whose family relocated from Lwów (Kresy) to Huta Zabrze (Silesia), recalls that native and migrant children were told to avoid one another and that migrants from the east "had for years demonstrated superiority to the autochthones, while the Silesians showed fear of strangers and kept their distance" (Maciorowski 2011, 43).

In some cases, the autochthonous population bonded with Ukrainians who were forcibly resettled during Operation Vistula over their shared experience of discrimination (Marcinkiewicz 2017, 40). Lidia Witkowska, a Mazurian living in Ełk, interviewed by Dariusz Zuber in 2021, recalls that Ukrainians displaced from Rogale, in southeast Poland, took some Mazurians "under their wing," sharing their flour and milk (Witkowska 2021). Similar to the common understanding that emerged in some places between forced migrants from Kresy and departing Germans, the rapport between Mazurians and displaced Ukrainians illustrates the role of shared suffering in shaping interpersonal relations.

## SOCIAL RELATIONS AND PROPERTY CONFLICT IN OFFICIAL DOCUMENTS

The challenges of coexistence portrayed in migrants' memoirs are also reflected in surveys conducted by the authorities. Despite the official position that the resettled territories' residents were all equally Polish, the government was nonetheless concerned that mixing populations from different regions could create conflict. In 1947, the Bureau for Resettlement Studies (*BSOP, Biuro Studiów Osadniczo-Przesiedleńczych*), a state agency tasked with gathering and analyzing statistical data about the resettled territories, conducted field-work to assess local conditions.[7] BSOP officials interviewed and observed migrants across the full expanse of the resettled territories. They ranked "the coexistence of groups of Polish people from different regions of origin" on a scale of 1 (good) to 5 (bad). Where they observed conflicts, they reported the groups involved, assessed the reasons for the conflict, and recommended remedial measures. Researchers disagree on whether the BSOP evaluation provides an accurate assessment of the situation on the ground. I would posit that if there is any bias in the data, it would present an overly positive picture of intergroup coexistence.

The BSOP concluded that the relationship between different groups was generally poor, particularly in Upper Silesia, which retained significant numbers of autochthones. The disparities in the economic circumstances among

---

[6] AAN, MZO, Sygn. 1255, p. 9–10.
[7] AAN MZO 1662, 99–115. The results were also analyzed in Szarota (1969, 301) and Kersten (1965, 11–13).

each migrant group (24.9 percent of responses), coupled with conflicts over German property (13.2 percent of responses), played a significant role in generating intergroup tensions. Overall, economic reasons for conflict were mentioned more frequently (54.8 percent of responses) than cultural differences (45.4 percent of responses). The repatriates and military settlers were reportedly jealous of voluntary migrants from central Poland, who had arrived earlier and had taken over better farms. According to one report, the repatriates were frustrated "because they often left their farms in a good condition beyond the Bug River, but received farms that were destroyed [in the west], while voluntary migrants from central Poland left their farms, relatives, and children in central Poland and received additional farms [in the west], getting rich like nobility" (Kersten 1965, 12–13). The settlement authorities were forced to intervene on numerous occasions, reminding the migrants of their common Polish identity.

It is important to remember that, despite these complaints, intergroup inequality in the resettled region was actually low. The expulsion of Germans allowed the government to redistribute land, granting plots to formerly landless migrants from central Poland. The largest German landholdings were either turned into collective farms and cooperatives or divided up. The amount of land redistributed to migrant families was tied to land quality and closely regulated. Finally, the amount of wealth prior to WWII had little bearing on the amount of property that individuals were allowed to keep after resettlement. In short, the differences in land ownership and housing were negligible by prewar standards.

State officials were particularly concerned about tensions between the incoming migrants and the native population. The head of Ostróda county observed: "The greatest obstacle in the area of re-Polonization of this population is ... the immigrant population, which uses any excuse of casting the autochthonous population as 'Germans'" [in order to exploit them] (quoted in Kulczycki (2016, 246)). In late 1949, officials in the Ministry of Public Administration (MAP) reported with concern that the autochthones were boycotting Polish schools and listening to German radio, resigned to their low status in Poland and convinced that they were "destined solely for manual labor with no chance for social advancement."[8]

In sum, there was a lack of unity among people in the resettled territories, even where they shared a common language, religious denomination, or a sense of "Polishness," which many did not. Several factors contributed to this. One was competition for land and farms: Migrants saw the native population and one another as an obstacle to obtaining these prized economic assets, and sought to obtain these assets through coordination with migrants of shared origin and/or migration history. The painful experience of displacement and

---

[8] AAN, MAP, Syg. 142, p. 22–23.

discrimination also produced cleavages. It created a strong sense of community among the displaced population from Kresy and among the autochthones, while at the same time complicating their interactions across group boundaries. Bemoaning the loss of their native villages, forced migrants sometimes identified with the departing German population more so than with their compatriots from central Poland. Similarly, the autochthones could not but identify with the experiences of their expelled German neighbors after experiencing discrimination by migrants from Kresy and central Poland.

In the next section, I ask whether the cleavages formed by mass resettlement affected the provision of public goods at the settlement level.

## HOMOGENEITY AND COOPERATION AT THE VILLAGE LEVEL

The resettlement process produced four types of communities:

1. Autochthonous (or "native") communities, where community bonds remained intact and the population was homogeneous. For these communities, only the broader institutional environment changed after 1945.
2. Homogeneous migrant communities that retained their communal bonds upon migration because the entire village migrated as a unit, as in the case of the village of Pyrzany (see the introductory section earlier).
3. Homogeneous migrant communities where residents came from different villages within the same region and shared social norms but not networks.
4. Heterogeneous migrant communities, where residents came from different regions and shared neither norms nor networks, as in the case of Kuniów (see the introductory section earlier).

These differences in community composition were a product of the arbitrary assignment process I described in Chapter 2. State officials in charge of resettlement were guided by the availability of housing, but they frequently overestimated local absorption capacity due to insufficient information about the region and wartime damage to its housing stock. As a rule, forced migrants traveled in larger groups than voluntary migrants, but in many cases a large group from the sending village in central Poland traveled together (Wierzbicki 2014). Nonetheless, many such groups were split into smaller units upon arrival because the destination villages were already partly occupied. How long the journey lasted determined how many houses were still available in a given village and thus how many migrants from one place of origin would be able to settle there. The situation was chaotic because, at the same time as forced migrants were already arriving from the east by train and voluntary migrants were crossing into the new territory from all directions and by all means of transport, the authorities were still deporting the Germans and taking stock of the autochthones, deciding who would be expelled and who would be allowed to remain.

I argue that the native communities as well as migrants resettled together with a large group from their village of origin had a particular advantage over heterogeneous migrant communities: shared norms and shared networks. In the native communities, the social structure remained unchanged after the war. In the few cases where an entire village was resettled from the USSR to Western Poland, the situation played out similarly. Homogeneous communities composed of migrants arriving from different villages within the same region encountered greater difficulties, but they were still able to replicate familiar patterns of associational behavior from their past lives and reestablish a semblance of social order because they shared social norms, even though their networks were disrupted. I expect heterogeneous communities, composed of migrants who shared neither norms nor networks, to have encountered the greatest obstacles to cooperation.

The advantages of homogeneity for bottom-up cooperation became evident in the creation of the first schools, the restoration of destroyed infrastructure, and the establishment of places of worship. The first schools in the region were created on the initiative of the native population. For example, as early as March 1945, a delegation from Dąbrówka Wielkopolska, an autochthonous village in Poznań voivodeship, contacted the nearby Poznań school district (which was on the Polish side of the pre-WWII Polish–German border) in search of teaching materials, opening a school for 160 children from the surrounding villages soon afterward (Magierska 1976, 204–205). The autochthonous population also played a key role in setting up Polish schools in Western Pomerania (now West Pomeranian voivodeship) and East Prussia (Olsztyn voivodeship) (Magierska 1976, 205). As the number of migrants in the region increased, schools began to appear in homogeneous migrant communities, whose members were able to band together to restore school buildings and provide lodging and food for teachers.

The collective efforts of migrant communities were also central to the rebuilding of churches and the restoration of spiritual life.[9] Forced migrants from Kresy often arrived with priests and religious artifacts from their native villages, including icons, bells, confessionals, and statues of saints. One migrant, Genowefa Kruk, born in 1930 in Obertyn (former Stanisławów voivodeship, now western Ukraine) and resettled to Siedlce (Silesia), emphasizes the role of the homogeneous community in maintaining religious traditions upon migration: "We brought all of our [religious] customs with us.... Here in Siedlce, the majority of people came from Obertyn, Dolina, and Stryj [Kresy villages], so all of the traditions were simply transported here. Nothing has changed ... What we did there, we do here" (Kruk n.d.).

---

[9] Whereas major church buildings in cities were subsidized by the state and the church authorities, the reconstruction of small parishes depended entirely on the voluntary efforts of migrants (Grabowski 2002, 242).

In heterogeneous communities, the resumption of religious life took longer, because intergroup antagonisms reduced the utility of attending shared services. Migrants from central Poland were also markedly less religious than repatriates from Kresy, an aspect that increased mutual suspicion (Lewandowski 2013). Aleksandra Hołubecka-Zielnicowa's research on Dziadowa Kłoda, a Silesian village populated by migrants of mixed origins, shows that migrants asked the priest to assign church benches based on regional origin and did not attend funerals or weddings of migrants from culturally different regions (Hołubecka-Zielnicowa 1970, 66).

A few representative cases illustrate the differences in cooperation levels between heterogeneous and homogeneous communities in the first years following resettlement.

An example of a successful homogeneous community is the village of Bieniów (Lubusz voivodeship), which was settled by about 250 USSR repatriates from two neighboring villages, Koniuszki Siemianowskie and Dołobow, near the city of Lwów. The migrants arrived in March 1946 with their priest Maciej Sieńko. In the summer of 1946, they opened a primary school. They proceeded to establish an informal committee of men from the village tasked with handling the restoration of the local church. The church building was rebuilt by 1948, and the presbytery building by 1950. Also in 1948, a volunteer fire brigade (*Ochotnicza straż pożarna, OSP*) and a sports club (*Ludowy Zespół Sportowy, LZS*) were established, and a German bakery was reopened for business, now selling eastern specialties. In other words, not long after resettlement, the community was able to provide a range of public goods (education, security, fire protection) and restore economic activities in the village, which had been disrupted by the war and the exodus of the German population.

Another example is the homogeneous community of Pyrzany (Lubusz voivodeship), mentioned at the beginning of the chapter. In order to protect the village from crime and fires, migrants formed a volunteer fire brigade that doubled as a militia. They then founded a preschool and reopened the German bakery and grocery stores – all within a year of resettlement (Halicka 2011). In this homogeneous migrant community, informal norms and networks ensured that the group's transition to a new location was orderly and allowed for the resumption of economic activity almost immediately following resettlement. The community organized collectively to provide a range of public goods, from security to repaired infrastructure to cultural activities. Father Józef Anczarski, who was visiting the village for a Lenten retreat in 1955, conveyed his impressions of the high level of cooperation in the village as follows: "They are not uprooted. They have their own traditions, their lives were not interrupted" (Witnica n.d.).

A striking contrast to Pyrzany was the nearby village of Oksza, settled by heterogeneous migrant groups from central Poland and the USSR in 1948. Stefan Cebulski, directed to Oksza by the PUR office in Gorzów, describes his first year in the village: "A lot of destruction could have been avoided through better organization of resettlement, but there was no oversight of the process: Everyone was looting and pillaging, like a hungry wolf would do to his prey" (Solinska and Koniusz 1961).

Another example of a dysfunctional heterogeneous community was Łęgowo (Lubusz voivodeship), a village settled by repatriates from a number of voivodeships annexed to the USSR as well as by migrants from central Poland. The new settlers arrived in several stages beginning in June 1945. Those who arrived first were able to acquire better houses. The new villagers struggled to cooperate, and an OSP was never established. The only social organization that functioned in the village during the 1940s and 1950s was a local sports club. An attempt to establish a Women's Circle (*Koło Ligi Kobiet*) in 1949 failed. Eventually, a dozen women joined a different women's club (*Koło Gospodyń Wiejskich*), but even this association fell into inactivity and dissolved in 1952 (Chmielewska 1965, 230). There was no church in the village until 1957, when it appeared thanks to the efforts of a priest from Gorzów Wielkopolski rather than of the migrants themselves.

These examples underscore that in the postwar years, the inhabitants of the resettled territories were often responsible for the provision of public goods before the arrival of state officials. In this context of self-reliance, homogeneous settlements proved more successful at providing public goods than heterogeneous settlements.

In the next section, I further demonstrate systematic differences in the cooperative provision of public goods between homogeneous and heterogeneous migrant communities using the example of the volunteer fire brigade.

## STATISTICAL ANALYSIS OF PUBLIC GOODS PROVISION IN OPOLE VILLAGES

### Volunteer Fire Brigades as an Indicator of Cooperation

The volunteer fire brigade (OSP) was one of the first organizations to emerge in the resettled territories, often preceding the state itself (Fiedler 2005; Kuta 1987). Its main role was protecting village residents from fires and criminals. For example, migrants from Kielce and Częstochowa (central Poland), who founded an OSP in the village of Dobroszyce (Lower Silesian voivodeship), explained that their decision had nothing to do with their attachment to the OSP's "traditions or vocational interests," and instead was motivated by an "instinct of self-preservation" (Skrzypkowski 1964, 12–13).

In addition to this primary purpose, OSP units initially fulfilled many social functions, including socializing young men into becoming loyal community members, performing at local festivals, and competing in sporting events (Bartkowski 2003). Over time, some of these functions were taken over by local clubs and associations, but the fire brigade remained the center of village life. The OSP was also closely connected to the local parish; most firefighting celebrations started with a Holy Mass, and the priest was sometimes a formal member of the fire department (Dzieniszewska-Naroska 2004).

Importantly, a successful OSP relied on reciprocity and social sanctions rather than formal law and external enforcement. Indeed, it took an entire community to support an OSP, even though OSP members themselves were predominately able-bodied men.[10] For example, to build a fire station in Mści-wojów in 1946, Polish migrants decided that each community member would contribute three days of labor or, if they could not work, 50 złoty per family (Szydłowska-Szczecińska 2017). In other cases, OSP members combined their savings to buy equipment, as happened in Dygowo.[11]

The volunteer fire brigade was one of the few voluntary associations to survive through the communist period, though its independence and ability to coordinate with neighboring units was restricted.[12] The OSPs remain common in the Polish countryside today, and they are now funded partly through local municipal budgets and partly through state subsidies.[13]

I expect the disruption of community bonds and the migrant population's regional diversity to undermine the establishment of volunteer fire brigades. As noted earlier, the OSP provides a local public good and relies on voluntary cooperation, which is more difficult among people who do not share social norms and networks. There is a risk of free riding: One group can disproportionately invest in the local fire brigade and pay for its equipment, yet all community members benefit from its presence. Regional diversity may also entail greater difficulty in coordinating organizational structure and procedures; members from one group may refuse to participate in a fire brigade headed by a competing group.

Historical accounts support this hypothesis. Migrants who arrived in large homogeneous groups were typically the first and the most effective at organizing an OSP (Fiedler 2005, 130). Some even brought OSP flags and banners from their places of origin. For example, a homogeneous group repatriated to Siedlęcin (formerly called *Bobrowice*) brought the banner (*sztandar*) of their home OSP from Lwów-Hołosko Małe (Fiedler 2005, 41). Another example is the OSP of Tarnowica Dolna-Stary Waliszów, which in 1958 celebrated its seventieth anniversary. This OSP was founded in Tarnowica Dolna in 1888 and was then reestablished in 1945 in Stary Waliszów, in the territory acquired

---

[10] In today's Poland, women can also serve as firefighters.
[11] Serwis Informacyjny Ochotniczej Straży Pożarnej w Dygowie. Historia. www.osp.dygowo .pl/historia.html.
[12] The Union of Voluntary Fire Brigades was liquidated in the spring of 1950, and the brigades were subordinated to voivodeship and county fire departments, which, in turn, were managed by the Headquarters of Fire Brigades at the state level. The state began to finance, train, and equip local units.
[13] Cities and towns rely on state-organized firefighting units (*Państwowa Straż Pożarna*), staffed by career firefighters rather than volunteers.

from Germany (Kuta 1987, 84). OSPs were also easier to organize in localities with a majority autochthonous population, which essentially reactivated the fire brigades that operated before the war. For example, the OSP in one such village, Żelazna (Opole voivodeship), celebrated its 100-year anniversary in 1998. At the time, every tenth Żelazna resident was either a member or an active supporter of the local OSP (Banik, Szwed, and Kobylarz 2009). By contrast, there were many heterogeneous migrant communities where the OSPs were either never formed or fell apart soon after they did, due to a lack of volunteers and to intergroup disagreements. Importantly, preexisting levels of familiarity with this organization among villagers from different places of origin cannot explain these patterns. The OSP had operated in all three imperial partitions of Poland from the mid-nineteenth century onward as well as in Imperial and Weimar Germany (where it was known as *Freiwillige Feuerwehr*) (Szaflik 2005).

I thus use the presence or absence of a volunteer fire brigade (OSP), as an indicator of successful cooperation for the provision of public goods in resettled villages. To compile the dataset on the creation of OSPs at the village level, I began with a list of OSPs that operated in the 1990s, based on registration data collected after the 1989 Law on Associations. The law encouraged all OSPs to register in order to receive equipment, funds, and training from the government. I then verified the date of founding for each OSP in the Opole voivodeship through online research (many OSPs have webpages with histories of their founding) or by contacting each organization in the summer of 2014 (if that history was unavailable online). Surveys estimate that 90 percent of all OSPs operating in Poland today existed prior to 1989 (Klon-Jawor 2013). Confirming the years of OSP founding through fieldwork and online sources, I established that 89 percent of OSPs in the dataset had been founded before 1949. Using this approach, half of all villages (52 percent) in the Opole voivodeship have an OSP that dates back to the 1940s or earlier.

It should be acknowledged that starting with a list of contemporary OSPs misses those OSPs that were established in the 1940s but dissolved in subsequent periods. Accordingly, the OSP dataset is not ideal for understanding the relationship between diversity and OSP presence *at the time* when the state was weak and OSPs were most needed. Nonetheless, it can speak, at the very least, to the implications of uprooting and diversity for the durability of social organizations created to provide collective goods at the village level.

## Measuring Diversity in Opole Villages

In order to formally test the hypothesis that weak community bonds and population heterogeneity undermined self-help collective action, I leverage a unique and detailed dataset on the composition of migrants in Opole voivodeship, southwest Poland. It was compiled by Elżbieta Dworzak and Małgorzata Goc (2011) based on property titles. This dataset is useful for two reasons.

First, it provides information about villages, the level of analysis at which daily interactions take place, and at which OSPs typically operate. Second and more important, the Opole dataset contains information about migrants' exact places of origin. This enables me to distinguish between two types of homogeneous communities: the one settled by the inhabitants from a single village of origin, who shared social norms and social networks; and the one settled by migrants from different villages from the same historical region, who shared social norms *but not* social networks. I am thus able to separate the effects of cultural differences from the effects of the disruption of social ties.[14]

The dataset encompasses 625 resettled villages (approximately two-thirds of all villages in Opole voivodeship). Repatriates from Kresy and settlers from central Poland made up 23 percent and 19 percent of the population, respectively. At the same time, the Opole voivodeship records a much higher share of the native population (49 percent) than other parts of the newly acquired territories (19 percent). I thus supplement data on migrant population with information about the distribution of the autochthones, collected from the Opole State Archive (*Archiwum Państwowy Opole*) and verified against data from the 1970s published by Robert Rauziński and Agata Zagórowska (2007). Such information is available for 938 villages (or 99 percent of all villages in the voivodeship).[15]

The presence of such a large number of autochthonous villages within the voivodeship presents a research opportunity, as such "preserved" communities serve as a suitable reference group to homogeneous resettled communities that did not experience any disruption of social ties. The native population was distributed unevenly across villages: My analysis suggests that about two-thirds of the villages had no autochthones, while in the remaining third, the autochthonous population made up more than 80 percent of the inhabitants.

To measure the diversity of the population in the villages dominated by migrants, I compute the fractionalization index based on the shares of migrants from the USSR, central Poland, and other countries as well as of the autochthonous population at the village level. The index estimates the probability that two individuals randomly drawn from the population came from different regions. It is computed using the following formula: Fractionalization $= 1 - \sum_{i=1}^{n} (s_i)^2$, where $s_i$ is the share of the population in each regional group and $n$ is the number of groups. Measured in this way,

---

[14] The 1948 population survey, used in other chapters, covers all of western Poland but is at the level of municipalities, which encompass multiple villages, and groups migrants into three large categories.

[15] In 1948, the current area of the Opole voivodeship was split between the Śląskie and Wrocławskie voivodeships. For this analysis, I focus on the voivodeship within its contemporary borders, which incorporates the following counties from the 1948 census: Brzeg and Namysłów (formerly located within the Wrocławskie voivodeship); Głubczyca, Grodków, Kluczbork, Koziel, Niemodlin, Nysa, Olesno, Opole, Prudnik, and Strzelce (formerly within the Śląskie voivodeship).

cultural diversity ranges from 0 (homogeneous) to 0.69 (diverse), with a mean of 0.29. The distribution of this indicator is bimodal: There is a large number of homogeneous villages as well as a considerable number of villages with a fractionalization index between 0.3 and 0.5.[16]

I also compute the share of migrant population, measured as the number of migrants to the total community population. This variable ranges from 0 to 1 with a mean of 0.58.

To further probe differences between the different types of villages described earlier, I create a factor variable *Village type* based on the size and diversity of migrant population in each village. I consider two alternative classifications. The simplest approach is dividing villages into four types: the autochthonous village (where the share of the autochthonous population is greater than 80 percent); the village settled by migrants from the same place of origin ("resettled as a whole"); the homogeneous migrant village (defined as a village where the migrant diversity index is below the mean of 0.23); and the heterogeneous migrant village (where the migrant diversity index is above the mean of 0.23). For robustness, I also consider an alternative, more fine-grained classification: the autochthonous village (where the share of the autochthonous population is above 80 percent); the village resettled as a whole; the homogeneous village (where migrant diversity is below 0.05); the moderately heterogeneous village (where migrant diversity is between 0.05 and 0.4), and the highly heterogeneous village (where migrant diversity is greater than 0.4). These categories were selected to test the argument about the role of shared norms and networks in cooperation with the additional consideration of keeping the number of settlements in each category similar.

## Estimation Strategy and Results of Statistical Analysis

I estimate the influence of migration history and diversity of the population on the prevalence of volunteer fire brigades using logistic regression with a dependent variable coded 1 for villages with an OSP and 0 otherwise. Each regression specification uses one of four alternative explanatory variables: the share of migrant population, the diversity of the population (*Fractionalization index*), and two alternative indicators of *Village type*. To account for preexisting differences between villages that may confound the effect of migrant presence or cultural heterogeneity on the establishment of volunteer fire brigades, all specifications control for the proportion of large farms (over 20 ha) and the prevalence of agriculture (*Share employed in agriculture*) in 1939, based on

---

[16] Since information is available on the precise origins of each migrant group, I was able to compute the fractionalization index on the basis of the imperial partition from which migrants originated and to compare the fractionalization based on pre-WWI empire of origin with the one based on the 1948 census categories. The correlation between the two indices at the village level is 0.68 ($p < 0.01$).

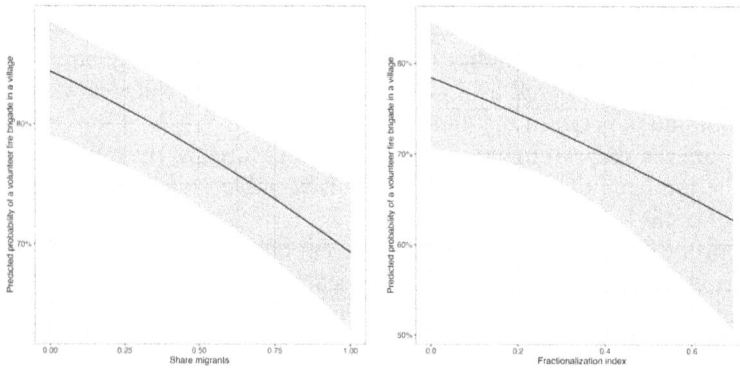

FIGURE 3.1 Predicted probability of the presence of a volunteer fire brigade. The estimates are based on Models 1 and 2 in Table A.2.

data from the 1939 German census.[17] I also include a natural logarithm of postwar population size as cooperation for the provision of public goods may be more challenging in larger settlements.

The results of logistic regression analysis are presented in Figure 3.1 and Table A.2. As expected, I find that the probability of OSP presence declined with the share of migrants to population. The predicted probability of an OSP in a majority autochthonous village is 20 percent higher than the predicted probability of an OSP in a village settled by migrants (see Figure 3.1). I further find that the diversity of the population in a given village is a negative and statistically significant predictor of the voluntary provision of fire protection. The predicted probability of an OSP in a village settled by a homogeneous migrant population (fractionalization index of 0) is 16 percent higher than the probability of an OSP established in a heterogeneous village (fractionalization index of 0.69), as shown in Figure 3.1.

Next, I investigate the prevalence of OSPs in villages of different types with autochthonous villages as an omitted category (see Models 3 and 4 in Table A.2). Results from Model 3 are presented graphically in Figure 3.2. The coefficient on the category "resettled together" is negative, but it does not reach statistical significance. Thus, the probability of establishing an OSP in a community that did not experience any disruption of social ties upon migration may not be that different from that observed in an autochthonous village. However, results in both models indicate that villages settled by homogeneous migrant groups, which experienced a disruption of social ties but could count on shared social norms, were less likely to establish an OSP than autochthonous villages (the coefficient on the "homogeneous" category is negative and significant in both models). The probability of an OSP is even lower

[17] The census includes information at the *Gemeinde* level. I matched each *Gemeinde* to a contemporary Polish village, now under a different name. A *Gemeinde* was typically smaller than a Polish *Gmina*.

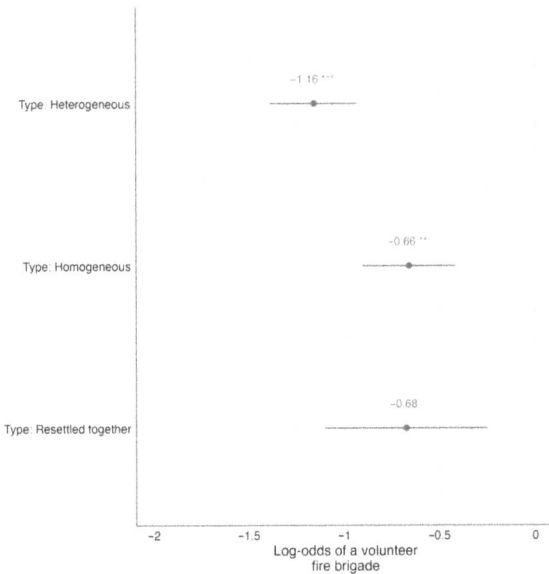

FIGURE 3.2 Predicted log odds of a volunteer fire brigade by type of village. Reference category is the autochthonous village. The estimates are based on Model 3 of Table A.2. Significant at $**p < 0.05$; $***p < 0.01$.

in villages settled by diverse migrant groups, which experienced both a disruption of social ties and a sudden diversification of social norms. I estimate that villages settled by diverse migrant populations were 20 percent less likely to establish an OSP than the autochthonous villages and 10 percent less likely to establish an OSP than homogeneous migrant villages.

My statistical analysis confirms the hypothesis that the disruption of communal ties in the process of migration as well as the heterogeneity of the migrant population presented an obstacle to the voluntary provision of collective goods in the resettled region. Cooperation levels were highest in villages that were both homogeneous and preserved their social bonds and lowest in villages populated by migrants from different places of origin.

## THE REAWAKENING OF GROUP IDENTITIES AFTER 1989

The Polish government sought to homogenize the population and instill nationalism through schooling and propaganda. It stoked fears of German aggression and emphasized the urgency of "restoring" the "original" Polish character of the resettled territories. The forced migrants from Kresy were prevented from forming associations and interest groups that could help preserve the memory of the lost homeland. The native population was likewise prohibited from organizing. The authorities also banned the use of German, Silesian,

and Kashubian and enrolled the autochthones in Polish classes. All names, sur-
names, and street signs were Polonized. After 1956, cultural expression became
possible in leisure activities, such as folk ensembles and choirs, but opportunities for speaking minority languages or commemorating the loss of eastern
borderlands remained limited.

These top-down homogenizing policies had mixed results. Among the
migrant population, intergroup differences gradually lost their salience, and
mixed marriages became common. Assimilation was facilitated by low levels of inequality and upward mobility: Forced migrants may have lost their
property in the East, but in the West, thanks to the expulsion of German
inhabitants, they acquired better houses and farms. The native population,
by contrast, grew increasingly alienated from the Polish state. When emigration became possible after 1956, significant numbers of autochthones left for
Germany, renouncing Polish citizenship.

After the democratic transition, the multicultural identity of western and
northern Poland reasserted itself in varied ways. Migrant origins of the population gave rise to evocatively titled electoral committees, such as "Settlers"
("*Osadnicy*," a term applied to migrants from central Poland); "The Lovers
of Lwów" ("*Miłośnicy Lwowa*," named after the Polish city transferred to
Ukraine in 1945); "Social Electoral Committee from beyond the Bug River"
("*Społeczny Komitet Wyborczy za Bugiem*"); and "People from Kresy" ("*Kre-
sowianie*," "*Kresowiacy*," "*Porozumienie Kresowe*," named after the territories
annexed by the USSR (Kresy) in 1945) in the early 1990s (Bartkowski 2003,
118). Kresy repatriates and their descendants also organized folklore groups
and festivals centered around their regional heritage. Nonetheless, these activities were predominantly nostalgic in nature; the social and political significance
of migrants' regional identities was marginal. In the 2002 population census,
the first to ask about nationality and language used at home, residents of the
resettled territories overwhelmingly self-identified as Polish.[18]

The autochthonous population, by contrast, retained a strong sense of cultural distinctiveness. The native population of Upper Silesia  has been most
active in reviving their language and reasserting political rights. In 1990, the
Silesian Autonomy Movement (*Ruch Autonomii Śląska*) was founded, aiming
to restore the prewar autonomy of Upper Silesia. In 1997, Silesian activists
applied for formal recognition of the Silesian nation by registering the Union
of People of the Silesian Nation (*Związek Ludności Narodowości Śląskiej*).
Other Silesians have rediscovered their German roots, with some 500,000
people declaring a German identity in the early 1990s. Beginning in 1993,
many applied for and were granted German citizenship.[19] A growing number

[18] See Szmeja (2000) for a sociological study of Silesian identity in Poland.

[19] This enabled them to work and reside in Germany and the EU before this opportunity became
available to all Polish citizens with Poland's accession to the EU in 2004. Even though dual
citizenship is permitted in neither German nor Polish law, the situation in Upper Silesia was
tacitly approved by both countries (Kamusella 2012).

of schools in Silesia have been choosing German as a language of instruction, and German clubs organize many cultural activities in the region. In the 2002 census, nearly 173,000 people declared Silesian nationality and another 136,000 – German nationality.

The Kashubian minority has likewise revived its language, which is now officially recognized by the Polish government and offered in schools. The Kashubian Association publishes books and magazines in Kashubian and organizes regular festivals and other cultural activities (Dołowy-Rybińska and Soria 2021). It has also called for the recognition of Kashubians as an ethnic minority in Poland. The less numerous Catholic Warmians and Evangelical Masurians, concentrated in former East Prussia, have created several organizations to foster their religious and cultural roots, including the Masurian Association, the Masurian Evangelical Association, and the Warmia House (Sakson 2008).

The reawakening of separate identities among the native community and the disappearance of differences between migrants from different regions raise the question of why some minority groups converged to the dominant culture, while others preserved their distinctive characteristics. The revival of Silesian identity, for instance, is puzzling because Silesians who remained in post-1989 Poland were those who decided against emigration in the 1940s, 1960s, and 1970s. Two important factors stand out: spatial concentration and a history of discrimination by Polish migrants and government officials. The autochthones clustered within two small historical regions, where they constituted the majority at the settlement level. They preserved their communal bonds and practiced endogamy. Furthermore, although they were declared to be Polish, the autochthones were treated as second-class citizens, confined to manual jobs, and underrepresented in state administration during the communist period (Kamusella 2012). Persistent discrimination likely encouraged the rejection of Polish identity.

DISCUSSION

This chapter has demonstrated that group origins played an important role in the organization of social life in the resettled region. Even though all those who resided in the territory east of the Oder–Neisse line were Polish on paper and shared the goal of reestablishing their lives after a destructive war, regional origins came to matter in everyday life. My analysis of personal narratives indicates that official classifications based on regional origin and migration status structured social relationships in the new environment. Group boundaries appeared particularly stark between migrants and natives, in part because of their conflicting economic interests. Furthermore, the origins of the population influenced how individuals treated one another, and whether they were able to work together to restore social order. I show that tight-knit homogeneous communities had a greater capacity than heterogeneous migrant communities to enforce cooperative behavior and to provide public goods.

Novel historical data on the origins of the population in Opole villages, combined with the presence of volunteer fire brigades, permit me to distinguish between the effects of shared networks and the effects of shared culture on the ability to cooperate for the bottom-up provision of collective goods. I find that both social ties and shared norms play a role in the ability of homogeneous communities to organize. Consistent with a large literature on the detrimental effects of cultural heterogeneity for voluntary cooperation (e.g., Habyarimana et al. 2007, 2009), homogeneous migrant communities appear to have been more capable of providing local public goods than heterogeneous migrant communities. In this respect, they were similar to communities that did not experience any mass uprooting.

# 4

# Cooperation in West German Communities

At the edge of many German towns today, there are neighborhood streets named after foreign places: Königsberger Straße (Kaliningrad, Russia), Breslauer Straße (Wrocław, Poland), Allensteiner Straße (Olsztyn, Poland), and Egerweg (Eger, Hungary). These streets serve as a reminder of the places expellees left behind at the end of WWII. Their considerable distance from German town centers is also emblematic of expellee marginalization. Situated in peripheral neighborhoods, expellees in postwar West Germany had scant opportunity to share public spaces with the native population. The latter may have preferred it that way. A telling example is Vreden, a municipality in North-Rhine Westphalia. In 1953, when introducing the planned construction of 110 new settlement sites (*Siedlerstellen*), Vreden's district housing association assured locals that the new properties would be situated far enough away to allow the rural community's independent life to continue undisturbed (Kossert 2008, 110). Eventually, some expellee settlements formalized their separation by establishing their own municipality (*Gemeinde*), which allowed them to make independent decisions about tax rates and municipal spending.

I begin this chapter by describing the boundaries – spatial, social, and symbolic – that separated expellees from the native population in West Germany after WWII. I show that the native population generally perceived expellees as foreigners. Dialects, clothing, and other markers made expellees easily identifiable in their new settlements. Cultural differences were amplified, moreover, as both expellees and natives intentionally resurrected long-forgotten traditions from their home villages. The expellees' poverty, a direct consequence of their expulsion, exacerbated intergroup tensions at a time of economic scarcity. The natives resented the obligation to accommodate expellees in their homes and were envious of the state support granted to expellees. Expellees, in turn, relied on their status to receive financial assistance and compensation for lost property. To defend its interests, each group coalesced around identity-based interest groups and parties, some of which survive to this day.

Next, I consider the implications of migration-based cleavages for cooperation at the community level. In Poland's resettled territories, migrants moved
into emptied-out settlements and confronted the challenge of organizing collective goods from the ground up. They had to come together to establish entirely
new organizations. By contrast, expellees in West Germany were distributed
across settled areas where formal and informal mechanisms of public goods
provision remained intact. Volunteer fire brigades and other prewar organizations simply resumed their activity following the end of wartime hostilities.
Municipal councils, elected shortly after the war in democratic elections, carried out their duties by levying local taxes and ensuring the provision of
collective goods. Accordingly, the nature of collective action differed from the
Polish case – rather than produce resources from the ground up, expellees in
West Germany struggled to gain access to existing resources and organizations
that were dominated by the native population. They were excluded from local
organizations, such as the volunteer fire brigade, and compelled to establish
their own self-help groups.

I end the chapter with a study of the relationship between local tax rates
and expellee presence. Local taxes were used to fund public goods. Since
the expellees owned virtually no land and few businesses in the immediate
postwar period, the tax burden fell disproportionately on the native population. Qualitative sources indicate that the natives were reluctant to pay
when municipal spending favored the expellees. In order to formally test my
hypothesis that high expellee presence reduced investment in public goods,
I use data for over 7,000 municipalities in Bavaria, the federal state that
received the largest number of expellees in West Germany and was the first
to hold local elections. Municipal councils set the tax rates on an annual
basis, yielding wide variation in rates across municipalities. My analysis
shows that in 1950, the first year for which data are available, communities
with a higher share of expellees set significantly lower tax rates. However,
by 1961, these negative effects disappeared. In other words, the negative
effects of migration-based cleavages on public goods provision were relatively
short-lived.

## THE EMERGENCE OF THE EXPELLEE–NATIVE CLEAVAGE

The arrival of expellees produced major cleavages in West German society. I
will demonstrate this using first-person accounts, media reports, secondary literature, and public opinion surveys. Notably, German researchers conducted
multiple studies on expellee integration starting in the 1950s. Unlike their Polish counterparts, they operated with a significant degree of freedom and faced
little to no external pressure to portray integration as a resounding success.
The relative absence of bias makes their studies an invaluable resource to assess
the effects of forced migration on societal cohesion. In addition, a number of

scholars in the 1990s conducted interviews with first- and second-generation expellees, which provide a useful window into the evolving status of expellees in their new settlements over time.

I also draw on rich data from public opinion surveys conducted shortly after the war. In October 1945, the Office of Military Government of the United States for Germany created a public opinion survey unit with the aim of understanding German political attitudes. Thanks to their administration of the food ration card program, the unit had access to a regularly updated list of all persons living in each community of the US-controlled zone and hence could design "a practically ideal sample under nearly worst possible conditions" (Merritt and Merritt 1970, xviii). The resulting surveys allow us to glean how widespread anti-expellee sentiments were and to learn what the average German citizen thought about the expulsions.

### Foreigners in Their Own Land

German ethnicity was the primary reason for the uprooting of expellees, and as many as 57 percent came from within the borders of pre-WWII Germany. Nonetheless, expellees were often perceived and treated as foreigners in their new communities in West Germany. According to a 1946 survey conducted in the US zone of Baden-Württemberg, only 49 percent of the native population considered the expellees to be German citizens. By the end of 1947, this proportion had increased to 67 percent, a deceivingly high number that still meant that one-third of native Germans did not acknowledge the expellees as compatriots (Merritt and Merritt 1970, 20). Correspondingly, many local and state governments were reluctant to enfranchise expellees or even grant them full access to the labor market and welfare benefits (Demshuk 2006; Carey 1951).

Indeed, if one took the natives at their word, postwar West Germany was inundated with "Poles," "Russians," and "Gypsies." These were some of the ethnic terms that the natives applied to the expellees, often in more derogatory forms (Kossert 2008, 49). Ingetraud Lippmann, whose family fled from Königsberg (East Prussia) to Kehdingen (Lower Saxony), recalls this painful experience: "When the arrival of a few more refugees was announced, [the locals] said: 'More Polacks are coming.' But we were also Germans and came from Germany..." (Lippmann 2001). An expellee who arrived from Silesia to Osnabrück with her family recounts: "[W]e had the feeling, and I had it very strongly, that the T. family thought we were foreigners. My little sisters said: 'Mom, hungry.' Then Mrs. T. said, 'Oh, you can speak German too!' (Bade et al. 1997, 124)." It is not hard to see the parallels to the situation in Poland's resettled territories, where accusations of German, Russian, and Ukrainian identity targeted families of Polish nationality, including those who had been forced out of their homes precisely because of their Polishness (see Chapter 3).

To differentiate themselves from the expellees, the natives fell back on regional and local identities. They presented themselves as Hamburgers, Württembergers, Bavarians, and so on; they considered the expellees to be Silesians or East Prussians, not fellow Germans. For instance, in February 1946, the Bavarian refugee commissioner reported with concern that leaflets "calling for the expulsion of Prussians, Silesians, and others" were circulated across Bavaria, and that the Bavarian population "firmly believed that they must [...] resist any interaction with the expellees who are imposed on them" (quoted in Krauss (2000, 30–31)).

The anti-expellee sentiment was sometimes expressed in racist terms. For instance, the administrator (*Landrat*) of Griesbach county claimed that the expellees were culturally inferior to the Bavarian people (Connor 2007, 67). In Schleswig-Holstein, political satire depicted the social democratic Prime Minister Hermann Lüdemann as a "Prussian" pied piper who brought the tens of thousands of "Slavic" refugees into the "Germanic" Southern Schleswig (Kossert 2008, 71–75). In October 1945, the population of southern Schleswig petitioned British field marshal Bernard Law Montgomery for the administrative separation of Schleswig and Holstein on the grounds that "[t]he flow of refugees from the eastern regions threaten[ed] to wipe out [...their] ancestral Nordic character..." (Kossert 2008, 74). At the same time, natives blamed expellees for prolonging the war. An expellee from Pomerania who found himself in Osnabrück recalled that "[e]veryone from the East was labeled as a Nazi" and sent to work in road construction (Bade et al. 1997, 160).

Different group markers became salient in different parts of Germany, but there is consistent evidence that first-generation expellees were easy to spot because of how they looked and spoke. Kossert (2008, 127) writes:

The rolling 'R,' the different dialects of East Prussians, Bohemian Forest people, Bessarabian Germans, and Danube Swabians, these were entirely new sounds to the locals. Through their clothing and language, the expellees stood out immediately; so did their dishes and household items. For example, the people from Düren, who slept under quilts, found the down beds of Silesians very peculiar and called them 'Silesian laundry'.

Dialect was perhaps the most durable signifier of outsider status. Historian Lutz Niethammer, a native of Schwabia, recalls that he and his classmates were "outraged to find out that they could not understand" their new third-grade German teacher, an expellee from Upper Silesia. "As I know today," he writes, "he spoke German, a guttural Upper Silesian, but we [Schwabian natives] organized ourselves to get rid of the 'Pollack,' especially for German class" (Niethammer 1987, 316).

Denominational differences also contributed to intergroup tensions, as it was often the case that Protestant expellees were settled in predominantly Catholic regions and Catholic refugees in predominantly Protestant regions. For instance, in Lower Bavaria, the Catholic natives sometimes referred to Protestant expellees as "Lutheran bloodhounds" (Spiegel-Schmidt 1959, 75). Even within the same denomination, religious customs and traditions appeared irreconcilable. Catholic Germans from Silesia did not recognize the Catholic hymns and rites of Westphalia, where they had been resettled (Connor 2007, 77). In Bavarian Viechtach, Protestant refugees refused to join the Bavarian Protestant State Church due to strained relations with the natives (Spiegel-Schmidt 1959, 49).

Cultural differences were purposefully amplified within groups in ways resembling Timur Kuran's "ethnification" process (Kuran 1998), whereby individuals invest greater resources in "ethnically meaningful" activities. For instance, some Bavarian villages moved to revive old customs, such as annual carnivals and county fairs, to emphasize their differences from the newcomers (Erker 1990, 404). The natives there also attempted to police group membership in the cultural realm by prohibiting expellees from wearing Lederhosen, traditional leather pants, with the argument that this was "a purely Bavarian costume" (Krauss 2000, 33). Likewise, the expellees revived old traditions that had been long forgotten in their places of origin, such as wearing folk costumes at celebrations and parades and singing folk songs, through which they created a new "homeland culture" (Pellengahr 2002, 62). As Süssner (2004, 7) argues, the "ethnified" collective memory of the expellees "became an important ideological tool for the closure of boundaries to other social groups, as the Germans from the east struggled against the danger of cultural assimilation in their new homes."

A central feature of expellee identity was the loss of the homeland. United by their shared trauma, expellees participated in pilgrimages to areas bordering the territories they had lost, where they could "sing and pray like at home," and see the outlines of the Heimat from afar (Melendy 2003, 43–44). Many of these activities were coordinated through a network of Homeland Associations (*Landsmannschaften*), organized based on regional origins. Thus, the trauma of expulsions contributed to the crystallization of expellee identity among individuals who came from the same country or province of origin.

To reinforce separation in economic and social life, the natives discouraged their children from marrying expellees. As a Bavarian resident recalled, "When in 1950 a farmer's son married a – let's use the unpleasant expression "refugee girl" (*Flüchtingmädle*) – the father initially thought about whether he should inherit the farm at all..." (quoted in Pellengahr (2002, 138)). Ingetraud Lippmann recalled a particularly shocking sign of physical separation: burying expellees on the edge of the cemetery, "namely in the dog cemetery" (Lippmann 2001). This was not an isolated occurrence; the creation of separate graveyards for the newcomers was reportedly a common practice in Bavaria until the government intervened to end it (Connor 2007, 79). An expellee from Silesia recounted that expellee children suffered from insults and beatings in school and were "treated a bit like second-class citizens" (Bade et al. 1997, 159).

Expellees' otherness persisted for a long time. "I must honestly say that it probably took at least 20 years to gradually shake off this feeling of being a stranger ... [N]ow after 40 years, one should assume that one is soon considered a local. But it is incredibly difficult, incredibly difficult" remembers an expellee from Posen-Westpreussen, who married a native woman (Bade et al. 1997, 165–166).

The above accounts illustrate how the arrival of expellees strengthened the sense of we-ness among the natives and expellees alike – producing symbolic and social boundaries that lasted for many years.

## ECONOMIC DIMENSIONS OF THE EXPELLEE–NATIVE CONFLICT

Housing was the principal consideration for assigning expellees to localities in West Germany. Since West German cities were crowded and damaged by the war, most expellees were sent to the countryside. There, they entered homogeneous communities with little prior exposure to outsiders, which had survived the war relatively unscathed. As Philipp M. Raup of the Food and Agriculture Organization wrote in October 1946: "The people who lost the most were suddenly in close contact with farmers who lost the least" (quoted in Kossert (2008, 79)). Correspondingly, the boundaries between expellees and natives were more salient and contentious in the countryside. As one expellee settled in rural Bavaria put it, "Because we, the expellees, do not own much, we are not highly regarded here. We stand here empty-handed" (quoted in Erker (1990, 384)). As reported by *Fränkische Zeitung* in the autumn of 1948, "in the towns and most larger communities ... a fruitful relationship between the original population and the newcomers is, in spite of all the difficulties, gradually developing, whilst in small communities and outlying villages meanness and intolerance is still often making the hard existence of the expellees more difficult" (quoted in Connor (2007, 64)).

Expellees may indeed have received a warmer welcome in cities. Many city dwellers had also lost their homes during the war, creating a shared sense of deprivation that served as a basis for mutual understanding (Connor 2007, 62). In addition, the expellee population in cities was smaller and more heterogeneous, and therefore appeared less threatening to the natives (Connor 2007, 62).

However, even in cases where expellees and natives had similar economic needs, altruistic behavior rarely crossed group boundaries. For example, in Greven, a 15,000-person town located in Westfalen, housing assistance was sought not only by expellees but also by many natives who had lost their homes during wartime. It would seem that the two groups shared an interest in rebuilding the community. Yet, they failed to come together to address the problem. Rather, the network of mutual aid mobilized immediately to assist the natives in rebuilding their damaged homes. Grottendieck (1999, 265–67) writes:

From the pulpits, pastors called for help, farmers cut wood free of charge for those in need, and furniture collections were initiated. Anyone planning a new building or an extension in the village was put under moral pressure to stop their construction activities so that all bricklayers and other building workers could be deployed in the north quarter [where the damaged houses were located].

Meanwhile, the expellees continued to live in crowded and squalid conditions in the surrounding countryside, spending their allowances on paying local farmers and struggling to get to the city for work. While the expellees' plight was of concern to the Refugee Committee in Greven, the local population was conspicuously absent from its meetings. Frustrated at the inaction of the municipal government, the expellees ended up forming the "Community of interests of the expellees from the East" to assist one another (Grottendieck 1999, 267).

Opinion polls indicate that native Germans did not feel responsible for supporting the impoverished expellees and had little empathy for their plight. In a November 1946 survey, only 28 percent of respondents said Germans should "care for the expellees"; 46 percent placed responsibility on the state expelling them and another 14 percent on the Allies (Merritt and Merritt 1970, 19).

At the insistence of the occupation governments, the expellees were billeted with the native population. The 1946 Housing law introduced stiff penalties – from fines to a year in prison – for refusing to share one's home with the expellees. The natives resented having to share their homes and often did so only under duress. An expellee from Silesia recalls: "Of course there were often complaints and sometimes even the use of police force and arrests [...] So the refugees were often accommodated with a lot of threats and insults" (Bade et al. 1997, 133). Another expellee recounts how she was turned away from the farm where she was supposed to stay by a woman who shouted: "We don't need gypsies [*Zigeuner*], go away, or I will call my husband home from the fields!" (Bade et al. 1997, 124).

A shocking headline from a 1952 newspaper offers a taste of how unhappy some natives were: "Quadruple suicide because of lodgers. Two rooms were to be given to an expellee family." The article reports that an elderly couple and their two daughters committed suicide on the day they had to vacate two rooms to expellees, having lost after almost two years of fighting with the local authorities.[1] This was an isolated incident – most of the time, the native population retaliated by charging excessive rent, requiring expellees to work on their farm in return for board and lodging, or challenging the allocation of expellees to their homes in administrative courts (Schraut 1995, 258). Sharing tight quarters further strained the expellee–native relationship.

[1] "Vierfacher Selbstmord wegen Untermieter. Zwei Räume sollten einer Flüchtlingsfamilie überlassen werden." 1952. *Eutiner Kreis-Anzeiger* (March 13).

Inequality between expellees and natives constitutes a key difference between the situation in West Germany and postwar Poland. The communist government reduced economic disparities by nationalizing, expropriating, and redistributing private wealth. There was no shortage of jobs in Poland's resettled territories, and although conditions were tough, even forced migrants from the eastern borderlands acknowledged an improvement in their economic situation following resettlement. Indeed, the autochthones in the resettled territories were the ones who could feel disadvantaged, whether due to state-mandated reductions in their landholdings or unequal access to the labor market owing to their suspected ties to Germany (see Chapter 3).

In West Germany, expellee status overlapped with poverty. Economic inequality between expellees and natives persisted for decades. In 1964, the average value of expellees' household wealth and savings amounted to 26,000 DM, just over half of that of the native population (47,000 DM), according to a nationwide survey (Kossert 2008, 108). As late as 1970, the first- and second-generation expellees still had lower earnings and home ownership rates than natives (Falck, Heblich, and Link 2012; Bauer, Braun, and Kvasnicka 2013; Kossert 2008).

State policies designed to assist expellees in regaining their economic status exacerbated intergroup tensions in the short term. The native population was concerned that expellees were getting more support from the state than they deserved. The chairman of the home and landowners association of Heidenheim claimed at a meeting in October 1950 that the refugees "who hadn't been Germans five years ago" now lorded over the native population and were the winners, whereas the natives were "treated like the Jews in the Third Reich" and were the real losers of the war (quoted in Kossert (2008, 105)). In a letter to the editor of the *Hamburger Allgemeinen Zeitung* in February 1950, one Hamburg resident lamented that the refugee craftsmen were receiving cash to establish their businesses and compete with the Hamburgers, while the native Hamburgers had to fend for themselves (Glensk 1994, 354–55). One of the main demands of the native evacuees from Hamburg, who founded the "*Bundesverband der Butenhamborger*" in April 1951, was receiving the same treatment as expellees and other displaced persons (Glensk 1994, 356).

When the refugee law stipulated that job placement should take into account the expellees' "greater need" for employment, the natives expressed concern that this would lead to the "disenfranchisement of the native population in favor of the refugees" (Krauss 2000, 32). In defiance of the law, the Munich City Council opted to give preferential treatment to native applicants ("*Heimatlichen*"), considering expellees for employment only as a last resort, "if no other candidates were readily available." When discussing the hiring of doctors, one member of the municipal council stated: "We are striving to employ only Munich residents or Bavarians. It would be advisable to consult the District Medical Association regarding the doctors so that we can eliminate people from the Sudetenland and Prussia who were only hired on a temporary basis" (quoted in Krauss (2000, 32)).

## ASSOCIATIONAL LIFE AS AN INDICATOR OF COOPERATION

Scholars view the propensity of individuals to form and join a wide range of voluntary associations as an indicator of their ability to cooperate with one another. According to Putnam (1995, 67), civic engagement "foster[s] sturdy norms of generalized reciprocity and encourage[s] the emergence of social trust." This section shows that, in the German countryside, associational networks did not cross group boundaries and, therefore, did not engender trust and collaboration between natives and expellees.

During the period of National Socialism, most religious, political, and supranational associations were banned and dissolved. Dissolution affected rifle clubs, church associations, and labor unions. Sports clubs were incorporated into Nazi associations for physical exercise, and volunteer fire brigades (*Freiwillige Feuerwehr, FF*) were converted into compulsory military service units and subordinated to the police. Their traditional social activities, including the organization of carnival balls and festivals and participation in religious processions, were restricted to a minimum (Pellengahr 2002, 39–40). After the war, clubs and hobby groups were allowed to operate as long as they registered with the district office. After August 1948, the registration requirement was lifted, and the German countryside experienced "explosive" associational growth (Pellengahr 2002, 45).

Pellengahr's (2002) in-depth research of four Bavarian municipalities (Offingen, Ichenhausen, Kissing, and Mehring) reveals that most prewar associations resumed their activity with largely unchanged membership and leadership structures. The organizational continuity within volunteer fire brigades, which combined the delivery of fire protection with recreational functions, is particularly striking.[2]

I digitized a list of all volunteer fire brigades in Bavaria that existed in 2007 ($N = 7,760$) to investigate how many were founded before and after WWII. I found that only 1 percent ($N = 98$) of volunteer fire brigades were established after 1945. The mean year of founding was 1885; that is, the average FF would have celebrated its sixty-year anniversary at the time of the expellees' arrival. Nazi policies failed to undermine the FF members' loyalty to their unit. Stories abound of FF flags that spent the war years hidden away in members' houses and were dusted off and solemnly unfurled after the war (Kyrieleis 1984, 137). To this day, membership in a volunteer fire

---

[2] As the name indicates, volunteer fire brigades are staffed with volunteers who perform firefighting duties and train in their spare time. They are more prevalent in the countryside, as the law requires all cities with more than 100,000 inhabitants to set up a professional fire department with full-time firefighters (Kyrieleis 1984, 131).

brigade goes back several generations; many firefighters know each other from a young age, and were born and raised in the community they serve (Kyrieleis 1984, 138).

While systematic data on membership are unavailable, ethnographic studies underscore the conspicuous absence of expellees among volunteer firefighters. Pellengahr (2002, 144) explains that FF "members mostly came from the ranks of long-established families," with "characteristics such as origin and social status" determining who could participate. As confirmed by Schulze's (2002, 43) interviews with expellees conducted half a century after the resettlement in the town of Celle, Lower Saxony, "admission to the natives' associations, in particular to the *prestigious volunteer fire brigades,* village church choirs, rifle associations and bowling clubs, was only granted hesitantly [emphasis added]" and some of these "traditional bastions of native rural elites" excluded expellees for decades.

Exceptions that prove the rule are those volunteer fire brigades founded after WWII in the so-called expellee communities (*"Vertriebenengemeinden"*), which accommodated a large number of expellees in one place. These include Geretsried (1949), Neutraubling (1948), Traunreut (1949), and Waldkraiburg (1950). The FF in Geretsried owes its existence to the devastating fire that started in one of the expellee barracks on July 3, 1949. By the time volunteer firefighters from nearby settlements arrived at the scene, the barracks were severely damaged and expellees had lost their belongings for the second time. To prevent this from happening in the future, the local expellees organized their own fire brigade. Due to a lack of resources, a portable pump and some hoses were all they initially had at their disposal. To build up the organization, each of the forty active members contributed a monthly fee of 50 Pfennig in the 1950s. In a show of solidarity, some members donated half of their earnings from building a local cemetery to the association's treasury, enabling the brigade to buy its first vehicle for 250 Marks (Schneider 2019).

In Waldkraiburg, the site of the former powder production facilities, hundreds of expellees were housed in wooden barracks at the Pürten refugee camp. The risk of fire was high, and the municipal council unanimously voted to establish a volunteer fire brigade in 1950. The flag-unfurling ceremony for the Waldkraiburg brigade was attended by other expellee brigades from Geretsried, Neutraubling, and Traunreut (Kern ND).

The divisions between expellees and natives were thus reflected in associational activity. Membership in many associations was restricted by the duration of residency, property ownership, and confessional life. For example, the statute of the local rifle association in Ottmarsbocholt (Westphalia) in the mid-1950s insisted that every member should belong to the Catholic

Church and further stipulated that anyone who wished to serve as the association's chairman should satisfy a ten-year residency requirement (Exner 1999, 82). Even when expellees were able to join, leadership roles were reserved for the natives.[3]

Expellees dealt with exclusion not only by retreating into the private sphere but also by founding their own associations and interest groups. Whereas in Communist Poland, the government sought to stamp out regional loyalties and control social activity, the West German authorities did not seek to constrain economic and cultural associations, and in 1950, they removed restrictions on all political activity among expellees.

Expellees took advantage of this new freedom of association by forming Homeland Associations (*Landsmannschaften*) based on their regions of origin, such as the Sudeten German Homeland Association, the Homeland Association of Pomerania, of Silesians, of East and West Prussia, and so on. The primary goal of such homeland associations was to advise and support members on legal and economic issues, such as submitting claims for the restitution of lost property (Exner 1999, 83). Over time, however, social and cultural activities came to the fore (Pellengahr 2002, 60–61).

Expellees were also active in organizations that provided economic assistance. They were overrepresented in the workers' welfare association (*Arbeiterwohlfahrt*), which was championed by the Social Democrats and focused on the procurement of food, clothing, fuel, and household items (Pellengahr 2002, 58). Since they did not have their own farms and gardens, expellees also organized gardening and fruit-growing associations (*Kleingartenkolonien, Obstbauvereine*) to supplement their rations (Kossert 2008, 131–32). Brelie-Lewien (1990, 209) writes that self-help was their driving force: "As an association, they [expellees] did not have to act as individual petitioners, whose requests were usually denied, but could submit applications to the city and local councils as group representatives." To the point, gardening associations "hardly had any social club life until the 1960s." Rather, their efforts were focused on representing expellee interests vis-à-vis the municipal government and on managing the gardens (Pellengahr 2002, 58–59).

A survey conducted in the early 1950s indicates that 20 percent of expellees participated in clubs alongside natives; 40 percent were active in expellee organizations; and the remaining 40 percent were entirely isolated (Wurzbacher 1954, 146).

---

[3] Organizations that were relatively more open included sports clubs and choral societies. In sports, performance mattered more than one's background, and local teams were in need of able-bodied male players to compete with the neighboring municipalities (Exner 1999, 83). Choral societies historically developed a more open structure, because they recruited members across multiple villages and municipalities (Pellengahr 2002, 143–144).

## Formalization of the Expellee–Native Cleavage in Identity-Based Organizations and Parties

In West Germany's more democratic political environment, competition over scarce economic resources encouraged the formation of identity-based political parties. Parties that catered to the native population and that ran on anti-expellee platforms included the Bavarian Party (*Bayernpartei*), founded in 1946, and the Schleswig-Holstein Homeland Association (*Schleswig-Holsteinische Heimatbund*), founded in 1947. The Bavarian Party united natives disgruntled by the requirement to host expellees in their homes (Connor 2007, 117). At a 1947 rally, its co-founder Jakob Fischbacher argued that "[t]he refugees have to be thrown out, and the farmers have to help vigorously" and likened the marriage between Bavarian farmers and refugee women to "incest."[4] The party won 17.9 percent of the vote in the 1950 state election. The Schleswig-Holstein Homeland Association sought to associate expellees with a set of pejorative traits, such as "reluctant to work," "know-it-all," "immoral," and "prone to theft." More fundamentally, the party underscored the Prussian origins of expellees and traced the roots of the Third Reich to Prussian militarism and expansionism, in order to exonerate Schleswig-Holstein natives from any possible sense of guilt over WWII (Andresen 2013).

Expellees also organized associations and political parties around their identity. In 1948, expellees in Bavaria organized a hundred Emergency Associations (*Notgemeinschaften*) to coordinate their political and economic activity. The German Emergency Association in Munich managed to secure a political party license by not referring to forced migration and emphasizing, instead, the establishment of a committee that would support war veterans and victims of the currency reform (Carey 1951, 197). Beginning locally, expellee political associations spread across West Germany and coalesced into the Central Association of Expelled Germans (*Zentralverband der vertriebenen Deutschen, ZvD*). At the end of the 1950s, every fourth expellee was a member of the expellee organization, that is, a total of 2.2 million expellees were organized (Süssner 2004). Once the ban on their political organization was lifted, the expellees established the Bloc of Expellees and Dispossessed Persons (*Block der Heimatvertriebenen und Entrechteten, BHE*), which campaigned on the promise of addressing the various injustices that expellees had been suffering in Germany.

Although their minority status in West Germany encouraged expellees to work together regardless of their regional origins, there were many divisions within this group as well, albeit less salient than the division between expellees and natives. As Ahonen (2016, 20) argues, "The far-reaching heterogeneity of

---

[4] "Bekannte Ängste." Oct 12, 2015. *BSZ. Bayerische Staatszeitung.* www.bayerische-staatszeitung.de/staatszeitung/politik/detailansicht-politik/artikel/bekannte-aengste.html#topPosition.

the various expellee groups perpetuated deep-seated divisions that proved difficult to overcome." Many political advocacy groups catered only to expellees from specific regions. These included the Aid Office for Sudeten Germans (*Sudetendeutschen Hilfsstelle*, banned by the US Military government in 1946), the Emergency Community of East Germans in Bavaria (*Notgemeinschaft der Ostdeutschen in Bayern*), and the Interest Group of the People Displaced from the East (*IGO*). Expellee Homeland Associations, as mentioned earlier, were also based on the region of origin. Germans from the annexed territories east of the Oder–Neisse line, which had historically been a part of Prussia, participated in cultural activities based on their former provinces.

While expellees shared the experience of displacement and the desire to return home no matter where they came from, their region of origin defined the means by which they hoped to achieve this goal. Germans from the territories annexed to Poland and the Soviet Union campaigned for the return of the annexed territories. The Sudeten Germans advocated for the formation of a new joint government of Bohemia, Moravia, and Silesia that would be blind to ethnic divisions, allowing them to return. Expellees from Danzig (Gdańsk) formed a government in exile, calling for the restoration of free status for their city. Expellees from other Central and Eastern European countries advocated for negotiations with their countries of origin to secure their return (Carey 1951). These disparate political interests ensured that expellees remained a heterogeneous group. Thus, strong regional loyalties and divergent political interests contributed to the coexistence of multiple expellee communities, united for some purposes and acting separately for others.

## LOCAL TAX RATES AS AN INDICATOR OF PUBLIC GOODS PREFERENCES

How did this uneasy coexistence between expellees and natives affect investment in collective goods at the municipality level? A suitable indicator of willingness to pay for the provision of public goods in the West German context is represented by local tax rates.[5] While the valuation procedure as well as the uniform minimum rate (*Steuermesszahl*) of local tax is set by the federal government, municipal governments vote on an additional rate (*Hebesatz*) that applies to taxes on land used for agriculture and forestry (*Grundsteuer A*), on other forms of immovable property (*Grundsteuer B*), and on local trade

---

[5] Municipal control over local taxes and spending was briefly curtailed during National Socialism. During this period, mayors and local council members were appointed, and tax rates were set by the appointed mayor. Guided by the aims of decentralization and democratization, the occupation authorities sought to make the local government more responsive to the population and thus introduced some democratic innovations. The mayor and local councils were now elected. By the end of 1946, municipal elections were allowed in all western occupation zones. From then on, West German municipalities enjoyed considerable fiscal autonomy. This system remains in place to this day.

(business) (*Gewerbesteuer*).[6] Although municipalities also receive additional transfers from the state and federal levels in response to both their population size and their economic condition, and can incur debt in order to finance their expenditures, their own tax revenues make up more than two-thirds of total revenue. In addition to setting the tax rate, the municipal council decides how the municipal budget will be spent. In 1950, some of the largest expenditures were on schools, hospitals, healthcare facilities, social welfare, infrastructure building and maintenance, and public safety. Ideally, I would have combined the data on tax rates with information on the spending allocated to specific public goods. However, information on spending was available only for cities, which received few expellees, as discussed in Chapter 2.[7]

In the early postwar years, the bulk of municipal taxes fell on native residents, who owned taxable property. At the same time, expellees received a disproportionate share of public funds because they were more dependent on social welfare and public housing. From 1948 onward, expellees were allowed to vote in municipal elections and thus gained the ability to influence the composition of the municipal council. In communities with a large expellee population, local elections were extremely contentious. Hoping to elect their representatives, expellees organized their own electoral committees, which had the effect of stimulating political activity among the natives, who panicked at the possibility of getting expellee mayors and councilors (Erker 1990, 411–412).

Once municipal councils were formed, agreeing on a tax rate was no easy matter. The issues of infrastructure improvement, welfare burdens and housing construction dominated the meetings. The native population was typically reluctant to increase spending on collective goods requested by the expellees. For example, in the Bavarian community of Mering, the natives rejected expellees' request for funding for a separate school and a volunteer fire brigade (Pellengahr 2002, 152–159).

To understand how expellee presence affected contributions to municipal budgets, I obtained data on municipal tax rates for 1950 and 1961 ($N = 7,092$) in Bavaria, which received the largest absolute number of expellees. The fiscal and political impact of an expellee presence has not been previously analyzed at this fine-grained level.[8]

---

[6] In addition, some communities may levy taxes on entertainment, beverages, dogs, and hunting.
[7] Chevalier et al. (2018), who analyzed city-level data, conclude that the arrival of expellees reduced spending on infrastructure and housing, but raised spending on welfare.
[8] Existing studies of forced migration in West Germany use county (*Kreis*) data (e.g., Braun and Kvasnicka 2014; Braun and Dwenger 2020; Menon 2022). Chevalier et al. (2018) focus on 400 German cities, which are smaller than counties but still significantly larger than an average municipality in Germany, an important limitation given that most expellees were allocated to small rural localities. Another microlevel study by Schumann (2014) exploits geographic regression discontinuity design to isolate the impact of expellee presence on population density, comparing municipalities on the opposite sides of the former border between the US and French occupation zones in Baden-Württemberg.

Statistics on expellee allocation are available from the 1950 census. The expellees (*Heimatvertriebene*) are defined as the population who on September 1, 1939 lived in the lost eastern territories or in the Saarland, as well as people who lived abroad (based on international borders from before December 31, 1937) but spoke German as a native language. Children from two-parent households are counted based on the father's identity. The distribution of the expellee population in Bavaria varied considerably across municipalities, from 0 to 0.88 with a standard deviation of 0.09 and mean and median at 0.25, which allows for an effective comparative analysis.

In addition to measuring the share of expellees, I collected data on local economic characteristics that influenced refugee allocation and fiscal policy from the 1939 and 1950 censuses. Descriptive statistics for the variables used in the analysis are presented in Table A.3.

## Estimation Strategy and Results

When estimating the effect of expellees on fiscal policy, it is important to consider selection bias. One concern is that more expellees settled in municipalities with more generous public services and thus with higher tax rates. As discussed in Chapter 2, expellees had little choice of their destination and the allocation policy was guided by the availability of housing. Nonetheless, a possibility remains that the availability of housing was positively correlated with tax rates. For instance, places that suffered less destruction during the war and had higher housing stock could afford higher tax rates on immovable property and also received more expellees. Importantly, this biases against finding a negative relationship between the share of expellees and tax rates, that is against confirming the hypothesis that forced migration reduced contributions to collective goods.

I estimate the following model, where $i$ stands for municipalities and $k$ stands for counties:

$$Y_{ik} = \beta_0 + \beta_1 \text{ Share expellees}_{ik} + X'_{ik}\beta + \gamma_k + \epsilon_{ik} \qquad (4.1)$$

The key explanatory variable is the share of expellees. I control for population size, denominational characteristics, agricultural employment, landholding inequality, the share of males, distance to the eastern border, and distance to the railway station (vector $X_{it}$). The model also includes fixed effects for counties (*Kreis*) to account for unobservable time-invariant differences between different parts of Bavaria ($\gamma_k$).

The results are presented in Table 4.1. I find that the share of expellees predicts lower tax rates in all three categories in 1950. The effects are sizable and statistically significant. A one-standard-deviation increase in the share of expellees (9 percent) results in a 3-percent decrease in tax rates on agricultural land, a 1-percent decrease in tax rate on real estate, and a 2-percent decrease in business tax. The results are in line with the reduced willingness to invest

TABLE 4.1 *Expellee share and tax rates in Bavarian municipalities.*

| | Tax rates in 1950 | | | Tax rates in 1961 | | |
|---|---|---|---|---|---|---|
| | Agriculture | Real estate | Business | Agriculture | Real estate | Business |
| Share expellees (1950) | −0.35*** (0.06) | −0.15** (0.07) | −0.22*** (0.08) | 0.12 (0.13) | 0.18 (0.13) | 0.21** (0.10) |
| Religious fractionalization (1950) | −0.00 (0.04) | 0.09* (0.05) | 0.05 (0.05) | −0.07 (0.09) | −0.06 (0.08) | −0.10 (0.07) |
| Share in agriculture (1950) | −0.07 (0.07) | −0.07 (0.08) | −0.34*** (0.10) | 0.68*** (0.14) | 0.57*** (0.14) | 0.22* (0.12) |
| Share in agriculture (1939) | −0.04 (0.14) | −0.30* (0.17) | −0.11 (0.19) | −0.46 (0.30) | −0.27 (0.29) | −0.23 (0.24) |
| Share male (1950) | −0.05 (0.05) | −0.14** (0.06) | 0.08 (0.07) | 0.15 (0.11) | 0.11 (0.11) | 0.11 (0.09) |
| Ln population in 1950 | −0.04*** (0.01) | −0.02*** (0.01) | 0.06*** (0.01) | −0.02 (0.01) | −0.00 (0.01) | 0.06*** (0.01) |
| Landholding Gini 1939 | −0.05 (0.05) | −0.01 (0.06) | 0.05 (0.07) | −0.07 (0.11) | −0.04 (0.10) | −0.01 (0.08) |
| Ln distance to the eastern border | 0.01 (0.01) | −0.01 (0.01) | 0.04*** (0.02) | −0.01 (0.02) | 0.01 (0.02) | 0.03** (0.02) |
| County fixed effect | ✓ | ✓ | ✓ | ✓ | ✓ | ✓ |
| Adj. $R^2$ | 0.44 | 0.32 | 0.25 | 0.36 | 0.33 | 0.18 |
| N | 7032 | 7024 | 6984 | 7037 | 7037 | 7008 |

*Notes:* All models are OLS with county fixed effects. Heteroskedasticity robust standard errors in parentheses. City counties (*Stadtkreise*) are excluded. Significant at *$p < 0.10$; **$p < 0.05$; ***$p < 0.01$.

in municipal budgets by the natives, who dominated municipal councils and disproportionately owned taxable property.

However, the relationship between expellee share and tax rates reversed in 1961. It appears that communities that received more expellees set higher tax rates on business, with a one-standard-deviation increase in expellee share leading to a 2-percent increase in business tax. Thus, the negative effect of expellee presence on contributions to local budgets was short-lived. It is important to note that by 1961, expellees were able to relocate within Germany. Bavarian municipalities that received the highest number of expellees per capita experienced some out-migration, which could further explain the reversal of the sign on *Share expellees* in regressions of tax rates measured in 1961.

## HOW LONG DID THE EXPELLEE–NATIVE CLEAVAGE PERSIST?

My analysis of local taxes suggests that the negative effects of expellee presence on investment in collective goods had disappeared relatively quickly. As expellees became more economically integrated, the confrontational aspects of the native–expellee cleavage lost their salience. In line with this interpretation, the Bloc of Expellees received only 4.6 percent of the vote in the 1955 election and dissolved in 1961.

Yet the cultural elements of expellee identity endured for many more decades. As argued by Süssner (2004, 12), expellees created "an imagined diasporic community within the German nation." Their cultural heritage was integrated into school curricula and reinforced through annual commemorative gatherings. In 1953, there were 234 expellee newspapers in West Germany, 84 of them serving Sudeten Germans, and another 69 Silesian Germans (Melendy 2003, 45–46). These newspapers often featured landscapes from the lost territories, allowing expellees to travel to the past. More than 500 small expellee museums (*Heimatstuben*) gathered material objects from towns and regions in Central and Eastern Europe and served as meeting places (Eisler 2018). In the 1990s, sociological studies in Celle concluded that more than half of all interviewed expellees viewed the place where they were born as their true home and undertook many visits there once this became possible in the 1970s (Schulze 2002, 46).

Expellees' efforts at cultivating a distinct culture were subsidized by the West German government. Whereas communist Poland sought to erase cultural differences in the resettled region, West Germany supported their preservation. The 1953 Expellee Law included a cultural paragraph that promised to fund archives, museums, libraries, exhibitions, and educational activities focused on spreading awareness about expellees' culture (Demshuk 2014, 230).

One of the binding elements for some expellees was their hope to recover lost homelands. In the 1950s and 1960s, all political parties in Germany supported the so-called "right to the homeland" (*Heimatrecht*). As a result of expellee pressure, West Germany did not recognize Poland's new western border until the 1970s. In 1985, the annual convention of the Silesian Homeland Association (*Landsmannschaft*) rattled nerves in Poland with the slogan "Silesia Remains Ours." Expellee grievances flared up during the negotiations about the EU accession of Poland and the Czech Republic in the 1990s. The Sudeten Germans demanded the right of return and restoration of lost property as a condition for Czech EU membership, straining the relationship between Germany and the Czech Republic. The Prussian Claims

Society (*Preussische Treuhand*) attempted to force Poland to pay compensation to expellees through European courts in 2006–2008 (Ahonen 2016, 122), activating counterclaims for reparations among Poles.

Menon (2022) shows that one-third of all districts in West Germany had an expellee organization as late as 2020. Indeed, the expellee organizations claim to have the same number of members today as they did in the 1950s, though researchers question their accounting practices (Ahonen 2016, 124). Whether the descendants of expellees differ in their cultural characteristics from native Germans without expellee backgrounds is an important question for future research.

## DISCUSSION

This chapter has shown that forced migration created a new cleavage in West Germany. Even though the expellees were German on paper and their plight was a consequence of WWII, they received a cold welcome. The native population did not see expellees as compatriots and resented having to support them financially. What were previously minor differences became sources of intergroup conflict when people were uprooted from one region to another and forced to share public resources with their new host communities. Thus, the population transfers designed to homogenize states and reduce interethnic conflicts ended up increasing socioeconomic heterogeneity and exacerbating tensions at the subnational level.

The literature on ethnic politics has emphasized how some ethnic markers are more effective than others in enforcing group membership because they are more visible (Caselli and Coleman 2012). Ethnic cleavages based on shared history and "linked fate" alone, without the additional differences of skin color, religious denomination, or language, are sometimes considered less powerful (but see Posner (2004a) for a contrasting view). From this perspective, natives and expellees are not that different. Indeed, many researchers have treated them as interchangeable. For example, Peters (2022) interprets the economic effects of forced migration in West Germany in terms of increased population size alone. However, my analysis of Bavaria shows that expellees' cultural distinctiveness mattered a great deal for their interactions with the native population and each other.

Using an original dataset from Bavaria, I also demonstrate that fiscal policy varied as a function of the expellee share of the population. The more expellees a municipality received, the less willing it was to tax land and businesses in 1950. These results are interesting in light of the expectations that come to us from political economy models on redistribution in economically unequal societies. The arrival of expellees changed the ratio of rich and poor at the local level, as expellees who had lost most of their assets were allocated to communities that had suffered little damage during the war. This shock to local economic inequality was largely uncorrelated with prewar economic and social structures, conditional on wartime destruction and the resulting housing availability. In a system with universal suffrage and majority rule, such a shift in the income of the median voter has been argued to increase taxation and public spending (Meltzer and Richard 1981).[9] I find that, although expellees supported greater spending, their presence reduced tax rates in the receiving communities.

The reason, I argue, is the coalescence of opposing group identities among expellees and natives after the expulsions. This interpretation aligns with the evidence observed in other contexts that social heterogeneity reduces support for redistribution and public goods provision, particularly in the presence of intergroup economic disparities (Baldwin and Huber 2010; Alesina, Harnoss, and Rapoport 2016; Suryanarayan and White 2020). For instance, Alesina and Glaeser (2004) suggest that when the poor belong to a different ethnic or racial group, the wealthy are less supportive of redistribution and public spending.

---

[9] Key assumptions of this model are the existence of universal suffrage, majority rule, balanced budget, and fully informed voters.

# PART III

# STATE BUILDING IN THE WAKE OF DISPLACEMENT

# 5

# State Building in the Polish Wild West

As Huntington (1968) argued over half a century ago, the fundamental distinction between states lies not in their form, but in their degree of government, that is, whether the government commands the loyalty of its citizens and possesses the power to tax, conscript, and govern. Most refugees come from countries with a limited degree of government. The uprooting of a population, in other words, has much to do with the instability and disorder that result from low state capacity.

However, the uprooting of a population also presents an opportunity to expand the infrastructural power of the state. The disruption of social ties in the process of forced migration as well as boundary-making processes after the resettlement undermine self-help collective action, generating demand for state-provided resources and reducing resistance to state policies. Relatedly, the loss of support networks and property leads individuals to turn to the state for various forms of support. Provided that ruling elites are willing and able to invest resources in the uprooted populations, they are able to strengthen the state. I thus expect a greater accumulation of state capacity in regions exposed to forced migration relative to regions that were unaffected by it. Furthermore, the reach and efficacy of the state should be greater where the uprooted population is more heterogeneous.

In this chapter, I evaluate these hypotheses using evidence from Poland. I begin by describing the weakness of the Polish state in the aftermath of WWII, which makes Poland a challenging test for the argument that mass displacement can contribute to the accumulation of state capacity. Weak states may not be able to meet increased demand for collective and private goods in the aftermath of mass displacement. Negative experiences with the state, in turn, may lead the uprooted population to turn to warlords, militias, kinship networks, and other nonstate sources of authority, further eroding state capacity (Bodea and LeBas 2016).

An important mitigating factor in Poland was the nature of the elite and other societal actors. Most Polish economic elites were expropriated by the Nazi and Soviet governments during WWII. German landlords and industrialists were expelled after the war, and prewar political elites were decimated. The remaining societal actors broadly shared the communist objective of strengthening Polish control over territories acquired from Germany, even if they disagreed on other issues. Unopposed, and even supportive, societal actors thus created a favorable basis for building state capacity – what one might describe as an absence of potential spoilers.

Yet, it was the large-scale turnover of the population that created the necessary conditions for building state capacity in the newly acquired territories. The deficit of informal cooperation in heterogeneous migrant communities increased demand for the state's presence, while also reducing resistance to unpopular economic reforms championed by the communist government. I demonstrate that uprooting made the population of the resettled territories more dependent on state assistance and also more legible to the state. I further show that migration weakened communal elites and alternative forms of authority, such as the Catholic Church, which successfully challenged communist rule in other parts of Poland.

To test the observable implications of my argument, I gathered statistics on various indicators of state capacity, including the number of state bureaucrats, the extent of collectivization, and state control over the economy. I exploit the placement of the 1919 border between Poland and Germany, established by the Treaty of Versailles, to estimate the causal effect of resettlement on the reach of the communist state. The border divided the territory of Prussia in two based on linguistic differences between Poles and Germans. I show that before WWI, counties on either side of the border had similar levels of economic development. The main difference between them was that counties west of the border experienced mass resettlement after 1945 while counties east of the border did not. In addition to comparing outcomes between resettled and non-resettled counties, I ask whether state capacity within the resettled territories covaries with the heterogeneity of the regional origins of the population.

I find that the communist state-building project in the resettled territories largely succeeded. Indeed, within a short span of time, the government accumulated more administrative capacity and control over the economy there than in other parts of the country. It also left behind a more secular and left-wing electorate. In line with the argument that migration-based cleavages create an opportunity for strengthening the state, I find that the heterogeneity of the population on the ground *within* the resettled region predicts higher administrative capacity during the communist period and stronger support for the ex-communist party in Poland's first democratic elections.

## BACKGROUND CONDITIONS

### State Weakness in the Aftermath of WWII

The Polish state ceased to exist in September 1939, when the country was split into the Nazi and Soviet occupation zones. The national government was forced into exile, first operating from France and later from London. The war devastated the country's infrastructure, economy, and institutions. It is estimated that two-thirds of industrial facilities were demolished or looted (Bräu 2016, 443). Most prewar elites were expropriated and/or killed.

The destruction of the Polish elite and state organizations was most extensive in the western and eastern voivodeships (*wojewodztwa*), which were incorporated into the Third Reich and the Soviet Union, respectively. In western voivodeships, Polish state institutions were replaced by the German civilian administration. These areas experienced five years of forcible Germanization – the Nazi government took over Polish banks, industrial firms, and farms, repressed the Catholic Church, closed Polish schools, conscripted Poles into forced labor, and deported Poles *en masse* (Bräu 2016). In the Special Pacification Operation (*Außerordentliche Befriedungsaktion, AB- Aktion*), the Nazi government executed some 100,000 Polish politicians, landowners, jurists, state officials, and political activists.

In the eastern borderlands, the Red Army established new administrations at the county and voivodeship levels. Polish economic elites were deported to Siberia and Kazakhstan. Land belonging to landowners, churches, and military officers was confiscated, redistributed, and later collectivized. Factories, railways, and banks were nationalized; craftsmen and light manufacturers were forced into state-controlled cooperatives (Wierzbicki 2014). The churches remained open, but some priests were arrested as "enemies of the people."

In the central voivodeships, incorporated into the General Government (*Generalgouvernement*), lower-level Polish civilian administration was preserved but placed under German military control. This territory served as a reservoir of forced labor and agricultural production and was not Germanized. Large Polish factories were taken over by state-owned enterprises or private German companies; railways and banks were nationalized (Bräu 2016). Polish farmers remained on their land, albeit subject to high delivery quotas and arbitrary requisitions. Churches, charitable organizations, and vocational and elementary schools remained open. Milder repression enabled the emergence of an extensive underground state with courts, universities, and the press (Gross 1979). After the failed Warsaw Uprising in August 1944, however, many of these underground institutions were discovered and decapitated (Prazmowska 2004, 144). Polish elites in the General Government eventually suffered the same tragic fate at the hands of the Germans as elites did in the western voivodeships.

The defeat of Nazi Germany did not lead to a swift reconstruction of Polish administrative structures. On the contrary, events in 1944–1945 further eroded them. Particularly damaging was the armed struggle between the Soviet-installed communist government and the anti-communist opposition.

As the Red Army advanced westward in 1944, it handed authority over Nazi-liberated areas to the Polish Committee of National Liberation (*Polski Komitet Wyzwolenia Narodowego, PKWN*). PKWN was established by the Polish communists with Soviet support in Lublin in July 1944 as an alternative to the Government Delegation of Poland (*Delegatura Rządu Rzeczypospolitej Polskiej na Kraj*), an agency of the Polish government-in-exile. Following the Red Army were special operational groups, tasked with dismantling administrative structures associated with the London government and creating alternative organizations (Prażmowska 2004, 120). It is estimated that between the fall of 1944 and the spring of 1945, the NKVD arrested 61,729 Poles in the military zone behind Soviet lines (Prażmowska 2004, 130).

On January 1, 1945, the PKWN became the Provisional Government of Poland, triggering protests by the government-in-exile. Tensions between the new Soviet-backed administration and supporters of the government-in-exile escalated into a full-blown civil war. The state of insecurity persisted for several years as neither side "had the ability to outright control and administer Poland" (Prażmowska 2004, 144). One of the common tactics of the anti-communist underground was infiltrating the local Citizens' Militia (*Milicja Obywatelska, MO*) and Security Offices (*Urzędy Bezpieczeństwa, UB*) (Prażmowska 2004, 158). The conflict weakened nascent police and security organizations and inhibited the expansion of state infrastructure.

### The Absence of the State in the Resettled Territories

While state capacity was low across Poland at the end of WWII, the situation was particularly dire in the resettled territories. This region in western Poland had neither Polish authority nor a large Polish population before the war. Moreover, over 82 percent of its original residents were gone after WWII. So too were all agencies of government: the police force, the firefighters, the local councils, and the municipal administration. The result was "a vacuum of state authority" (Douglas 2012, 256).

After the region was officially transferred to the Polish government in 1944, Soviet armed forces for several years retained "unlimited authority over everything and everyone" (Sakson 2011, 198). Despite official proclamations, Soviet commanders were reluctant to share power with Polish officials. Maintaining social order in the occupied areas was not among the Red Army's priorities; instead, the Army units themselves undermined security by engaging in looting, drunkenness, and wanton violence (Zaremba 2012, 153–158). Some strategic outposts remained under Soviet control until the late 1940s (Techman 2000).

The resettled territories became known as the "Wild West" (*Dziki Zachód*), a nod to the American frontier, which conveyed the mixture of lawlessness and economic opportunity that characterized the region's early years under Polish authority. As Grabowski (2002, 152) writes, the lack of state oversight led to the emergence of an entirely "new profession" – *szabrownik*, derived from the German *schabemack*, which involved "shuttling between the Western Territories and central Poland, looting abandoned or semi-abandoned workshops, factories, and apartments, and selling thus-acquired treasures for profit." Theft and looting were so widespread that post-1945 damage to movable and immovable property may have rivaled the level of destruction during the war (Kociszewski 1993).

The new Citizens' Militia was particularly feckless in the resettled territories.[1] Its units lacked manpower and proper training. A June 1945 report by the head of Iława county in East Prussia described the status of the local MO unit as "tragic," noting an incident in which a militiaman accidentally shot himself because he did not know how to use his gun (Plotek 2011, 143).

The Polish state was so weak in the aftermath of WWII that it could not provide even basic public services. The situation was most dire in the resettled territories. As the next section shows, the Soviet-backed government was determined to change this reality and found allies in unexpected places.

### Coalition-Building to Strengthen the State

Turning the "Wild West" into an orderly, well-governed region was among the top priorities for the Polish Workers' Party (*Polska Partia Robotnicza, PPR*). The party strategically named the region "Recovered Territories" (*Ziemie Odzyskane*), reinforcing the claim that it had once belonged to the Polish Piast dynasty in medieval times and was now being taken back by Poland. It touted the territorial changes as the "greatest gain from the war" (quoted in Curp (2006, 589)) and called for national unity to guard against a continual German threat from the west. Władysław Gomułka, the party's First Secretary, stated at a May 1945 meeting of the Central Committee:

The western territories are one of the reasons the government has the support of the people. This neutralizes various elements and brings people together. Westward expansion and agricultural reform will bind the nation with the state. Any retreat would weaken our domestic position (Quoted in Kersten (2001, 80)).

Gomułka recognized that having suffered tremendous hardships during the occupation, Poles across the political spectrum favored expropriating the Germans (Curp 2006). The PPR could legitimize its rule in Poland by positioning itself as responsible for reclaiming the "Piast lands" from Germany (Curp

---

[1] The communist government changed the structure of the prewar police organization, strategically naming it Citizens' Militia to underscore the role of "ordinary citizens" in policing their own communities.

2006, 46). Gomułka argued that in returning these lands to Poland, the government was "not only repairing the injustices done by Germany over the centuries but also weakening Germany, all in the name of preserving international peace" (quoted in Sudziński (1997, 9)). Furthermore, the imperative to defend the new status quo against future German aggression provided a convenient justification for strengthening Poland's alliance with the Soviet Union.

The party's interest in the region was also rooted in its economic potential for realizing the communist vision of state-led industrialization and collective farming. The newly acquired territories were more economically developed than the eastern borderlands and rich in natural resources, including coal and iron ore deposits. The annexation also granted Poland access to the ports of Gdańsk and Szczecin. As Hilary Minc, the chairman of the Economic Committee of the Council of Ministers, argued at the meeting of the Council of Ministers:

If we tried to imagine the model of the Polish economy without the Recovered Territories, this model would come out as the worst nightmare: low consumption, huge overpopulation, chronic unemployment, a country so weak that its independence would have to be questioned. Without the Recovered Territories, there is no economic reconstruction of Poland. Without the western lands, there is no Poland as a sovereign state. (Quoted in Łach (1993, 25).)

Conveniently, German land, plants, and factories were nationalized under the April 1945 decree. Due to the expulsion of the original owners, the state obtained these properties for free and with minimal administrative effort.

As Gomułka anticipated, the annexation of the German territories was broadly popular. Both the government-in-exile and the opposition parties supported the new western border, even though they initially stood by the inviolability of Poland's 1939 border in the east. The Polish People's Party (*Polskie Stronnictwo Ludowe*, the PSL), the main competitor of the PPR after the war, campaigned ahead of the 1946 referendum arguing that the new western and northern territories would "satisfy the essential need of the Polish nation" for land in light of displacement from the east and the repatriation of Poles from around the world. Just like the PPR, the PSL further claimed that taking over this land would reduce Germany's economic and military potential and thereby guarantee peace (Domke 2010, 69). Echoing Gomułka, PSL leader Stanisław Mikołajczyk also stressed the German threat: "Germany is the eternal enemy of the Polish and Slavic lands, whose intention is to destroy our country and our people" (quoted in Sudziński (1997, 7)).

The plan to expel the Germans also attracted right-wing nationalists associated with the interwar National Democrats (*Endecja*) movement. Formerly arch-enemies, nationalists saw eye to eye with communists with respect to the "historic mission of the Polish government" in recovering lost "Piast lands" (Curp 2006, 46). They joined the newly created Association for the Development of the Recovered Territories (*Towarzystwo Rozwoju Ziem Zachodnich, TRZZ*) and the reactivated Polish Western Union (*Polski Związek Zachodni, PZZ*) to provide the new government with practical support in appropriating the new region.[2]

The Polish Catholic Church likewise welcomed the territorial changes as an opportunity to expand its influence into a former Protestant area (Osekowski 1994; Zaryn 1997; Curp 2006). Upon his return from exile, Poland's primate Cardinal August Hlond used the special powers granted him by the Pope to reform the Church administration and appoint new Polish priests in the newly acquired parishes. As Curp (2006, 60) observes, "[I]n contrast to the growing conflict between church and state in the old voivodeships of Wielkopolska, in the pioneer conditions of Ziemia Lubuska [former Germany], a spirit of cooperation reigned between the newly established religious and political authorities."

The annexation of German territories thus fostered an unlikely coalition between communists and other political actors. The communist government hoped to preserve this consensus in preparation for the June 1946 People's Referendum. The referendum posed three questions, covering: (1) the abolition of the Senate; (2) the nationalization of basic industries and agricultural reform; and (3) the consolidation of the western border of the Polish state on the Oder–Neisse line. The PPR campaigned with impassioned slogans: "YES is a sign of your Polishness, you are a Pole - say YES"; "Remember the Silesian people - Silesia was Polish, it will be Polish, a sign of a Pole - three times YES"; "3 times YES - the Germans don't like it." A slogan prepared for the referendum, but eventually excluded, read: "3x yes – this is Poland without national minorities" (Zaremba 2001, 153–154). Although the Communists and their opponents disagreed on the first two questions, they were unanimous in their support for the appropriation of German territories.[3]

The results of the referendum were manipulated, but historian Andrzej Paczkowski (1993) used the original records preserved in the Polish Central Archives of Modern Records (*Archiwum Akt Nowych*) to estimate that two-thirds (66.9 percent) of the Polish population supported the western border revision (Paczkowski 1993).[4] The proportion was particularly high on the frontier itself, where 78 percent of the Polish population voted yes on this question.

---

[2] These organizations conducted research to justify Poland's rights to the annexed areas, assisted the government in verifying the nationality of German citizens wishing to stay in Poland after the war, sponsored the renaming of place names, and helped develop settlement plans (Curp 2006).

[3] The PSL advocated a "no" on the abolition of the Senate and "yes" on the other two questions. Catholic groups advocated "no" on the abolition of the Senate, "yes" on the western border and left the nationalization question for voters to decide. The anti-Communist WiN advocated "yes" on the western border and "no" on the other two questions.

[4] This is considerably lower than the official result of 91.4 percent.

There was considerably less enthusiasm for communist dominance and the accompanying political and economic changes. Paczkowski (1993) estimates that only 27 percent of the population supported the abolition of the Senate and only 42 percent supported the proposed economic reforms.[5]

As the communist government set about cementing its power, it benefited from the weakening of the elite and property structures during the war. Polish economic elites, who arguably had the most to lose from the communist redistributive agenda, had been killed or expropriated. In the newly acquired territories, the main losers of government expropriation – Germans – had been expelled by the Red Army and the Polish People's Army. Only 30 percent of prewar senators were still alive and on Polish territory after the war (Pakulski 2016).

The PPR also benefited from access to Soviet coercive resources. Repression did what propaganda could not accomplish. After the manipulated 1947 parliamentary elections, the remaining opposition leaders left the country, fearing for their lives. The PPR absorbed the remaining left-wing groups and was renamed the Polish Worker's Party (*Polska Zjednoczona Partia Robotnicza*, PZPR). The PZPR would retain a monopoly on power until 1989.

## UPROOTING AND THE DEMAND FOR STATE PRESENCE

### The State as a Provider of Resources and Intermediary

While the government worked to forge a new order in the resettled territories, a steady stream of migrants entered the region from different directions. As I discussed in Chapter 3, migrants' diverse regional origins and experiences impeded their cooperation in many areas of civic life, such as safeguarding property, repairing communal buildings, and organizing economic activity. These deficiencies increased reliance on the state. In other words, uprooted communities had more to gain from the expansion of state capacity than more stable communities because they lacked alternative forms of social control and had lower levels of voluntary cooperation. Furthermore, the loss of economic resources and social ties in the aftermath of migration made the population of the resettled territories more likely to turn to state organizations for credit, insurance, and other forms of support.

Below, I use qualitative evidence to illustrate the processes leading to the accumulation of state capacity in the resettled territories.

After an initial period of uncontrolled resettlement, the State Repatriation Office (PUR) began to direct migrants to specific locations selected on the basis of housing availability, providing them with food and supplies during the long

---

[5] The officially published numbers suggested that 68 percent of voters supported the abolition of the Senate and 77.2 percent supported the nationalization of basic industry and agricultural reform.

journey west. The government offered material support in order to make relocation more appealing and to reduce the potential settlers' upfront investment. Those relocating from other Polish territories enjoyed the most generous treatment: They received a certificate of resettlement that entitled them to a free one-way train ticket as well as ration cards, cash, and other material benefits. Countless bureaucracies emerged to manage the distribution of land, apartments, ration cards, and jobs. Stanisław Dulewicz, the first mayor of Darłowo (Rügenwalde), recalls the assistance rendered to new arrivals by his municipal office: "They had to be supported at the city's expense, as they had no livelihood. In the first days of living in Darłowo, sometimes within three or four weeks, until they got a job, they were not only fed completely free of charge by the city council, but also, if possible, provided with clothes, underwear, and shoes" (Dulewicz 2016, 218).

The exodus of German landowners enabled the government to redistribute thousands of hectares of land to Polish peasants. In a typical case, migrants settled on the land first, often with the permission of the local PUR office, but turned to the state to register their properties a year or two later once the corresponding government agencies were in place. To receive a land title, voluntary migrants bought land directly from the state. Only 10 percent of the cost had to be paid immediately; the remaining value could be paid over the next ten years, in cash or in kind. Forced migrants from eastern borderlands were entitled to receive property comparable to what they left behind, though few felt properly compensated or received valid ownership rights (Ther 1996, 799).

In the vast majority of cases, settlers did not receive grant deeds or, if they did receive grant deeds, no judgments were issued confirming the execution of the grant deeds. This meant that settlers did not acquire ownership rights to the occupied German property. To resolve these issues, in 1951 a decree on the protection and regulation of ownership of peasant farms in the Recovered Territories was issued. The decree granted settlers ownership rights, but these rights were rarely formalized in the land register.[6] These incomplete property rights made migrants even more dependent on the state as they feared that any day they could lose their land. In a pattern Michael Albertus observed in other autocracies, distributing land without full property rights served to bind the recipients of land to the incumbent government and made the state "central to citizens' strategies for economic survival" (Albertus 2021, 21–22).

Cultivating the land was extremely difficult due to the lack of seeds, draft animals, and agricultural machinery. These resources too would have to come from the state. Migrants' memoirs about their early years in the resettled territories frequently mention the various forms of support that the state and state-affiliated organizations provided. They also refer to donations from the

---

[6] To this day, the legal status of many properties has not been regulated in land registers and has to be resolved via administrative courts when disputes arise.

United Nations Relief and Rehabilitation Administration (UNRRA), which
were redistributed by state organizations.[7] For example, a forced migrant from
the eastern borderlands writes that his family managed to make it through
the first year thanks to the "post-German" cow, a "UNRRA" horse, and several tons of grain from the Polish government. After the first harvest was
destroyed by mice, he writes that "the government provided further assistance in both money and seeds" (Jarecka-Kimlowska 1968, 224). He also
mentions support from the state-owned Agriculture Bank (*Bank Rolny*), the
Association of Peasant Self-Help (*Związek Samopomocy Chłopskiej*), and the
Savings and Loan Cooperative (*Spółdzielnia Oszczędnościowo-Pożyczkowa*)
(Jarecka-Kimlowska 1968, 225–226). Another migrant recalls:

As the surrounding villages became more populated, the national councils and the PPR
organization allocated one cow each, first to families with small children, then to all
others who, for whatever reason, did not have livestock. We received some horses from
the [Polish] army and later UNRRA [...], delivered on credit. We were also provided
with cereal and potato seeds on credit. This was the most needed state aid for agriculture here in the West because without it the development of these lands would have
taken at least two to three years longer. Many farmers would give up developing their
farms if it were not for state aid. (Jarecka-Kimlowska 1968, 286.)

Notwithstanding the biased nature of the memoirs published during the
communist period, they do bear testament to the considerable resources the
government put toward assisting settlers. Obtaining resources from the state,
in turn, made migrants more legible. The government knew exactly how many
seeds the farmers borrowed, how many horses they received, and so on. This
knowledge later served as the basis for extracting revenue through land taxes
and deliveries of agricultural products.

The state's presence was also welcomed because of the dire security situation. In the 1940s and 1950s, crime rates in the former German territories
were many times higher than elsewhere in Poland, and the migrant population
lived in permanent danger (Banasiak 1965, 122; Chuminski 1993, 64). The
disruption of social networks and the diversity of settlers increased both the
prevalence of crime and the challenges associated with addressing it through
bottom-up cooperative endeavors. Only tight-knit homogeneous communities
were successful in establishing effective neighborhood watches, volunteer fire
brigades, and other security-oriented organizations. Residents of less cohesive
communities were more likely to support the creation of the Citizens' Militia
(MO), despite its ineptness in solving crimes. For instance, one migrant recalls
that after multiple cows were stolen in his [heterogeneous] community and he
found them at the local butcher, he successfully brought the cows back "with
the help of the MO" (Jarecka-Kimlowska 1968, 271). The migrant had to find

---

[7] UNRRA delivered two million tons of various goods to Poland between 1945 and 1947, including agricultural machinery, grain, farm animals, and clothing. Subsequently, the Communist
authorities withdrew consent to UNRRA activities in the country.

the cow on his own first, but the MO had to convince the butcher to surrender it. In many cases, migrants joined the MO units themselves.

During the initial postwar years, the key to survival lay in the spirit of neighborly assistance and collaborative resource-sharing. And yet, the diversity of settlers made these essential cooperative economic relationships difficult to sustain. State-affiliated organizations filled the gap – as Zaneta Stasieniuk (2011, 154) notes, "[formal] institutions [in the resettled territories] not only represented state authority but also served as an intermediary between different societal groups. Social relations were established on the basis of these institutions."

A notable example is the Peasant Self-Help Association (*Związek Samopomocy Chłopskiej*, ZSCh), a form of rural cooperative endorsed by the communist authorities. Prior to WWII, peasants formed voluntary consumer and production cooperatives to negotiate prices, manage resources, and coordinate harvests. While cooperatives in the "old" Poland persisted after the war, the population in the resettled territories encountered hurdles in launching new cooperatives due to mutual distrust among migrants originating from different regions. The communists took advantage of this void to establish the ZSCh, which differed from independent cooperatives in that it encompassed the entire village and served as an arm of the local government. The ZSCh's economic functions included supervising credit allocation, supplying peasants with seeds and draft animals, organizing threshing events, and providing agricultural machinery (Gross 2018). In 1947, the ZSCh further introduced a compulsory system of neighborly assistance, which obligated wealthier farmers to share their agricultural tools and livestock (Gross 2018, 211).

Communist efforts at establishing ZSCh were more successful in the newly created communities, which were less likely to cooperate independently and had fewer resources. A migrant from Wielkopolska describes the emergence of ZSCh in his village:

There was one displaced person every few houses, there was no village head or any shop, and there were plenty of looters. [...] On Sundays, we gathered for meetings to discuss how to continue farming without horses and cattle. Once, a representative of the Peasant Self-Help Association came to our meeting in the uniform of a Polish lieutenant. He told us a lot about the People's Republic of Poland, land reform, and the nationalization of industry, explaining that it was necessary to organize the Association in the village. (Jarecka-Kimlowska 1968, 279).

### Cooperation or Coercion?

That the success of the communist government on the frontier was facilitated by the uprooting of the population and by the weakening of social ties between migrants is a view shared by many Polish scholars. It is, however, typically imbued with a negative evaluation of the Communist regime's treatment of migrants, who are seen as victims. For example, Kersten (1991, 165) writes that forced migration "was an important cause in weakening resistance to the Communist authorities." Sakson (2011, 332) notes that the resettled communities were easy to manipulate because they "lacked the strength of a long tradition, a sense of solidarity, and social ties."

While it is true that the disruption of communal ties weakened opposition to collectivization and other unpopular economic reforms during the Stalinist period, the relationship between state and society in the resettled territories was at first more cooperative than adversarial. The communist regime attracted numerous people to join its organizational structures with the promise of material and social advancement. In a sense, it was creating state institutions *together* with the incoming migrants. As one migrant wrote in his diary: "I arrived in the village as the first settler and found myself honored with the appointment as the village elder. Thus, I became a representative of the state, with the duty of assisting other newcomers" (Jarecka-Kimlowska 1968, 224). Migrants were enlisted to participate in various areas of local administration, social welfare, and education, irrespective of their prewar professions or educational backgrounds. The Citizens Militia, the Peasant Self-Help Association, and other state-affiliated organizations were mostly staffed by migrants themselves, even though the impetus for forming these organizations originated from the communist authorities.

Migrants' personal accounts reveal the potential for significant upward mobility: A primary school teacher became a school inspector; an engineer became a factory director; and the first peasant to arrive in a given village became its elder (*sołtys*) (Dulczewski and Kwilecki 1970, 11–12). For example, Dulewicz, the mayor of Darłowo quoted earlier, had no administrative experience, as he had worked as a teacher before the war. However, the new Polish head of the Darłowo county, himself a former teacher, "convinced [him] that [his] ignorance in the field of administration should not scare [him]," and that he would "undoubtedly learn" on the job (Dulewicz 2016, 207). Dulewicz continued to gather new responsibilities: he soon became the acting headmaster of a new secondary school and secretary of the city committee of the Polish Socialist Party.

Even before the communist regime was able to muster any coercive power, the pro-Communist parties enjoyed greater support in the former German territories than in central and eastern Poland. In a study of Polish workers, Kenney (1997, 136) observed that "two very different Polands [existed] in the years 1945–50: Łódź, an example of Poland of the past, where prewar traditions strongly influenced social relations; and Wrocław, the Poland of the future, where social relations were reconstructed in a communist context." Kenney shows that in Wrocław, 50–60 percent of workers joined the party, compared to only 18 percent nationwide and 14 percent in Łódź (167). Work in Wrocław was often tied to party membership and strikes were nearly absent, despite harder working conditions on the frontier. Kenney (1997, 137) concludes that "the task of creating, physically and culturally, a Polish community in an alien land [...] resulted in a society much more hospitable to communists."

To be sure, many people on both sides of the pre-1945 Polish border eschewed politics and feared all things communist. For example, a January 1947 report of Olsztyn Voivodeship Office characterized settlers in Braniewo county as "apathetic and passive" toward politics. They viewed "all parties and organizations with distrust and avoid[ed] joining parties [...] Being in a party is considered as something very bad" (McNamara 2013, 99). It is no coincidence that the names of the parties associated with communist ideology – the Polish Workers' Party, the Polish Socialist Party, and later the Polish United Workers' Party – had no "communism" in them. However, differences played out at the community level: In a stable homogeneous community, joining the party could be punished with ostracism; whereas in an uprooted heterogeneous community, ostracism was not a credible threat, and indeed, the benefits of a party-state presence were readily apparent to migrants seeking order and stability.

## Weaker Alternative Forms of Authority

Could diverse uprooted communities turn to organizations other than the state following the erosion of traditional social structures? In Eastern Europe, the Catholic Church is credited with enabling the bottom-up resistance to the party-state during the Communist period (e.g., Nalepa and Pop-Eleches 2022; Wittenberg 2006). Churches had long been responsible for enforcing social norms, funding charities, educating children, administering justice, and enforcing marriage contracts. The Catholic Church was the most formidable institution, with organizational structures extending across welfare, schooling, and other social services.

Although the Polish Catholic Church lost 28.8 percent of its priests and 13.6 percent of its buildings during WWII (Osa 1989, 276), it remained powerful enough for the Communist regime to avoid challenging its authority until the end of the 1940s. The fusion between Polish nationalism and Catholicism, furthermore, raised the costs of repressing the Church during the Stalinist period (Grzymała-Busse 2015). Although the government confiscated Church lands and took over the Catholic welfare organization, *Caritas*, it did not prohibit religious services. Catholic priests remained influential in their communities throughout the communist period.

In the resettled territories, the parish was initially the only place where migrants of different origins interacted on a regular basis (Majka 1971, 145). No matter their regional origins, migrants flocked to mass, seeking in it, in addition to spiritual succor, endorsement of their decision to migrate (Osekowski 1994, 218). The church was also important for the autochthones who were deprived of other social institutions and organizations following the change from German to Polish government (Nowakowski 1957, 113). Correspondingly, some Polish scholars credit the Catholic Church with enabling cooperation among migrants from different cultures and organizing the first schools and hospitals (Wejman 2007; Osękowski 2001; Osa 1989).

Nonetheless, the influence of the Church was much weaker in the resettled territories than in other parts of Poland. Like the Polish state, the Polish Catholic Church was a stranger to this region. Its efforts to expand influence into previously Protestant areas were hampered by a shortage of priests. As late as 1952, only 288 out of 500 parishes in the resettled territories had a priest (Cichocka 2013, 53). The shortage contributed to the "laicization of social life" in the region (Kowalski and Śleszyński 2000). In the 1954–1955 academic year, just 4 percent of schools in the region taught religion, compared to 18 percent of schools in the non-resettled territories (Konopka 1997).

The scarcity of priests was exacerbated by the communist government's disagreement with the Vatican over the appointment of new bishops to replace the German bishops expelled after the war. Church affairs in the resettled territories were managed by temporary apostolic administrators who had less authority than bishops (Nalepa and Pop-Eleches 2022). The vacancies at various levels of the Church hierarchy enabled the communist regime to infiltrate the Church with so-called patriot priests (*księża patrioci*). The state recruited roughly 1,000 clergy who sympathized with the communist regime on account of a conflict with higher Church authorities, a history of Nazi repression, or simply a positive inclination toward communist ideology. The "patriot priests" were expected to disseminate communist ideology from the pulpit. They received direct assignments from the party and state security organizations. Table 5.1 shows that, in 1954, the proportion of pro-regime priests was much higher in the resettled voivodeships. As Nalepa and Pop-Eleches (2022) argue, communities "disrupted by the inflow of migrants" where "parishioners had less familiarity with each other" were less able to detect communist infiltrators. The result was that even the Catholic clergy was more likely to cooperate with the communist government in the resettled territories.

## A FORMAL COMPARISON OF RESETTLED AND NON-RESETTLED VOIVODESHIPS

In the remainder of the chapter, I compare the degree of state presence in the former frontier region to that observable in the neighboring western voivodeships as well as in the migrants' regions of origin. I also examine whether variation in the heterogeneity of the population *within* the resettled region predicts the level of state capacity.

There are many reasons to expect differences between western and eastern Polish territories, only some of which relate to displacement. Already in the interwar period, an unofficial distinction existed between the so-called "Poland A" in the west – considered to be the more developed and better-governed

TABLE 5.1  *Influence of the Catholic Church in 1954–1955 by voivodeship.*

| Voivodeship | Schools | | | Priests | | | Priests per 1,000 people |
|---|---|---|---|---|---|---|---|
| | Total | Teach religion | Share | Total | "Patriot" | Share | |
| Kraków | 57 | 18 | 0.32 | 1,630 | 62 | 0.04 | 0.69 |
| Rzeszów | 52 | 11 | 0.21 | 945 | 42 | 0.04 | 0.62 |
| Lublin | 56 | 16 | 0.29 | 630 | 31 | 0.05 | 0.29 |
| Poznań | 58 | 17 | 0.29 | 965 | 52 | 0.05 | 0.42 |
| Białystok | 28 | 2 | 0.07 | 382 | 21 | 0.05 | 0.37 |
| Łódź | 62 | 5 | 0.08 | 673 | 43 | 0.06 | 0.39 |
| Warszawa | 116 | 15 | 0.13 | 1,206 | 88 | 0.07 | 0.37 |
| Stalinogród | 80 | 5 | 0.06 | 988 | 76 | 0.08 | 0.33 |
| Kielce | 45 | 11 | 0.24 | 736 | 60 | 0.08 | 0.42 |
| Zielona Góra* | 20 | 0 | 0 | 230 | 21 | 0.09 | 0.34 |
| Opole* | 27 | 0 | 0 | 424 | 39 | 0.09 | 0.48 |
| Bydgoszcz | 43 | 0 | 0 | 635 | 60 | 0.09 | 0.40 |
| Koszalin* | 18 | 2 | 0.11 | 146 | 20 | 0.14 | 0.23 |
| Gdańsk* | 38 | 17 | 0.45 | 355 | 54 | 0.15 | 0.33 |
| Olsztyn* | 22 | 3 | 0.14 | 249 | 42 | 0.17 | 0.31 |
| Wrocław* | 53 | 1 | 0.02 | 555 | 110 | 0.20 | 0.28 |
| Szczecin* | 17 | 0 | 0 | 128 | 35 | 0.27 | 0.19 |
| Resettled | 157 | 6 | 0.04 | 2,087 | 321 | 0.15 | 0.16 |
| Non-resettled (Prussia) | 181 | 22 | 0.12 | 2,588 | 188 | 0.07 | 0.47 |
| Non-resettled (other) | 454 | 95 | 0.21 | 6,202 | 347 | 0.06 | 0.67 |

*Notes:* The voivodeships located primarily in the formerly German territories are marked with an asterisk.
*Sources:* Konopka (1997) and Zurek (2009).

region, and "Poland B" or even "Poland C" in the east and south – known for their economic backwardness and conservative attitudes (Lewandowski 2013, 208).

   These differences go back to the late eighteenth century, when the Polish-Lithuanian Commonwealth (*Rzeczpospolita*) was divided among the Russian, the Austro-Hungarian, and the Prussian Empires (see Map 5.1). During the 125 years of its rule, the Kingdom of Prussia industrialized its Polish territories far more than either the Russian or the Austrian empires did (Wolf 2007). Thus, the Prussian partition had better infrastructure and a more capable bureaucracy compared to the Russian and Austrian partitions – assets that would positively influence state capacity in subsequent periods. At the same time, Prussian officials pursued marginalization policies – suppressing Polish

Map 5.1 Imperial partitions and territorial changes in Poland. Partition boundaries are based on MPIDR and CGG (2013).

national identity, excluding ethnic Poles from state administration, and limiting Polish schooling (Davies 2005). The legacies of imperial partitions persist to this day and are visible in physical infrastructure, voting preferences, religiosity, bureaucratic quality, and schooling (Grosfeld and Zhuravskaya 2015; Zarycki 2015; Bukowski 2018; Vogler 2019). Differences in railway density, an indicator of economic development, are plotted in Figure A.3.

In 1919, the Second Polish Republic was born out of the parts of the three defeated empires. Its eastern border would not be finalized until 1921, following the Polish victory in the Russo-Polish War (1919–1920). Its western border was established by the Treaty of Versailles in 1919, and it traversed the former Prussian territory. The port of Danzig (Gdańsk), inhabited predominantly by Germans, was placed under the administration of the League of Nations. The surrounding area, sandwiched between Germany proper in the west and

German East Prussia in the east, was given to Poland despite Germany's protes-
tations. The exact border between the two countries was drawn in such a way
as to separate German and Polish speakers, per Woodrow Wilson's principle
of "national self-determination." Economic considerations came "third, after
history and nationality" (Schultz 2002, 111–115).

Given the fluidity of identities and the mixed settlement patterns in the
region, classifying individuals into ethnolinguistic categories was far from
straightforward, and the final boundary failed to satisfy either side (Ther
and Siljak 2001, 63). In the Polish case, in particular, the language divide
between Poles and Germans was fuzzy after a long period of forced Germanization and internal migration. The resulting border did not follow preexisting
boundaries of Prussian provinces and counties, splitting some units in half (see
Figure A.2).[8]

Constituting an exception to this top-down process of partition, two short
segments of the border in East Prussia and Upper Silesia were determined by
plebiscites, held in July 1920 and March 1921, respectively. In East Prussia,
most of the population, including Polish-speaking Masurians, voted to remain
in Germany. In Upper Silesia, the outcome of the plebiscite was more even,
with 60 percent of the population voting for Germany. This result provoked
an insurgency by pro-Polish forces and, eventually, a partition of the region
between Poland and Germany.[9] East Prussia and Upper Silesia were the two
provinces where Poland would claim autochthones as newly minted Polish
citizens after 1945 (see Chapter 2).

I use Prussian census data from 1907 to 1910 to verify that the post-
WWI border within Prussia, which in 1945 would mark the new frontier,
ran through communities that were economically and demographically similar. The dataset was originally compiled by Galloway (2007) and is at the level
of counties (*Kreise*). It provides information about the size and density of the
urban and rural population as well as its religious affiliation and occupational
characteristics. Regression discontinuity analysis with distance to the border
as a forcing variable confirms that the Prussian counties transferred to Poland
after the Treaty of Versailles were similar to the counties west of the border
that remained in Germany in terms of their levels of economic development,
urbanization rates, and prevalence of large landholdings (see Table A.4). The
only noticeable, though statistically insignificant difference – a higher share of
Protestants west of the border and a higher share of Catholics east of the border – is consistent with the Versailles objective to separate ethnic Poles from
ethnic Germans.[10]

---

[8] The outline of the border roughly followed the sixteenth-century borders of the Polish-
Lithuanian Commonwealth.
[9] The urban areas of Kattowitz (Katowice) and Konigshütte (Chorzów) went to Poland, despite
the outcome of the plebiscite, to even out the division of industrial assets (Urbatsch 2017).
[10] Ethnic Germans were more likely to be Protestant, whereas ethnic Poles were more likely to be
Catholic.

Although the counties east and west of the 1919 border appear to be economically indistinguishable before WWI, the territory east of the border (Wielkopolska) experienced twenty additional years of Polish rule (1919–1939). Polish state organizations therefore had a longer history in this region. During WWII, communities east of the border were reincorporated into the Reich, as part of the Wartheland Reichsgau and the Danzig-Westpreussen Reichsgau (see Figure A.4). Polish administration was dismantled, the Nazi regime forcibly resettled thousands of local Poles into the General Government, and many others were sent to Germany as forced laborers. Their farms were taken over by nearly 500,000 *Volksdeutsche*, or Germans who had lived as minorities in other parts of Poland and Eastern Europe. After the war, the Poles returned, and the *Volksdeutsche* were expelled to Germany, just like the *Reichsdeutsche*, or Germans who had lived west of the 1919 border.

By the end of WWII, Polish state institutions were absent on either side of the Versailles boundary, though for different reasons. In the counties on the eastern side, they were destroyed by the Nazi regime; in counties on the western side, they never existed. Furthermore, counties on either side of the border experienced mass displacement. Still, the extent of displacement was much higher west of the Versailles border. For instance, within the former Poznań voivodeship that traversed the border after 1945, 91 percent of the population east of the Versailles boundary lived in the same voivodeship in the year 1950 as in 1939. By contrast, only 29 percent of the population west of the Versailles border was living in the same voivodeship in 1950 (GUS 1950). As shown in Figure 5.1, the differences in population turnover were still visible at the end of the Communist period. According to the 1988 census, the share of the population born outside the region was 10 percent higher just west of the 1919 border, a statistically significant difference.[11]

The comparison of state presence between the post-1945 frontier and the nearby Wielkopolska region constitutes a harder test for my argument than the simple comparison between the newly acquired German territory and the rest of Poland. Not only do the two regions share economic, institutional, and infrastructural commonalities, but Polish rule also has a longer history in Wielkopolska, which should bias against my hypothesis that the communist state achieved higher state capacity in the newly acquired region over time. Furthermore, Wielkopolska experienced a significant degree of forced migration, in contrast to the territories in central and eastern Poland. The difference in the intensity of "displacement treatment" on either side of the Versailles border is smaller than that between the resettled territories and central Polish voivodeships, which may bias the estimated effect of displacement downward. However, this comparison allows me to hold constant many confounding factors, including the level of economic development and urbanization, the

---

[11] It is important to take into account that children born in the resettled territories immediately after resettlement would be in their early forties in 1988.

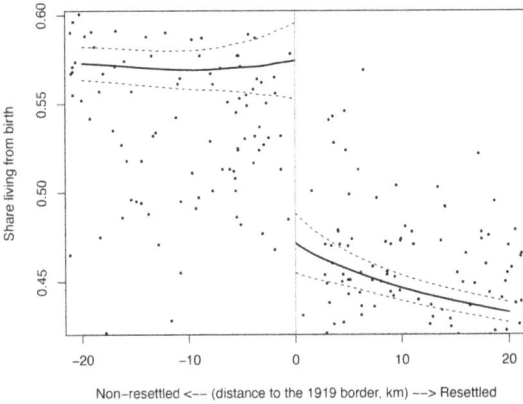

FIGURE 5.1 Discontinuity in the share of the population living in a municipality from birth in 1988.

legacy of Prussian and Nazi governance, the absence of Polish administrative structures at the start of communist state building, and the weakness of the anti-communist underground in the final stages of WWII.

While my main focus is on the differences between districts within the former Prussian partition for the reasons outlined earlier, I also discuss the differences in outcomes between the newly acquired territories and the former Austrian and Russian partitions of Poland, that is, the areas where the majority of migrants came from. Because migrants brought attitudes toward the state with them, it is informative to compare their political and economic behavior in a new environment to that in their regions of origin. To foreshadow my findings, the differences between the resettled region and migrants' regions of origin are much larger than the differences between the resettled region and the former Prussian partition.

VARIATION IN ADMINISTRATIVE CAPACITY

To the extent that forced displacement facilitated the accumulation of state capacity in the newly acquired territories, we should observe a discontinuity in the number of state employees at the 1919 border. To measure administrative capacity, I digitized occupational data from the 1950 Polish census. I consider the following occupational categories as related to state capacity: (1) state administration, social organizations, and banks (*administracja, organizacje społeczne i banki*) and (2) municipal services (*gospodarka komunalna*). The number of state employees in both categories ranges from 10 to 128 per 1,000 people ($\mu = 32$, $\sigma = 19.71$) in the frontier region. County-level variation in this variable is mapped in Map 5.2. The map shows that state capacity increased from east to west, and that it was particularly low in the former

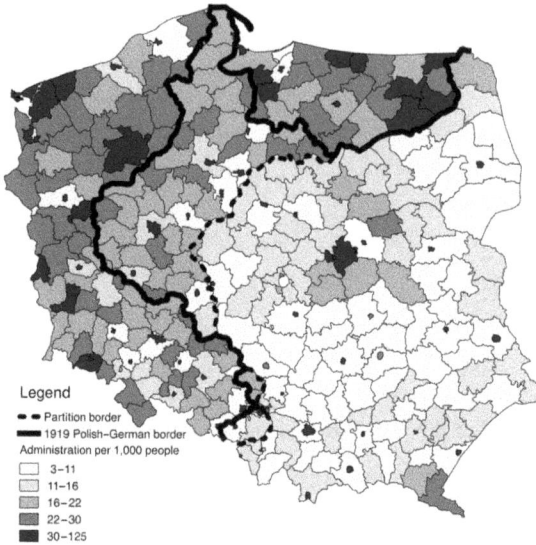

Map 5.2 Administrative capacity in Polish counties in 1950. Polygon boundaries created by the author based on the map from Central Office for National Measurements (*Główny Urząd Pomiarów Kraju*).

Russian and Austro-Hungarian partitions – where the majority of migrants came from – even though the war had ended a year earlier in this region.

To estimate the effects of displacement on administrative capacity, I use a geographic regression discontinuity (GRD) design.[12] The key assumption is that counties on either side of the Versailles boundary shared a similar socioeconomic makeup before 1945, except for their experience, or lack thereof, of a massive uprooting of their population. As shown earlier, this assumption holds for the Prussian period. The forcing variable in the analysis is the Euclidean distance to the 1919 border from the centroid of each county. Specifications control for city indicator, area, liberation month, and the latitude and longitude of each county. To select the distance to either side of the border within which to perform the local linear regression, I use two approaches for robustness: the Imbens-Kalyanaraman optimal bandwidth calculation in the *RDD* package in R by Dimmery (2016) as well as the MSE-optimal bandwidth from package *rdrobust* in R by Calonico et al. (2015).

Figure 5.2 shows the discontinuity in size of the state administration at the Versailles border graphically (see Table A.5 for full estimation output). The analysis indicates that administrative capacity was significantly higher on the western side of the border, that is, in the resettled territories. The local average treatment effect for counties within 10 km around the border is 12.72 and

---

[12] This is a sharp regression discontinuity because placement on either side of the border perfectly predicts treatment (mass resettlement of the majority of the population).

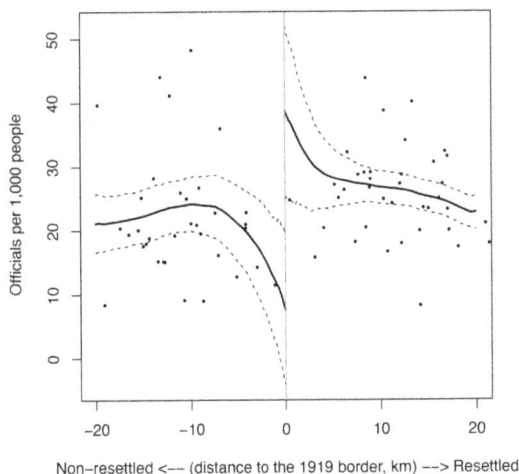

Non–resettled <–– (distance to the 1919 border, km) ––> Resettled

FIGURE 5.2 Discontinuity in the number of state officials in 1950.

statistically significant at a 99-percent level. The differences are substantively meaningful: On average, there were nearly 13 additional state officials per 1,000 residents in the frontier counties just west of the 1919 border compared to counties just east of the border. There were also 10.21 additional municipal servants per 1,000 people in counties just west of the 1919 border, a difference that exceeds two standard deviations in this variable ($\mu = 3.08$; $\sigma = 4.00$). The effect sizes are smaller, at 10.10 and 5.29, but remain statistically significant when using an alternative RDD package and wider bandwidth (see Table A.6).

These differences cannot be explained by lower population density, which does not change sharply at the 1919 border. As shown in Table A.5, the frontier was also similar to the nearby region in urbanization rates and in the prevalence of nonagricultural occupations.

To further test whether mass uprooting and intergroup differences facilitated the expansion of state authority on the frontier, I make use of the information recorded in the 1948 census on the origins of the population. As discussed in detail in Chapter 2, migrants had little say in their final destinations. The proportion of migrants from the same region – and thus, the level of societal cohesion in a given area – depended on an arbitrary assignment process by PUR and was unrelated to the preexisting socioeconomic characteristics of the area. To measure the heterogeneity of the population, I compute a fractionalization index at the county level based on the shares of the population from four different regions – central Poland, the USSR, Western Europe, and the former German territories (i.e., autochthones). The index estimates the probability that two individuals randomly drawn from the population came from different regions. Results of the multivariate regression analysis, which controls for urbanization, the share of industry, the size of landholding, the distance to the new Polish–German border, and logged population size, are in

TABLE 5.2 *Cultural diversity and administrative capacity* within *the resettled region.*

| | Officials | | Municipal servants | |
|---|---|---|---|---|
| | Per 1,000 people | | | |
| | (1) | (2) | (3) | (4) |
| Fractionalization index | 22.83 | 22.65* | −0.25 | −2.99 |
| | (14.49) | (13.44) | (3.53) | (2.24) |
| Share farms over 100 ha | | 20.18 | | −2.86 |
| | | (80.13) | | (16.15) |
| Share in industry | | −43.59** | | 0.08 |
| | | (17.03) | | (3.61) |
| City | | 32.68*** | | 8.60*** |
| | | (6.79) | | (0.94) |
| Ln distance to Germany | | −3.23** | | −1.49*** |
| | | (1.35) | | (0.46) |
| Ln population | −5.61 | −4.70* | 2.48** | 1.37* |
| | (3.43) | (2.46) | (1.08) | (0.82) |
| Province fixed effect | ✓ | ✓ | ✓ | ✓ |
| Adj. $R^2$ | 0.03 | 0.48 | 0.11 | 0.76 |
| N | 132 | 123 | 132 | 123 |

*Notes:* Analysis at the county level. All models are OLS, with fixed effects for German provinces. Fractionalization index ranges from 0 to 1. Heteroskedasticity-robust standard errors in parentheses. Significant at $*p < 0.10$; $**p < 0.05$; $***p < 0.01$

Table 5.2.[13] The coefficient on *Fractionalization index* is positive and statistically significant at a 10-percent level in regressions of state officials per 1,000 people with a full set of covariates. The estimate suggests that one standard deviation increase in the heterogeneity of postwar population translates into two additional officials per 1,000 people in 1950 ($\mu = 28.28, \sigma = 17.42$). This pattern is consistent with the argument that the mixing of settlers from different regions of origin facilitated state building. At the same time, I observe no relationship between the fractionalization index and the number of municipal servants per 1,000 people.

Ideally, I would trace changes in administrative capacity over time, particularly because the 1950 census was conducted shortly after the population transfers were completed. Unfortunately, other censuses from the communist period do not use sufficiently detailed occupational categories. For instance, the 1960 census groups administration and municipal services with "other."

[13] Including population size on the right-hand size of the equation allows me to account for the economies of scale in public administration (Gehlbach 2008).

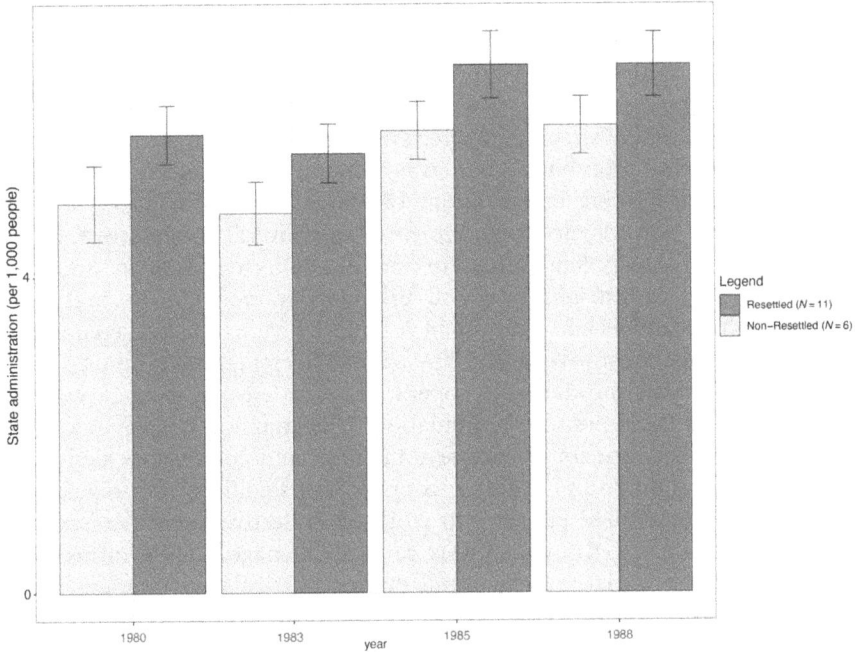

FIGURE 5.3 Differences in the number of state officials in resettled and non-resettled voivodeships in the Prussian partition.

Information about the number of state officials reappeared in statistical yearbooks (*Roczniki Statystyczne Województw*) in the 1980s at the level of forty-nine voivodeships, only sixteen of which were in the newly acquired territories.[14] Comparison using these less fine-grained data suggests that the differences in administrative capacity between the resettled territories and the neighboring voivodeships persisted over time, as shown in Figure 5.3. There were consistently more state officials relative to the population in the frontier region through the 1980s. The residents of western Poland were therefore more likely to come into contact with state officials and more likely to work for the state themselves.

## STATE DOMINANCE IN THE ECONOMY

The data on administrative capacity do not tell the full story. A distinctive characteristic of the communist state was its control over the economy. In the resettled territories, the communist regime was able to pursue its main objective – nationalization of the means of production – without resistance from the original owners, the expelled German natives. Elsewhere in Poland, the

---

[14] Two voivodeships are split by the frontier boundary and are excluded from the analysis.

state had to contend with millions of private property holders. Even when the original owners were deceased, as in the case of three million Polish Jews, their land and assets had already been expropriated by other private actors and were difficult to recover.

The majority of Polish migrants received individual farms. Any talk of collectivization was prohibited, as it was unpopular among Polish settlers. Rather, to enable farming in conditions of scarce livestock and agricultural equipment, settlers were encouraged to form agricultural cooperatives. After 1948, however, state policy shifted to forcible collectivization in order to support state-led industrialization and urbanization policies. To that end, cooperatives that settlers had established voluntarily were transformed into the new "production cooperatives" (*spółdzielnie produkcyjne*) modeled on Soviet kolkhozes. Additional production cooperatives were created through various forms of economic and political intimidation. One common strategy was subjecting independent farmers to excessive taxation and compulsory deliveries of agricultural products and granting cooperatives significant tax relief. The government also recruited peasants to work on collective farms (*Państwowe gospodarstwa rolne (PGR)*), which were centrally managed. These farms were typically created from large agricultural estates, particularly common in the resettled territories. By the end of 1955, the state had established 6,185 state farms and 9,076 agricultural cooperatives.

State pressure was more effective in regard to migrants who had lost their social networks and lived in diverse communities. Migrants' memoirs underscore the role played by social dislocation and mutual distrust in allowing the state to take over. Adolf Juzwenko, whose family migrated from Kresy to Lisowce in Silesia, writes: "Collectivization in these areas was also favored by the fact that in the villages there was a mix of people from different areas of Poland. They were often distrustful of one another, and there was no bond or understanding between them" (Juzwenko 2011, 54). Because migrants in the resettled territories had received their farms from the state, they had fewer opportunities to misrepresent their income and reduce their tax burden. The state had detailed information about the size and quality of their land as well as their agricultural equipment. Voluntary migrants were particularly vulnerable to economic pressure because, in addition to standard taxes and compulsory deliveries, they were still paying for their newly acquired land.

In line with the argument that the communist regime was more successful in transforming property relations in the resettled region, I find that cooperatives were much more prevalent west of the 1919 border (see Figure 5.4). At the end of the collectivization period (mid-1956), about 6 percent of all peasant families in the country were organized in cooperatives. This low rate hides substantial subnational variation: the degree of "incorporation" of peasant farms ranged from 0.8 percent in Kielce voivodeship to 31.8 percent in Szczecin voivodeship (see Table A.8). Half of all production cooperatives in Poland in

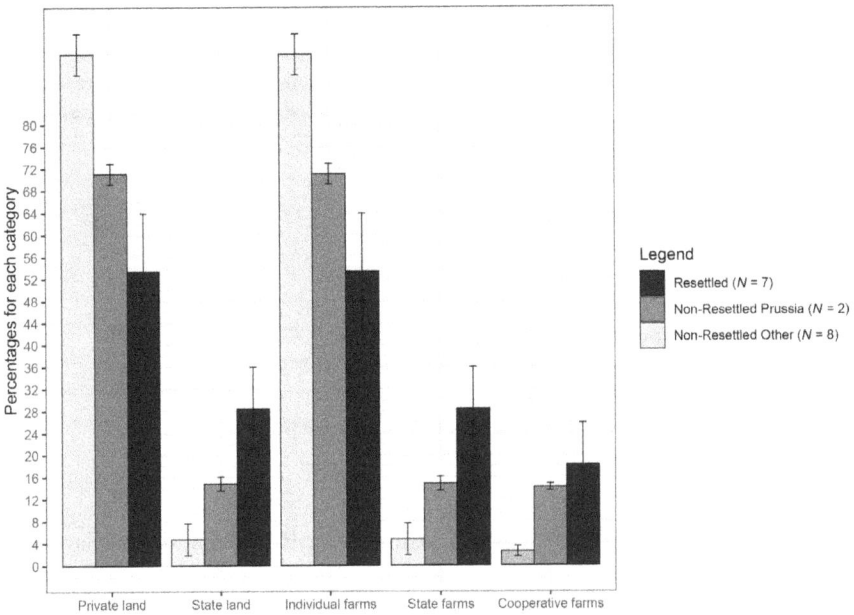

FIGURE 5.4 Differences in land and farm ownership in resettled and non-resettled voivodeships.

1955 (5,019 out of 9,963) were thus located in the resettled territories, which accounted for only a third of postwar Polish territory.

Additional evidence that mass uprooting increased state capacity to organize peasants into agricultural cooperatives comes from the variation in the turnover of the population within the Wielkopolska region. Wielkopolska settlements that had a large German population at the end of WWII also experienced expulsions and large-scale resettlement. In the early 1950s, these repopulated villages accounted for a disproportionate share of cooperative farming. For instance, in 1951, 1,219 out of the 1,315 cooperatives registered within Poznań voivodeship had been established on the basis of parceled land estates or former German farms, and only 96 were established in villages with continuous Polish settlement. Furthermore, individuals who had received land from the government were overrepresented among the members of production cooperatives. According to Dobieszewski (1993, 63), out of a total of about 30,000 cooperative members, only about 5,000 had owned farms before the war.

The government was also more successful in creating state farms in the resettled territories relative to other parts of Poland (see Table A.8). In the resettled voivodeships, 28.4 percent of farms were managed by the state. In the neighboring non-resettled Prussian areas, the figure was 14.8 percent. The

TABLE 5.3 *Stalinism in the resettled territories and elsewhere in Poland.*

|  | Resettled voivodeships | Non-resettled voivodeships |
|---|---|---|
| State agricultural farms (PGR) in 1955 *per 10,000 people* | 5.82 | 1.10 |
| Output of private industry in 1955 *per capita, in złoty* | 3.52 | 10.91 |
| Output of state industry in 1955 *per capita, in złoty* | 1,451 | 1,571 |
| Private Crafts Workshops in 1957 *per 1,000 people* | 4.49 | 4.88 |

*Sources:* Rocznik Statystyczny (1956); Rocznik Statystyczny (1958).

lowest proportion of state farms was in the former Russian and Austrian partitions, at 4.7 percent. This pattern reflects not only the legacy of uprooting but also the historical prevalence of large landholding in the region. Properties left behind by the German landed nobility in East Prussia and Pomerania were unsuitable for individual farming due to their size and infrastructure. Therefore, they were appropriated by the Polish state before official collectivization policies were even adopted.

The communist regime was also more successful in quashing private economic activity in the newly acquired territories (see Table 5.3). Recall that all large industries and infrastructure in this region were nationalized in 1946. In 1949, the communist government introduced Soviet-style centralized planning. Capitalist enterprises were destined for elimination through numerous legal, administrative, and economic restrictions (Przybyla 1958, 323). Perhaps the most destructive measure was the October 1950 currency reform, which devalued cash holdings and caused a wave of liquidations. All entrepreneurs in handicrafts, industry, and trade were also forced to join the organizations of entrepreneurs and pay the obligatory membership fees. These measures were more far-reaching in the newly acquired territories. In 1955, the output of private industry in this region was 3.52 Zł. per person, nearly three times lower than the output of 10.90 Zł. per person in the rest of Poland. Private retail outlets made up just 5.6 percent of the total number of retail outlets, compared to 11.82 percent in the non-resettled voivodeships. The overall share of employment in the so-called socialized sector (*sektor uspołeczniony*) was also higher, at 98.69 percent of the total workforce in 1955, compared to 96.62 percent in the non-resettled voivodeships (see Table A.7).

Collectivization and industrialization efforts peaked in 1952–53 and declined after Stalin's death. A decisive break with Stalinism was facilitated by the death of the PZPR's First Secretary Bolesław Bierut in March 1956 and his replacement by Gomułka.[15] After October 1956, most agricultural cooperatives dissolved, and restrictions on private entrepreneurship declined. In Chapter 7, I investigate whether these policies had different implications for economic performance in homogeneous and heterogeneous areas within the resettled region.

COMMUNIST VICTORY IN THE BATTLE FOR HEARTS AND MINDS

How did uprooting and the resulting dominance of the communist state in the resettled region affect political attitudes and behavior? One proxy for the ability of the communist regime to shape preferences is church attendance. Although the government did not ban church services outright, it discouraged church attendance and sought to weaken the authority of the Catholic Church. As mentioned earlier, in the resettled territories, these efforts were particularly successful due to the absence of bishops and the scarcity of priests.

To understand the long-run consequences of these policies, I compare the frequency of attending Mass and receiving Holy Communion in 1991, the earliest available date, in municipalities on either side of the pre-1945 Polish–German border. The outcome variable is calculated as the share of all Catholics in the parish who (1) attended Mass on a specific day or (2) received Holy Communion.[16] The statistics are based on surveys conducted at the parish level and were purchased from the Institute of Statistics of the Catholic Church (*Instytut Statystyki Kościoła Katolickiego*). Full results from the geographic regression discontinuity analysis are presented in Table A.9. I find that the share of Catholics attending Mass and receiving Holy Communion decreases by 16 percent and 7 percent, respectively, just west of the 1919 border. The differences in religious behavior between the frontier municipalities and the nearby non-resettled communities are substantively large. The magnitude of the effect is particularly striking because nearly half of the population settled in this region arrived from the eastern borderlands, known for their religiosity and conservative values.

Next, I examine whether the dominance of the communist state enabled it to shape voting behavior in the long run by comparing preferences for ex-communist parties on the opposite sides of the 1919 border. Until 1989, Poland was a one-party state. It held regular elections to the legislature, with voter turnout that hovered around 95 percent, but only the PZPR and its satellites, the United People's Party and Democratic Party, were allowed to compete. The first fully free and fair parliamentary elections for which fine-grained data exist

---

[15] Gomułka was one of the few communists untainted by involvement in Stalinist repression because he was dismissed in 1948.

[16] Holy Communion is received by baptized Catholics who have made their First Holy Communion and confessed their sins. Thus, the frequency of receiving Holy Communion varies with religious devotion.

were held in 1991.[17] At least 111 different parties participated in this election. Although the political system was extremely fragmented and unstable, there was a clear divide between ex-communists and the heirs of the Solidarity trade union movement (Chan 1995). The former was represented by the Democratic Left Alliance (*Sojusz Lewicy Demokratycznej, SLD*), a successor to the PZPR, and the PSL (*Polskie Stronnictwo Ludowe, PSL*), whose predecessor was the United Peasant Party (*Zjednoczone Stronnictwo Ludowe, ZSL*), a PZPR satellite. The latter group was comprised of multiple small parties, including the religiously conservative Christian National Union, the more secular Democratic Union (UD), and the Congress of Liberal Democrats (KLD).

For my analysis, I focus on the SLD, which benefited from the PZPR's structure and resources. The SLD's leader Aleksander Kwaśniewski held high-level government positions during the communist period.[18] In short, the party's ties with the old regime were clear to voters despite its attempts to rebrand itself as a "social democratic" party in the 1991 election.[19]

After 1989, the SLD advocated for a "social market economy," envisioned as a third way between the centrally planned economy and a fully liberalized market economy. It promised greater support from the state in the face of economic hardships caused by the transition to capitalism (Millard 1992). In the 1991 campaign, the SLD criticized the proposed reductions in pensions and child support. In the 1993 campaign, the SLD charged the Solidarity leaders with failing to cushion the population from the negative aspects of the liberal economic reform and neglecting the interests of industrial workers, farmers, state employees, and pensioners (Chan 1995). The party performed surprisingly well. In 1991, at 11.98 percent of the vote, the SLD came second after the Solidarity Bloc, which gained 12.31 percent of the vote. In 1993, the SLD became the largest party in the Sejm, winning 171 out of 460 seats.

Electoral data from the first two post-transition elections (1991, 1993) to the lower house of the Polish parliament (*Sejm*) are available at the municipal level. Accordingly, the sample size is much larger than in the analyses of administrative capacity for the year 1950 presented earlier in the chapter. To examine the aggregate effects of uprooting and subsequent communist policies in the frontier, I again exploit the 1919 border placement. I estimate the effect of uprooting using a geographic regression discontinuity design that employs the Euclidean distance from the municipality centroids to the 1919 border between Poland and Germany as a forcing variable (see Table A.10).[20]

---

[17] The results of the 1989 election are available only at the voivodeship level.

[18] In 1985–87, Kwaśniewski served as a Minister for Youth Affairs; in 1988–89 he served as a Cabinet Minister.

[19] The PSL, on the other hand, participated in the Solidarity government and emphasized its pre-communist roots.

[20] I adjust for the urban status of a municipality, its distance to the railway in 1939, latitude, longitude, and their interaction.

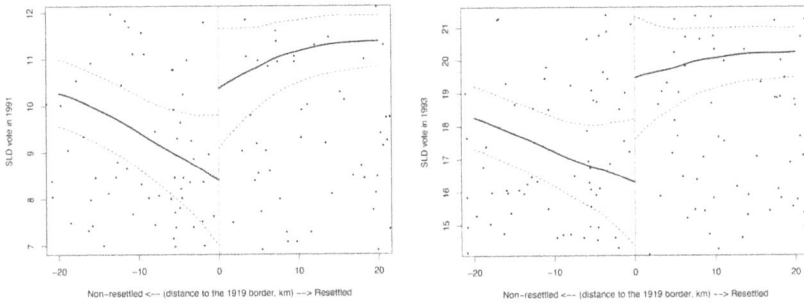

FIGURE 5.5 Discontinuity in support for the communist successor party.

The discontinuity in the SLD vote share on either side of the 1919 border is plotted in Figure 5.5. My analysis shows that support for the ex-communist SLD was higher west of the border, in the resettled municipalities, by 2.4 percent and 3.7 percent on average in the 1991 and 1993 elections, respectively. This seems like a small difference, but in 1991, the highest vote share secured by a single party was a mere 12 percent.[21] In 1993, the SLD secured 20 percent of the vote and was the best-performing party in Poland. Correspondingly, support for the Solidarity Bloc west of the border is lower by 2.6 percent in the 1991 election. The differences are highly statistically significant.

Higher support for the SLD in the resettled territories is notable also because many of its residents originated from the former Russian and Austrian partitions of Poland, which disproportionately supported the Solidarity Bloc, rather than from the Prussian partition, where the SLD was more popular overall.

I further look at whether support for the communist successor party varies with the diversity of the population *within* the resettled territories. As an indicator of diversity, I again use a fractionalization index computed from 1948 census data on the numbers of autochthonous residents, migrants from the eastern borderlands, migrants from central Poland, and migrants from abroad. As mentioned earlier, this index measures the probability that two individuals randomly drawn from the population of a given municipality came from different regions. I also use the share of the migrant population as an alternative indicator, which captures uprooting as such. In this analysis, I condition on variables that affected the resettlement process, including distance to the 1939 railway and the post-1945 German border as well as the prominence of industry and large landholdings, as measured in the 1939 German census.

The coefficient on *Fractionalization index* is positive for both the 1991 and 1993 SLD vote (see Table 5.4). The results indicate that support for the ex-communist party was higher in municipalities populated by people of more heterogeneous regional origins after WWII. A standard deviation increase in heterogeneity (0.14) predicts a 1-percent increase in the SLD vote ($\mu = 0.11$, $\sigma = 0.05$) in 1991 and a 2-percent increase in the SLD vote ($\mu = 0.19$,

---

[21] SLD and UD both secured 12 percent of the vote in that election.

TABLE 5.4 *Cultural diversity and support for the communist successor party.*

|  | SLD vote in 1991 | | SLD vote in 1993 | |
|---|---|---|---|---|
|  | (1) | (2) | (3) | (4) |
| Fractionalization index (1948) | 0.08*** | 0.06*** | 0.15*** | 0.13*** |
|  | (0.02) | (0.01) | (0.02) | (0.02) |
| Share urban |  | 0.08*** |  | 0.10*** |
|  |  | (0.01) |  | (0.01) |
| Share in industry (1939) |  | 0.04** |  | 0.15*** |
|  |  | (0.02) |  | (0.02) |
| Share over 100 ha (1939) |  | 0.36*** |  | 0.65*** |
|  |  | (0.09) |  | (0.12) |
| Distance to German border |  | 0.00 |  | 0.00*** |
|  |  | (0.00) |  | (0.00) |
| Distance to railway |  | 0.00** |  | 0.00 |
|  |  | (0.00) |  | (0.00) |
| Ln population |  | −0.01*** |  | −0.01** |
|  |  | (0.00) |  | (0.00) |
| Province fixed effect | ✓ | ✓ | ✓ | ✓ |
| Adj. $R^2$ | 0.06 | 0.37 | 0.10 | 0.47 |
| N | 629 | 610 | 632 | 613 |

*Notes:* All models are OLS, with fixed effects for German provinces. Heteroskedasticity-robust standard errors in parentheses. $*p < 0.1$; $**p < 0.05$; $***p < 0.01$.

$\sigma = 0.07$) in 1993. While these are substantively small differences, they support the hypothesis that the communist regime was more successful in attracting support in places where the population did not share social norms and networks.

## DISCUSSION

Gomułka's 1945 promise that Poland's westward expansion would "bind the nation with the state" seemed anything but assured at the time. Polish claims on the new territory remained tenuous until at least 1970, when West German Chancellor Willy Brandt signed a treaty normalizing the relationship between the two countries. Yet Gomułka was right, at least in some respects. Just five years after the war, the party-state could boast greater administrative capacity in a region where it had previously not existed, relative to neighboring counties that had enjoyed a longer history of Polish rule but experienced less uprooting after 1945. It was also able to implement far-reaching economic transformation in line with the ideology of state socialism and marginalize the Catholic Church, its main contender for moral and political authority. Remarkably, party-state dominance in this region did not turn the population against it:

In the 1990s, in Poland's earliest free and fair elections, the descendants of migrants from regions that endorsed the Solidarity Bloc were more likely to vote for ex-communist parties instead.

How was this possible? I argue that by rupturing communal ties and placing individuals in a culturally heterogeneous environment, postwar population transfers created an opportunity to strengthen state capacity. Resettled communities lacked effective collective action mechanisms to oppose state intervention and had much to gain from the state's presence. Communal elites were weakened and non-state organizations were dissolved through the process of migration, leaving the communist state with little competition from other societal actors.[22] At the same time, the expulsion of the native German population provided the communist government with land and other property that could be redistributed to Polish migrants. In this way, societal dislocation of both Poles and Germans contributed to state building.

The communist state-building project in the resettled territories was facilitated by the absence of potential spoilers. Not only did WWII weaken political and economic elites who could have challenged state authority, but the rest of society supported the communist goal of controlling the formerly German territories. In addition, the disappearance of German government agencies effectively produced a clean slate for the new regime to build on. As a result, the government enjoyed considerable freedom of action despite starting with a low stock of state capacity.

The findings are notable in light of the existing research on state capacity in frontier regions. After WWII, the newly acquired territories constituted a scarcely populated frontier, and the parallel to the American West was not lost on contemporary observers, who called it the Wild West. All frontiers start as regions where state institutions are largely absent. In some cases, state reach remains tenuous even after the population grows (e.g., Foa and Nemirovskaya 2016). For example, studies of the American West credit the frontier environment with forging an ethos of individualism and reinforcing opposition to state regulation (Turner 1920; Bazzi, Fiszbein, and Gebresilasse 2017). Yet in Poland, settling the frontier allowed the regime to consolidate its authority and accumulate greater administrative capacity.

In Chapter 6, I consider the rather different role played by mass uprooting in postwar state building in West Germany. There, forced migrants arrived into densely populated communities, and both newcomers and natives could express their demands on the state under inclusive political institutions.

---

[22] This point builds on Joel Migdal (2001), who argues that forced migration and mass resettlement can be conducive to state domination because they weaken competing alternative forms of social organization.

# 6

## Expellees and the State in West Germany

In Chapter 5, I showed that mass displacement facilitated state building in Poland's resettled territories, enabling the government to accumulate greater infrastructural power, redistribute land, and implement far-reaching economic reforms. The communist regime operated as a hegemonic actor, benefiting from the weakening of prewar elites and the expulsion of the German population. This chapter shifts the focus to West Germany, which differs from Poland in two key respects relevant to my argument: It experienced less social upheaval during the war, and it had in place a democratic political system with a multiparty government.

My contention is that the uprooting of Germans increased the demand for state intervention via two interrelated channels. First, communities that received expellees experienced greater conflict, which called for state intervention. Second, the loss of property and social ties made expellees more dependent on state-provided resources. In contrast to Polish migrants in the annexed territory, German expellees were distributed across populated settlements. I expect the native population in these settlements to have a lower demand for state presence than the expellees because the natives retained their social ties and property. Furthermore, the extent to which increased demands on the state will lead to an increase in state capacity hinges on the motivations of governing elites. In line with prior research, I expect governing elites to be more supportive of strengthening the state in response to domestic unrest or external conflict (Darden and Mylonas 2016; Slater 2010).

The chapter begins with an overview of the effects of WWII and subsequent military occupation on state capacity in West Germany. Following Germany's defeat, the central government's institutions crumbled, and infrastructure and public facilities lay in ruins. The occupation authorities – comprised of the USSR, the United States, Britain, and France (the "Allies") – initially sought to weaken the state further. They dissolved the police and military organizations and removed civil servants affiliated with the Nazi regime. They also planned to divide large landholdings, dismantle heavy industry, and break up industrial conglomerates.

And yet, by the end of the military occupation in 1949, a majority of local bureaucrats had resumed their positions, and agricultural and industrial assets remained with their original proprietors. Thus, in contrast to Poland's resettled territories, where Polish state institutions did not exist until after the war and all property was nationalized, West German settlements preserved their pre-1945 administrative and economic structures. Furthermore, because the Allies delayed the formation of state and federal governments, local authorities achieved a high degree of autonomy.

Next, I consider the preferences expressed by both the Allies and German political elites in relation to the size and functions of the German state. I show that, in the immediate postwar period, the majority of German policymakers believed that building a powerful central government was necessary to deal with the devastating consequences of WWII. There were widespread fears that, without significant state intervention, expellees would radicalize, endangering political stability. The Allies held a different view: While they shared concerns about expellee radicalization, they also preferred to limit the powers of the central government and minimize state intervention in the economy. Once the West German government regained full sovereignty, the governing elites' consensus on bolstering the state's authority unraveled. Nevertheless, the majority of political stakeholders continued to support the allocation of administrative and fiscal resources toward expellee needs in order to mitigate social unrest and preempt more extreme demands.

In the second part of the chapter, I use qualitative and quantitative evidence to demonstrate that economic deprivation and the lack of support from receiving communities increased expellee demand for state intervention. I show that expellees skillfully leveraged concerns about political radicalization to further their interests and utilized a range of influence channels available to them in a democratic system, from turning out to vote to organizing protests. Most of the expellees' appeals were directed to state and federal governments, since the receiving communities lacked sympathy for the newcomers. My quantitative analysis shows that in the 1949 federal election, counties with a larger expellee population had higher levels of political participation and delivered more votes to the Social Democrats, a party that advocated for greater state intervention in the economy.

I then review governmental policy toward the expellees and the communities that accommodated them. I discuss policymaking during the military occupation (1945–49) and after the creation of the federal government (1949–89) separately, highlighting the constraints that the governing elites faced when seeking to intervene on behalf of expellees, enforce expellee laws, and redistribute economic resources. Before 1949, the authority of German policymakers was limited in its scope by the Allies, who either blocked or watered down several early initiatives designed to compensate the expellees' economic losses. Their authority was also curbed by the native population in receiving communities, which subverted pro-expellee measures and organized to protect their own economic interests. From 1949 onward the Allies could no longer veto German policy, but the government remained constrained by the interests of native property owners, who outnumbered the expellees. As a result, the final Equalization of Burdens Law (*Lastenausgleich*) imposed a very modest property tax, failing to satisfy expellee demands on the state. Nonetheless, by setting up a formidable bureaucratic apparatus to gather information about property losses and disburse compensation, the federal government succeeded in strengthening its administrative reach and informational capacity.

The chapter concludes with a quantitative analysis of the effects of expellee presence on administrative capacity at the county level. I show that the number of civil servants per capita increases with the expellee share of the population. This pattern aligns with the creation of specialized bureaucracies in high-inflow regions, tasked with enforcing expellee laws and frequently staffed by the expellees themselves. I further show that, relative to their population share, expellees were overrepresented in state and federal governments, while being underrepresented in local administration. This is consistent with the difficulties faced by the federal government in enforcing expellee representation laws in receiving communities.

## BACKGROUND CONDITIONS

### The Division of Germany

The unconditional surrender of German troops was announced on May 8, 1945. The German state would be reconstructed under military occupation by the USSR, the United States, Britain, and France. Disagreements and compromises between the Allies would shape the process of state-building, expellee policy, and the choice of political and economic institutions.

The Allies initially planned to establish centralized bureaucratic structures at the national level. However, French and Soviet opposition derailed this plan. The resulting decentralization of governance had several repercussions. It hindered inter-zone trade, exacerbated food scarcity, and impeded the process of economic reconstruction. Additionally, it produced marked regional disparities in the distribution of expellees: France closed its occupation zone to expellees because it did not view the Potsdam Agreement as binding (see Chapter 2).

In December 1946, the US and British governments unified the economies of their respective occupation zones, creating the Bizone. The French occupation zone was added in January 1948. Meanwhile, relations with the Soviet Union deteriorated, leading to the creation of two German states in 1949: the German Democratic Republic and the Federal Republic of Germany.

## State Capacity in the Aftermath of WWII

As British and US troops entered German territory in the spring of 1945, they encountered little resistance. The central government had ceased to exist. German cities lay in ruins, and the country's industrial assets were significantly damaged. Public order disintegrated and looting spread. In large cities, liberated prisoners of the Nazi regime roamed the streets seeking revenge (Marshall 1988, 28). In this moment of total breakdown, millions of expellees and other displaced persons streamed into overcrowded communities.

The first order of business was to establish a headquarters and deploy military units to key cities. These units assumed control over local governance, reporting to higher-ranking authorities. Prominent Nazis were arrested and new local administrations were appointed to carry out essential functions, including the organization of food supplies, the maintenance of public health and safety, and the restoration of critical infrastructure. Hence, the reconstitution of local administration took place almost immediately after the war, well in advance of the establishment of administrative bodies at the state and federal levels. These developments resulted in a high degree of bureaucratic continuity with the pre-1945 era and also had the effect of circumscribing the subsequent influence of state (*Länder*) governments and the federal government on local policy.

The German population was generally cooperative with the Allies. The absence of underground resistance facilitated the establishment of the new order. At the same time, the Allies' dependence on German administrators for implementing reforms had the effect of tempering the most ambitious initiatives. To quote a reflection by a US military government official on the failure of land reform in Baden-Württemberg, "[I]f a task is left up to the Germans, and the Germans don't want to do it, then they won't do it" (quoted in Schraut (1995, 140)).

The Allies initially worked to weaken German state capacity with the goal of averting potential future aggression. To that end, they oversaw demobilization and disarmament. They also seized German military and industrial assets. Germany's steel and coal production was capped, and equipment was removed from 706 manufacturing plants in West Germany (Gareau 1961, 530). These measures, reminiscent of Soviet actions in the newly incorporated regions of Poland before the establishment of the Polish administration, had the unintended consequence of delaying economic recovery and hampering the capacity of state governments to generate public revenue. By 1948, however, the Allies had recognized the negative effects of these measures and changed their approach. In the same year, moreover, Germany began receiving assistance through the Marshall Plan.

The Allies agreed to implement land reforms to weaken the societal foundations of German militarism and facilitate the integration of millions of expellee farmers. Thus, in September 1947, the Allied Council issued Ordinance No.

103, which limited land ownership to 150 ha, later reduced to 100 ha. The responsibility for implementing this ordinance was delegated to *Länder* governments; however, they made little progress in dividing large landholdings, as will be discussed later in the chapter.

Decartelization, another well-intentioned policy, faced similar setbacks. The 1947 decartelization laws – which denied cartels access to legal support, established bureaucratic measures to dissolve cartels, and designated enterprises with over 10,000 employees for decartelization and asset sale – did not yield the anticipated results (Cho 2003). Despite the identification of seventy-one firms or cartel organizations by the Decartelization Branch of the US military government, only the notorious IG Farben underwent dissolution, rendering the prohibition on cartels largely ineffective (Hayse 2003, 106–107).

## The Democratization of Political Institutions

One of the central objectives of the occupation authorities was to lay the groundwork for democracy. To that end, the Allies attempted to remove German officials with ties to the Nazi regime. In 1945, approximately 55,000 civil servants were discharged pending denazification proceedings (Rigoll 2018). The De-Nazification policy was most far-reaching in the US occupation zone, where each adult was required to fill out questionnaires about his/her Nazi past (Capoccia and Pop-Eleches 2020). The British government pursued a more pragmatic approach, purging a smaller number of individuals in order to maintain a functioning administration (Biddiscombe 2007, 115). The French, while sanctioning a larger number of individuals compared to the US and British governments, imposed relatively mild penalties (Capoccia and Pop-Eleches 2020).

In parallel with removing public officials associated with the Nazi regime, the Allies appointed individuals perceived to be "capable of assisting in developing genuine democratic institutions." These so-called "45ers" would fill many of the key political, social, and cultural positions in the new Federal Government after 1949. They included Konrad Adenauer, Willy Brandt, and Gustav Heinemann, who today are considered the founding fathers of West Germany (Rigoll 2018, 252, 264).

The Allies also introduced democratic elections, first at the local level, then at the *Land* and eventually the federal level.[1] The unintended consequence of

---

[1] The timing of the elections and the degree of intervention into the political process varied by occupation zone. The US military government was the first to hold local elections. District and municipal governments in the US occupation zone were elected between January and May 1946, while state parliaments (*Landtage*) were elected in December 1946. The *Länder* governments in the US zone also achieved greater autonomy relative to their counterparts in other zones, though the US government retained the right to veto policies. Britain was more interventionist, introducing a system of "indirect rule," whereby a body of German officials at the municipal (*Gemeinde*) and *Länder* level operated under its supervision. In the British zone, local elections

this process was the enabling of local elites to successfully resist *Land* and federal policies aimed at facilitating the integration of expellees. A significant delay between the creation of lower and higher levels of government was in line with the Allies' decentralization objective. The reconstruction of the administration from the ground up would contribute to a permanent shift in the balance of power away from the political center.

To prevent extremist parties from running for office, the Allies imposed a ban on expellee parties (lifted in 1950) and additionally introduced a licensing system. Party organizers were required to fill out personal questionnaires and submit programs and reports on party activity in order to receive a license for operating in a given district or *Land*. Of the sixteen political parties founded in the late 1940s, only four – the SPD, the CDU/CSU, the Free Democratic Party (FDP), and the Communist Party of Germany (KPD) – obtained licenses in all three Western zones and were thus able to operate as national parties (Kreuzer 2009, 678). With the exception of the KPD, which was banned in 1956, these early parties would continue to dominate West German politics for decades.

In a manner similar to political parties, all voluntary associations were required to obtain licenses from the military government. At first, such associations were only allowed to operate at the municipal level. Over time, their organization came to be permitted at the regional and *Länder* levels. In a relatively short time, native economic elites managed to reestablish powerful associations, reminiscent of those in the Weimar era (Hayse 2003, 119).

## CONFLICTING BLUEPRINTS FOR THE RECONSTRUCTION OF THE GERMAN STATE

After Germany received millions of expellees, German elites across the political spectrum agreed that addressing the dual challenges of mass displacement and wartime destruction required a degree of state intervention in the economy (Overy 2012, 66). Behind this consensus was a concern that, if the state did not offer enough support, expellees would radicalize. For instance, Willibald Mücke, co-chairman of the Main Committee of Refugees and Expellees in Bavaria, argued in March 1948 that "people who have nothing to lose ... are a highly explosive source of tension in any human society" (quoted in Connor (1986, 133)).

The preferred degree of state intervention varied by party. The German left, which included the Communists and the Social Democrats, has traditionally

were held only in the fall of 1946 and state elections in April 1947. Even after the creation of state governments, the British continued to exercise centralized authority over policy-making. The German authorities retained some responsibility for policy implementation and could make recommendations to the occupation authorities, but they could not initiate policy on their own. The French took the longest to reconstitute electoral institutions and granted the least autonomy to German officials. In their occupation zone, local elections were held in October 1946 and elections to state governments in May 1947.

endorsed a larger state and a more redistributive policy. In the immediate post-war period, some Social Democrats advocated for a regulated market economy with partial nationalization, while others aligned with the Communist Party and endorsed a planned economy and the full nationalization of industry. The center-right, represented by the ideologically heterogeneous CDU/CSU, like-wise accepted the need for greater state authority (Nicholls 1994, 131). In the British zone, the Ahlen Program of the CDU promoted "a socialist economic order," calling for the decartelization and nationalization of large industries. The CDU argued that "planning and guidance of the economy would be nec-essary on a large scale for a long period of time" (GHDI n.d.). Only the liberals, represented by the FDP, preferred a more limited government; yet even the FDP supported an increase in public spending so as to prevent the emergence of "a revolutionary and revolutionizing [expellee] estate" (quoted in Hughes (1999, 33)).

Against the backdrop of this broad domestic consensus, West German pol-icymakers were constrained by the Allies' opposition to a powerful central government. The United States, in particular, frequently used its veto power to thwart policies perceived to be granting the state too much control over the economy (Hughes 1999, 132).

During the drafting of West Germany's Basic Law (constitution), the Allies mandated the devolution of fiscal and administrative authority to the *Länder*. They also insisted on establishing a robust bicameral legislature capable of safeguarding the individual *Land* interests. Rejecting various proposals from the German side as excessively centralizing, the Allies played a pivotal role in shaping the limited powers of the contemporary German federal government (Bernhard 2005, 43, 50).

After the foundation of the Federal Republic, the Allies no longer held veto power over German policy. However, by then domestic preferences had shifted away from building a strong central government. The 1949 federal election brought the neoliberal CDU/FDP coalition to power, which moved quickly to reduce state intervention in the economy. Concerns about expellee radical-ization became less urgent, and native property owners grew less willing to shoulder the costs of the expellees' economic integration. The expansion of Soviet power in Eastern Europe as well as reforms in East Germany increased fears of a "creeping socialism" (Hughes, 1999, 132). In short, the window of opportunity for strengthening the state narrowed.

## EXPELLEES AND THE DEMAND FOR STATE INTERVENTION

The expellees' demand for state intervention in the aftermath of WWII was, to a large extent, the product of their desperate economic circumstances. The majority of expellees struggled with extreme poverty for many years after reset-tlement. In a survey conducted in the fall of 1947, 80 percent of expellees reported insufficient access to food (Connor 2007, 26). A subsequent survey from September 1949 revealed that 90 percent of expellees lacked basic cooking and household utensils. During winter, expellee children had to miss school because they lacked adequate clothing. For instance, in Oldenburg (Schleswig-Holstein), 12.9 percent of expellee schoolboys had no socks, and 25 percent lacked waterproof shoes (Connor 2007, 24). The expellees' economic situation worsened following the 1948 currency reform, which depleted their savings, increased rents, and undermined their fledgling businesses.

Due to the mismatch between their skills and local conditions, as well as the discrimination encountered in the labor market, a significant number of expellees remained unemployed. The higher the number of expellees residing in a given locality, the higher their unemployment rate. In the three *Länder* with the largest number of expellees to population – Schleswig-Holstein, Lower Saxony, and Bavaria – expellees were almost twice as likely to be unemployed as the native population (Connor 1989, 190). Economic deprivation increased the need for social welfare, which the local authorities were initially reluctant to provide.

The receiving communities were unsympathetic to expellee needs, as shown in Chapter 4. Indeed, the majority of municipalities grudgingly accepted expellees only under pressure from the occupation authorities. The absence of local support compelled expellees to seek assistance outside their immediate community, including from the occupation forces, from *Länder* governments, and, after 1949, from the federal government.

Expellees depended on external intervention from the very beginning. For instance, it was not uncommon for expellees to move in "under the protection of the machine guns" (Kossert 2008, 52). Expellees who were accommodated in natives' homes endured cramped conditions and sometimes took native homeowners to court for violating the Housing Law (Connor 2007, 69). At the end of 1946, the Liaison and Security Office (LSO) of Buchen, a town in Baden-Württemberg, observed: "The expellees consider the natives and not the occupation power their oppressors. It is a matter of fact that the expellees go only to MG [Military Government], for they cannot gain anything by going to the German officials" (quoted in Grosser (1996, 300)). The *Badische Neueste Nachrichten* reported that expellees appealed to district Resident Officers "to use their detached position in their communities to aid in the assimilation of refugees by encouraging their representation in local government and civil groups" (quoted in Grosser (1996, 325)).

Upon the establishment of *Land* and federal governments, expellees directed their appeals toward these German institutions. For example, the Bavarian state received more than 500 complaints and protest resolutions, accusing the State Secretary for Refugees of not doing enough to alleviate the expellees' economic hardships (Connor 2007, 178–79). In August 1948, the expellees housed in the Dachau concentration camp organized a hunger strike, demanding larger food rations, repairs to camp buildings, and pocket money. They were soon joined by the expellees housed in the Rosenheim, Berchtesgaden, and Augsburg camps. The strike of more than 72,000 camp occupants ended only after the Bavarian government made significant economic concessions (Connor 2007, 178–79).

In October 1951, a refugee commissioner in Schleswig-Holstein came up with the idea of organizing a self-help trek across Germany to force the hand of the federal government into providing employment and housing. In preparation for the march, trek associations emerged in Bavaria, Lower Saxony, and Schleswig-Holsten. In Schleswig-Holstein alone, some 34,000 expellees and their families signed up for the trek by March 1952. The expellees threatened to camp on the marketplaces of the "conquered communities" until they were given accommodation or a job (Kittel 2020, 54).

Expellees recognized that they could use the widespread fear of political instability to their advantage. In their appeals to authorities, they often invoked the specter of radicalization. A representative of the expellees in Herzebrock (North Rhine-Westphalia), for instance, concluded the petition with the following warning: "We are aware that unless the current situation changes soon, the plight of the expellees ... will and must create an outlet, and that vent is called radicalism or chaos" (quoted in Wiesemann (1995, 218)). William Mattes, the head of the Central Association of Bomb and Currency Damage (*Zentralverband der Flieger- und Währungsgeschädigten, the ZvF*), argued in 1948 that if expellees were not compensated for their property losses, they would "turn to political radicalism and join the ranks of those who are fundamental opponents of private property" (quoted in Hughes (1999, 33)). The landless farmers from Pomerania and East Prussia in Schleswig–Holstein wrote letters to the *Landtag* threatening that, if they did not receive their fair share of land, they would turn to arson.[2]

Despite the restrictions on their political activity, expellees began to organize. In Hamburg, Linus Kather founded the Emergency Association of East Germans in June 1945 (renamed the Association of German Refugees in early 1946). Expellees from Czechoslovakia established the Sudeten Germans Relief Office. In Münster (Nordrhein-Westfalen), a clerical councilor from Silesia set up the "Main Committee of the East Representatives" in June 1947, uniting 24 professional and cultural associations (Wiesemann 1995, 222). The expellees' mobilization around shared economic problems accelerated after the 1948 currency reform and the lifting of restrictions on associational activity. In October 1948, they established "The War Burden Compensation Committee of the regional associations of the expellees and the general representation of the expellees from the East." The committee's efforts contributed to the founding of the Central Association of Expelled Germans (*Zentralverband Vertriebener Deutschen, ZvD*) on April 9, 1949, to which it became formally subordinate (Schillinger 1985, 148–150).

---

[2] "Das alte morsche Ding." June 28, 1950. *Der Spiegel*. 26/1950.

Once expellees obtained the right to vote, they used it in record numbers. At around one-fifth of the electorate, they made up a considerable political force. Due to the ban on expellee parties, expellees initially channeled their demands via parties that also represented the native population. Notably, the expellees' political activism reportedly spurred the natives to mobilize. As the LSO of Buchen reported:

With the influx of expellees the native people are confronted with the necessity of engaging in some kind of politics even against their 'better judgment' because only on the battlefield of politics will the native people be able to throw in their weight against the rising claims of the politically more active (forced by circumstances rather than innate interest) expellee population. (Quoted in Grosser (1996, 316).)

Expellee appeals to government officials indicate that they viewed the state as morally obligated to remedy their losses. They argued that they had a legitimate claim to compensation and should not be dependent on state welfare (Hughes 1999, 97). For example, one frustrated expellee applicant for a development loan wrote: "Please take into account whatever business I had, I lost not through my fault, but through state action [...] After all, I don't want anything for free." Another applicant argued: "Our fight is about legal entitlement and not about the principle of need" (quoted based on Müller (1997, 339)).

### Expellees and Support for an Interventionist State in the 1949 Bundestag Election

The introduction of free and fair elections in West Germany offers an opportunity to examine how expellee presence affected support for parties with varying positions on the state's role in the economy. Of particular interest is the 1949 Federal Parliament (*Bundestag*) election, which offered voters a choice between two competing visions for Germany's future: the first advocating a planned economy and the second advocating a social market economy (Spicka 2002).

The electoral platform of the SPD promoted economic planning, full employment, and socialization of specific industries (Spicka 2002, 83). The party explicitly rejected communism but argued for redistributive policies to reduce economic inequality within Germany. The CDU endorsed an alternative vision of the social market economy and sought to discredit SPD policies by likening them to "Soviet-style" economic controls (Hughes 1999, 66). Despite its association with a generous welfare state today, in postwar Germany, the social market economy represented a reaction against a statist economic tradition. Its main architect, Minister of the Economy Ludwig Erhard, argued that state intervention in the 1930s had paved the way to National Socialism. Erhard's neoliberal policies were endorsed by the German business community and the United States alike (Hughes 1999, 66–67).

By 1949, the two parties' platforms on expellee issues were quite similar. Land reform, initially supported by the SPD but not the CDU, was no longer on the agenda. Both parties had expellees on their lists, although the proportion was higher within the SPD (25 percent of the mandates) than within the CDU/CSU (13 percent of the mandates) (Schoenberg 1970, 135).[3] Both parties supported the balancing out of burdens (*Lastenausgleich*) created by the expulsion by partially compensating expellees' economic losses. One difference was that the SPD endorsed a "social" approach, which would redistribute wealth based on the current material needs of expellees and other war-damaged individuals, whereas the CDU (and its Bavarian counterpart the CSU) was divided on the issue but leaned toward an "individual" approach, which would take previous property ownership into account.[4]

As a proxy for the demand for state intervention, I use the SPD vote. In the 1949 election, support for this party fluctuated from 6 percent to 52 percent at the county (*Kreis*) level. I also examine turnout to find out whether expellee presence increased political participation.

I assembled an original dataset that combines county-level (*Kreis*) electoral and demographic data from Weimar Germany with information on the distribution of expellees after the war as well as the vote in the 1949 election. Data on the Weimar elections come from the Inter-university Consortium for Political and Social Research (ICPSR 1999) and were aggregated to the level of 1950 counties. I also digitized data from the 1939 census to condition on the characteristics of German counties prior to the arrival of expellees. The data on expellees in 1946 come from Braun and Franke (2021).[5] The results of the 1949 election were digitized based on separate statistical publications in each *Land* listed in Appendix B.

I estimate the following model:

$$Y_{il} = \beta_0 + \beta_1 \text{ Share expellees}_{il} + X'_{il}\beta + \gamma_l + \epsilon_{il}. \tag{6.1}$$

In this model, $Y_{il}$ captures electoral outcomes, such as turnout, the share of the SPD vote, or the share of the CDU vote in 1949. The main explanatory variable is the share of expellees. It is measured in 1946, a few years before the election. This measure closely tracks the share of expellees in the 1950 census ($\rho = 0.96$, $p < 0.001$) and is used here because it avoids posttreatment bias.[6] The vector of controls $X'_{il}$ includes support for the Social Democrats in the 1933 election (the last Weimar vote), which allows me to isolate the changes in electoral outcomes following the arrival of expellees. I also condition on the

---

[3] CDU/CSU was the center-right union between the Christian Democratic Union of Germany (CDU) and the Christian Social Union in Bavaria (CSU).

[4] The individual approach was more popular among expellees.

[5] Information on expellee presence is unavailable for twenty-two counties in Südbaden Regierungsbezirk. This district was in the French occupation zone and did not have many expellees.

[6] Some scholars argued that the 1946 expellee share carries an additional advantage over the 1950 share in that it is not contaminated by expellees' selection into specific counties, which became possible after the restrictions on internal migration were relaxed (Braun and Dwenger 2020).

extent of wartime destruction, the share of the population employed in agriculture, and the distance to the eastern border. As noted in Chapter 2, these factors affected the allocation of expellees and likely also influenced electoral preferences. In some models, I control for the 1939 share of the Catholic population because the CDU originated from the Catholic Center Party in Weimar Germany and confessional differences continued to influence support for the CDU and SPD in the postwar period. Finally, I add fixed effects for *Länder* ($\gamma_l$) and an indicator variable coded 1 for the French occupation zone and 0 for the other two zones.[7]

The results of regressing electoral outcomes on the share of expellees and covariates are presented in Table 6.1 and plotted in Figure 6.1. The table shows that support for the SPD was higher in counties that received more expellees. One standard-deviation increase in the share of expellees, equivalent to 10 percent, translates into a 2-percent increase in the SPD vote share ($\mu = 26$, $\sigma = 10$). By contrast, the CDU secured fewer votes in high-inflow counties: one standard-deviation increase in the share of expellees predicts a 5-percent decrease in the CDU/CSU vote share ($\mu = 33$, $\sigma = 16$). Expellee presence also increases turnout: A 10-percent increase in the share of expellees is equivalent to a 2-percent increase in turnout. Thus, opposing preferences between the natives and the expellees increased political participation.

Interpreting these results as an increase in support for statist policies due to forced migration is challenging for two reasons. First, it is possible that expellees a priori had different political preferences than the native population. For instance, expellees coming from the more urbanized regions of Sudetenland and Silesia supported the SPD in the 1930s. Second, the electoral outcomes are measured for all eligible voters and do not separate the expellee and native votes. Correlating population shares and vote shares thus presents an ecological fallacy problem, understood as inferring individual preferences from aggregate data. Aggregate-level relationships may not hold for individuals: For instance, the presence of expellees could increase support for the SPD among the native population, even as the expellees themselves support other parties.

To address these two issues, I estimate the effect of expellee presence on the 1949 vote using municipal-level data from Schleswig-Holstein. Seventy-one percent of expellees in Schleswig-Holstein originated from East Prussia and Pomerania, agricultural areas that voted for the conservatives in the Weimar period (Connor 2006, 177), just like the native population of Schleswig-Holstein. In the 1930s, both regions were the strongholds of the German National People's Party and eventually of the Nazi Party.[8] If the share of

---

[7] The effects of the British occupation zone are captured by *Länder* indicators because this zone was contained within the borders of Schleswig-Holstein, Lower Saxony, and Hamburg. The French zone included the southern part of Baden-Württemberg, with the northern part of this *Land* was allocated to the US zone, which is why a separate indicator is necessary.

[8] The German National People's Party (*Deutschnationale Volkspartei, DNVP*) was a national-conservative party that allied with the NSDAP in 1933.

TABLE 6.1 *Expellee share and voting in the 1949 federal election.*

| | Turnout | | SPD vote share | | CDU/CSU vote share | |
|---|---|---|---|---|---|---|
| | Outcomes in the 1949 election: | | | | | |
| | (1) | (2) | (3) | (4) | (5) | (6) |
| Expellee share (1946) | 0.16*** (0.06) | 0.14*** (0.04) | 0.15** (0.07) | 0.13** (0.06) | −0.87*** (0.12) | −0.53*** (0.10) |
| Share in agriculture | 0.03*** (0.01) | −0.01 (0.02) | −0.23*** (0.02) | −0.17*** (0.03) | 0.40*** (0.03) | 0.12*** (0.03) |
| Share destroyed | 0.03* (0.02) | 0.03* (0.01) | −0.04 (0.03) | 0.05** (0.02) | 0.10** (0.04) | 0.16*** (0.03) |
| Ln dist to the Eastern border | −0.01*** (0.002) | −0.01*** (0.003) | −0.02*** (0.005) | 0.001 (0.004) | 0.002 (0.01) | −0.03*** (0.01) |
| SPD vote in 1933 | | 0.21*** (0.04) | | 0.47*** (0.05) | | −0.30*** (0.09) |
| Share Catholic | | 0.10*** (0.01) | | −0.12*** (0.01) | | 0.22*** (0.02) |
| Ln population | | −0.01*** (0.004) | | 0.01** (0.005) | | −0.03*** (0.01) |
| City | | −0.02*** (0.01) | | −0.05*** (0.01) | | −0.09*** (0.02) |
| French zone | | −0.06** (0.02) | | 0.05*** (0.02) | | 0.12*** (0.03) |
| State FE | ✓ | ✓ | ✓ | ✓ | ✓ | ✓ |
| Adjusted $R^2$ | 0.36 | 0.54 | 0.43 | 0.68 | 0.54 | 0.73 |
| N | 526 | 525 | 526 | 525 | 526 | 525 |

*Notes:* All models are OLS, with fixed effects for German states. Heteroskedasticity-robust standard errors in parentheses. Significant at $^*p < 0.10$; $^{**}p < 0.05$; $^{***}p < 0.01$.

expellees has a similar effect on support for the Social Democrats in Schleswig-Holstein as in West Germany as a whole, then we can be more confident that the shift to the left reflects the consequences of the expulsions rather than pre-existing partisanship. Furthermore, Schleswig-Holstein offers significant variation in the share of expellees from one municipality to another, which is helpful for estimating the support for the SPD among expellees and natives separately.

I thus repeat the analysis of the 1949 election using municipal data from Schleswig-Holstein. There are fewer prewar indicators available at this more fine-grained level of analysis; I compensate for this to some extent by including county-fixed effects and restricting comparisons to communities that are proximate to each other and thus share prewar economic characteristics.

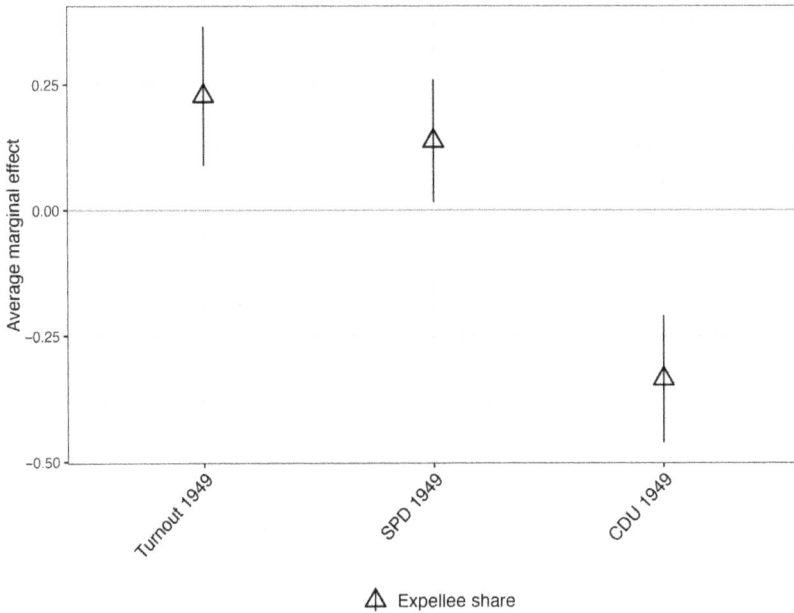

FIGURE 6.1 Expellee share and voting in the 1949 federal election. The standardized coefficients are based on estimates in Table 6.1.

As expected, I find that expellee presence increases support for the SPD and lowers support for the CDU (see Table A.11). The coefficient on *Expellee share* is positive but insignificant in regressions of turnout. Next, I use ecological inference techniques to investigate whether the increased support for the SPD is driven by the voting behavior of expellees or by the natives' vote in municipalities that received more expellees. The idea is to combine information about the numbers of expellees and natives and support for different political parties in each municipality to estimate mean support for the SPD separately for each group. I do this using *eiR* program in R, developed by King and Roberts (2012). The ecological inference analysis indicates that the mean support for the Social Democrats is more than twice as high among expellees, at 42.9 percent ($\sigma = 3.05$), than among the natives, at 21.8 percent ($\sigma = 1.5$). Support for the Christian Democrats, by contrast, is more than eight times as high among the natives, at 40.2 percent ($\sigma = 0.3$) than among the expellees, at 5.8 percent ($\sigma = 0.6$). We also see that the estimated turnout among expellees, at a striking 89.8 percent ($\sigma = 1.1$), was significantly higher than turnout among the native population, at 79 percent ($\sigma = 0.6$).

This analysis confirms that in the 1949 election, the inflow of expellees benefited the Social Democrats, who advocated for a more active role of the state in the economy, and increased turnout. This result is consistent with my argument that mass uprooting increases the demand for state intervention. This result aligns with other studies of the expellees' political preferences (Connor 2006; Bösch 2016). Importantly, researchers observe that by 1949, expellees were already growing disillusioned with the Social Democrats, particularly in Schleswig-Holstein where the SPD had served as a governing party (Connor 2007, 117). Thus, the expellees who supported the SPD in 1947 sometimes defected to support independent expellee candidates or other parties in 1949 (Connor 2006). Still, the SPD support remained significantly higher among expellees than among natives as late as 1949.

With the formation of the Bloc of Expellees and Dispossessed Persons (*Block der Heimatvertriebenen und Entrechteten, BHE*) in 1950, expellee support for the SPD and other established parties plummeted. The BHE described itself as a "non-Marxist social party" (Hughes 1999, 35). Its program and pronouncements reflected the expellees' many demands on the state. BHE candidate Hans-Adolf Asbach claimed that the party's goal was "to create a social Germany which would not break apart with the first assault" (quoted in Lattimore (1974, 60)).[9] *Der Spiegel* described the campaign of BHE politician Waldemar Kraft in Schleswig-Holstein in these words:

[He] promises everyone help and healing: sufficient minimum wages, social tax policy. Adjustment of social benefits to the purchasing power of the DM, fair distribution of housing, upgrading of the expellees' Eastern savings, accelerated collection of emergency aid also from ailing agriculture.[10]

At the same time, the BHE was careful to emphasize the expellees' entitlement to compensation from the state over their economic needs. For instance, Kraft argued that the expellees were neither "supplicants" nor "charity recipients," but "creditors" with rights vis-à-vis the state. Balancing out the burdens of expulsion was framed as necessary for the expellees to become masters of their own fate and avoid dependence on "welfare, public assistance, or benefits" (Hughes 1999, 97). Nonetheless, it is evident that the BHE platform also envisioned an interventionist and redistributive state, despite fundamental differences from the SPD's platform.

EXPELLEE POLICY DURING THE MILITARY OCCUPATION

### The Influence of the Occupation Authorities

The Allied Control Council viewed expellees as a "German problem," and hoped to get involved only when negotiating the distribution of expellees

---

[9] Asbach soon became the Minister for Social Affairs, Labor and Issues for Displaced Persons in Schleswig-Holstein.

[10] "Kraft für jeden," *DER SPIEGEL* 27/1950, July 5, 1950. www.spiegel.de/politik/kraft-fuer-jeden-a-1b7a51a9-0002-0001-0000-000044448848.

across different occupation zones (Report to H. Res. 238 1950, 21). Nonetheless, the Allies ended up influencing expellee policy a great deal. Writing about the US occupation zone, Sylvia Schraut (2000, 115) argues that "traces of American influence on the German refugee problem can be found in nearly all the sources and at all levels of decisions concerning refugees."[11]

Three factors contributed to the oversized role of the occupation governments in handling the matter of expellees. First, most expellees arrived in 1945–46, when only local and district governments were in place. The occupation governments had to coordinate expellee allocation across different areas, deciding how to direct expellee transports. Second, German local governments were reluctant to accommodate expellees. They refused to enfranchise the newcomers or grant them full access to the labor market and welfare benefits (Demshuk 2006; Carey 1951). The Allies' intervention was necessary to ensure that expellees were housed, fed, and employed. As the US working group on the expellee problem conceded in May 1946: "[The expellees] have no official status at this time – they neither desire to come here, nor do the Germans want them; nevertheless, they require housing, food, and employment, which, though it is a German responsibility, ultimately falls upon the shoulders of the U.S." (quoted in Schraut (2000, 118)). Third, until 1949, German policymakers did not have full decision-making autonomy, and the federal government did not exist. All major legislative initiatives regarding expellee care at the *Land* level had to receive approval from the occupation authorities.

As a result, the foundational laws on expellee rights were drafted with the heavy involvement of the occupation governments. In March 1946, in response to the local government's failure to accommodate expellees, the Allied Control Council passed the Housing Law (*Wohnungsgesetz*), which set new standards for housing density in order to improve the spatial allocation of expellees. The law stipulated that the municipal authorities could requisition living quarters, enforce the registration of vacant housing, and order compulsory rental contracts to house expellees (Connor 2007, 31). The Allies believed that order could be maintained only if the expellees became equal citizens, so they urged the reluctant German authorities to grant citizenship and the right to vote to expellees (Demshuk 2006, 387). The occupation authorities also urged German authorities to extend social welfare benefits to expellees. Erker (1988, 47–48) writes that had it not been for the US's intervention, expellees settled in Bavaria would have been entitled to no more than temporary emergency aid.

---

[11] One exception is the French occupation government, which refused to accept expellees into its zone altogether.

The Allies' recommendations also led to the formation of advisory boards for expellee affairs at all levels of government. In the US zone, expellee commissions were introduced at the district (*Regierungsbezirk*) and county (*Kreis*) level. In the British zone, ministers for expellees were set up at the *Länder* level, and expellee committees (*Flüchtlingsausschüsse*) were set up at the district, county, and municipality (*Gemeinde*) levels. These new entities were staffed by expellees and would "advise" local officials on matters concerning expellees.

In contrast to migrants in Poland's resettled territories, the majority of expellees in West Germany were settled in communities where social structures remained intact and local governments were already in place. Such communities could muster considerable resistance to pro-expellee measures. US officials observed that the local mayors in their occupation zone "passively" defied *Länder*-level laws mandating expellee rights and acted instead in the interest of their native electorates (Grosser 1996, 296). When reviewing the expellee situation in Baden-Württemberg, one US official concluded: "The authorities on the lower level of *Kreise* and *Gemeinden* more than the central government in the *Länder* are to blame for the failure to promote assimilation" (quoted in Grosser (1996, 293)). The situation was similar in the British occupation zone. For example, a Landrat in Osnabrück (Lower Saxony) refused to publicize a ministerial directive that invited expellees to apply for financial assistance, while the local government in Dossenheim (Baden-Württemberg) misrepresented the availability of unoccupied rooms to avoid accommodating expellees (Connor 2007, 67). In the town of Eutin (Schleswig-Holstein), the local elites resisted the appointment of a full-time Expellee Agent required by law for a town of that size, arguing that the town could not afford to do so (Lattimore 1974, 62).

The Allies did not always play a constructive role in the development of expellee policy. Their interference led to significant delays in drafting legislation to address expellees' property losses. In 1948, a coalition between SPD, CDU, and CSU in the bizonal Economic Council drafted the first Equalization of Burdens Law. The law would levy a 2–3 percent tax on property in order to support expellees economically and reduce pressure on the social welfare system at the municipal level. Under this law, the expellees would receive a monthly allowance of 70 DM, subsidies for education, training, and housing, as well as targeted loans for setting up businesses (Schillinger 1985). This assistance would come directly from central funds to even out the fiscal burden between regions with higher and lower expellee inflows. However, the Allies refused to approve the bill. The US government objected to the bill's "socialistic tendencies," and insisted on framing it as a "pure relief" measure rather than a redistributive one (Hughes 1999, 80–81). The French government was concerned about the potential reduction in the amount of compensation it would be able to extract from its occupation zone (Hughes 1999, 81). As a result of the Allies' pressure, the law was amended to reduce its redistributive aspects and renamed the Immediate Aid Law (*Soforthilfegesetz*). It came into force only in August 1949, nearly a year after it was drafted. The delay is particularly significant in light of the urgency of the expellees' material needs.

### Resistance from Native Economic Elites

Once the expellees obtained the right to vote, they could elect their representatives. While they were typically outnumbered at the municipal level, in some *Länder* they were numerous enough to shape the composition of the parliaments. Yet when the parties in power sought to act on behalf of expellees, they faced pushback from native elites.

A notable example of the limitations that *Länder* governments faced in assisting expellees was the failure of land reform. As discussed in Chapter 5, land reform in Poland was facilitated by the exodus of Germans, whose land and farms were redistributed to Polish migrants. Large estates were converted into state farms and agricultural cooperatives, alleviating land scarcity and strengthening state control over the economy. In 1945, far-reaching land reform was also introduced in East Germany. At first, it seemed that West Germany would follow this precedent. As mentioned above, the Allies viewed land reform as necessary for reorganizing German society.

The circumstances for implementing the reform seemed most propitious in Schleswig-Holstein, a *Land* with a disproportionate share of expellees (45 percent in 1946) and high levels of landholding inequality. In May 1946, the agriculture minister of Schleswig-Holstein, Erich Arp (SPD) declared that the expropriation of large landowners was "a prerequisite for democratization" (Gerolimatos 2014, 114). Hoping to preserve at least some of their land by cooperating with the authorities, large estate owners preemptively offered to give up 10,000 ha of their land for state needs (Gerolimatos 2014, 114). In the parliamentary elections of 1947, the expellees supported the rise of the pro-reform SPD, which secured 44 percent of the vote. The party's support was highest among expellees in the localities where the planned land reform areas were located (Lorenzen-Schmidt 2009; Connor 2006).

Despite this promising start, the SPD's three years in power failed to bring about meaningful reform. Native landowners engaged in organized lobbying to block the bill. *Das Bauernblatt*, published by the National Farmers' Association, claimed that the reform "treated private property with eastern methods," marked the "moral decline of western culture," and would backfire by undermining the production of food (Gerolimatos 2014, 117).

The SPD draft legislation encountered bitter opposition in Schleswig-Holstein's parliament. The CDU, initially open to redistributing land, pulled back, accusing the SPD of introducing the "beginning of the kolkhoz" (Lorenzen-Schmidt 2009). A modified bill was passed by the SPD majority in 1948, but new challenges arose when the government moved to settle the issues around compensation. Following extensive negotiations with the Working Group for Landowners in Kiel, the parliament in 1949 adopted watered-down legislation that compensated landowners in full and made optional previous regulations prohibiting the ownership of multiple estates. The new law faced significant implementation challenges, as large landowners refused to fill out the obligatory registration forms. Between November 1949 and April 1950, only 30,000 ha of land were transferred, costing the government twenty-eight million DM in compensation payments (Lorenzen-Schmidt 2009).

The land reform also failed in the American occupation zone, despite considerable pressure from the military government, which viewed the establishment of "the greatest possible number of [... expellees] in their own homes on the land, in the shortest possible time ... [as] essential for the promotion of a secure and democratic social system" (Schraut 1995, 142). Commenting on the failure of land reform in Württemberg-Baden, the Chief of the F&A Branch of the military government ruefully observed that the *Land* government "bends its political ear to these powerful [landowners'] interests" and the Minister-Präsident was particularly determined to shield the properties of the "royal" family of Württemberg, on whose support he had depended during the war (quoted in Schraut (1995, 140)).

As these examples illustrate, expellee demand for state support did not always translate into effective policy solutions. Even in cases where expellees succeeded in electing political parties aligned with their interests, those parties' actions were circumscribed by various domestic and international stakeholders. Although expellees enjoyed greater influence on government policy than Polish migrants, West German democratic institutions also empowered native property owners, who ultimately succeeded in limiting redistribution.

EXPELLEE POLICY AFTER THE CREATION OF THE FEDERAL
GOVERNMENT

In the 1949 election, the CDU/CSU secured 31 percent of the vote, narrowly beating the Social Democrats at 29 percent of the vote. Konrad Adenauer of the CDU sought to make the best of this narrow victory, interpreting it as a mandate for implementing neoliberal economic reforms. He rejected the grand coalition of the CDU and the SPD, proposed by some of the CDU elites who favored a more interventionist government, forming instead a coalition with the liberal FDP (which had garnered 11.9 percent of the vote). In his inaugural address to the parliament, Adenauer signaled his government's priorities as follows: "The reconstruction of our economy is the foremost, indeed the only, basis for any social policy and for the integration of the expellees. Only a prosperous economy can bear over the long run the burdens from the Lastenausgleich" (Hughes 1999, 85).

With the center-right coalition in power, many of the redistributive initiatives envisioned at the height of concerns about expellee radicalization were no longer feasible. Nevertheless, the first *Bundestag* passed a high volume of socially oriented legislation. In 1950, West Germany had the highest level of social spending to GDP in Europe, at 19.2 percent (Leisering 2001).[12] In this broader context, the Federal Parliament passed a series of important measures in response to expellee demands, mobilizing considerable fiscal and administrative resources.

One of the first steps of the new government was the creation of the independent Federal Ministry for Expellees (*Bundesvertriebenenministerium*), headed by Hans Lukaschek. The ministry would coordinate the integration of expellees and refugees across *Länder*, oversee the distribution of economic aid to expellees, and participate in the design of the final Equalization of Burdens Law (see below). The Adenauer government also created a committee for displaced persons in the Bundestag, chaired by Linus Kather (CDU).

Starting in 1950–51, the federal government sponsored the construction of affordable housing through both direct subsidies and tax relief (Führer 2005). Private contractors received additional subsidies if they built houses for refugees and expellees. The money came from federal and *Länder* budgets as well as from foreign aid (Connor 2007, 141).

Special banking institutions were created to facilitate the expellees' economic integration. In May 1950, the Refugee Bank (*Vertriebenenbank*), a central credit institution for expellees, was established in Bad Godesberg.[13] Another new state-sponsored organization was the Reconstruction Loan Corporation (*Kreditanstalt für Wiederaufbau, KfW*). Motivated by the need to increase the volume of affordable housing for expellees, the bank was tasked with providing long-term investment funds. The KfW allowed the government to intervene directly in the market when necessary (Guenbacher 2004). It is one of Germany's biggest banks today.

In 1953, the Federal Expellee Law was passed. The Law amended prior *Länder* legislation concerning expellees by clarifying their legal standing and reinforcing their claims to German citizenship. The law also set forth material and administrative provisions to facilitate expellee integration into the labor market. For instance, it stipulated that federal and *Länder* governments contribute to the preservation of expellees' culture and customs by sponsoring research on their expulsion and funding special archives and libraries (Wolfs 2003, 75).

---

[12] The welfare state continued to expand in subsequent decades, with social spending reaching 26 percent of GDP in 1970 and 32.2 percent in 1980.

[13] After the adoption of the Equalization of Burdens bill in 1953, the bank was renamed the Equalization of Burdens Bank (*Lastenausgleichsbank*) and began to serve all parties affected by the war.

## The Equalization of Burdens Law

In August 1952, the *Bundestag* adopted the Equalization of Burdens Law (*Lastenausgleichsgesetz, LAG*).[14] The LAG was intended to balance out the burdens created by WWII, by providing economic aid as well as partial compensation for property losses to expellees and other war-damaged persons. It became the main instrument for advancing the social and economic integration of expellees for the next three decades.

Producing a bill that could secure a majority in the *Bundestag* took three years. The political process was so fraught that Federal Finance Minister Fritz Schäffer reportedly claimed that the "burden sharing [would not be possible] without a civil war" (quoted in Schillinger (1985, 202)).

By delegating the drafting of the LAG to the Finance Ministry, the Adenauer government ensured that the decision-making process would be dominated by fiscal concerns. In line with the government's focus on economic reconstruction, the Finance Ministry strived to limit the capital levies needed to finance the bill at a level deemed sustainable for the economy. Schäffer's draft thus envisioned only a moderate tax on business and property owners, in contrast to the more radical redistributive proposals advocated by expellee organizations and the "Unkeler Circle."[15]

German business associations largely supported Schäffer's proposal, because they feared that its failure would empower "extremist expellee groups" and lead to even higher tax rates (Schillinger 1985, 202). Only the most conservative business circles did not abstain from criticism, proposing several amendments that would strengthen the protection of private property.

Opposition to the draft came primarily from expellee organizations, which were disappointed by the limited amount of compensation offered by the bill and demanded a right to direct participation (*Mitwirkung*). With the aim of exerting pressure on the lawmakers, in May 1951, the Central Association of Expelled Germans (ZvD) mobilized tens of thousands of expellees in protest. Linus Kather, an expellee politician who chaired the ZvD and was elected on the CDU list in the *Bundestag*, castigated the draft as "a clear denial of [expellees'] legal claims" and "the negation of the idea of equalization of burdens in general" (Kittel 2020, 53–54). The demonstrators resorted to intimidation tactics, exploiting concerns about expellee radicalization to win more concessions. Some held signs saying "Lastenausgleich with Adenauer – or by Stalin," threatening to support the Soviet invasion if their demands were not accommodated (Hughes 1999, 146). In a bid to influence the government, expellee deputies in the *Bundestag* linked support for the LAG with support for the remilitarization bills favored by the CDU. When his amendments to

---

[14] The LAG replaced the provisional Immediate Aid Law, adopted before the formation of the Federal Government.

[15] The Unkeler Circle was a circle of coalition-party experts that drafted guidelines about the scope and nature of the levy.

the bill were rejected, Kather threatened to leave the CDU for the BHE. The tactic worked, securing additional federal funding for the bill alongside other concessions (Schillinger 1985, 277). However, the Finance Minister rejected the expellees' demands for immediate compensation payments, arguing that grappling with hundreds of thousands of expellee petitions was beyond the capacity of the German administration (Hughes 1999, 153).

In August 1952, out of 353 members of the *Bundestag*, 208 voted in favor of the law and 139 against it.[16] With some amendments, the bill was later passed by the Federal Council (*Bundesrat*). The final version of the bill was much less redistributive than the expellees had hoped. As Schillinger (1985) observes, "[N]o one seemed particularly happy. But at least the protests that had characterized earlier phases of the burden-sharing policy did not materialize." He argues that widespread rejection of the LAG was averted, in part, because the implementation of the bill required a large number of additional regulations and instructions, which gave various stakeholders reasons to hope that their unmet demands would be addressed during the implementation stage.[17]

Although the LAG failed to satisfy expellee organizations, it stipulated a diverse set of policies that proved important for expellee integration. The law provided for two categories of payments: (1) quick integration assistance based on need, granted without legal entitlement, and (2) various forms of compensation based on legal entitlements that had to be documented and processed by subnational burden-sharing offices (Kittel 2020, 58–63). Notably, federal spending on the Lastenausgleich would exceed spending on rearmament and foreign debt (Bach 2011).

Integration assistance made up the bulk of LAG spending and was paid out first. Some 49.71 billion DM, in the form of pensions and maintenance aid (*Unterhaltshilfe*), was granted to individuals who could not support themselves in the aftermath of displacement or suffered from other consequences of the war (Kittel 2020, 61). Another 25.47 and 9.74 billion DM were spent to compensate for the loss of land, real estate, and businesses (*Hauptentschädigung*) and to provide household allowances (*Hausrathilfe, Hausratentschädigung*), respectively (Kittel 2020, 61). In a compromise between the need- and loss-based approaches, losses below 5,000 DM were indemnified at a 95-percent level, while larger losses were compensated at progressively lower levels, down to 8 percent for damages exceeding one million DM.

Compensation payments were issued starting in the 1960s, much later than the expellees and other war-damaged groups had hoped. Still, they benefited nearly two million families, approximately nineteen million people total in the mid-1960s. As a share of the property value, the restitution averaged 22 percent, with a maximum of 30 percent (Kittel 2020, 15). A total of 113.9 billion DM were disbursed by 1979 (Schillinger 1985, 289). By the end of

[16] Six deputies abstained. Opposition was concentrated among SPD deputies.
[17] In the early years, the LAG and related laws were amended on average once a year. By 1987, some thirty-one amendments had been passed (Kossert 2008, 98).

the 1960s, twenty-six amendments to the law were passed, expanding and adapting its provisions to changed circumstances.

The transfers were financed by a mixture of contributions from private tax-payers and the public sector. A prominent feature of the bill was a 50-percent levy on capital, selected to symbolize the equal division of WWII "burdens." In reality, the tax on capital owners was "nowhere near its nominal rate," because the Adenauer government opted for a twenty-seven-year amortization period (Hughes 1999, 151–52). In practice, 6-percent annual tax rates were levied on business assets and properties, 5-percent rates on mixed-use properties, and 4-percent rates on land, forestry, and residential properties (Kittel 2020, 67). This one-off tax diminished over time because the taxable amount was fixed at the valuation of assets at the time of the 1948 currency reform. As a result, the distribution of wealth within Germany was largely unaffected; large and small property holders alike preserved their assets.

Despite this modest tax rate, native property owners began to petition the responsible state organizations for exemptions as soon as the bill was passed. Interest groups such as the Emergency Community of Native People and Taxpayers, the German Farmers' Association, and the Central Association of German House and Landowners beset federal ministries in West Germany's capital Bonn, seeking to extricate themselves from payment (Kittel 2020, 194–201). Many native property owners viewed themselves as unfairly burdened. For instance, the local paper covered a protest against the LAG organized by the residents of Coburg (Bavaria) under the title "Blood Donor Dead – Patient Lives," implying that the natives' welfare was sacrificed for the expellees' benefit (Hughes 1999, 120). The natives argued that expellees did not deserve assistance because they had "not yet paid a penny in taxes to the German state" (letter from Frieda M. to the LAG office in Mannheim in 1954, quoted in Müller (1997, 360)). Some property owners sought to evade the new tax by concealing their incomes. A tax officer in 1950 claimed that, if the government were able to compare farmers' real income with their tax returns, it could finance the equalization of burdens from tax evasion penalties alone (Kittel 2020, 197).

The LAG had a significant impact on the capacity of the German state. Implementing the law and verifying property claims required an expansion of the bureaucratic apparatus. At the end of the 1950s, there were 590 municipal equalization offices nested within 10 equalization offices in each federal state (*Land*), subordinated to the headquarters in Bad Homburg. Approximately 25,000 civil servants were employed to sift through claims. The federal government covered 50 percent of the personnel costs, and the districts and cities had to each bear the other half themselves. The decisions of the compensation offices were checked by several additional bodies, including 117 supra local complaints committees (*Beschwerdeausschüsse*), whose decisions could be appealed in administrative courts (Kittel 2020, 85). In addition, thirty-five homeland information centers (*Heimatauskunftstellen, HASt*) were created.

The centers were closely connected to expellee associations and manned by expellees. They were given the task of examining expellees' applications for damage assessment, providing information or naming witnesses and experts in order to facilitate approval of the application by the compensation authorities (Kittel 2020, 94). The expellees were thus included in the processing of compensation claims as an auxiliary bureaucracy. After all, only the expellees themselves "could verify extremely complicated expellee claims for restitution" (Schoenberg 1970, 154).

By offering partial compensation for WWII losses, the government induced expellees and other war-damaged individuals to share detailed information about prewar assets and postwar economic circumstances. It learned about its citizens' education, finances, and employment histories. The native property owners, who were obligated to pay the new tax, were similarly required to provide detailed information about their assets and earnings. This they did, albeit less willingly than the expellees. The informational capacity of the federal government thus expanded considerably. In turn, the collected data would facilitate all sorts of planning and subsequent political interventions.

The LAG restitution process stretched out over nearly three decades and involved increased and sustained interaction with state institutions. The President of the Federal Equalization of Burdens Office set a high bar for this interaction. He urged the bureaucrats working at local LAG offices to exercise "understanding, helpfulness, and community spirit," and to ensure that "the ultimate recipient of a service also feels the political and human intentions of the legislator" (quoted in Müller (1997, 342)). The LAG bureaucrats were instructed to be aware of the sensitivities of the people they served. Recognizing that the process was draining their "moral and mental strength," some offices had, as part of their permanent inventory, "a wool blanket, a vomiting bowl, a glass of water and valerian drops to control fainting and nausea" (Müller 1997, 345).

Nonetheless, the experience was rarely without conflict. Expellees were often frustrated with their LAG offices and threatened to complain to third parties, be it the press, "a lawyer well versed in expellee matters," the Federal Equalization Office, the Higher Administrative Court, or even the President [of the Federal Republic] (Müller 1997, 351).

## EXPELLEES AND ADMINISTRATIVE CAPACITY

As discussed earlier, *Land* and the federal government responded to the needs of expellees by creating advisory boards, new administrative departments, and new ministries for expellee affairs. This new administrative layer went all the way down to the local level, and it often employed the expellees themselves. Expanding the state bureaucracy was necessary to adjudicate disputes between expellees and natives over housing, to advise expellees on their legal rights, to verify their eligibility for government benefits, and, after the LAG was passed, to process expellees' property claims.[18]

At the same time, expellees were allocated to settlements where state administration was already in place. In contrast to *Land* and federal authorities, which were weakened by territorial reorganization and delayed establishment, local and district administrations survived the war largely intact. As described above, they resisted regulations from the higher levels of government. This makes it important to verify that the inflow of expellees corresponded to increased administrative capacity at the local and district levels.

To do so, I use occupational data from the 1950 German population census compiled by Braun and Franke (2021). My main outcome is the (logged) number of employees in public service (*Beschäftigte in Öffentlicher Dienst*) per 1,000 people. Variation in the size of the state bureaucracy at the county level is mapped in Map 6.1.[19] The census also distinguishes between native and expellee public servants. I therefore use two additional outcomes: the number of expellees in public service per 1,000 residents and the share of expellees in public service.

I estimate the following model, where $Y_{il}$ is log public employees per 1,000 people:

$$Y_{il} = \beta_0 + \beta_1 \text{ Share expellees}_{il} + X'_{il}\beta + \gamma_l + \epsilon_{il}. \qquad (6.2)$$

My key explanatory variable is the share of expellees in 1950, published in *Statistisches Taschenbuch über die Heimatvertriebenen* (1953).[20] When relating state capacity to the size of the bureaucracy, it is important to account for the economies of scale in public administration (Gehlbach 2008). Therefore, I include the logged population size in 1950 as a right-hand-side variable. In addition, the vector of controls $X'_{il}$ includes the extent of wartime destruction, the share of the population employed in agriculture, the type of county (city or rural), and the logged distance to the eastern border (same as in the section above). These variables capture the fact that higher numbers of expellees were allocated to areas that were more rural, remote, and suffered little war destruction. To account for the differences in state policy as well as for divergent effects of occupation in different zones, I add fixed effects for *Länder*, $\gamma_l$, and an indicator coded 1 for French occupation zone and 0 for other zones.[21]

---

[18] In the 1950s, the Adenauer government also committed to providing jobs to expellee civil servants in connection with Article 131 of the German Basic Law. The federal government, *Länder*, and municipalities were all obligated to fill at least 20 percent of their offices with the so-called 131ers, or the "displaced members of the public service and dissolved offices."

[19] Information about public service employment is missing for the Hannover and Südbaden districts (*Regierungsbezirke*).

[20] The results are very similar when using expellee share from 1946.

[21] Adding a dummy for counties in the French zone accounts for the variation in the occupation authority within Baden-Württemberg, the only *Land* that was divided between two occupation zones, as noted earlier.

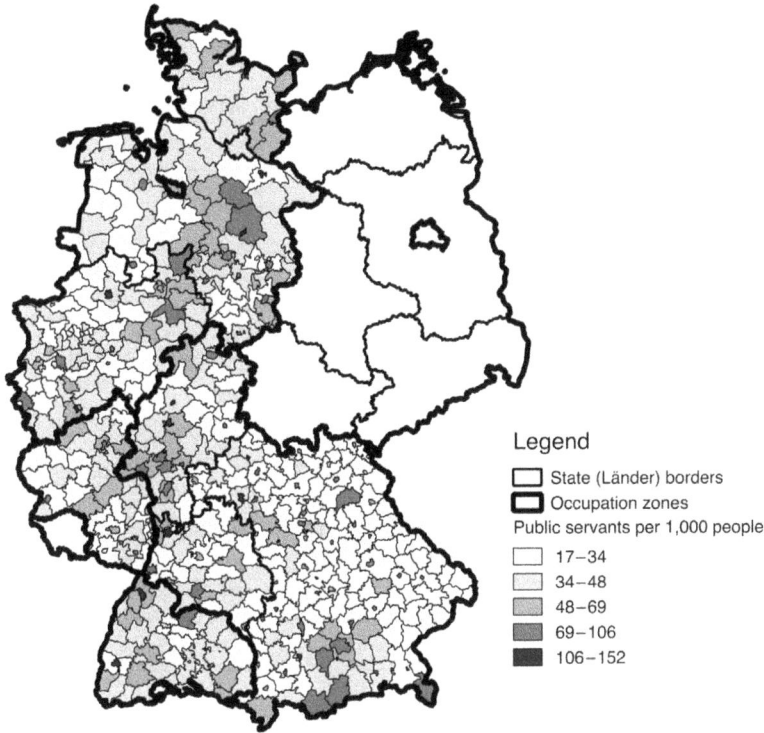

Map 6.1 Administrative capacity in West German counties in 1950. County boundaries are based on shapefile from MPIDR and CGG (2011).

The results are presented in Table 6.2, and the estimates for logged outcomes are represented graphically in Figure 6.2. First, we see that expellee presence increases administrative capacity at the county level (Models 1–2). One standard-deviation (10 percent) increase in the share of expellees translates into one additional public servant per 1,000 people in 1950. In response to expellee needs, state administration expanded at a higher rate than necessary to adjust to a larger population. This pattern appears to be driven by expellees rather than natives joining public service in greater numbers (Models 3–4). Relatedly, expellee share to population is a strong predictor of expellee share in public service: A 10-percent increase in this explanatory variable increases the share of expellees in administrative positions by 5 percent (Models 5–6). This is consistent with *Land* and federal governments hiring expellees to fill new offices and boards tasked with expellee-related functions while retaining most of the native administrators in their original jobs.

To further understand how expellee presence affected state bureaucracy, I analyze the representation of expellees among civil servants across various government levels. In 1952, expellees made up 20 percent of civil servants at the

TABLE 6.2 *Expellee share and administrative capacity in 1950.*

| | Ln(public employees per 1,000) | | Share expellees in public service | | Ln(expellees in public service per 1,000) | |
|---|---|---|---|---|---|---|
| | (1) | (2) | (3) | (4) | (5) | (6) |
| Expellee share | 1.12*** (0.41) | 1.12** (0.50) | 4.74*** (0.46) | 3.92*** (0.53) | 0.53*** (0.10) | 0.50*** (0.14) |
| Share destroyed | | −0.20 (0.17) | | −0.70*** (0.17) | | −0.04 (0.04) |
| Share in agriculture | | −0.94*** (0.21) | | −1.54*** (0.24) | | −0.16** (0.06) |
| Ln dist to Eastern border | | 0.05** (0.03) | | −0.03 (0.02) | | −0.02 (0.02) |
| Ln population | | −0.04 (0.03) | | −0.15*** (0.04) | | −0.01 (0.01) |
| City | 0.80*** (0.06) | 0.62*** (0.08) | 0.67*** (0.06) | 0.42*** (0.08) | −0.03** (0.01) | −0.06** (0.02) |
| French zone | 0.36*** (0.09) | 0.31*** (0.10) | 0.08 (0.12) | −0.09 (0.14) | −0.04*** (0.01) | −0.04** (0.02) |
| State FE | ✓ | ✓ | ✓ | ✓ | ✓ | ✓ |
| Adjusted $R^2$ | 0.41 | 0.43 | 0.50 | 0.57 | 0.17 | 0.18 |
| N | 409 | 407 | 409 | 407 | 409 | 407 |

*Notes:* All models are OLS, with fixed effects for German *Länder*. Heteroskedasticity-robust standard errors in parentheses. Significant at $*p < 0.10$; $**p < 0.05$; $***p < 0.01$.

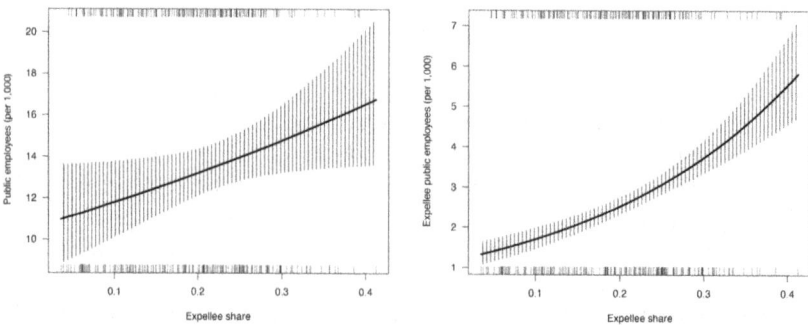

FIGURE 6.2 Expellee share and administrative capacity in 1950. The estimates are based on Models 2 and 4 in Table 6.2.

TABLE 6.3 *Expellees employed in Länder and municipal administration in 1950.*

| | Proportion of expellees (percent) in administration | | | |
|---|---|---|---|---|
| | To population | State | Municipal | Total |
| Schleswig-Holstein | 33 | 36.2 | 25.1 | 30.9 |
| Hamburg | 7.2 | 7 | – | 7 |
| Niedersachsen | 27.2 | 29.7 | 21.7 | 26.3 |
| Bremen | 8.6 | 9.1 | – | 9.1 |
| Nordrhein-Westfalen | 10.1 | 13 | 7 | 9.4 |
| Hessen | 16.7 | 18.8 | 13.1 | 15.8 |
| Rheinland-Pfalz | 5.1 | 4.1 | 2.2 | 3.8 |
| Baden-Württemberg | 13.4 | 11.9 | 9.8 | 11 |
| Bayern | 21.2 | 20.8 | 12.4 | 17.2 |

*Source: Statistisches Taschenbuch über die Heimatvertriebenen* (1953, 76).

federal and *Länder* level, but only 13 percent of civil servants at the county level (Schoenberg 1970, 133). Table 6.3 breaks down these statistics by *Land*, showing that the expellee share in state administration slightly exceeded their share in the overall population in five out of nine *Länder* (Schleswig-Holstein, Lower Saxony, Hessen, Bremen, and North Rhine-Westphalia). Within West Germany, expellees were most likely to work for offices that dealt with the consequences of the war (27.1 percent), with finance and tax administration (20.7 percent), in schools (20.6 percent), and in social welfare offices (18.5 percent). Their presence in federal civil service further increased in subsequent years (Schoenberg 1970, 134). Thus, for a considerable proportion of expellees, *Land* and federal governments became not only important allies in the struggle vis-à-vis local authorities but also immediate employers.

Integrating expellees into the local bureaucracy, on the other hand, proved much more challenging. In all *Länder*, the share of expellees in the municipal administration was significantly lower than their share in the population. At the local level, expellees were the least likely to work for the finance and tax administration (6.9 percent) and for the local police (7.4 percent). The low levels of expellee presence within the ranks of local-level bureaucracy reflected the broader pattern of local resistance to state and federal regulations designed to facilitate expellee integration.

DISCUSSION

This chapter has demonstrated that the arrival of expellees increased demands on the state. The reluctance of local communities to accommodate expellees amplified the importance of intervention from higher authorities: Government officials played a crucial role in securing housing, providing economic relief, and resolving numerous conflicts that arose between expellees and natives.

Motivated by concerns about expellee radicalization, they created an additional layer of state administration to oversee expellee matters and, with some delay, passed laws that taxed native property owners to alleviate the expellees' economic deprivation. Implementing these measures led to an expansion of administrative capacity: I show that, as early as 1950, counties that received more expellees relative to the overall population had more public officials per capita. Opportunities to receive assistance and compensation for property losses made expellees and other war-damaged persons more legible to the state and placed them into sustained contact with state bureaucrats.

The introduction of inclusive political institutions by the occupation authorities enabled German expellees to influence governmental policy through both voting and extra parliamentary activities. Although they were outnumbered by the natives and could not form their own political party until 1950, expellees succeeded in electing their representatives into the *Landtag* and *Bundestag*. Reflecting their support for an interventionist central government, they initially endorsed the Social Democrats. Even the expellees from East Prussia, the stronghold of the conservative right before WWII, voted for the SPD in the 1949 election. When expellee issues were debated in the first *Bundestag*, expellee politicians advocated for expellee interests, even when they were elected as candidates from bourgeois parties such as the CDU. In 1950, expellees founded the BHE, which allowed them to champion their interests more effectively.

While the democratic West German government was more responsive to expellee needs than the communist Polish government, it was also accountable to a greater number of stakeholders with diverse interests. Those different stakeholders constrained the government's ability to implement pro-expellee policy. One constraint was posed by the occupation governments, which sometimes encouraged state intervention on behalf of expellees, but just as often vetoed measures perceived to be "socialist" in spirit. Another constraint originated in the native population, and especially its economic elites, who retained their economic assets and were well organized. The native population outnumbered the expellees five to one. Consequently, the 1949 election brought a center-right coalition into power, which devoted more attention to economic reconstruction than to addressing economic inequality.

As a result, many of the expellees' economic needs remained unmet. Economic disparities produced by postwar expulsions would remain visible for decades, affecting not only first-generation expellees but also their children. Correspondingly, some expellees grew dissatisfied with the mainstream parties. Menon (2022) shows that, in the long run, the radical right would secure more votes in counties that had received greater shares of expellees. At the same time, the dire predictions of expellee radicalization never materialized. And, as will be shown in Chapter 8, expellees wound up benefiting the receiving communities economically in the long run.

PART IV

# LONG-RUN ECONOMIC CONSEQUENCES
# OF UPROOTING

# 7

# Economic Implications of Diversity in Poland

This book has so far explored how forced migration impacts cooperation and state–society relations in receiving communities. I have shown that, by rearranging ethnically homogeneous populations in space, population transfers in Poland and West Germany after WWII increased diversity within communities, at the same time eroding voluntary cooperation and facilitating the expansion of state capacity. I now turn to the final set of questions raised in the introduction: What were the short- and long-term effects of mass migration on economic development? Did it matter where migrants came from?

I argue that communities that have been diversified by migration can achieve superior economic outcomes in the long run. First, higher state capacity and greater supply of market-supporting public goods increase gains from productive economic activity and enable entrepreneurs to expand operations beyond their immediate social circle. Second, the broader range of skills and perspectives found in diversified communities stimulates innovation and the creation of new businesses. Importantly, these outcomes are possible only where national institutions are *inclusive*; in particular, where a formal legal system protects property rights and enforces contracts of all citizens in an unbiased way. When formal institutions are *extractive*, on the other hand, individuals living in more heterogeneous communities with a stronger state presence find it more difficult to engage in entrepreneurial activity than those in more homogeneous communities with a weaker state presence and stronger social ties.

This chapter interrogates these claims using micro-level data from Poland's resettled territories. Chapter 8 will focus on West Germany. A crucial difference between these two cases is that the West German government encouraged private economic activity from the 1940s onward, whereas the Polish government restricted it until the country's transition to a market economy in 1989. In other words, Poland's national institutions were *extractive* for the first forty-five years after the arrival of migrants in the resettled territories.

The large time gap between resettlement and the market transition makes Poland a difficult test case for my argument. By the time the restrictions on private economic activity were lifted in 1989, the cultural differences among migrants of different regions, as well between migrants and the native population, had diminished. Furthermore, as shown in Chapter 5, the communist government was particularly successful in quashing private economic activity in the resettled territories. The resettled territories thus entered the market economy with higher levels of state ownership and greater dependence on the government than other parts of Poland.

At the same time, the sudden shift in 1989 from extractive to inclusive economic institutions – within the same country – enables me to examine the scope conditions of my argument. I am able to compare the economic performance of the *same* communities in different institutional settings, just before and after the transition to a market economy.

To this end, I use a novel dataset based on a range of archival sources, including the unpublished 1948 population census conducted in the newly acquired territories preserved in the Polish Archive of Modern Records. I also collected data from the 1939 German census at the commune (*Gemeinde*) level shedding light on the premigration occupational structure as well as farm sizes. I digitized historical maps on railway lines and municipal borders. I link these historical indicators to the statistics compiled by the Central Statistical Office of Poland on economic outcomes for the 1980s and 1990s.

Because the composition of the migrant population was a product of exogenous factors (see Chapter 2), this new dataset enables me to isolate the economic effects of migrant diversity in the 1940s from prior levels of economic development and other confounders. My quantitative analysis shows that the economic benefits of diversity are contingent on the nature of formal institutions. During the communist period, municipalities settled by migrants from different regions of origin had slightly lower levels of wealth than their more homogeneous counterparts, but they were otherwise economically similar. However, municipalities with greater diversity did achieve superior outcomes after the country's transition to a market economy; in particular, incomes and entrepreneurship rates were higher in 1995–2000 in places settled by a more heterogeneous migrant population than in places characterized by a more homogeneous population.

Importantly, these results are based on the analysis *within* former German provinces; that is, they cannot be explained either by the legacies of German rule or by the differences in communist policy toward the resettled territories. I further show that my findings are driven neither by the presence of migrants from a particular region nor by sorting after the initial migrant allocation.

I proceed by tracing changes in the macro institutional environment of post-WWII Poland. I show that while it was possible to pursue private economic activity in select sectors of the economy, the communist government imposed numerous restrictions on the private sector and taxed it at higher rates than state-owned enterprises. Small-scale private businesses were able to function, in part, thanks to their use of informal networks to obtain raw materials, capital, and protection. Formal legal institutions became truly inclusive only after 1989, when the remaining administrative barriers to private entrepreneurship were removed, and preferential treatment of state enterprises ended.

I use this overview of the institutional environment to derive expectations regarding the effects of cultural heterogeneity in migrant communities on private economic activity, both before and after the transition to a market economy. In the second part of the chapter, I introduce the dataset I use to test these expectations, explain my empirical strategy and measurement, and present my findings.

## FROM STATE SOCIALISM TO A FREE MARKET ECONOMY

Institutional constraints on private economic activity in Poland changed significantly over time. During the communist period, the state owned the key branches of industry, services, and trade, while private ownership prevailed in agriculture, retail, crafts, and services, particularly after 1956. Successful private entrepreneurship depended on strong informal norms and connections to the nomenklatura rather than on formal state institutions, which were extractive and favored the state sector. Furthermore, the government placed many restrictions on the types of activity that businesses could legally engage in. State policy reduced incentives to accumulate capital, innovate, and grow, pushing economic activity underground. In the 1980s, restrictions on private initiative were gradually removed, and, in 1990, the Balcerowicz Plan ushered in fundamental economic restructuring. Economic liberalization increased potential gains from entrepreneurial activity and reduced the role of informal networks in solving supply and enforcement problems. This contributed to a boom in new business activity.

### Reversal of State Policy toward Private Industry in 1946–1956

In January 1946, when the Polish Workers Party (PPR) was still establishing itself, the government promulgated two decrees with contradictory implications for entrepreneurs and the private sector. The first was a decree on the nationalization of key sectors of the economy, which transferred to the state all industrial, mining, transportation, insurance, commercial, and banking enterprises owned by Germans and by declared traitors of the Polish nation. The nationalization proceedings were a formality, because these entities had already been in state hands since the end of the war (see Chapter 5). However, the nationalization decree did not extend to craftsmanship and trade, which were covered by a separate decree on the establishment of new enterprises and of support for private initiative in industry and commerce.

The government thus signaled its commitment to a mixed economy, whereby private ownership would continue to coexist side-by-side with state and cooperative ownership.[1] The state would control industry, banking, foreign trade, and transportation, while small-scale industry, domestic trade, agriculture, and craftsmanship remained in private hands. In 1947, the contribution of different ownership forms to the national income was distributed as follows: The state-owned sector accounted for 49.6 percent, local ownership for 2.2 percent, cooperatives for 4.3 percent, and the private sector for 43.9 percent (Kaliński 2019, 37). The PPR justified this mixed-ownership system as the "Polish Road to Socialism," contrasting it to the fully nationalized Soviet economy.

As soon as the PPR achieved a monopoly on power, it began to marginalize private ownership. During the so-called Battle for Trade (*Bitwa o Handel*), launched in April 1947, the party cracked down on private retail with exorbitant taxes, administrative controls, and licensing restrictions. Private wholesale trade collapsed, and by 1950, 76 percent of private retail outlets would close. This policy not only hurt the commodity trade but also left many small towns and settlements without access to supplies and agricultural produce. The functions of private shops were taken over by a mix of socialized retail outlets and the black market (Kaliński 2015, 184).

Despite the assurances made in the 1946 decree, the government also moved to undermine private industry and craftsmanship. The average tax burden on the individuals working in these sectors doubled, and mandatory savings were introduced. Production volume and product assortment were regulated. Between 1947 and 1949, the number of private enterprises and workshops fell by 53 percent, from approximately 19,100 to 9,000 (Kaliński 2015, 184).

In 1949, the Six-Year Plan introduced Soviet-style centralized planning and prioritized large-scale industrial production at the expense of light industries and crafts. The resulting shortages of raw materials and equipment, combined with high taxes, further raised the costs of running a private business. Many private craftsmen and traders were pressured into joining cooperatives. By 1955, the share of private retail trade had plummeted to just 2.7 percent of total production and turnover (Przybyla 1958, 316). Private handicrafts and industries (*zakłady rzemiosła prywatnego*) survived, but their number decreased further, from 118,470 in 1949 to 89,627 in 1955. The remaining workshops employed just one to three persons and specialized in producing small quantities of products for local consumption (Kaliński 2015, 184).

In addition to these restrictions on private business, the government manipulated wages, prices, and taxes to achieve centrally mandated economic targets (Los 1990, 28). A new crime emerged, that of profiteering or speculation, defined as buying or selling a good with the purpose of reselling at a higher price, by a person not authorized to conduct such business.

---

[1] At the same time, large landowners were expropriated and their land was redistributed.

## Liberalization of Economic Policy after October 1956

Restrictions on private economic activity were partially reversed after worker protests in Poznań in October 1956. From then on, the "socialist" economic model was gradually modified with market elements. Private sector activity expanded, but the number of registered private enterprises continued to fluctuate, as craftsmen and merchants transitioned in and out of the shadow economy in response to state policy (Kochanowski 2010, 171). Furthermore, not all new enterprises produced products and services. Some were predominantly speculative in nature – they were set up for brief periods to take advantage of the three-year period of tax relief granted to new enterprises and were later reestablished in another area (Chmielewski, Kamiński, and Strazalkowski 1990, 304).

Constraints on private economic activity continued to loosen with each successive crisis. By the late 1970s, hoping to attract foreign currency, the government allowed the establishment of the so-called Polonia firms (*firmy polonijne*), or enterprises with the involvement of foreign capital and Polish employees. The Polonia firms enjoyed foreign exchange and tax privileges and could determine their own prices. They were typically established by Poles who managed to persuade their relatives abroad to create semi-fictitious foreign entities with representation in Poland. The number of Polonia firms rose from just a few dozen in 1981 to some 700 firms with over 100,000 employees at the end of the 1980s (Bałtowski and Żminda 2005, 57).

In 1981, Resolution No. 112 of the Council of Ministers established equal treatment of private handicraft workshops and other small-scale private industries vis-à-vis socialized industry (Los 1990, 29). Restrictions on the sale of agricultural goods to state companies by private producers were lifted and, in 1983, the legislature passed a constitutional amendment recognizing farmers' rights to land (Los 1990, 30). In response to these incremental institutional changes, the number of registered private economic entities increased by over 50 percent between 1981 and 1988, reaching a total of 572,448. Most of these early private enterprises were involved in the production and sale of handicrafts and services as well as in small-scale trade, the two sectors outside agriculture where private initiative had been tolerated during state socialism.

Still, the legal environment left much to be desired. Janos Kornai (1990, 136) argues that "half-hearted reform caused [...] difficulties due to the absence of legal institutions for the consistent protection of private property and the enforcement of private contracts." In this environment, the reliance on state enforcement carried few advantages, because the legal protections afforded to private property remained inadequate. Informal norms and networks, on the other hand, facilitated access to scarce goods and increased opportunities for economic exchange. Even registered private businesses had to rely on informal connections to obtain tools and supplies (Kochanowski 2010, 185).

The incidence of recorded speculation offenses rose in tandem with the growth of the private sector. At first, the anti-speculation committees mainly dealt with illegal trade in food and alcohol. Over time, the range of goods sold on the black market expanded to include cars, gasoline, refrigerators, pianos, and even "credits for young couples and vouchers facilitating purchases for veterans." Speculation was particularly common in small towns, where "informal networks, mainly within family and social circles, limited or even prevented proper [state] control and repressive actions" (Kochanowski 2010, 235–236). About half of the convicted speculators worked in state-owned enterprises, while the other half consisted of "petty traders, retirees, and elderly women" (Kochanowski 2010, 248). Thus, legal and illegal private economic activity were inextricably linked during the period of state socialism.

### Transition to a Market Economy

Formal institutions continued to evolve, with the most important changes occurring between 1988 and 1990. In January 1989, the Act on Economic Activity, popularly called Wilczek's bill, came into force. The Act declared that "economic activity was free and permitted to everyone on an equal basis," thus removing all remaining barriers to private entrepreneurship and establishing equal treatment of private and state-owned enterprises under the law. Still, entrepreneurs' access to foreign markets remained restricted by the concession system and currency regulation; the state retained a monopoly on the distribution of many scarce goods and raw materials, and it continued to control prices in some sectors (Bałtowski and Żminda 2005).

This situation improved in 1990 with the passing of the so-called shock therapy economic reforms. Under the Balcerowicz Plan, named after Finance Minister Leszek Balcerowicz, price controls were abolished, banking and financing sectors were restructured, state-owned businesses no longer enjoyed fiscal privileges, and insolvent firms were liquidated or reorganized. The reforms were designed to stabilize the economy and create an environment that would be more business-friendly. They removed the remaining obstacles to private entrepreneurship and contributed to the explosive growth of new companies.

The economic and political reforms did not generate a void in formal enforcement. While the "party" element of the party-state disappeared, state capacity increased due to a series of administrative reforms and an overhaul of the tax system. Under state socialism, taxation was largely indirect, and the state extracted large revenues from industrial enterprises it owned or controlled. By the late 1980s, as the system unraveled, state enterprises stopped making payments into the state budget. During the transition to a market economy, the state was forced to contend with outstanding debt and a rising fiscal deficit. This deficit was addressed by the introduction of personal and corporate income tax in 1992. In that year, the government collected just ten million tax returns from a workforce of sixteen million. By 1996, sixteen million were received, suggesting that over 90 percent of the workforce began contributing to the state's coffers (Easter 2010). Tax collection depended largely on taxpayers' compliance, which was itself secured in part through the continual provision of public goods and services (Easter 2002). Maintaining sufficient tax revenue, in turn, enabled the government to expand its administrative capacity and to strengthen the institutions for the protection of private property and the enforcement of contracts. Between 1990 and 1995, the number of state administration employees increased by 88 percent, from 75,229 to 141,494. The size of the local government rose by 66 percent, from 83,583 to 139,295, during the same period (Ekiert 2003, 310).

The Law on Local Self-Government passed in March 1990 constituted a watershed intervention for improving state capacity at the local level. It gave Poland's 2,380 municipalities greater authority and responsibility. From then on, local bureaucrats were accountable exclusively to elected local councils, and they were paid out of municipal budgets. Municipalities were now authorized to collect and spend their own fiscal revenues from immovable property, agricultural income, and vehicles, within caps that were set at the national level.[2] They became responsible for financing the maintenance and improvement of local infrastructure, primary education, healthcare, and social assistance.

The increased fiscal autonomy and responsibilities of municipal governments widened subnational differences in the degree and quality of governance. Some municipalities negotiated numerous tax exemptions and special deals, yielding to local interests, while others set high tax rates and increased spending on key public goods, supporting private economic activity (Swianiewicz 1996). The ability to pay bureaucrats affected the privatization of communal property, the distribution of social benefits, and the process of licensing new businesses and regulating private economic activity more broadly. Localities with the highest levels of fiscal and bureaucratic capacity also promoted entrepreneurship by funding business incubator programs, guaranteeing start-up loans, and offering training programs for the unemployed (Misiag 2000).

The Law on Local Self-Government also transferred the rights to local commercial properties from the central government to the municipalities, enabling the latter to lease real estate to private businesses. In 1990–91 alone, some 33,800 municipal properties were leased to private businessmen, and another 1,000 were sold (Bałtowski and Żminda 2005, 61). In this manner, properties that were previously part of the socialized economy became the basis

---

[2] Municipal revenues also included shares of personal and corporate income tax, which was collected by the central government at rates constant across Poland.

for private entrepreneurship, before the formal privatization of state-owned enterprises occurred.

In October 1991, the parliament passed the State Agricultural Property Management Act, which provided for the privatization and dissolution of state agricultural enterprises (PGRs). The majority of state farms were dissolved and dismantled between 1992 and 1994. However, the privatization of state-owned enterprises did not follow, as the government feared a potential spike in unemployment.

The fundamental changes in the quality and quantity of state enforcement in the early 1990s led to the rapid growth of the private sector. Between 1989 and 1994, the share of the private sector in total employment increased from 12 percent to 61 percent. By the mid-1990s, Poland achieved the highest growth in Europe, at 5 percent in 1995 and 7 percent in 1996.

GUS data indicate that between 1990 and 1994, there were about 1.9 million private enterprises employing up to 5 employees, and 56,948 enterprises with more than 5 employees. Among the latter, 5 percent of companies had been established with foreign capital (Bałtowski and Żminda 2005). Thus, the majority of private sector firms were small in size, employing one to two people on average. They were created from scratch rather than from the privatization of state enterprises. Many of the new companies sold imported goods and borrowed Western marketing strategies (Johnson and Loveman 1995). These businesses were concentrated in construction, trade, and services, though there were also some manufacturing companies that produced textiles, wood, leather, printing, food, and beverages. They supplied products and services that had not been available during the shortage economy of state socialism.

Private businesses that emerged in the 1980s continued to exist alongside these new firms, though they sometimes experienced challenges in trying to adjust to the new rules of the game. Many "Polonia firms," for example, lost their advantages following the introduction of internal convertibility of the Polish złoty and the entry of international corporations, and disappeared from the scene.

Private entrepreneurship increased economic growth in the long run by creating new jobs and generating wealth for entrepreneurs as well as their employees. As businesses grew, they generated more tax revenue for local governments, which could be funneled back into the provision of public goods and services.

While private businessmen were the clear winners of the transition, the majority of state employees and agricultural workers were not. In 1990/1991, the gross national product decreased by 18 percent. Real wages fell, and economic inequality increased. The collapse of unprofitable industrial plants increased unemployment rates. The liquidation of PGRs not only left thousands without jobs but also precipitated the collapse of local infrastructure, including canteens, nurseries, hospitals, and schools. The so-called agro-towns surrounding PGRs became "hotbeds of accumulated problems" (Błąd 2022, 46–47). In 1989–91, Poland witnessed 1,455 strikes and 912 collective protest actions (Kubik 1994).

## UNDERSTANDING THE REVERSAL OF FORTUNES IN WESTERN AND NORTHERN POLAND

As noted in Chapter 5, the Communist regime left the biggest imprint on the economy in the resettled territories. Although in the prewar period the region was known for its small industry, crafts, and services, by the end of the Stalinist era, in 1955, the output of private industry per capita in the resettled territories amounted to just one-third of that registered in other parts of Poland. Anzelm (1970, 199–200) estimates that in Poland as a whole, between 1948 and 1954, the number of private handicraft workshops declined by 51 percent and the number of their employees by 65 percent. In the resettled voivodeships, the number of workshops dropped by 74 percent and the number of their employees by 83 percent.[3] Only agriculture remained predominantly in private hands. However, even private farmers were not fully independent, because the prices at which they could sell their products were set by the government.

Gubin, a historic county in Lower Lusatia, was a poignant example of this decline in private industry. In the summer of 1945, Polish migrants there identified seventy-seven agricultural and industrial facilities, many of which had been damaged by war and looting. Only twelve mills, two brickworks, and two distilleries, or 22 percent of the total facilities, were successfully repaired and put into operation under private managers between 1945 and 1947. By 1949, in turn, every single facility in Gubin had either been taken over by a cooperative, nationalized, or simply shut down (Kurowska 2022).

Restrictions on private economic activity loosened after October 1956, when the number of workshops rebounded and eventually overtook prewar levels. Figure 7.1, reproduced based on data in Muszkiewicz (2020, 25, 92), plots the number of crafts workshops (*zakłady rzemieślnicze*) and employment in crafts industries (*rzemiosło*) in Lower Silesia, located in the resettled territories, and in the country as a whole. It shows that private industry in the resettled territories experienced both a greater decline during the Stalinist period and a stronger resurgence in the 1980s, relative to other regions.

The patterns are similar when we look at the growth of employment in the private nonagricultural sector at the voivodeship level (see Map 7.1). In 1970, a lower share of the population in the resettled voivodeships was employed in the private nonagricultural sector compared with the rest of Poland, as measured by the number of private handicraft enterprises per 1,000 people (*zakłady rzemiosła prywatnego*). By 1990, however, subnational patterns of

---

[3] This estimate is based on data from three voivodeships (*województwa*): Olstynskie, Szczecińskie, and Wrocławskie.

Increase in the number of workshops over time

Increase in employment in craftsmanship over time (including students)

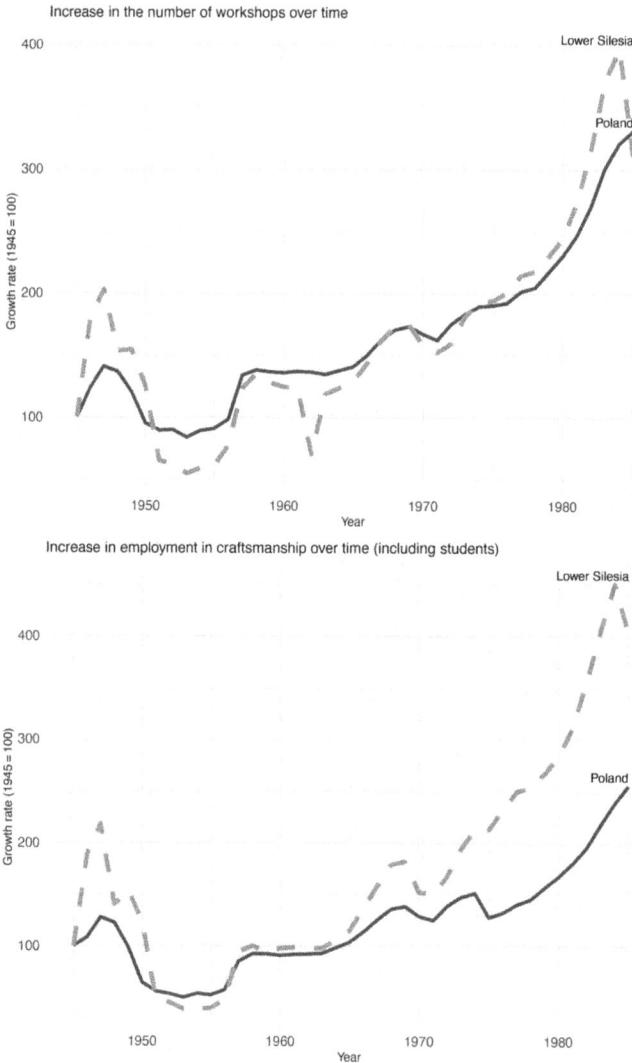

FIGURE 7.1 Craft workshops and employment in craft industries over time. Source: Muszkiewicz (2020, 25, 92).

private economic activity had changed considerably. The resettled voivodeships were now bustling with private initiative, despite their delayed start.

What explains these differences in private economic activity between the resettled territories and other parts of Poland? As I contend below, postwar migration and resulting cultural heterogeneity played an important part. But first, it is important to address economic fundamentals.

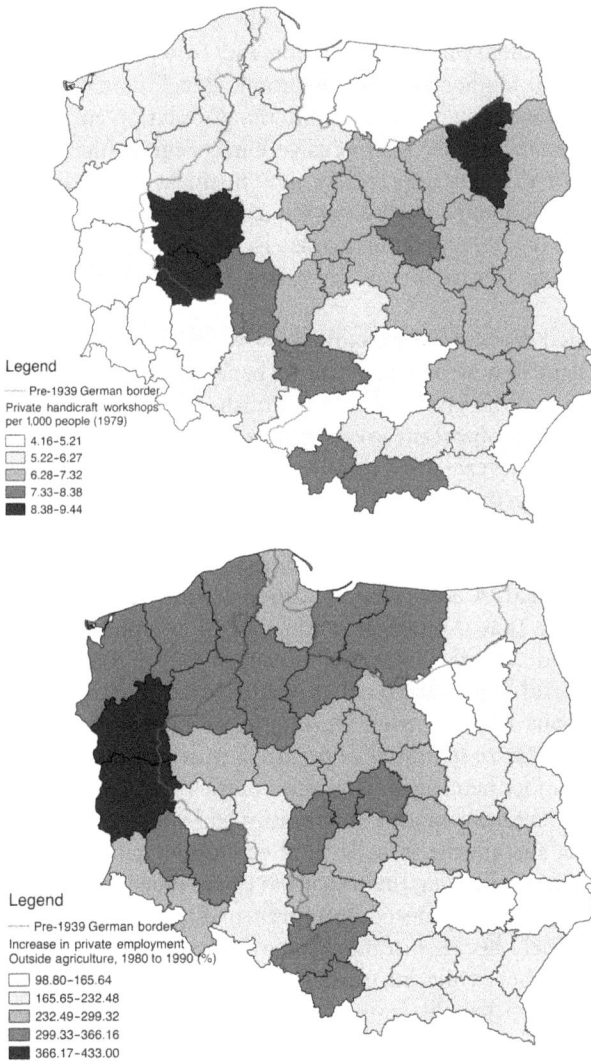

Map 7.1  Private employment outside agriculture in Polish voivodeships. The top map depicts the prevalence of workshops in 1979. The bottom map depicts the change in private employment outside agriculture from 1980 to 1990. Polygon boundaries were shared by Thomasz Zarycki.

The territory that Poland acquired from Germany was both more urbanized and had better infrastructure than other Polish regions. Services, trade, and small-scale industry had dominated in this region before the war. In 1939, 32 percent of the population in the soon-to-be annexed German provinces was employed in industry and construction, and 39.8 percent of the population worked in services. By contrast, in 1930s Poland, only 19.2 percent of the population was employed in industry and construction and 19.9 percent in services (Muszkiewicz 2020, 59). Higher levels of economic development in the resettled territories likely persisted over time, despite the population turnover. Indeed, the location of German knowledge-intensive entrepreneurship in the 1920s is a good predictor of the average rates of new business formation in contemporary Poland (Fritsch, Pylak, and Wyrwich 2021). Thus, the rapid growth of private firms in the resettled territories is, to some extent, the product of superior economic infrastructure persisting from the pre-WWII period.

Furthermore, the resettled territories' proximity to western markets and German heritage placed them in a strong position to benefit from the transition to the market economy and the improvement in Polish–German relations. After 1989, Germany became an important source of foreign direct investment, with German firms establishing several joint ventures with Polish counterparts.

It is important to keep these economic fundamentals in mind when comparing the growth of new businesses between the resettled territories and other parts of Poland. The remainder of this chapter examines more closely the second explanation for the reversal in economic conditions, namely, the effects of postwar migration. I argue that the different trajectories exhibited by the resettled territories before and after the country's transition to a market economy owe in part to the cultural heterogeneity that resulted from the inflow of migrants from different regions and countries. During the years of state socialism, when the government sought to marginalize private businesses, the greater reach of the state within the more heterogeneous communities was detrimental to private economic activity. Heterogeneous communities had weaker informal ties and as a result could not sustain the same level of economic activity.

The role of the state changed following the transition to the market. Starting in the late 1980s, the government promoted entrepreneurship and protected private property rights. Precisely because in more heterogeneous communities state capacity was already higher while informal institutions were less effective, such communities stood to benefit from the transition from extractive to inclusive formal institutions to a greater extent than more homogeneous communities. Economic actors in heterogeneous communities could now take advantage of institutional changes to engage in market transactions and register new firms.

Higher state capacity in more heterogeneous communities enabled them to finance a greater range of services necessary to support private economic activity. For example, in the town of Bartoszyce, home to a more heterogeneous community, the municipal government created the Department for the Promotion and Social Affairs, which centralized information about all registered businesses and offered training to the unemployed (Gorzelak and Jałowiecki 1996). In the town of Dzierzgoń, another more heterogeneous community, the government established the Society for the Development of Dzierzgoń to offer legal and economic advice to those interested in starting new firms, along with the Mutual Guarantee Fund to help small- and medium-sized enterprises overcome capital barriers (Gorzelak and Jałowiecki 1999).

Furthermore, the advantages of cultural heterogeneity, such as skill complementarity, are more likely to manifest under inclusive institutions, which protect private property and allow all citizens to exercise their skills and knowledge in a work environment, as argued in the introduction. Under state socialism, much of citizens' ingenuity was directed toward nonproductive economic activities, such as hiding profits, negotiating supply shortages, and bribing the right officials. Because there were caps on the profitability of private businesses and the risk of expropriation remained high, there was little incentive to innovate and grow. Self-employment was often a way to survive in the shortage economy and make ends meet. The situation changed with the transition to the market, when property rights became more secure and potential gains from running a successful business increased. Both channels – higher state capacity and complementary skills – would increase private entrepreneurship and incomes in more heterogeneous communities under a market economy.

The implications of the argument are particularly relevant for subnational variation within the resettled territories. Before 1989, I expect entrepreneurship and incomes to be lower in more heterogeneous migrant communities, which, in contrast to more homogeneous migrant communities, lacked strong norms and networks that could provide an alternative to state enforcement and facilitate economic exchange. It is also possible that there may not be any observable differences in the economies of homogeneous and heterogeneous communities, given the restrictions on most forms of private economic activity at this time. After 1989 and the switch to a market economy, I expect entrepreneurship and incomes to be higher in historically more heterogeneous migrant communities. I also expect to see higher fiscal capacity in more heterogeneous communities in the 1990s, once the decentralization reforms had taken place.

EMPIRICAL APPROACH AND MEASUREMENT

In order to compare economic outcomes in homogeneous and heterogeneous resettled communities, I compiled an original dataset on migrant history and economic performance in Poland's resettled territories at the level of municipalities. This is the smallest unit for which both historical and contemporary data are available. Municipalities are small enough to ensure that migrants from one region will interact with migrants from a different region at high levels of migrant diversity. Furthermore, contemporary municipalities are self-contained social units with legislative and governing bodies and are therefore appropriate for studying the effects of diversity on social and economic outcomes.

One challenge of conducting the analysis at the municipal level is that municipal boundaries have changed considerably since 1939. To account for these changes, I digitized historical maps of administrative borders and aggregated historical communal (1939) and municipal (1948) data for 630 contemporary municipalities, which are larger than historical units. In cases where contemporary municipal borders split historical municipalities, I weighted the historical data by the proportion of the overlapping area.[4] This approach produces a dataset that spans over sixty years and can be used to understand the effects of migrant composition on economic development in the short and long run.

## Measuring Economic Outcomes before and after 1989

Comparing the effects of migration and diversity before and after the market transition presents a challenge due to the distinct forms that private economic activity assumed during these two periods.

Quantifying the extent of entrepreneurship before 1989 is particularly challenging due to the prevalence of the shadow economy. Many private businesses operated informally and the state restricted the number, size, and type of firms that could be established. Ideally, one would measure the size of the shadow economy alongside registered private firms, yet informal transactions are not directly observable and existing approaches to measuring their volume cannot be replicated at the micro level. Instead, I measure the rates of legal private economic activity using data on (1) the population engaged in *Socialized Economy*, regardless of occupation, and in (2) *Private Handicrafts* as well as (3) the number of *Shops* per 1,000 people in 1980-82 (earliest available).[5] Even such legal forms of economic activity typically depended on informal connections (Kochanowski 2010). I also use the number of (4) *TV-sets* and (5) *Phones* per 1,000 people for the same period as an indicator of wealth. TVs, in particular, were luxury items that were accurately counted by the state because the state was the sole provider of programming. All of these measures are indirect, and employment in the private sector is likely measured with error. I expect to see a positive relationship between *Migrant Diversity* and employment in the socialized economy and a negative relationship between *Migrant Diversity* and the remaining four indicators.

Assessing the economic impact of migrant diversity is more straightforward following the transition to a market economy. To measure private economic activity in this period, I use data on *Private Enterprises* (per 1,000 people) and per capita *Personal Income Tax* in złoty (zł.). The earliest measures are available from 1993 and 1995, respectively. Personal income tax has the same rate

---

[4] The number of municipalities used in the analysis is slightly lower because of incomplete data, and it varies over time due to administrative changes.

[5] Only some shops were privately owned.

TABLE 7.1 *Measurement of key outcomes and hypothesized effects of migrant diversity.*

| Measures of economic activity | Hypothesized effect |
|---|---|
| *Extractive state institutions (1980s)* | |
| Shops | − |
| Phones | − |
| TVs | − |
| Employment in socialized economy | + |
| Employment in private handicrafts | − |
| *Inclusive state institutions (1990s)* | |
| Personal incomes | + |
| Entrepreneurship rates | + |

across all municipalities and closely tracks incomes.[6] It is generally collected by employers, which lowers but does not eliminate concerns about measurement error due to variation in tax compliance. I expect a positive relationship between historical levels of migrant heterogeneity and post-1989 economic outcomes. The indicators and hypothesized effects of migrant diversity are summarized in Table 7.1.

## Measuring Diversity

Information about the origins of migrants and the distribution of the autochthonous population comes from an unpublished survey conducted in December 1948, when the population transfers were largely complete. The data span all 1,217 historic municipalities (*gminy*) in the resettled territories, and is contained in the Polish Archive of Modern Records (*Archiwum Akt Nowych*).

The census recorded the sizes of four distinct population groups: repatriates from the USSR, settlers from central Poland (understood to encompass all migrants from within post-1945 Polish borders), reemigrants from abroad, and the autochthonous population. These categories do not encompass all cultural cleavages and, accordingly, they underestimate the heterogeneity on the ground. Fortunately, measurement error in this case biases against finding significant differences in economic outcomes across homogeneous and heterogeneous communities.[7]

---

[6] One exception is the tax on agricultural activity, excluded from this indicator.

[7] For example, reemigrants from abroad were a diverse group originating in several states including France, Germany, and Yugoslavia. The repatriates from rural Galicia (Ukrainian SSR)

I decompose diversity into (1) the diversity of the migrant population and (2) the share of migrants, following Alesina, Harnoss, and Rapoport (2016). The first component, $Div_{mig}$, measures the diversity of migrant groups in each municipality. If $s_j$ is the share of migrants from region $j$ from the total population of migrants, with $j = 1, \ldots J$, then migrant diversity can be expressed as $Div_{mig} = \sum_{j=1}^{J} [s_j * (1 - s_j)]$. This expression does not depend on the share of the autochthonous population. The values of migrant diversity are a product of factors largely unrelated to migrants' preferences or local economic conditions, as discussed in Chapter 2 and verified formally in the next section.

The second component, $Div_{resettled}$, measures the share of migrants in the total population. This variable captures the extent of uprooting and thus also the presence of the native population that had lived under German institutions and differed from Polish migrants in multiple respects (rootedness, language, informal norms, experience with Polish institutions, and ability to emigrate). In 82 percent of the local communities, the share of migrants exceeded 80 percent, that is, most of the settlements in the annexed region experienced a nearly complete turnover of the population. The autochthonous population was concentrated in two regions, Upper Silesia and East Prussia, where national identities were historically ambiguous. After the war, the Polish government allowed the autochthonous population in these regions to stay and apply for Polish citizenship. In other words, unlike $Div_{mig}$, $Div_{resettled}$ is the product of historic nation-building processes as well as postwar incentives to declare Polish nationality.

## Empirical Strategy

To estimate the impact of migrant presence and heterogeneity on economic outcomes, we first need to understand why some communities wound up more heterogeneous than others. If more economically developed German communities received more migrants or more diverse migrant populations, the effect of migrant diversity would be confounded by preexisting economic conditions.

As discussed in more detail in Chapter 2, most migrants could not select into specific destinations, and a great many were uprooted against their will. Both forced and voluntary migrants were assigned to specific settlements based on the availability of housing at the time of their arrival at PUR distribution points. Migrants who arrived earlier were more likely to settle together with their communities than migrants who arrived later in the resettlement process, by which time housing was scarcer. The time of arrival, in turn, varied based on registration procedures in places of origin, access to transportation, and the unpredictable duration of the journey.

included both Catholic and Greek Orthodox populations and had few cultural similarities with repatriates from the more urbanized Lithuanian SSR. The settlers from central Poland arrived from all three former imperial partitions.

Nonetheless, historical accounts point to patterns that can be confirmed in the data (see Table 7.2). First, migration proceeded from east to west and places closest to the post-1945 German border were the last to be repopulated. For security reasons, military families were encouraged to settle in the border regions, while migrants of certain origins (Ukrainians and Lemkos) were prohibited from settling near the borders. I calculated the distance to the international border, in kilometers (km), from the centroid of each municipality, to account for these relationships. Indeed, distance to the post-1945 Polish–German border is negatively correlated with *Migrant diversity* and explains 11 percent of the variance in this variable.

Second, localities near the railway lines were easier to reach for migrants from any point of origin and were settled sooner than less accessible destinations. Proximity to the railway also facilitated state control and economic development, so it is important to control for this variable in regression analysis. Thus, I control for distance to the nearest railway station, measured in 1948, which explains 9 percent of the variance in *Migrant diversity*.

Third, the Polish government was particularly keen to resume coal mining, shipbuilding, and machine building in the resettled territories. To this end, it sought to attract migrants from industrial areas within Poland and abroad and also to temporarily retain skilled Germans. To account for the role of preexisting levels of development, I collected data on the size of industrial employment (*Share in industry*) from the 1939 German census as a proxy for industrial potential.[8] The share of industrial employment to population in 1939 explains 12 percent of the variance in *Migrant diversity* and 4 percent of the variance in *Migrant share*.

In rural areas, the resettlement process was influenced by the presence of large German estates. Wealthy German landowners were expelled and their properties were divided up or transformed into state-owned farms in the early 1950s.[9] Thus, the share of migrants is positively correlated with the presence of farms over 100 ha. State farms attracted primarily landless migrants from central Poland and, in addition to employment, provided important social services during the communist period. After 1989, the closure of state farms increased unemployment rates. It is therefore important to include this covariate when studying the impact of migrant composition on private economic activity.

Building on this discussion, I use the following model to estimate the effect of migrant heterogeneity on economic outcomes:

$$Y_{ij} = \beta_0 + \beta_1 \, Div_{mig_{ij}} + \beta_2 \, Div_{resettled_{ij}} + X'_{ij}\beta + d_j + \epsilon_{ij}, \qquad (7.1)$$

where $Y_{ij}$ is the outcome in municipality $i$ and German province $j$, $Div_{mig}$ and $Div_{resettled}$ are the two components of diversity discussed earlier, $X'_{ij}$ is a set

---

[8] Data from the immediate postwar period are less reliable: Many factories were damaged and did not operate until the 1950s.

[9] This affected most farms above 50 ha, but only data on the share of farms above 100 ha are available from the 1939 census.

TABLE 7.2 *Correlations between the share and diversity of migrants and characteristics of receiving municipalities.*

|  | Migrant diversity | | Migrant share | |
|---|---|---|---|---|
|  | Correlation | $R^2$ | Correlation | $R^2$ |
| Migrant diversity (1948) | – | – | −0.009 | 0.000 |
| Share urban (1948) | 0.077 | 0.006 | 0.119 | 0.014 |
| Share in industry (1939) | 0.340 | 0.115 | −0.189 | 0.036 |
| Share farms over 100 ha (1939) | −0.076 | 0.006 | 0.267 | 0.071 |
| Ln population (1948) | 0.136 | 0.018 | −0.185 | 0.034 |
| Distance to county seat (1950) | −0.117 | 0.014 | 0.001 | 0.000 |
| Distance to railway (1948) | −0.293 | 0.086 | 0.029 | 0.001 |
| Distance to German border | −0.332 | 0.110 | 0.050 | 0.002 |

*Note:* Analysis is at the level of contemporary municipalities.

of municipality-level covariates, $d_j$ is a vector of province-level fixed effects, and $\varepsilon_{ij}$ are errors. The intuition is that the assignment was as-if random, conditional on covariates discussed earlier, and thus the estimated coefficient on *Migrant diversity* can be interpreted causally. I also consider the association between *Migrant share* and economic outcomes. Because the size of the migrant population depended on the size of the "verified" autochthonous population, which was not randomly distributed across space, the coefficient on *Migrant share* cannot be interpreted causally. Nonetheless, as shown in Table 7.2, the share of the autochthonous population is only weakly correlated with most socioeconomic indicators.

In addition to the variables that are known to have influenced migrant allocation and are discussed above, $X'_{ij}$ includes access to state public goods provision proxied by the distance (in km) between the center of each municipality and the county seat, which hosted the state police and fire brigade, hospitals, and courts (*Distance to county seat*).[10] Two additional covariates are population size and the share of the urban population. To address divergent historical patterns of development within Germany, I include dummies for German provinces (Silesia, East Prussia, Brandenburg, and Pomerania) as well as a dummy for Gdańsk and surrounding municipalities.[11] To account for spatial autocorrelation, I estimate Conley standard errors within a 100-km radius, in addition to heteroskedasticity-robust standard errors.[12]

Sources and descriptive statistics for all historic and contemporary variables used in the analyses are presented in Table A.13.

[10] I use county centers in existence from 1950 to 1975, though most county seats from 1945 to 1949 are the same as the post-1950 county seats.
[11] These areas belonged to West Prussia before 1918 and became part of the Free City of Danzig in the interwar period.
[12] The results are robust to choosing alternative distance cutoff for Conley standard errors.

## DIVERSITY AND ECONOMIC OUTCOMES BEFORE 1989

I expect that heterogeneity yielded few economic advantages and may even have hampered private entrepreneurship during state socialism. On the other hand, informal norms and networks, historically stronger in more homogeneous communities, created additional opportunities for economic exchange and provided access to scarce resources. Regressions in Table 7.3 explore the observable implications of this argument using data from the early 1980s, when private entrepreneurship was legal but market-supporting formal institutions remained inadequate. The estimates for the key variables of interest are plotted in Figure 7.2.

The coefficient on *Migrant diversity* is negative and marginally significant in Model 3, which regresses *Shops* on diversity and historic covariates. The estimate suggests that an increase in diversity by one standard deviation translates into a decrease in the number of shops by one-tenth of a standard deviation. *Migrant diversity* does not predict any other economic indicators. The analysis further indicates that the state sector was larger in communities that received more migrants and thus experienced greater population turnover after the war (Model 1), though there are no significant differences in the prevalence of private handicrafts (Model 2) or the number of shops (Model 3). Models 4 and

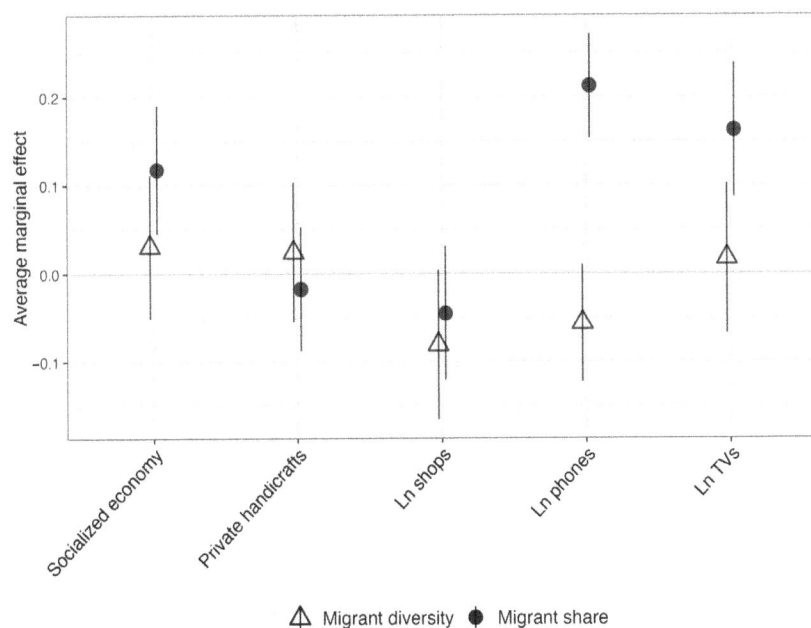

FIGURE 7.2 Share and diversity of migrants and economic outcomes during state socialism. The standardized coefficients are based on municipality-level analysis in Table 7.3.

TABLE 7.3 *Share and diversity of migrants and economic outcomes during state socialism.*

|  | Socialized economy | Private handicrafts | Ln shops | Ln phones | Ln TVs |
|---|---|---|---|---|---|
|  | (1) | (2) | (3) | (4) | (5) |
| Migrant | 28.39 | 1.28 | −0.14* | −0.23 | 0.02 |
| diversity | (36.19) | (2.18) | (0.08) | (0.15) | (0.06) |
|  | [32.46] | [2.51] | [0.08] | [0.18] | [0.05] |
| Migrant | 57.16*** | −0.48 | −0.04 | 0.46*** | 0.12** |
| share | (18.61) | (1.01) | (0.04) | (0.08) | (0.05) |
|  | [13.16] | [1.09] | [0.05] | [0.11] | [0.04] |
| Covariates | ✓ | ✓ | ✓ | ✓ | ✓ |
| Province fixed effects | ✓ | ✓ | ✓ | ✓ | ✓ |
| Adjusted $R^2$ | 0.33 | 0.33 | 0.24 | 0.55 | 0.27 |
| N | 602 | 602 | 601 | 599 | 601 |

*Note:* All models are OLS. All outcomes are measured in 1980–82 and divided by population (in thousands). Heteroskedasticity-robust standard errors in parentheses. Conley standard errors in brackets. Significant at *$p < 0.10$; **$p < 0.05$; ***$p < 0.01$.

5 suggest that communities that received more migrants in the 1940s were slightly wealthier, with more TVs and phones per 1,000 people.

The conclusions we draw about the economic implications of migration thus depend on which outcome we consider. The sign of the coefficients on both *Migrant diversity* and *Migrant share* changes from one model to another. It is safe to conclude from the regressions in Table 7.3 that although places with more migrants were better off on select indicators, heterogeneity produced no economic advantages during the communist period.

## DIVERSITY AND ECONOMIC OUTCOMES AFTER 1989

After 1989, formal institutions became more inclusive. Institutional transformation increased the security of private property rights, allowed for relatively free registration of private businesses, and created incentives for founding private firms. Unlike some other postcommunist countries, Poland did not experience a weakening of state institutions or political instability following its transition to a market economy. The combination of market reforms and political stability contributed to steady economic growth starting in 1992, at an average annual rate of 4.2 percent. I expect historical levels of heterogeneity to be beneficial for economic productivity in this institutional environment. In particular, I expect more heterogeneous migrant communities to register higher entrepreneurship rates and incomes than more homogeneous communities after 1989.

Table 7.4 evaluates these predictions using indicators for income levels and entrepreneurship rates for 1993–2000. As noted earlier, tax rates on personal incomes do not vary across municipalities, so the latter measure closely tracks municipal differences in individual earnings. All regressions include a full set of covariates and fixed effects for German provinces.

I plot estimates for key explanatory variables in Figure 7.3. Model 1 indicates that *Migrant diversity* does not predict *Personal income tax* in 1993, the earliest year for which data exist and a year after the tax was introduced. Income differences across resettled communities gradually widened over time, however. The coefficient on *Migrant diversity* is positive and reaches statistical significance in the other three models (Models 2–4). An increase in diversity by one standard deviation predicts an increase in personal income tax by nearly one-fourth of a standard deviation (approximately 5 zł) in 1995 and one-fifth of a standard deviation (approximately 10 zł) in 2000. This is a conservative estimate within historic German provinces. In 2000, the predicted differences in personal income tax collected from homogeneous and most heterogeneous communities reached nearly 50 zł. per 1.000 people. The coefficient on *Migrant share* is negative in regressions of personal income tax in 1993, 1995, 1998 and becomes positive in 2000. It is statistically significant only for the 1995 outcome.

Models 5–7 further show that *Migrant diversity* leads to higher rates of private entrepreneurship. Substantively, Model 5 implies that an increase in

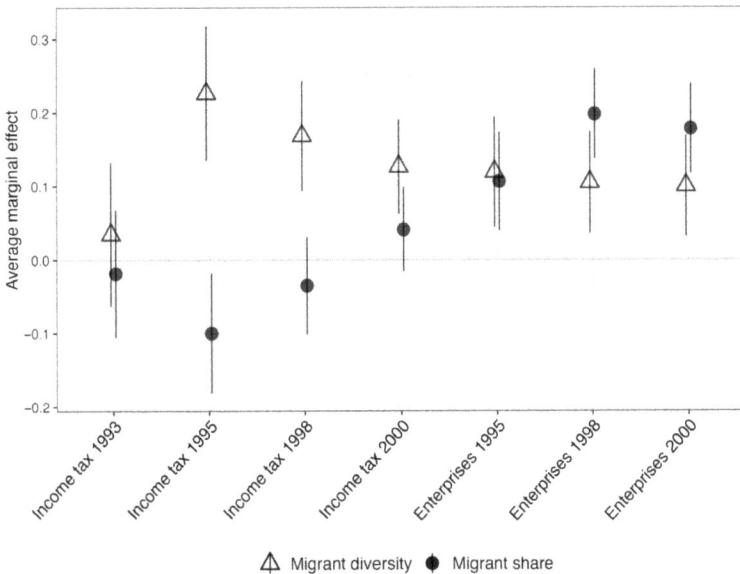

△ Migrant diversity ● Migrant share

FIGURE 7.3 Share and diversity of migrants and economic outcomes in a market economy. The standardized coefficients are based on municipality-level analysis in Table 7.4.

TABLE 7.4 *Share and diversity of migrants and economic outcomes in a market economy.*

| | Ln personal income tax | | | | Ln private enterprises | | |
|---|---|---|---|---|---|---|---|
| | 1993 | 1995 | 1998 | 2000 | 1995 | 1998 | 2000 |
| | (1) | (2) | (3) | (4) | (5) | (6) | (7) |
| Migrant diversity | 0.16 | 0.37*** | 0.36*** | 0.32*** | 0.43*** | 0.32** | 0.29** |
| | (0.20) | (0.08) | (0.08) | (0.08) | (0.16) | (0.13) | (0.12) |
| | [0.20] | [0.10] | [0.09] | [0.10] | [0.24] | [0.18] | [0.17] |
| Migrant share | −0.05 | −0.09** | −0.04 | 0.05 | 0.20*** | 0.32*** | 0.27*** |
| | (0.10) | (0.04) | (0.04) | (0.04) | (0.06) | (0.05) | (0.05) |
| | [0.10] | [0.08] | [0.07] | [0.05] | [0.11] | [0.11] | [0.10] |
| Covariates | ✓ | ✓ | ✓ | ✓ | ✓ | ✓ | ✓ |
| Province fixed effects | ✓ | ✓ | ✓ | ✓ | ✓ | ✓ | ✓ |
| Adjusted $R^2$ | 0.02 | 0.15 | 0.32 | 0.52 | 0.42 | 0.47 | 0.48 |
| N | 607 | 611 | 611 | 611 | 611 | 611 | 611 |

*Note:* All models are OLS. Personal income tax is measured per capita. Private enterprises are measured per 1,000 people. Heteroskedasticity-robust standard errors in parentheses. Conley standard errors in brackets. Significant at **$p < 0.05$; ***$p < 0.01$.

historical levels of heterogeneity from 0 (homogeneous) to 0.66 (most heterogeneous) translates into five additional private enterprises (per 1,000 people), equivalent to nearly a quarter of a standard deviation in this outcome variable ($\mu = 36.64$, $\sigma = 21.31$). These differences remain statistically significant and substantively meaningful over time. In 2000, the estimated effect of the same increase in migrant heterogeneity is eight enterprises per 1,000 people, on average. In the Appendix, I show that the coefficient on *Migrant diversity* nearly doubles in size when excluding cities, which have both high levels of migrant diversity and private entrepreneurship (see Table A.14). One possible interpretation is that migrant heterogeneity and resulting state capacity matter more in rural areas, where interactions with outgroups and the state are otherwise less frequent.

Entrepreneurship rates are also higher in municipalities with more migrants: The coefficient on *Migrant share* is positive and statistically significant in all models with enterprises as the outcome variable. In 1995, one standard deviation in the share of the migrant population, equivalent to 26 percent, predicts an increase in the number of enterprises by one-tenth of a standard deviation in this outcome. The estimated coefficient on *Migrant share* increases in magnitude for entrepreneurship measures in 1998 and 2000.

We thus see a reversal of fortune after the transition to more democratic, pro-market institutions. Communities that received more migrants and were more heterogeneous due to the patterns of migrant settlement after WWII outperformed communities that were more homogeneous and economically similar under state socialism. More than half a century after WWII, heterogeneity increased the levels of private entrepreneurship and incomes. Because the analysis is concentrated *within* the formerly German territories and conditions on pre-WWII economic characteristics, these findings cannot be explained by historical legacies of German rule or by the allocation of a more heterogeneous migrant population into more developed communities.

## COMPARING THE EFFECTS OF FORCED AND VOLUNTARY MIGRATION

So far, my analysis has focused on the heterogeneity of the migrant population. In this section, I consider whether places populated by a larger number of forced migrants are systematically different in entrepreneurship and income levels from places populated by voluntary migrants.

Forced migration is a traumatic experience marked by the loss of property and disruption of social networks, which could disincentivize entrepreneurial undertakings. Indeed, qualitative accounts suggest that forced migrants from Kresy were initially reluctant to invest in their new dwellings and instead mourned the loss of their native villages (Mach 1998).[13] Migrants from within post-1945 Poland chose to relocate voluntarily, often in the hope of acquiring German property. In contrast to Kresy repatriates, this population may have been more motivated to invest in their new acquisitions. Migrants from within Poland may have also benefited from preserving social ties in their places of origin, which could be leveraged for entrepreneurial activity later on. There is some evidence that personal ties can pay off economically in other contexts: Burchardi and Hassan (2013) show that the population of West Germany that lived in areas with strong ties to the East experienced a rise in personal incomes and entrepreneurial activity after the fall of the Berlin wall. To the extent that first-generation migrants transmit their economic behaviors to their children, we should see lower entrepreneurship rates and incomes after the transition to a market economy in municipalities where forced migrants are more numerous.

Another reason why the form of migration may matter for long-run economic outcomes is selection. Recall that migrants from central Poland included landless peasants, who did not have farms or businesses to lose in their places of origin. This group likely had below-average skills and education levels.

---

[13] At the same time, Becker et al. (2020) argue that the loss of their immovable property encouraged forced migrants to invest in their children's education, leading to superior levels of human capital.

Forced migrants from Kresy, on the other hand, were not selected based on their socioeconomic characteristics. If anything, the selection was positive: Belarusian and Lithuanian governments were encouraging the emigration of urban, educated Poles whom they perceived as less assimilable. The selection mechanisms suggest that we should see higher entrepreneurship rates and incomes in places with more forced migrants relative to places with more voluntary migrants.

To explore which of these opposing hypotheses holds in the data, I replace *Migrant diversity* with the share of forced migrants from Kresy (*Share forced*) to the total migrant population as the alternative explanatory variable. The share of forced migrants ranges from 0 to 0.87 in my dataset. The results of these alternative regression specifications are presented in Table A.15. I find that places that received more forced than voluntary migrants in the 1940s had higher incomes in the 1990s. One standard-deviation increase in the share of Kresy migrants ($\mu = 0.33$, $\sigma = 0.18$) increases income by one-tenth of the standard deviation. At the same time, places that received more forced migrants do not differ in entrepreneurship rates or education levels from places that received more voluntary migrants. These patterns are consistent with the negative selection of voluntary migrants, but not with the positive effects of forced migration on the accumulation of human capital and entrepreneurship.

## ALTERNATIVE EXPLANATIONS AND MECHANISMS

### Diversity and Fiscal Revenue

By the early 1990s, residents of the resettled territories had experienced more than four decades of homogenizing policies under communist rule. Their children had been exposed to the same curricula and held similar skills and perspectives. While the descendants of migrants who originated from different historical partitions had retained partition-specific cultural traits, particularly when they were settled in large groups (Charnysh and Peisakhin 2022), it is fair to say that the diversity of skills and perspectives that characterized migrant populations in the 1940s was much reduced.

What I argue persisted, instead, is higher state capacity in municipalities with a more historically diverse population, which in turn influenced the state's ability to enforce rules and regulations after 1989. To shed some light on the plausibility of this hypothesis, I look at fiscal capacity at the municipal level. Starting in 1990, municipalities were able to collect their own taxes from immovable property and other assets. The base tax rate was set at the national level, but municipal governments were able to raise it and determine how the revenue was spent. Higher taxes would enable municipalities to maintain local infrastructure, fund primary education and healthcare, and provide greater social assistance during the period of economic restructuring. The introduction of fiscal autonomy widened subnational differences in the degree and quality of governance across Poland. In Table A.16, I examine whether fiscal policy varied with historical levels of heterogeneity in the resettled region. I find that migrant diversity did not have a significant effect on tax rates but increased average fiscal revenues in 1993–95. One standard-deviation increase in diversity increased fiscal revenues by one-seventh of a standard deviation in the outcome. Furthermore, higher fiscal revenues predict higher municipal spending per capita in the same period (Model 3) and higher per capita incomes and entrepreneurship rates five years later (Models 4–5). These results are consistent with the argument that higher state capacity in municipalities settled by more heterogeneous migrant populations paid off economically after the market transition.

## Differences in Migrants' Culture

Migrants came from regions with various levels of economic development, which could, in turn, influence their long-run economic productivity. Historical research on resettled territories indicates that forced migrants from Kresy and migrants from the Russian and Austrian partitions were less familiar with German material culture than the native population and migrants from the former Prussian partition (Burszta 1995). They were thus less likely to take advantage of mechanized agriculture, electricity, and other German technology. To examine whether the regional origins of the dominant group matter for long-run economic outcomes, I add an indicator for the regional origins of the largest population group in each municipality into the regression models. I find that the coefficient on *Migrant diversity* is robust to controlling for migrants' regional origin (see Table A.17). Thus, the beneficial effects of heterogeneity cannot be explained by the presence of migrants from a specific region. This analysis further indicates that places dominated by migrants from Kresy or migrants from central Poland are outperforming places dominated by the autochthonous population in the prevalence of private enterprises but have statistically indistinguishable income levels. I thus find no evidence for the claim that familiarity with German material culture, which was highest among the autochthones, improved economic performance.

## Human Capital

Could preexisting differences in human capital explain the economic success of more heterogeneous resettled communities following the transition to a market economy? While detailed occupational statistics are lacking, the 1978, 1988, and 2002 national censuses contain data on education at the municipal level. If the differences in education between more heterogeneous and more homogeneous migrant communities existed in 1948, they should still be visible in the 1978 census and may either fade away or increase in subsequent periods. I find no statistically significant differences in education across different levels of heterogeneity in 1978 or 1988. The coefficient on *Migrant diversity* is a positive and significant predictor of education levels only in 2002 (see Table A.18). This suggests that incentives to acquire human capital changed following the transition to a market economy. A related possibility is that prosperity in more heterogeneous communities increased human capital.

### Sorting after the Resettlement

It is possible that migrants from the more heterogeneous communities gradually sorted into more homogeneous communities, which were superior in terms of voluntary public goods provision? This dynamic could explain the reversal of fortunes after 1989. To evaluate this alternative mechanism, I collected data on migration history from the 1988 Census. The census distinguishes between the population living in a given municipality since birth, the population that arrived in the 1970s, and the population that arrived in the 1980s. I use these data to proxy for sorting from one community into another and regress various indicators of sorting (see Table A.19) on *Migrant diversity*, *Migrant share*, and historic control variables.

I find a positive relationship between *Migrant diversity* and the share of the population *Not living from birth* in 1988, that is, communities populated by more diverse migrant groups are receiving more newcomers over time. Regressions that use alternative outcome variables, the share of the population that *Arrived in the 1970s* and *Arrived in the 1980s*, confirm this pattern. Thus, there is some evidence of posttreatment sorting into more heterogeneous communities, perhaps because these communities have better-functioning state institutions, which would make these communities even more heterogeneous. The predicted differences in the share of the population not living from birth at minimum versus maximum heterogeneity are small: at just 5 percent of the population.[14] Importantly, the estimated effects of *Migrant diversity* do not change when these new variables, *Arrived in the 1970s* and *Arrived in the 1980s*, are included in the model. While sorting is present, it does not weaken the economic effects of starting levels of migrant heterogeneity.

### DISCUSSION

This chapter offers evidence for the "diversity bonus" – communities diversified by migration can achieve superior economic outcomes in the long run. I support this argument using an original historical dataset on the composition of the migrant population in the territories transferred from Germany to Poland in 1945. I show that in the 1990s and 2000s, municipalities that

---

[14] Note: all regressions control for the share of migrant population, which by definition is not living in a given municipality from birth.

received more heterogeneous migrants after the war reached higher per capita incomes and entrepreneurship levels. I also show that historical levels of heterogeneity predicted greater fiscal revenues following the decentralization reform in Poland, which allowed municipalities to collect their own property tax. These patterns cannot be attributed to different attitudes toward entrepreneurship among migrants from a particular region, differences in migrants' human capital, or sorting.

The analysis highlights an important precondition for economic development in heterogeneous societies: institutions that protect property rights and enforce contracts of all citizens. In other words, diversity is more likely to advance economic development in states with inclusive institutions (Acemoglu and Robinson 2012; Besley and Persson 2014). My findings question the focus on social capital as an explanation for poor economic performance in heterogeneous societies. Municipalities populated by migrants from different regions started with lower levels of intergroup cooperation and trust, but this did not prevent them from achieving greater economic prosperity in the long run.

Of course, it is also plausible to attribute these outcomes to the nature of state socialism or the post-1989 market reforms, which may have benefited more heterogeneous areas to a greater extent. In addition, there is no municipal data on pre-1980 private economic activity, and economic performance is measured differently before and after the market transition. I acknowledge a degree of uncertainty regarding the short-run economic impact of mass migration and cultural heterogeneity, and hence, the possibility that differences in economic indicators used for the analysis are at least partly responsible for divergent findings before and after 1989. The Polish case is also *sui generis* in that the relatively more developed region of the country experienced a near complete population turnover and its new residents received comparable amounts of German property from the state. Low levels of economic inequality and plentiful land and housing smoothed the process of economic integration.

In Chapter 8, I will explore whether mass resettlement had similarly positive long-run economic consequences in West Germany. The West German case was quite different. Migrants were allocated to preexisting communities and were significantly poorer than the native population. Formal institutions were also more inclusive from the start. I test my argument using more extensive data for postwar West Germany at the national and subnational levels.

# 8

# Economic Implications of Diversity in West Germany

In 1950, *Der Spiegel* magazine reported on the remarkable success of expellee coat manufacturer Bernhard Liening. In 1945, he arrived in Kappeln (Schleswig-Holstein) on foot with "a shabby corporal uniform" as his sole possession; by 1950, he was employing 893 people in his new factory, 90 percent of whom were expellees, producing an average of 1,000 coats per day.[1] How representative were such expellee success stories in West Germany? How did the arrival of expellees affect entrepreneurship and income levels in West German receiving communities? Did it matter where expellees came from, or how diverse an expellee population in a particular region was?

In Chapter 7, I showed that in Poland's resettled territories, heterogeneous migrant communities were initially worse off, but after Poland's transition to a market economy, they achieved higher incomes and greater entrepreneurship rates than more homogeneous communities. This pattern suggests that cultural heterogeneity resulting from migration generates long-run economic benefits.

The case of West Germany allows me to evaluate the generalizability of this pattern in a different institutional setting. As argued in the introduction, higher state capacity in migrant-receiving communities and the diversity of skills and experiences that comes with the mixing of individuals from different regions are more conducive to entrepreneurship under *inclusive* formal institutions – that is, institutions that protect the private property rights of all citizens and enable broad participation in the economy (Acemoglu and Robinson 2012, 144). Unlike in Poland, West German institutions were already inclusive prior to 1989. The social market economy model, adopted at the end of the 1940s, incentivized entrepreneurship and promoted economic competition and free trade. At the same time, some protections were put in place to both cushion

---

[1] "Flüchtlingsbetrieb. Bei Schallplattenmusik." *Der Spiegel* 35/1950. August 30, 1950. www .spiegel.de/wirtschaft/bei-schallplattenmusik-a-9928c71d-0002-0001-0000-000044449568.

the negative impact of market competition on vulnerable population groups and create a more level playing field. Notably, the Equalization of Burdens Law to support expellees was itself designed to incentivize and enable private initiative. The West German case thus allows me to examine the short- and long-term effects of mass migration on private economic activity under inclusive economic institutions.

West Germany conducted regular censuses, which enabled me to consistently measure economic outcomes in different periods. To that end, I assembled two datasets that combine data on the expellee population with occupational statistics from 1939, 1950, 1961, 1970, and 1987. Key outcomes of my analysis are the rate of self-employment, the size of the agricultural sector, and the share of the population with higher education. One dataset covers over 10,000 municipalities in Bavaria, the *Land* that received the highest absolute number of expellees, at 1.9 million. The same economic outcomes can be measured before and after the arrival of expellees, accounting for unobserved time-invariant characteristics of the receiving municipalities in a difference-in-differences design. The second, cross-sectional dataset covers all of West Germany and is at the (larger) county level. For this unit of analysis, in addition to the size of the expellee population, I obtained data on the expellees' countries of origin and measured the diversity of the expellee population in each county, replicating the empirical approach adopted for the analysis of Polish municipalities in Chapter 7. The county-level dataset has the added advantage of capturing a broader range of economic outcomes for the contemporary period, including household incomes and the number of enterprises in different economic sectors.

In the first part of the chapter, I describe the postwar institutional environment of West Germany. I highlight the ways in which formal institutions incentivized entrepreneurship and investment in human capital and enabled the majority of citizens, including expellees, to participate in the economy. I also discuss the effects of expulsion on expellees' economic behavior, using aggregate data from the microcensus and secondary sources.

In the second part, I employ regression analysis to examine how the arrival of expellees and the regional composition of the expellee population influenced economic activity in the receiving communities. I find that places with a larger and more heterogeneous expellee population experienced a reversal of economic fortunes similar to the one that occurred in Poland's resettled territories, albeit with an earlier start. While the arrival of expellees dampened self-employment rates in the first two decades after the war, over time the trend reversed. In Bavaria, high-inflow municipalities achieved greater self-employment rates than low-inflow municipalities by 1970, exceeding their prewar baseline. Across West Germany, the relationship between the share of expellees and self-employment rates became positive by 1987. Furthermore, both the size and the diversity of expellees had the effect of increasing entrepreneurship rates, education, and household incomes.

This analysis demonstrates that in the long run, forced migration can benefit the receiving economies, even as it economically disadvantages the migrants themselves.

## INSTITUTIONAL ENVIRONMENT IN WEST GERMANY

When discussing Germany's future economic system, German elites generally accepted the need for a more interventionist state and, with it, the adoption of a social economy as a way to facilitate economic reconstruction and avoid a resurgence of political extremism. They believed that only government intervention had the power to support economic reconstruction, improve living conditions, and integrate the millions of uprooted and war-damaged persons in the economy (see Chapter 6). The sentiment began to shift away from state planning only after the 1948 currency reform, adopted at the insistence of the US government. The reform increased the availability of goods by removing price controls and stabilizing the currency, even as it further widened the gap between property owners and have-nots, including the expellees.

The US influence was important in lending strength to the proponents of free-market competition, organized around Ludwig Erhard in the Bizonal Economic Council. Erhard and his followers viewed working-class collectivism and economic cartels as the two main sources of Germany's economic problems in the interwar period (Erhard 1958, 117). They recognized the significance of upholding social justice but remained cautious about excessive state regulation. They argued that only a "market-conforming" social policy – an alternative to both laissez-faire capitalism and state socialism – would enable economic reconstruction.

Erhard began to implement his vision as a Director of Economic Affairs in the Bizone. After the 1949 federal election, Adenauer appointed him as the Minister of Economics, a position in which Erhard served until 1963. Under Erhard's guidance, the Adenauer government removed price controls in most economic sectors except for coal, iron, steel, and energy, and also lifted trade barriers.

At the same time, the government continued to use fiscal policy, targeted spending, and strategic subsidies to manage the economy. It created incentives to work and save. Tax allowances were put in place to encourage private investment in machinery and equipment (Carlin 1996). Approximately 25 percent of total gross capital investment came from public funds, much of it spent on housing (Smith 1893, 28).

Despite its neoliberal tendencies, West Germany had the highest level of social spending to GDP in Western Europe, at 19.2 percent, in 1950. Social spending increased to 21.7 percent of the GDP in 1960, 26 percent in 1970, and 32.2 percent in 1980 (Leisering 2001). In 1953, more than 25 percent of the population received some monthly benefit from the state (Hughes 1999, 168). The emphasis on private initiative and individual responsibility was reflected not so much in the level of spending, but in the reliance on the pay-as-you-go system financed through employers' and employees' contributions and managed by non-state bodies (Leisering 2001).

Erhard's and Adenauer's views on private responsibility and the overarching importance of economic reconstruction affected the design of the Equalization of Burdens Law (LAG). As discussed in Chapter 6, the LAG imposed only a modest tax on capital and property holders. To encourage private initiative among expellees and other war-damaged groups, the law introduced tax breaks for new businesses, business loans, and education grants. Short-term loans were given at particularly favorable terms to expellees who were self-employed and would use the loan to restore their livelihoods (Kittel 2020, 58) and to natives whose firms would create long-term jobs for expellees and other war-damaged individuals (Hughes 1999, 158). The law thus relied on "market-conforming" measures to promote private economic activity rather than simply compensate for wartime losses or provide social welfare.

These policies – together with a conducive international environment and aid from the Marshall Plan – bore fruit, as the West German economy experienced an "economic miracle" (*Wirtschaftswunder*). Between 1950 and 1959, the country's real GDP grew at an annual rate of 8 percent. The unemployment rate plummeted from 11 percent in 1950 to just 1 percent in 1960. Economic growth fueled the demand for labor, which, in turn, created employment opportunities for expellees and soon necessitated the recruitment of millions of "guest workers" (*Gastarbeiter*).[2]

State intervention in the economy increased somewhat after the 1965 federal election made the SPD the largest single party in the Bundestag. Government expenditure rose from the baseline of 32–34 percent in 1950–1960 to 43.6 percent of the GNP in 1974 (Duwendag 1975, 18). The government deployed fiscal measures to stabilize the economy and provide aid to specific regions. Notwithstanding the shift in state policy, for the entire postwar period the state protected private property rights and actively fostered private initiative by encouraging broad segments of the population to participate in the economy and acquire education.

THE EXPELLEES' ECONOMIC PLIGHT

Expellees were the last to benefit from the social market economy policies. In 1950, 34.3 percent of expellees were unemployed, compared to 16.6 percent of the native population.[3] The allocation of expellees to the countryside, where fewer jobs were available, exacerbated the problem. The mismatch between

---

[2] In 1955, West Germany signed an agreement with Spain and Greece to supplement domestic labor with immigrant workers.

[3] This is probably an underestimate, as expellees were also more likely than the natives to retire early.

local opportunities and expellee skills was greatest in Bavaria, a predominantly agricultural state that accommodated over a million Sudeten Germans and some 461,000 Germans from the Silesian coal basin, most of whom had held industrial occupations (Connor 2007, 38–39). Expellees were also discriminated against in the labor market, despite the fact that preferential treatment for expellees was legally mandated (Kossert 2008, 93).

Self-employed expellees fared the worst. Few expellee farmers were able to return to independent farming due to the failure of the land reform (see Chapter 6), and the majority remained unemployed, performing odd jobs as agricultural workers. Expellee business owners lost their economic assets along with their supply and trading networks. They were allocated to areas where there was little demand for their skills and products and could not afford the equipment and materials necessary for rebuilding their livelihoods. In a vicious circle, their access to credit was initially limited because they had no equipment to use as collateral (Dittrich 1951, 359). The expellees' ability to get back on their feet was further set back by the 1948 currency reform, which increased real estate prices and reduced the supply of credit and other forms of assistance from state governments (Connor 2007, 47).

It is a notable contrast that among the natives, the self-employed appear to have weathered the uncertainties of the postwar economy best (Lüttinger 1989, 85). Native farmers continued to barter or sell their food on the black market, and native craftsmen were able to trade with each other to obtain raw materials.

The loss of assets, coupled with discrimination in the labor market, pushed some expellees into early retirement. In 1950, 44.5 percent of expellees in the 61–73 age group were pensioners, compared to just 35 percent of the native population in the same age group. In the 51–60 age group, 10.3 percent of the expellees and only 5.1 percent of the natives were pensioners (Lüttinger 1989, 86). The expulsions and related property losses reduced the proportion of the economically active population, even as they expanded the size of the labor force in absolute terms.

This brief review shows the extent to which the expellees' economic situation in Germany differed from that of both forced and voluntary Polish migrants settled in the territory east of the Order–Neisse line. In Poland's resettled territories, jobs, houses, and land were abundant. Correspondingly, Polish migrants typically experienced economic advancement upon resettlement, even when they were forced to leave their property behind. Conversely, in West Germany, the arrival of expellees overcrowded the receiving communities and increased unemployment rates. Expellees lost their socioeconomic status. Even after the adoption of the Equalization of Burdens Law, economic disparities between expellees and the native population persisted. As proof, the expellees' incomes remained significantly lower than the natives' incomes a quarter century after displacement (Bauer, Braun, and Kvasnicka 2013).

HOW FORCED MIGRATION RESHAPED LOCAL ECONOMIES

In this section, I highlight two ways in which the arrival of expellees bene-fited the West German economy in the long run. First, the arrival of expellees increased cultural diversity in receiving communities. As argued in the intro-duction, people from different cultures bring new skills and knowledge that can stimulate entrepreneurship and innovation in receiving economies. The returns to cultural diversity are particularly high under inclusive state insti-tutions. Yet, the question remains as to whether German expellees were sufficiently distinct from the native population to generate these economic benefits. Second, forced migration changed expellees' economic incentives. In particular, qualitative accounts about German expellees highlight that the loss of immovable assets and communal networks motivated expellees to change occupation, relocate for a job, and invest in the education of their children. If these behaviors were prevalent enough, then expellee presence would result in a better-educated, more flexible workforce, benefiting the receiving economies.

### New Skills and Technologies

The argument that diversity increases entrepreneurship appears least plausi-ble in relation to expellees originating from the former Reich, a group that made up 57 percent of all expellees in West Germany. After all, this group had lived under institutions identical to those of the native population from the late nineteenth century onward. And yet, there are many examples where expellees from the former German territories brought with them new skills and technologies. For example, fishermen from Pomerania and West Prussia introduced new salmon fishing techniques to Schleswig-Holstein, significantly expanding the routes and range of fishing trips and, thereby, strengthening the state's fishing industry (Kossert 2008, 125). East Prussian farmers brought a new potato variety to Schleswig-Holstein, soon to be exported to Morocco and Algiers.[4] Expellees from Silesia contributed new technologies to the textile industry as well as coal mining and steel production (Lassotta 2005).

The remaining 43 percent of expellees originated from outside the former Reich and were, therefore, more culturally distinct from the native population, and also more likely to diversify skills and perspectives in the receiving commu-nities. Expellees from Sudetenland (24 percent), known for its small industries and handicrafts, were recognized as an economically productive population early on.

Hoping to benefit from their technical skills, state governments in West Germany went to great lengths to attract the displaced Sudeten craftsmen. In 1945, the Bavarian State Ministry of the Economy commissioned expellee rep-resentative Fred Wilfer, a renowned Schönbach violin maker, to gather Sudeten

---

[4] "Exportartikel im Flüchtlingsstreck." *Eutiner Kreis-Anzeiger*. October 13, 1954.

violinmakers in the county of Erlangen. The mayor of Bubenreuth, a predominantly agricultural town, apportioned a large piece of land to construct a new settlement for violinmakers, in the hopes of kickstarting the local economy. The credit for the construction of new apartments and workshops came from the Bavarian government, and the expellees received generous resettlement grants to reduce relocation costs (Cairns 2016, 112–120). State governments also sought to revive the famed glass and jewelry industries, recruiting expellees from Gablonz, Haida, and Steinschönau to settle in Waldkraiburg and Kaufbeuren (Bavaria) as well as Trappenkamp (Schleswig-Holstein).

By 1952, Sudeten Germans had established 55,000 handicraft shops and 8,000 small- to mid-sized industrial enterprises, turning Bavaria into "Germany's Workshop." Of these, 993 enterprises originated from just one Sudeten town – Gablonz – employing 14,400 people in 7 localities (Connor 2007, 147). As Jakob Kaiser, the Federal Minister for All-German Affairs, noted in a 1952 report: "Bavaria managed to draw 25 percent of the West German industrial expansion ... due partly to a very constructive economic promotion through the Bavarian government and partly to a large number of Sudeten German industries."[5] Indeed, German scholars have attributed Bavaria's economic growth and urbanization in the 1950s and 1960s to the arrival of expellees (Krauss 2008, 32–33).

The Sudeten industries were ideally suited for postwar conditions because they consisted of multiple small- and medium-sized enterprises with highly specialized workers, who relied on cheap raw materials and therefore required little capital investment. Seeking to emphasize the newcomers' industriousness and initiative, the media covered their economic successes in highly positive terms. In 1954, *Eutiner Kreis-Anzeiger* wrote about Trappenkamp (Schleswig-Holstein), the former munitions depot settled by a group of Sudeten Germans:

The hard-working Sudeten Germans went to work eagerly. Soon they were producing so much that the German Federal Post Office felt compelled to set up its own modern post office on the Heidefeld. The Trappenkamp residents also had their own school and, above all, their own glassworks.[6]

However, many handicraft industries failed due to either inadequate infrastructure, insufficient capital, or suboptimal locations. The famed Trappenkamp manufacturers, for example, struggled to turn a profit after the 1948 currency reform, losing their best-performing firms to the larger concentration of glass blowers in Bavaria. The settlement stagnated until 1959, when the federal government committed to building 600 new housing units, attracting new businesses and residents (Wendt 2009).

[5] "Where Freedom Begins," OMGUS WIB, No. 208, November 1952, 8. Quoted in Cairns (2016, 126).
[6] "Exportperlen aus ehmaligen Munitionsdepot. Sudetendeutsche Glasbläser fanden in Trappenkampf eine neue Heimat." *Eutiner Kreis-Anzeiger* No. 179. August 5, 1954.

In addition to introducing high-skilled handicraft industries to the West German countryside, Sudeten Germans are also credited with instigating school reform in Lower Saxony, which made a ninth school year compulsory for all children in 1962, as well as with establishing secondary and professional schools (*Realschulen* and *Fachschulen*), public libraries, and adult education centers in Bavaria (Keil 1967; Krauss 2008).[7]

## Changes in Expellees' Economic Behavior

The majority of expellees experienced a sharp deterioration of their social and economic status in West Germany. As noted earlier, many were dependent on social welfare and were forced into early retirement. The education of some expellee children was cut short, as they were forced to join the labor force to supplement their parents' incomes. At the same time, German researchers have observed that expellees responded to the loss of their land and immovable property by transitioning to nonagricultural occupations and investing in the education of their children.

The analysis of generational cohorts by Lüttinger (1989) demonstrates that whereas the native population changed occupation mainly from one generation to another, occupational changes among expellees also occurred *within* cohorts. The largest occupational shifts were documented between the agricultural and manufacturing sectors: Expellees left farming for secondary sectors, including energy, mining, manufacturing and construction, in higher numbers than the native population.

Data from the Microcensus Supplementary Survey of 1971, focused on the economic and social integration of expellees, allow me to trace this process (see Figure 8.1). Twenty-two percent of the expellees surveyed in 1971 had been employed in the agricultural sector in 1939, compared to 14.4 percent of the native population. In 1950, only 11 percent of expellees were still working in agriculture, compared to 13.8 percent of the natives.[8] By 1971, agricultural employment among expellees dropped to just 2.1 percent, significantly lower than the 7.7 percent of the native population (Lüttinger 1989, 294). The Microcensus shows that while only 45.8 percent of expellees were employed in the secondary sector in 1939, the number had risen to 61 percent in 1950 (and stayed the same in 1971). Among natives, secondary sector employment remained constant, at 54.6 percent in 1939 and at 54 percent in 1971 (Lüttinger 1989, 295). Unfortunately, subsequent micro-censuses do not separate expellees as a category, so it is impossible to trace this out over a longer period.

---

[7] Some of these schools were specific to their trade, such as a school for glass and jewelry making in Kaufbeuren and a school for violin production in Erlangen, while others had broader curricula. In Nazi Germany, these types of schools had been abolished.

[8] The proportions are slightly different in the 1950 census, with 13.6 percent of expellees employed in agriculture.

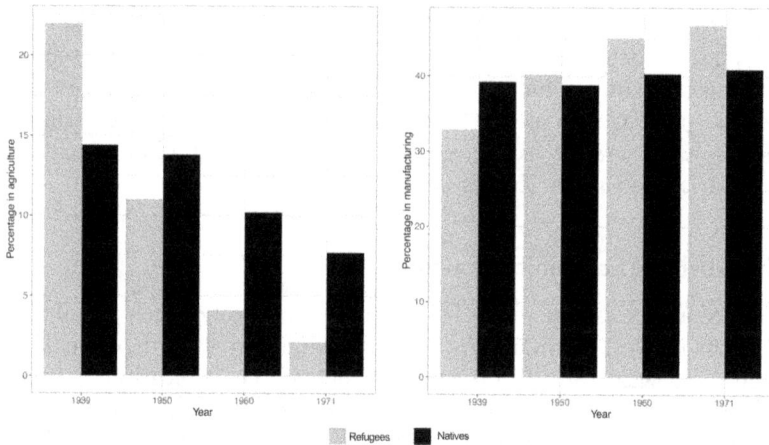

FIGURE 8.1 Occupational differences between native and refugee populations. The refugee category includes both expellees and refugees from East Germany. Sources: 1971 Microcensus and Lüttinger (1989).

Survey data on individual occupational trajectories analyzed by Herlemann (1959) show that only 21 percent of employed male expellees who had been farmers before WWII still worked in agriculture at the time of the survey in 1956. The percentage is even lower, at 12 percent, when we consider expellees who were no longer economically active. More than half switched to other sectors, particularly in manufacturing and construction.[9]

The transition to nonagricultural occupations did not necessarily lead to the expellees' social advancement, as they were forced to take on jobs with low qualification requirements, poor pay, and/or low popularity with the natives (Ambrosius 1996, 52). Instead, this occupational shift likely benefited local economies and West Germany as a whole. These changes reportedly increased labor productivity per employee by 16 percent over the period 1950–1967 (Lüttinger 1989, 99).

There is also some anecdotal evidence that expellees were more likely than natives to invest in the education of their children. According to a 1950 survey conducted in Bavaria, having accepted their own loss of social status as irreversible, expellees hoped that at least their children would regain their former social standing (Pfeil 1951, 97). Echoing these sentiments, a teacher in Schleswig-Holstein observed that expellee parents "demanded a solid good education for their children from us, since they saw it as their only capital investment" (Hotlander school chronicle, quoted in Kossert (2008, 131)). One expellee, born in 1936, recounts that, as the oldest son, he faced enormous

---

[9] The likelihood of occupational change decreased with age: While 23 percent of people aged 36 and older in 1956 were still employed in agriculture, this proportion drops to only 9 percent among those aged 16 to 26 (Herlemann 1959, 113–116).

pressure to earn good grades, because his parents realized that only with good education would he be able to overcome his expellee background (Hillenstedt 2009, 12). Although expellee parents had limited resources, the West German government provided short-term loans as well as support for schooling and job training under the Equalization of Burdens Law. By 1959, over a million young people, 83.5 percent of whom were from displaced households, had benefited from education grants provided by the LAG (Kittel 2020, 60).

In sum, there is some evidence that expellees introduced new skills and technologies that increased economic productivity in agriculture and industry, that they were more likely to change their occupation in response to available labor market opportunities, and that they invested in education. Most examples in this section also showcase the role of the government in enabling these economic behaviors. Specifically, state loans were essential for enabling the Sudeten Germans to rebuild their handicraft workshops, for attracting new business to the struggling expellee community of Trappenkamp, and for funding schooling and occupational training of expellees and their offspring.

Moreover, the arrival of expellees increased the size of the labor force, which proved beneficial for the growth of manufacturing in the 1950s and 1960s. As Erhard observed in 1958, "The countless refugees who during the first postwar years exacerbated the terrible plight of our people, now in a time of full employment have become an asset" (Erhard 1958, ix).

## THE EFFECTS OF FORCED MIGRATION ON BAVARIAN MUNICIPALITIES

In the remainder of this chapter, I will draw on five decades of quantitative data to test my hypotheses that the arrival of expellees proved economically beneficial in the long run by increasing entrepreneurship rates and economic prosperity, and further, that the diversity of the expellee population was in part responsible for this effect.

### Bavarian Municipalities: Dataset and Empirical Strategy

I begin my analysis at the municipal level in Bavaria, the state that received the largest absolute number of expellees, at 1.9 million (20.6 percent of the population). Bavaria is where cultural differences between the expellees and the natives loomed largest since 69 percent of the expellees allocated to Bavaria had originated from abroad, including the Sudetenland, which had historically belonged to the Austro-Hungarian empire and then Czechoslovakia. Moreover, expellees settled in Bavaria typically had higher human capital than the receiving communities because they arrived from more urbanized regions. Bavaria thus presents the most likely case for finding a positive impact of forced migration on local economic activity.

210 *Part IV Long-Run Economic Consequences of Uprooting*

I collected original data on the size of the expellee population, prewar demographic and economic characteristics, and postwar economic outcomes for over 7,000 Bavarian municipalities (*Gemeinden*) using data from the 1939, 1950, 1970, and 1987 censuses. I constructed a panel dataset, which allows me to examine the *change* in economic outcomes from 1939 to 1950, 1970, and 1987. Since WWII, Bavaria underwent several reforms of its administrative divisions, including a consolidation of municipalities from 7,099 in 1950 to 2,056 in 2011. I conduct my analysis at the level of 2011 municipalities, which are larger than historical units. I used the coordinates of historical municipalities from the 1950 census to construct a spatial crosswalk between historical data and the corresponding contemporary units. This spatial matching was supplemented with qualitative research on municipalities with ambiguous coordinates.

My key explanatory variable is the share of the expellee population as measured in the 1950 census at the municipal level. The expellee group includes both Germans from the pre-WWII German territories and Germans from abroad. Unfortunately, information on expellees' regions of origin is unavailable at the municipality level. However, I am able to explore the role of diversity among expellees in Bavaria using a county-level dataset at the end of the chapter.

The distribution of expellees within Bavaria is presented in Map 8.1. Although the average share of expellees stood at 25 percent of the total population, in five municipalities (<1 percent) expellees comprised the majority of the population in 1950.[10] Many of these localities were formerly part of the military infrastructure with barracks for forced laborers, which became available for housing expellees after the war. For instance, Waldkraiburg had an armaments plant with many administrative buildings and living barracks and was settled by expellees from Sudetenland, who planned to use the former factory buildings for a glass-making plant. A large number of expellees also settled in the barracks of the former Buchberg and Stein forced labor camps near Geretsried, which housed two explosives factories during the war.

My main dependent variable is the share of the self-employed (*Selbständige*) in the total workforce. This indicator is commonly used as a proxy for entrepreneurship, although it is a heterogeneous category that includes business owners and co-owners, independent craftsmen and sales representatives, freelancers, contractors, and members of parliament.[11]

[10] These are Geretsried (Bad Tölz-Wolfratshausen), Waldkraiburg (Mühldorf a. Inn), Kirchham (Passau), Dörfles-Esbach (Coburg), and Poxdorf (Forchheim). Note these are contemporary municipalities that sometimes incorporate multiple historic municipalities.
[11] A full list of employment categories in German is as follows: *Eigentümer, Miteigentümer, Pächter von Arbeitsstätten, selbständige Handwerker oder Handelsvertreter, die freiberuflich Tätigen sowie Abgeordnete in den Parlamenten des Bundes und der Länder, Hausgewerbetreibende, Zwischenmeister und Werkvertragspartner.* In 1971, farmers accounted for 2.8

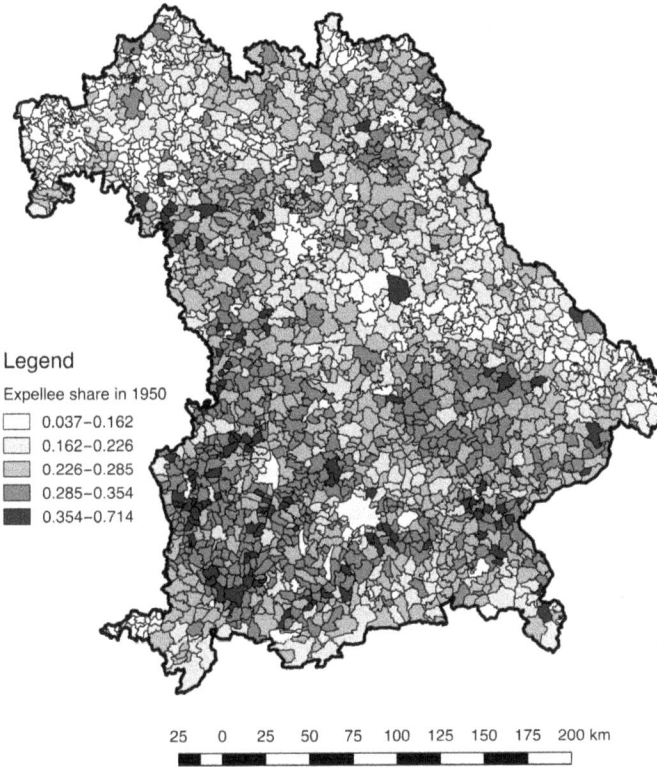

Map 8.1 Distribution of expellees in Bavarian municipalities in 1950. The map represents 2011 administrative divisions based on the shapefile provided by GeoBasis-DE / BKG (2011).

I also examine the changes in the share of the population employed in agriculture to estimate the effect of expellee presence on the occupational structure. The transition to nonagricultural jobs seems particularly likely in Bavaria, which received expellees from the more industrialized regions. Note that while the 1971 Microcensus indicates that expellees were more likely than the natives to exit the agricultural sector, it is an open empirical question whether these within-group occupational shifts correspond to changes in the aggregate occupational structure of a given locality, since expellees may have moved in order to work outside agriculture.

Because I observe the share of self-employed and agricultural-sector workers before and after the arrival of expellees, I estimate a causal effect of receiving expellees using a two-way fixed effects analysis with a continuous treatment (*Share expellees*). The panel structure of the data allows me

percent of the population; the self-employed in nonagricultural sector – for 7.1 percent (Lüttinger 1989, 301).

to account for municipalities' unobserved time-invariant characteristics. The regression model takes the form

$$Y_{it} = \beta_0 + \beta_1 \text{ } Share \text{ } expellees_{i1950} * Year_{1950} + \beta_2 \text{ } Share \text{ } expellees_{i1950}$$
$$* Year_{1970} + \beta_3 \text{ } Share \text{ } expellees_{i1950} * Year_{1987} + X'_{it}\beta + \lambda_i + Year_t + \epsilon_{it}$$
$$(8.1)$$

where $Y_{it}$ is the outcome in municipality $i$ and year $t$, regressed on the interaction of expellee share in municipality $i$ and year dummies $Year_{1950}$, $Year_{1970}$, and $Year_{1987}$. To exploit variation within municipalities over time, I control for municipality fixed effects $\lambda_i$. Year dummies ($Year_t$) are included to absorb changes in economic outcomes that are common to all municipalities in Bavaria. I chose 1939 as a base year. Therefore, my coefficients of interest $\beta_1$, $\beta_2$, and $\beta_3$ measure the effects of the expellees' arrival on the change in the rate of self-employment and agricultural employment in 1950, 1970, and 1987, relative to the base year 1939. In addition to municipal fixed effects, I account for time-varying covariates ($X'_{it}$), such as the share of men, the share of Catholics, and population size (logged), as well as time-invariant covariates, such as the (logged) distance to the sending regions in the east[12] and urban status, interacted with the year dummies. I cluster standard errors at the municipal level.

Summary statistics on all variables are presented in Table A.3.

## Bavarian Municipalities: Results

The estimates from the two-way fixed effects regression models are reported in Table A.20. Figure 8.2 plots the estimated coefficients on the main explanatory variable, the share of expellees from the total population. The analysis shows that places that received more expellees to the population experienced a decrease in self-employment rates in 1950 relative to the 1939 baseline. A standard-deviation increase in the share of expellees, equivalent to 7 percent, predicts a 0.7-percent decrease in the share of self-employed in 1950 ($\mu = 20$, $\sigma = 4$). As noted earlier, expellees lost their immovable assets and were initially more likely to work in dependent positions than the native population.

In subsequent periods, however, the rates of self-employment rebounded and exceeded prewar levels. This is an interesting pattern because the overall prevalence of self-employment declined in West Germany after the war in response to the strong demand for labor in manufacturing. The coefficients on the interaction term between *Share expellees* and the 1970 and 1987 year dummies are positive and statistically significant. A standard-deviation increase in the share of expellees predicts a 0.4- to 0.6-percent increase in the share

---

[12] I measure this as the distance to East Germany or the border with Czechoslovakia, whichever is closest.

Change in self-employment rates from 1939 in Bavarian municipalities

Change in agricultural employment from 1939 in Bavarian municipalities

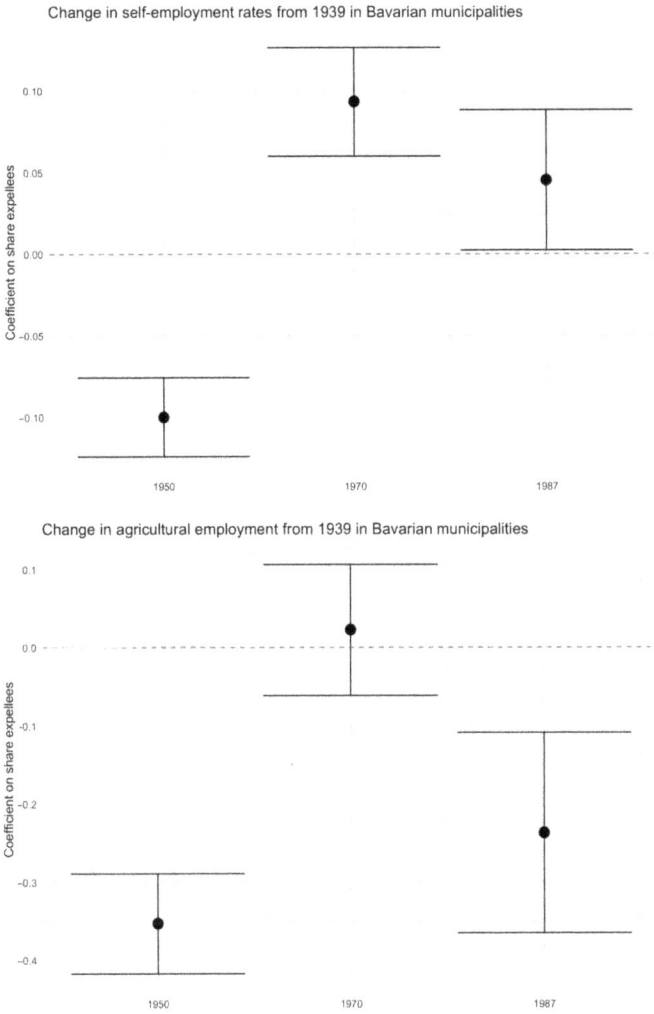

FIGURE 8.2 Share of expellees and economic outcomes in Bavaria. Change for each year is measured relative to the 1939 baseline. Estimates are based on municipality-level analysis in Table A.20.

of the self-employed in 1970 and 1987. To sum up, the reduction in self-employment in the aftermath of displacement was short-lived, and the rates of private economic activity in higher-inflow municipalities overtook the 1939 baseline approximately one generation later. The analysis does not allow me to separate expellees from the natives, so this finding may be a product of two related trends: the creation of new businesses by expellees and the increased rates of entrepreneurship among the natives in receiving municipalities.

The estimated effects of expellee inflow on changes in agricultural employ-ment are more ambiguous. The coefficient on *Share expellees* is negative and statistically significant in 1950 and 1987, but not in 1970. The regression esti-mates suggest that a standard-deviation increase in the share of expellees to population decreases agricultural employment by 3 percent in 1950 ($\mu = 27$, $\sigma = 16$) and by 2 percent in 1987 ($\mu = 10$, $\sigma = 8$), statistically significant and substantively large effects. By contrast, in 1970, the estimated coefficient on *Share expellees* is close to 0. To understand this pattern, I ran separate regres-sions in subsets of Bavarian municipalities with above and below the median *Share expellees*. Dividing the sample in this way reveals divergent trajectories between municipalities with high and low shares of expellees to population. Agricultural employment consistently decreased in high-inflow municipalities, with the largest decline observed between 1939 and 1950. By contrast, the predominance of agriculture actually increased in low-inflow municipalities. These countervailing trends in high- and low-inflow localities account for the null average treatment effect in the full dataset.

In sum, regression analysis indicates that hosting expellees had short-term costs, but benefited the Bavarian economy in the long run by increasing aggregate rates of entrepreneurship. Communities that received particularly high numbers of expellees also experienced a greater decline in agricultural employment.

## THE ECONOMIC EFFECTS OF FORCED MIGRATION AT THE COUNTY LEVEL

I supplement the analysis of Bavarian municipalities with cross-sectional regressions at the county (*Kreis*) level for the entire West Germany. County-level data allow me to disaggregate the explanatory variable, forced migration, into two components, the size and heterogeneity of the expellee population. In addition, I am able to use a more diverse set of economic indicators as dependent variables.

To construct this new dataset, I start with the data collected and merged by Schmitt, Rattinger, and Oberndörfer (1994), which include variables from the 1950, 1961, 1970, and 1987 censuses at the level of 1987 counties. I supple-ment this dataset with data from the 1950 census in North Rhine-Westphalia, which were missing, as well as with indicators from the 1939 census. I used spatial interpolation to harmonize 1939 and 1950 units (smaller) to the level of 1987 units (larger). County boundaries are based on shapefiles created by MPIDR and CGG (2011).

### Explanatory Variables

In addition to computing the population share of expellees, I construct an indi-cator for the heterogeneity of the expellee population to capture the diversity of skills and knowledge that expellees brought with them. The information about expellees' countries of origin was digitized from the Statistical Handbook about the Expellees (*Statistisches Taschenbuch über die Heimatvertriebenen*), published in 1953.

Following the empirical approach in Chapter 7, I measure the heterogeneity of the expellee population as an inverse Herfindahl (or fractionalization) index ($Div_{mig} = \sum_{j=1}^{J} [s_j * (1 - s_j)]$), where $s_j$ is the share of expellees from the same region of origin out of the total expellee population. The index is computed based on the categories provided in the German census: expellees from the former German territories (*Reichsdeutsche*), expellees from Sudetenland, and expellees from other countries. It measures the probability that two randomly selected expellees come from a different country of origin. The index ranges from 0.22 to 0.67 in the dataset ($\mu = 0.49$, $\sigma = 0.12$). County-level variation in the heterogeneity of the expellee population was mapped in Chapter 2.

Concrete examples are helpful for interpreting the substantive meaning of high and low values of the expellee diversity index. Rural county Lingen in Niedersachsen had the lowest fractionalization index in the dataset, at $Div_{mig} = 0.20$. Ninety percent of all expellees there came from the annexed German territories; expellees from Sudetenland and from other countries made up just 2 and 9 percent of all expellees, respectively. Conversely, the city of Munich and the rural county of Passau in Bavaria had the highest fractionalization index values for West Germany, at just over 0.66. In Munich, expellees from territories east of the Oder–Neisse line made up 35 percent of all expellees, expellees from Sudetenland 33 percent, and expellees from other countries the remaining 32 percent. In Passau, expellees from Germany's pre-1937 territory made up 38 percent, while expellees from the other two categories made up slightly more than 30 percent each. The population share of expellees was not correlated with the heterogeneity of the expellee population: Expellees made up only 10 percent of Munich's total population despite being an extremely heterogeneous group.

These categories do not represent the full extent of diversity among expellees. For one, the census data lump Germans from various countries together (with the exception of Sudeten Germans, a group that is large enough to have its own category). Furthermore, the census does not capture variation in the origin of *Reichsdeutsche*, a large group that came from provinces as diverse as rural East Prussia and industrialized Lower Silesia.

## Economic Outcomes

My first dependent variable is the number of self-employed (*Selbständige*) per 1,000 people, as measured in the 1950, 1961, 1970, and 1987 censuses.[13] As

---

[13] Note the variable is measured to the population as opposed to from total workforce because data on the total workforce are unavailable for some states in the dataset compiled by Schmitt, Rattinger, and Oberndörfer (1994).

noted earlier, this indicator includes not only business owners but also independent farmers and unpaid family workers. I also collected data on the highest completed level of education from the 1970 and 1987 censuses to compute the share of the population aged 15 and older with higher or professional education (*Hochschule, Fachhochschule*).

I examine whether forced migration affected agricultural employment, following the analysis in Bavaria. Data availability on occupational characteristics varies by year. For 1950 and 1961, I use information on the share of the labor force in agriculture and forestry (*Erwerbspersonen in Land- und Forstwirtschaft*). This indicator includes both employed and the unemployed, and as discussed earlier, expellees were significantly more likely to be unemployed in 1950. Using this outcome allows me to establish whether the arrival of expellees shifted the broader occupational structure at the county level. For 1970 and 1987, I use the number of people actually employed in agriculture and forestry (*Erwerbstätige*). This indicator does not include the unemployed.

I was able to leverage an even broader range of economic indicators for more recent periods. The Federal Institute for Building, Urban and Spatial Research (*Bundesinstitut für Bau-, Stadt- und Raumforschung*) provides county-level data on a number of economic indicators, including household income (starting in 2000) and the number of companies by economic sector (starting in 2008).[14] In light of the hypothesis that forced migration affected innovation, of particular interest for the analysis are companies in the knowledge industry, which requires intensive use of human capital and technology. Thus, in addition to examining the total number of enterprises per 1,000 people, I separately consider companies classified as belonging to the professional, scientific and technical activities sector (*freiberufliche, wissenschaftliche und technische Dienstleistungen*), which encompass the provision of highly specialized services that require a high level of training and expertise. Among companies included in this sector are those engaged in legal and accounting activities, management consulting, architecture, engineering, testing and analysis, scientific research and development, advertising and market research, and veterinary activities.[15] Two other potentially relevant sectors are information and communications, which include publishing and broadcasting as well as computer programming, consultancy, and related activities, and the education sector (*Erziehung*). I also look at the size of the transaction costs sector, which includes administrative and support services, that is, companies that facilitate economic activity in other sectors.

---

[14] Information on the number of companies is available for earlier years only for a couple of states.
[15] See details in "Klassifikation der Wirtschaftszweige, Ausgabe 2008 (WZ 2008)." Statistische Ämter des Bundes und der Länder. Accessed December 22, 2021. www.klassifikationsserver .de/klassService/jsp/item/grouping.jsf.

## Empirical Strategy

Estimating the effects of forced migration in 1950 on economic outcomes entails several empirical challenges. Most importantly, we need to understand the process of expellee allocation and account for pre-1945 economic characteristics of the receiving communities that confound the relationship between expellee inflow and economic indicators. Recall that French occupation authorities refused to accept expellees, so most of the expellees were settled in the US and British occupation zones. Within these two zones, the allocation of expellees was based on the availability of housing rather than on economic characteristics that would facilitate expellee integration. Most expellees wound up in small rural communities, which suffered less destruction during the war because they were predominantly agricultural. Furthermore, because the largest sending region was in the east, counties closer to Germany's eastern borders received more expellees. As shown in Table 8.1, the share of expellees is correlated with the level of postwar destruction, agricultural employment, population density, and distance to the eastern border. It is important to condition on these characteristics in a regression analysis to estimate the economic effects of expellee presence, because counties that were more agricultural and less affected by wartime bombing likely experienced different growth trajectories than more industrial and war-damaged counties.

At the same time, the expellees' origins played little role in the allocation decisions; the proportion of expellees from a specific region relative to the overall expellee population depended on idiosyncratic factors. This null relationship is confirmed in Table 8.1, which shows that the fractionalization index based on expellees' countries of origin is uncorrelated with prewar socioeconomic characteristics. To be sure, geography still influenced which groups of expellees reached a given destination. In particular, Northern Germany received expellees from East Prussia and Poland, who traveled by sea from the port of Danzig to the ports of Lübeck and Kiel in Schleswig-Holstein. The expellee population in the north was large but relatively homogeneous. Southern states, such as Bavaria, received a more heterogeneous expellee population because of their proximity to three distinct sending regions: Sudetenland, Silesia, and Hungary. Western states, including Rhineland-Palatinate, and southwest Baden-Württemberg, had a small, if heterogeneous, expellee population because they were in the French occupation zone. Finally, North Rhine Westphalia had a small and relatively homogeneous expellee population because it was dominated by industry and suffered greater destruction after the war.

Building on this discussion, I estimate the following OLS model at the county level:

$$Y_{is} = \beta_0 + \beta_1 \text{ Share expellees}_{is} + \beta_2 Diversity_{is} + X'_{is}\beta + \gamma_s + \epsilon_{is}, \quad (8.2)$$

TABLE 8.1 *Correlations between the share and diversity of expellees and characteristics of receiving counties.*

|  | Diversity of expellees | | Expellee share | |
|---|---|---|---|---|
|  | Correlation | $R^2$ | Correlation | $R^2$ |
| Share expellees (1950) | −0.273 | 0.075 | 1.00 | — |
| Share destroyed (1946) | −0.020 | 0.000 | −0.618 | 0.381 |
| Share Catholic (1939) | 0.281 | 0.079 | −0.211 | 0.045 |
| Share in agriculture (1939) | −0.004 | 0.000 | 0.450 | 0.203 |
| Ln distance to Eastern border | −0.018 | 0.000 | −0.493 | 0.243 |
| Population density (1939) | 0.015 | 0.000 | −0.427 | 0.182 |
| Ln population (1950) | −0.338 | 0.114 | −0.086 | 0.007 |

where $Y_{is}$ is outcome in county $i$ and state $s$ and the two coefficients of interest are $\beta_1$ and $\beta_2$, signifying the share and heterogeneity of the migrant population at the county level. The vector of covariates ($X'_{is}$) includes pretreatment variables that are correlated with the share of expellees (see Table 8.1). I also include state fixed effects ($\gamma_s$) in all models to account for unobserved differences between German states.

An additional challenge for county-level analysis is the presence of spatial autocorrelation in both outcome and treatment variables. Counties with higher shares of expellees sometimes cluster near each other. Most economic outcomes likewise cluster in space. To address spatial autocorrelation, in addition to heteroskedasticity-robust standard errors, I also estimate Conley standard errors within a 500-km cutoff.[16]

## Results

How did the size and diversity of the expellee population affect occupational structure at the county level? As shown in Figure 8.3, counties with a larger and more heterogeneous expellee population experience a reversal of fortune over time (see Table 8.2 for full regression results). Consistent with the results from Bavarian municipalities, I find a negative relationship between the size of the expellee population and self-employment rates in the immediate postwar period. An increase in the share of expellees by one standard deviation (9.7 percent) reduces the number of self-employed by 4.30 per 1,000 people in 1950. By 1961, however, the coefficient on *Share expellees* becomes smaller and no longer reaches statistical significance. The relationship between *Share expellees* and self-employment rates becomes positive for self-employment rates in 1970

---

[16] The results are similar with alternative cutoff distances. For plots in the rest of the chapter, I use heteroskedasticity-standard errors because they turn out to be larger.

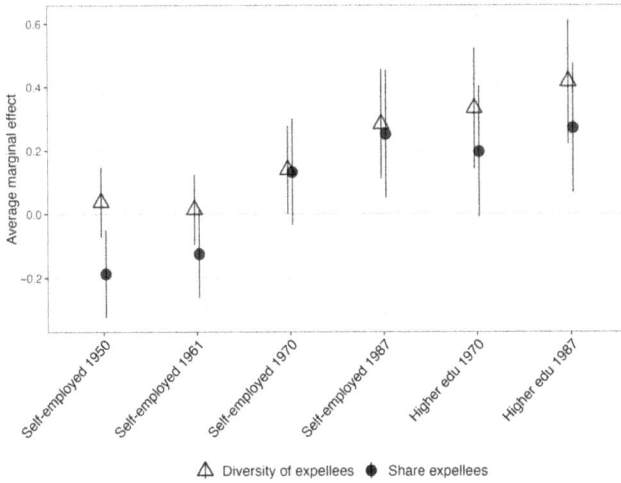

FIGURE 8.3 Share and diversity of expellees and economic outcomes in West German counties. The standardized coefficients are based on county-level analysis in Table 8.2.

and 1987. The estimates indicate that a standard-deviation increase in the population share of expellees increases self-employment rates by 2.05 people per 1,000 in 1970 and by 2.56 people per 1,000 in 1987, equivalent to a quarter of a standard deviation. This result demonstrates that, even though the inflow of expellees reduced economic initiative immediately after WWII, a quarter-century later counties with more expellees relative to their population achieved higher levels of entrepreneurship.

Counties with more expellees also attained higher levels of human capital by 1970 and 1987. In 1970, a standard-deviation increase in the share of expellees raises the share of the population with higher education by one-fourth of a standard deviation ($\mu = 6.52$, $\sigma = 2.28$).[17] Note this does not necessarily mean that the expellees themselves had higher self-employment rates or education levels. These effects are estimated for the combined population in the receiving county.

The analysis in Table 8.2 further shows that the diversity of the expellee population had an independent positive effect on entrepreneurship and education levels. The coefficient on *Diversity of expellees* is positive in all models and reaches statistical significance in regressions of the 1970 and 1987 outcomes. One standard-deviation increase in this variable ($\mu = 0.49$, $\sigma = 0.12$) raises self-employment by 2.17 people per 1,000 in 1970 and 2.88 people per 1,000 in 1987. *Diversity of expellees* also has positive effects on human capital. One standard-deviation increase in this variable raises the share of the

---

[17] The average county-level shares of population with higher education are low because higher education is measured to the total population as opposed to population above the age cutoff.

TABLE 8.2 *Share and diversity of expellees and economic outcomes in West German counties.*

| | Self-employment rates | | | | Education | |
|---|---|---|---|---|---|---|
| | 1950 | 1961 | 1970 | 1987 | 1970 | 1987 |
| | (1) | (2) | (3) | (4) | (5) | (6) |
| Share expellees | −44.34*** | −29.64* | 21.20 | 26.37** | 2.27* | 6.36*** |
| | (16.59) | (16.57) | (13.67) | (10.79) | (1.22) | (2.44) |
| | [12.93] | [6.97] | [8.26] | [4.72] | [0.56] | [1.12] |
| Expellee diversity | 7.02 | 2.59 | 17.92** | 23.83*** | 3.08*** | 7.83*** |
| | (10.73) | (10.75) | (9.06) | (7.43) | (0.90) | (1.89) |
| | [7.85] | [6.19] | [6.97] | [6.77] | [0.94] | [1.95] |
| Share destroyed | 0.65 | −1.59 | −0.59 | −4.31 | −0.50 | −0.71 |
| | (6.45) | (6.43) | (4.96) | (3.77) | (0.45) | (0.90) |
| | [2.05] | [2.48] | [2.39] | [2.61] | [0.23] | [0.69] |
| Share Catholic | −3.72* | −3.62* | −1.60 | 2.28 | 0.81*** | 1.35*** |
| | (2.16) | (2.13) | (1.84) | (1.43) | (0.19) | (0.40) |
| | [2.05] | [1.14] | [1.00] | [1.06] | [0.13] | [0.35] |
| Share in agriculture | 92.35*** | 101.69*** | 61.77*** | 19.65*** | −2.44*** | −6.20*** |
| | (6.77) | (7.44) | (5.78) | (4.24) | (0.53) | (1.11) |
| | [9.97] | [8.40] | [4.26] | [3.18] | [0.69] | [1.17] |
| Ln dist to Eastern border | 3.14*** | 2.59*** | 4.15*** | 4.69*** | 0.21*** | 0.72*** |
| | (0.89) | (0.89) | (0.70) | (0.58) | (0.07) | (0.15) |
| | [0.56] | [0.85] | [0.37] | [0.48] | [0.09] | [0.19] |
| Pop density 1939 | −0.00 | −0.00 | 0.00 | 0.00 | −0.00** | −0.00 |
| | (0.00) | (0.00) | (0.00) | (0.00) | (0.00) | (0.00) |
| | [0.00] | [0.00] | [0.00] | [0.00] | [0.00] | [0.00] |
| Ln population 1950 | 0.66 | 2.08 | 1.41 | 0.60 | 0.33** | 0.62* |
| | (1.79) | (1.59) | (1.28) | (1.07) | (0.15) | (0.32) |
| | [1.26] | [1.04] | [0.86] | [0.24] | [0.11] | [0.22] |
| City-district | 2.19 | 4.10 | 4.30 | −2.30 | 1.15*** | 0.74 |
| | (3.56) | (3.91) | (2.99) | (2.33) | (0.41) | (0.79) |
| | [1.94] | [2.47] | [2.31] | [2.83] | [0.53] | [0.83] |
| French zone dummy | 2.60 | 1.73 | 4.97* | 2.60 | 0.52 | 0.80 |
| | (3.28) | (2.85) | (2.79) | (2.15) | (0.37) | (0.67) |
| | [1.34] | [0.73] | [0.97] | [0.55] | [0.09] | [0.16] |
| State fixed effects | ✓ | ✓ | ✓ | ✓ | ✓ | ✓ |
| Adjusted $R^2$ | 0.81 | 0.83 | 0.74 | 0.60 | 0.38 | 0.34 |
| N | 310 | 310 | 310 | 310 | 310 | 310 |

*Note:* All models are OLS. Heteroskedasticity-robust standard errors in parentheses, Conley standard errors within a 500-km radius in brackets. Significant at *$p < 0.10$; **$p < 0.05$; ***$p < 0.01$.

population with higher education by 0.37 percent in 1970 and 0.95 percent in 1987, which is nearly double the effect of *Share expellees*.

Regression results summarized in Figure 8.4 indicate that the arrival of expellees did not reduce agricultural employment. In fact, the coefficients on both *Share expellees* and *Diversity of expellees* are positive, though not significant for 1950 and 1961. In both 1970 and 1987, counties that received more expellees to population had slightly higher levels of agricultural employment. Thus, industrialization trends observed in Bavaria do not generalize for West Germany as a whole.

How long did the economic legacies of uprooting last? Are counties that received a larger and more heterogeneous expellee population still different from counties that received fewer expellees or a less heterogeneous expellee population today? To answer these questions, I compare the number of companies in different sectors of the economy and household income levels in the 2000s, the earliest period for which such data are consistently available for all of West Germany. The results of cross-sectional regressions of contemporary outcomes with a full set of covariates and fixed effects for German states are reported in Table A.22. I plot the coefficients on the main variables of interest in Figure 8.5. We see that the effects of postwar displacement remain visible in the present, despite the fundamental economic and demographic shifts following the reunification of Germany. Both the size and heterogeneity of the expellee population have beneficial long-run consequences.

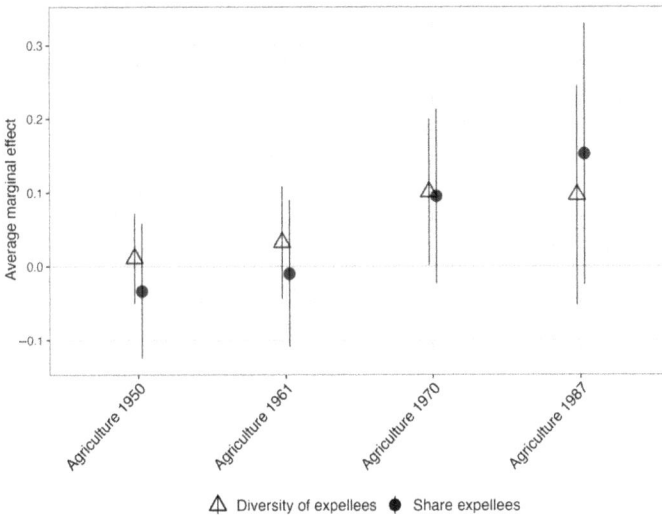

△ Diversity of expellees  ● Share expellees

FIGURE 8.4 Share and diversity of expellees and agricultural employment. The standardized coefficients are based on county-level analysis in Table A.21.

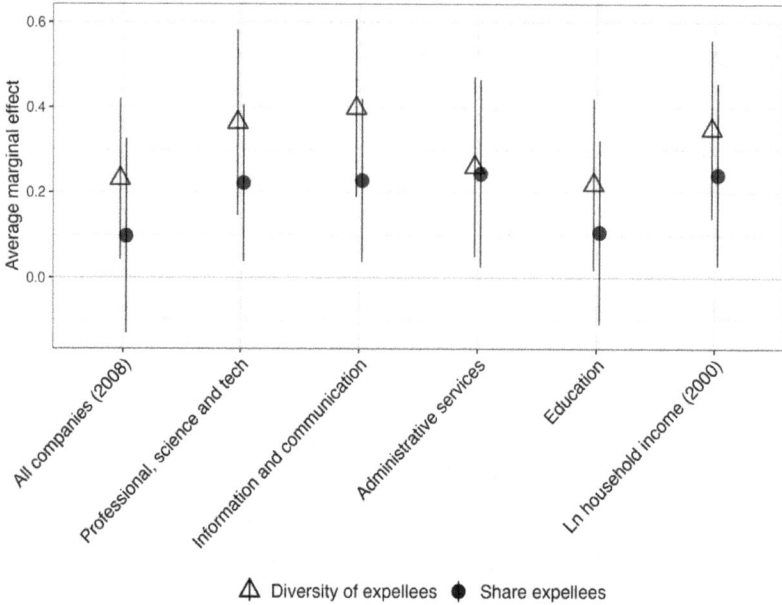

△ Diversity of expellees   ● Share expellees

FIGURE 8.5   Share and diversity of expellees, entrepreneurship, and household income. Firms in each sector are measured in 2008. Household income is measured in 2000. The standardized coefficients are based on county-level analysis in Table A.22.

The coefficient on *Share expellees* is positive in all models, but – with the more conservative heteroskedasticity-robust standard errors – reaches statistical significance only for enterprises in specific sectors of the economy. One standard-deviation increase in the share of expellees predicts an increase in the number of companies in the professional, scientific and technical activities sector and in the communications and technology sector by just under a quarter of one standard deviation each. An increase in *Share expellees* by one standard deviation also raises household income by approximately 40 euros per resident, a considerable amount.

The coefficient on *Diversity of expellees* is positive and statistically significant for all indicators. Counties that had received a more heterogeneous mix of expellees after WWII registered more enterprises per capita, particularly in economic sectors that require a high-skilled workforce and produce knowledge, and also had higher household income. An increase in *Diversity of expellees* by one standard deviation (0.12) translates into an increase in the total number of firms by 1.87 per 1,000 people, equivalent to a quarter of a standard deviation ($\mu = 46.03$, $\sigma = 8.16$). This means that counties that wound up with the most heterogeneous expellee population are estimated to have seven additional companies, on average, relative to counties that received expellees from one region.

The benefits of heterogeneity are even larger for companies in the professional, scientific, and technical activities sector and in the information and communications sector. One standard-deviation increase in the diversity of expellees increases the number of companies in these two sectors by more than one-third of a standard deviation each. This means, for example, that counties that had the most heterogeneous expellee population (*Diversity* = 0.67) are predicted to have 3.11 additional companies in the professional, scientific, and technical activities sector and 1.20 additional companies in the information and communications sector than counties with the most homogeneous expellee population (*Diversity* = 0.22). Historic levels of expellee diversity also increase the number of companies in the education and in administrative services sectors.

Finally, regression analysis shows that counties that had received a more heterogeneous expellee population after the war were also significantly wealthier in 2000, the year for which household income is measured. An increase in the diversity of expellees by one standard deviation increases logged household income by a third of a standard deviation, equivalent to 54 euros per person.

Altogether, I find that receiving forced migrants, particularly from diverse countries of origin, increases economic productivity, innovation, and welfare. Conclusions based on contemporary economic indicators are more tentative given the many decades that passed between the period when expellees were allocated to specific counties and the period when economic activity is measured. Most notably, approximately 800,000 East Germans arrived in West Germany between 1989 and 1990, at the peak of emigration from the GDR (Prantl and Spitz-Oener 2020, 82). Still, it is unlikely that the economic migration of East Germans followed the same spatial pattern as the top-down allocation of expellees after WWII, which would confound the relationship between expellee characteristics and contemporary economic outcomes.

## ADDRESSING ALTERNATIVE EXPLANATIONS

### The Origin of the Dominant Expellee Group

Expellees arriving from more economically developed, urbanized regions may have been more beneficial to receiving economies. As discussed earlier, Sudeten Germans typically stood out among other expellees due to their craftsmanship and received considerable support from state governments interested in their technical skills. To ensure that my main findings are not driven by expellees from a particular place of origin, I construct an indicator variable for the origins of the largest group. In 196 counties (61 percent), Germans from the annexed territories predominate; another 109 counties (34 percent) are dominated by Sudeten Germans, and the remaining 16 (4 percent) by Germans from other regions. The coefficients on the main explanatory variables, *Share expellees* and *Diversity of expellees*, do not change when the dummy for the largest group of expellees in a given county is included in the analysis (see Tables A.25 and A.26). The beneficial effect of expellee diversity thus cannot be explained away by the outsized economic impact of a particular expellee group.

## Increased Labor Supply

Counties that received more expellees experienced a positive shock to their population size, which persisted for decades after the expulsions (Schumann 2014). Is it possible that an increase in population size alone was responsible for the increase in entrepreneurship and income? Using West German data, Peters (2022) shows that the inflow of expellees increased the supply of labor and in this way contributed to the growth in manufacturing employment in the 1950s and 1960s, increasing aggregate income per capita in the long run. To account for this alternative mechanism, all analyses in this chapter included logged population size in 1950 as a covariate. Thus, the conclusions based on the expellee population share are conditional on the size of the labor force in each county. Furthermore, while the share of expellees is mechanically correlated with the overall population increase in receiving localities, the diversity of the expellee population is independent of both, as shown earlier in the chapter.

## Migration after the Initial Allocation

In response to unemployment and the mismatch between their skills and local economic structure, as many as 915,000 expellees eventually took advantage of the official resettlement programs to move to states with better employment opportunities, particularly to North Rhein–Westphalia, Baden–Württemberg, and Rhineland–Palatinate (Nahm 1971, 115). The exit of expellees in the 1950s from the most overpopulated counties could explain the gradual improvement of economic conditions in counties that received more expellees after the war. At the same time, if enough expellees had relocated from their initial counties to make a difference, then we should expect the effect of expellee presence to disappear over time rather than turn positive.

To examine whether my conclusions about the beneficial long-run impact of displacement on entrepreneurship and human capital are robust to these changes in the initial allocation of expellees, I use data on expellee shares in 1961 as an alternative explanatory variable. It is important to keep in mind that this measure of expellee presence is endogenous to local economic conditions, unlike earlier measures: After 1950, some expellees relocated to areas with better job opportunities, often with state assistance. Another limitation of using this later indicator of expellee presence is the absence of information on expellee origins. However, the heterogeneity of the expellee population is uncorrelated with the change in expellee shares from 1950 to 1961 ($\rho = 0.09$,

$p = 0.12$). That is, expellee relocation patterns were comparable in counties with a more (or less) heterogeneous expellee population.

I rerun the regression analysis, substituting the share of expellees in 1961 for the share of expellees from 1950. The results are presented in Tables A.23 and A.24. For self-employment rates in 1970 and 1987, the coefficient on the share of expellees in 1961 remains negative, unlike the coefficient on the share of expellees in 1950. This alternative specification indicates that the effects of expellee presence turned positive after a longer period than suggested by the analysis using the 1950 expellee share. One possible explanation for these divergent results is that more entrepreneurial expellees were more likely to move to more developed counties, leaving behind those who were less entrepreneurial. At the same time, the estimates on *Share expellees* in 1950 and *Share expellees* in 1961 are broadly similar for education levels and contemporary economic outcomes, supporting the previous conclusions about the positive long-run impact of expellee presence on entrepreneurship rates, human capital, and household income in the receiving communities. These results appear robust to accounting for the shift in the number of expellees within West Germany due to state-sponsored resettlement programs.

EXPLORING THE CHARACTERISTICS OF EARLY EXPELLEE FIRMS

The state of Bavaria published data on expellee firms in 1950 by sector for each county, digitized by Braun and Franke (2021). The data offer a snapshot of expellees' entrepreneurial activity shortly after the 1948 currency reform, which disproportionately hurt expellee firms. As discussed earlier, in 1950, counties that received a larger expellee population were economically worse off relative to the counties that received fewer expellees. Nonetheless, the data are useful for understanding the effects of expellee allocation policies – which resulted in varied size and diversity of the expellee population – on entrepreneurial activity among expellees. In particular, it can be used to examine (1) how the number or size of expellee firms varies with the size and the composition of the expellee population and (2) whether places that received expellees from different countries have a more heterogeneous mix of expellee firms in 1950.

Full regression results for this analysis are presented in Table 8.3. The analysis shows that the number of expellee firms increases with the share of expellees but is unrelated to the heterogeneity of the expellee population. In other words, a more diverse expellee population did not generate more firms than a more homogeneous expellee population in the short run. We further see that all three categories of expellees – *Reichsdeutsche* from the annexed German territory, Germans from Czechoslovak Sudetenland, and Germans arriving from other countries – contribute to the creation of expellee companies. That is, the coefficients on the share of each group are positive and statistically significant in regression analysis (Model 2). The proclivity toward entrepreneurial activity

TABLE 8.3 *Share and diversity of expellees and expellee-founded firms in Bavarian counties in 1950.*

| | Ln expellee firms to population | | Employees per firm | Diversity of firms |
|---|---|---|---|---|
| | (1) | (2) | (3) | (4) |
| Share expellees | 24.08*** | | −0.90 | −0.16*** |
| | (3.90) | | (2.27) | (0.04) |
| Expellee diversity | −3.88 | | −1.60 | 0.07** |
| | (2.59) | | (1.10) | (0.03) |
| Share Reichdeutsche | | 17.86*** | | |
| | | (3.59) | | |
| Share Sudetendeutsche | | 30.47*** | | |
| | | (6.54) | | |
| Share other expellees | | 14.95*** | | |
| | | (5.55) | | |
| Covariates | ✓ | ✓ | ✓ | ✓ |
| Adjusted $R^2$ | 0.62 | 0.63 | 0.18 | 0.21 |
| N | 187 | 187 | 187 | 187 |

*Note:* All models are OLS. Heteroskedasticity-robust standard errors in parentheses. Significant at *$p < 0.10$; **$p < 0.05$; ***$p < 0.01$.

does not appear to vary by group. I also find that the number of employees per expellee firm cannot be explained by the size or diversity of the expellee population (see null coefficients on both *Share expellees* and *Expellee diversity* in Model 3).

Finally, I use data on expellee firms in different economic sectors to probe the hypothesis that expellees from different countries bring complementary skills and knowledge. I expect to observe a more diverse mix of expellee firms in counties with a more diverse expellee population relative to counties with a more homogeneous expellee population. I use the number of firms in each sector to compute the inverse Herfindahl index of sectoral diversity. The index ranges from 0.61 to 0.80, suggesting low sectoral concentration among expellee companies. The two most popular sectors are manufacturing (36 percent of expellee companies) and trade (30 percent of expellee companies). Regression results are presented in Model 4 in Table 8.3. I find that an increase in expellee diversity by one standard deviation translates into an increase in the sectoral diversity of expellee firms by one-fifth of a standard deviation ($\mu = 0.74$, $\sigma = 0.03$). The share of expellees, on the other hand, decreases the diversity of expellee firms. While these results are only provisional given the lack of data on companies founded by expellees in later periods, they suggest that expellees coming from different countries of origin brought different skills.

DISCUSSION

When communities become more heterogeneous through mass migration, private economic activity increases in the long run. This chapter presents qualitative and quantitative evidence from West Germany to support this claim.

The arrival of millions of expellees presented an unprecedented economic challenge. Postwar deprivation in the receiving communities was extreme, and the expellees bore the brunt of the burden, whether in the form of food scarcity, unemployment, or reduced purchasing power. To boot, expellees lost most of their assets and capital and were assigned to rural areas, where their occupational skills were often irrelevant. For a decade and a half after WWII, self-employment rates remained lower in municipalities that had received larger numbers of expellees. In this regard, the situation for migrants in postwar West Germany was markedly worse than in Poland's resettled territories, where jobs and housing were plentiful, intergroup inequality was low, and both forced and voluntary migrants experienced upward mobility.

Within a relatively short time, however, the presence of expellees wound up benefiting the receiving communities in West Germany. Both the size and the diversity of the expellee population contributed to higher rates of entrepreneurship and education (although expellee diversity had a more consistently positive effect on all economic indicators examined). In Bavaria, municipalities with a higher share of expellees achieved higher self-employment rates and education levels within a generation. This pattern also holds for the rest of West Germany, where the initially negative consequences of displacement began to reverse by the 1970s. The positive economic legacy of uprooting remains visible in West Germany to this day, notwithstanding subsequent internal migration. In the 2000s, more than half a century after WWII, counties that had received a more heterogeneous mix of expellees had higher average incomes and registered more companies in the knowledge industries, which require highly educated employees.

Viewed together, the long-run benefits of heterogeneity that resulted from mass migration appear to be very similar in West Germany and Poland's resettled territories. However, they took more time to manifest in Poland: Until the late 1980s, migrants there had few opportunities to apply their ingenuity and complementary skills under communist rule. By contrast, in West Germany, expellees' entrepreneurial spirit as well as their new skills and knowledge could be applied right away, often with state encouragement in the form of start-up loans, education grants, and partial compensation for lost assets. In many cases, workshops and businesses that expellees were forced to leave behind were reestablished in West Germany. The comparison of findings in Chapters 7 and 8 thus underscores that the economic effects of migration-based diversity are conditional on the presence of *inclusive* institutions that protect private property rights and ensure access to education and economic opportunity for all citizens.

# 9

# Conclusion

In November 1989, West German Chancellor Helmut Kohl attended Mass in the small Silesian village of Krzyżowa (*Kreisau*), side by side with Poland's Prime Minister Tadeusz Mazowiecki. The location was proposed by the Wrocław Catholic Intelligentsia Club because during the war Krzyżowa was where the Kreisau Circle, a German anti-Nazi group, used to meet. Poland was just emerging from communism, and the Berlin Wall had fallen three days prior.

The first German leader to visit the territories transferred from Germany to Poland after the war, Kohl arrived to advocate for more rights for the German minority in Poland. Mazowiecki, in turn, hoped to finally secure West German recognition of the Oder-Neisse line as the permanent border between the two countries.

The ceremony was briefly interrupted by a demonstration of the Silesian-German community. Thousands of protesters used Kohl's visit to demand official minority status from Warsaw, carrying banners such as "Helmut you're our Chancellor too" and "We Demand German Schools and Church Services." A part of the crowd began to shout "Mazowiecki!" and another loudly chanted "Helmut!"

Notwithstanding the commotion, the two leaders embraced in a gesture of peace. This image would become an icon of German-Polish relations for years to come, even though the issues that brought Kohl to Poland would not be resolved for another year, with the signing of the German-Polish Border treaty. "We don't want to forget history. We want to learn from history," urged Kohl in his address at Krzyżowa.[1]

In this final chapter, I consider what we have learned from mass migration in the aftermath of WWII. I return to the questions set up at the beginning of

---

[1] Tagliabue, John. 1989. "Clamor in the East: A Rite of Healing." *The New York Times*, November 13. Section A, Page 1.

this book about the effects of uprooting on intergroup relations, state capacity, and economic performance. I then discuss the implications of the analysis for broader debates in the fields of comparative politics and political economy and the applicability of my findings to other cases of forced migration.

REVIEWING THE ARGUMENT AND EVIDENCE

Modern Poland and Germany are a product of WWII, which redrew European borders and uprooted approximately one-fifth of each country's population. Using fine-grained statistical data and narrative evidence from these two countries, the book traced the varied and sometimes contradictory effects of this mass displacement on the receiving communities, state institutions, and economic performance over time. I argued that postwar population movements diversified Polish and German societies in profound ways and in doing so, influenced the trajectory of their social and economic development for decades to come. Counterintuitively, mass displacement ended up strengthening the state and improving economic performance in the long run.

I first showed that simply reorganizing ethnically homogeneous groups in space created new cleavages, with consequences for cooperation in the provision of collective goods at the community level. Coming into contact with people from other regions helped define the contrasting identities of repatriates, settlers, and autochthones in Poland. In West Germany, the exposure to expellees led natives to close their ranks; expellees, in turn, united around their regional identities and migration status. The expellee–native cleavage overshadowed all other social divisions, not least between former Nazis and opponents of the Nazi regime. These patterns support the view that social identities are constructed and situational (e.g., Posner 2004b) and that people's relationships with others are often more important than their cultural attributes for the formation of group boundaries (Barth 1969, 10).

In both cases, the uprooted population groups received full citizenship rights, which enabled them to make claims on the state and motivated the incumbent governments to invest in their integration. Using qualitative and quantitative analysis within each country, I showed that mass displacement and its discontents shored up the role of the central government in mediating local conflicts and providing collective and private goods, thereby increasing subnational administrative capacity. In Poland's resettled territories, the state served as an organizer of social and economic life and as the guarantor of Polish control over formerly German property. Weak collective action in uprooted, culturally diverse communities was an important reason why the communist government was able to implement far-reaching economic reforms in the resettled territories.

The authorities in West Germany were less than enthusiastic about the inflow of forced migrants, whom they viewed as potentially dangerous. The initial measures implemented to provide financial support to expellees arose from concerns that, in the absence of state assistance, these individuals might become radicalized. Once the expellees formed their own political party, their impact on government policy increased considerably. In contrast to the Polish migrants and autochthones, who wielded little influence on state policy, the expellees in West Germany secured considerable concessions from the federal government. As a result of expellee pressure, Germany would pay out some DM145.3 billion to the expellees and their descendants over a period of nearly half a century (Borutta and Jansen 2016, 3). Until the 1970s, all political parties supported the expellees' right to return to lost homelands. Expellees were also well represented in federal and state governments. Still, many pro-expellee policies were diluted or sabotaged by resistance from the native population.

Using statistical data that span more than half a century, the book also traced out the economic effects of displacement at the subnational level. In Poland, mass uprooting was followed by over four decades of communism, which restricted private economic activity. Up until the 1990s, I found no economic differences between places that varied in terms of migrant composition. However, after Poland transitioned to a market economy, communities settled by more heterogeneous migrant groups achieved higher per capita incomes and entrepreneurship rates than communities settled by more homogeneous groups.

Subnational statistical analysis in West Germany, which adopted the social market economy model, allowed me to trace the consequences of mass displacement and resulting heterogeneity over time, while holding the institutional environment constant. I found that the negative effects of expellee presence on aggregate levels of entrepreneurial activity were limited to the first two decades after the war. It took just over a generation for the effects of expellee presence on entrepreneurship and education levels to become positive. In the long run, both the size and the diversity of the uprooted population increased entrepreneurship rates, education levels, and average household incomes. The reversal of fortunes in West Germany was not accompanied by institutional change, which suggests that mass displacement and cultural heterogeneity have divergent effects in the short and in long term.

In sum, the inflow of heterogeneous migrants eventually benefited the receiving economies, even when they settled in areas with scarce employment opportunities and inadequate housing. However, the positive economic effects of displacement were contingent on the quality of formal institutions. New skills and knowledge brought by forced and voluntary migrants from different places of origin translated into economic payoffs only when the state protected property rights and encouraged private entrepreneurship. The comparison of Poland and West Germany thus allowed me to pin down the scope conditions under which the hypothesis on the long-run economic benefits of migration and cultural diversity holds and to examine how long it takes for the negative externalities of mass uprooting to disappear.

What can my findings tell us about migration and cultural heterogeneity more broadly? The biggest takeaway is that under the right conditions, hosting displaced persons can benefit the host society, particularly in the long run. My research further shows that the effects of forced migration unfold over generations rather than years and may change over time. At first, the arrival of refugees put pressure on public resources and reduced social cohesion in the receiving communities. Over time, however, refugees' presence translated into higher incomes and entrepreneurship rates. These divergent short- and long-run effects indicate that developing a comprehensive understanding of the consequences of migration requires a longer time frame than in most prior studies.

My analysis also suggests that the economic effects of migration and resulting heterogeneity are conditional on the broader institutional environment: the inflow of heterogeneous migrant populations advances long-run development only in states with inclusive formal institutions, that is institutions that protect property rights and enforce contracts of all citizens (Acemoglu and Robinson 2012).

## EXTENDING THE FRAMEWORK TO OTHER CASES

How far does my argument travel? Would we expect forced migration and resulting heterogeneity to have similarly positive effects on state building and long-run economic outcomes in other contexts?

Although I expect my general approach to apply widely, my findings are drawn from cases involving migrants who are sometimes described as "privileged" because they received full citizenship rights upon arrival (Žmegač 2005). Shared citizenship enabled the uprooted Poles and Germans to make claims on the state and compelled the receiving governments to react. This form of migration occurred in many places in the twentieth century following the dissolution of multiethnic states and overseas colonies. In this section, I draw on existing research on similar historical cases to probe the generalizability of my findings.

### Migration Following the Dissolution of Multiethnic States and Empires

To start, let us consider three twentieth-century cases of mass uprooting: Orthodox Christians in Greece; Pakistani Mohajir in India; and French Pied-Noirs in France. Each of these involve migration following the dissolution of a multi-ethnic state or empire.

The first case served as a model for the Allies contemplating the transfer of ethnic Germans at the end of WWII. In the aftermath of the Greco-Turkish War 1919–1922, 1.2 million Orthodox Christians from Turkey were resettled to Greece and 350,000 Muslims from Greece were resettled across the Aegean to Turkey. Refugees from Turkey amounted to nearly a quarter of the Greek population at the time. Despite the common view that population exchanges homogenized Greece, the Asia Minor refugees had a distinct linguistic, cultural, and ideological background that set them apart from the mainland Greeks (O'Sullivan 2010, 52). The natives greeted them with widespread animosity upon arrival, and tensions between the two groups occasionally escalated into violence (Kontogiorgi 2006, 259). Some fifty years after the resettlement, the repatriated Greeks appeared to have preserved a separate identity from the native population (Hirschon 1989, 4–5).

The inflow of the Orthodox Christian refugees threatened to destabilize Greece. The government responded by spending over 40 percent of the national budget to parcel out land to facilitate refugee settlement and integration (Kontogiorgi 2003, 74). This added spending imposed a substantial burden on the Greek economy. Additionally, the refugees received assistance from the Refugee Settlement Commission, established by the League of Nations with the aim of enabling refugees to achieve self-sufficiency (Murard and Sakalli 2019). Still, many problems remained unresolved. Although the Treaty of Lausanne gave refugees the right to compensation for the property they left behind, many refugees remained destitute decades later.

While costly for the receiving state in the short term and traumatic for the affected individuals, the inflow of Asia Minor refugees benefited the Greek economy in the long term. Using a geocoded dataset that locates refugee settlements in Greek municipalities, Murard and Sakalli (2019) show that places that had received more refugees in 1923 exhibited higher average earnings, a more extensive manufacturing sector, and higher night-light luminosity in 1991. The authors theorize that the refugees brought complementary skills that fostered long-run growth by facilitating technology transfers and increasing human capital, skill complementarities, and the size of the labor force.

Another case with similar characteristics is the uprooting of 17.9 million people during the partition of British India in 1947–51. After the sudden creation of the international border between India and Pakistan, millions of people found themselves stranded far away from their supposed new homeland. Refugee movements were accompanied by widespread communal violence that left an estimated half a million dead. The Partition increased religious homogeneity within each country and at the same time increased heterogeneity within the affected communities in terms of education, social status, and occupation (Bharadwaj, Khwaja, and Mian 2008). It gave rise to new ethnic categories, such as the Mohajirs, or Muslims who migrated from India to Pakistan.[2]

In the short run, the Partition and subsequent displacement had adverse economic repercussions for the affected communities, disrupting trade, shattering

---

[2] In Urdu, the term 'Mohajir' means a migrant or refugee who has left their homeland to preserve their faith. Initially, the category applied to all refugees from India, but later it came to signify Urdu speakers. Over time, Mohajirs mobilized politically and established several Mohajir parties (Shah and Sareen 2019).

lives, and triggering a humanitarian crisis. The long-run economic effects of displacement at the subnational level appear to be positive, however, at least on the Indian side of the border. Bharadwaj and Mirza (2019) find that the Indian districts that accommodated a greater number of refugees post-Partition witnessed a rise in agricultural productivity during the Green Revolution.[3] The authors attribute this finding to the refugees' high levels of human capital, as well as to the inflow of governmental aid, which reached nearly 90 percent of the displaced population in some districts.[4]

Finally, we can examine the case of the French Pied-Noirs – the postcolonial repatriation of French settlers from Algeria to France following the Algerian War of Independence in the early 1960s. In a recent volume edited by Borutta and Jansen (2016), the authors write that the repatriates were "perceived as culturally different, if not inferior, and were rejected by many of their fellow citizens" even though they were of French origin and attended French schools in Algiers (Borutta and Jansen 2016, 1). Over time, these so-called Pied-Noirs developed a separate identity, just like German expellees (Schioldo-Zürcher 2016, 208–209). In 1999, they created their own political party, Parti des Pieds-Noirs.

The French state took care of the repatriates from Algeria on an unparalleled scale because it perceived them as a potentially dangerous group. It set up a massive administrative apparatus to provide jobs, housing, and social security benefits in order to reduce tensions between the Pied-Noirs and the local population. In particular, the Pied-Noirs received a "Repatriation Package" covering their travel and moving expenses and were prioritized over other French citizens in the allocation of farmland and business premises, in an attempt to facilitate their economic integration. Civil servants were entitled to employment in equivalent posts in France; private-sector employees received monthly allowances (Schioldo-Zürcher 2016, 99). Borutta and Jansen (2016, 3) conclude that the integration programs set up by the French government were an important driving force behind the expansion of the French welfare state.

The economic effects of the Pied-Noirs' postcolonial repatriation remain underexplored, although there is some indication that these effects varied over time. According to Edo (2019), the influx of Pied-Noirs initially led to a decline in natives' wages from 1962 to 1968; however, it subsequently exerted a more substantial positive effect on wages from 1968 to 1976.

These three cases underscore that shared ethnicity and nationality cannot guarantee that the refugees are viewed as compatriots upon arrival. Even

---

[3] There is no comparable research on economic outcomes in Pakistani districts.

[4] The Indian government distinguished refugees based on their potential for rehabilitation and timing of arrival into groups with varying deserving-ness to receive aid. All refugees from West Pakistan, who experienced the highest incidence of violence, were entitled to relief and rehabilitation benefits. By contrast, refugees from East Pakistan received very little aid from the government (Chakravarty 2014).

though the refugees were ostensibly returning "home," they were perceived as outsiders by the local population. In other words, forced displacement created new cleavages and generated conflict, regardless of how culturally similar migrants and natives were. In two of the three cases – Pakistani Mohajir and French Pied-Noirs, – migration-based cleavages remained politically salient in the 2000s. There is also some evidence that the arrival of refugees and repatriates improved long-run economic performance. In other words, the inflow of forced migrants was a "blessing in disguise" from the perspective of the receiving societies, particularly in the medium to long term.

What about the effects of these migrant flows on state capacity? This is an important direction for future research, but these cases fit the scope conditions of my theory. In each of the three cases, the receiving governments appeared willing to mobilize considerable administrative and fiscal resources to integrate the refugee populations. The sheer scale of each displacement episode – and the realization that the uprooting was permanent – compelled state officials to react. It is plausible that dealing with the newcomers increased each state's capacity.

## Settling the Frontiers

The causal mechanisms I discussed in Chapter 5, regarding the buildup of state capacity in Poland's resettled territories, are also likely to operate following the settlement of state frontiers, understood as regions with extremely low population density (Bazzi, Fiszbein, and Gebresilasse 2017). Scholarship on state development in frontier regions has reached divergent conclusions with respect to the effect of mass immigration for outcomes related to state capacity. In Canada, Russia, Brazil, and the United States, self-organized society in the frontier regions appears to have "crowded out" the state (Foa and Nemirovskaya 2016) and engendered opposition to state regulation in the long run (Bazzi, Fiszbein, and Gebresilasse 2017). By contrast, in the Middle East, Southeast Asia, and elsewhere frontiers appear to have strengthened state authority and benefited the incumbent government politically (Migdal 1989). For instance, the Israeli state offered Jewish settlers protection and economic resources in exchange for their willingness to secure the contested territories of the West Bank, the Golan Heights, and Gaza. These "pioneers" developed a strong sense of Jewish identity and grew dependent on state support (Troen 1999). In Rwanda, the government resettled some 450,000 persons to new farms in the region previously controlled by Tutsi landlords. The resettlement increased state control over the border region and bound the Hutu settlers to the incumbent regime (McNamee 2018). In Indonesia, the uprooting of two million people from the Inner Islands of Java and Bali to the Outer Islands via the state-sponsored Transmigration program has been shown to facilitate the convergence toward new forms of shared national identity, advancing state-building goals (Bazzi, Fiszbein, and Gebresilasse 2017).

These divergent findings may be the product of differences in state policy in the frontier regions. Settling the frontier appears to strengthen state capacity when the governments take an active role in assisting the settlers, providing a wide range of collective goods. By contrast, when settlers are left to fend for themselves and set up organizations for the provision of public goods before the arrival of the state, state capacity in the frontier remains tenuous.

**Contemporary Refugee Crises**

In the last decade, European states have been dealing with a record number of refugees from Syria, Ukraine, Afghanistan, and other countries. The situation facing Europe today is unlike the post-WWII period in several respects. A pivotal distinction lies in the fact that present-day refugees do not automatically acquire full citizenship rights upon their arrival and are generally expected to return to their home countries once the conflicts subside. My findings about state–society relations in migrant-receiving communities do not translate well to such contexts. For instance, refugees who cannot vote face greater barriers to making claims on the receiving governments, rendering the "demand" channel less relevant. Additionally, refugees' ability to sustain themselves and contribute to the local economy is compromised when they are excluded from the formal labor market or housed in temporary settlements isolated from the native population. Furthermore, the economic behavior of refugees is likely to be influenced by the anticipated duration of their stay in host communities.

Nonetheless, my book offers broadly applicable lessons. First, I contribute to the discussion about the relevance of cultural similarity for successful integration of refugees. One of the key concerns about refugees in today's Europe is their impact on culture and way of life in receiving societies. The arrival of Syrians in 2015–2016 sparked anti-immigrant protests across Europe. By contrast, much more numerous Ukrainian refugees received a warm welcome in 2022. In a survey of 18,000 eligible voters in fifteen countries in Western Europe, Bansak, Hainmueller, and Hangartner (2016) show that Europeans are more willing to accept Christian rather than Muslim asylum seekers, all else equal.

Analysis in this book questions the preoccupation with refugees' culture by drawing on two different pieces of evidence. On the one hand, I show that no matter how culturally similar refugees are to each other and to the native population, their arrival increases tensions and reduces cooperation in the short term. The migrant–native conflict was equally acute in the German state of Schleswig-Holstein, where the majority of expellees came from within prewar Germany and shared religious denominations and institutional backgrounds with the natives, as it was in Bavaria, where the majority of expellees came from Czechoslovak Sudetenland and where many expellees did not share religious denomination with the native population. The key takeaway from my historical cases is that large-scale population movements can create new cleavages even within ethnically homogeneous societies. Other studies reach similar conclusions. In a thoroughly researched book on immigration and conflict in contemporary Germany and the UK, Dancygier (2010, 292) finds that "resource scarcity – not ethnic difference – is the key driver of immigrant conflict."

On the other hand, I show that the more heterogeneous migrant inflows are, the better for long-run economic performance. Conditional on the share of migrants, Polish and West German communities that received migrants from more diverse places of origin wound up more economically successful than communities that received migrants from the same region of origin. Refugees coming from different cultures are more likely to bring complementary skills and novel experiences, which can increase economic productivity and entrepreneurship (e.g., Ortega and Peri 2014; Alesina, Harnoss, and Rapoport 2016; Bove and Elia 2017). Conversely, scholars have yet to find any evidence that migrants' "cultural baggage" undermines the functioning of formal and informal institutions in receiving societies (Nowrasteh and Powell 2021).

My research suggests that state policy toward the displaced population is ultimately more important than cultural distance in shaping the long-run social and economic consequences of displacement. Governments often impose greater restrictions on migrants from more distant and less developed countries, which discourages integration and feeds stereotypes among the native population. As noted earlier, Syrian refugees face greater restrictions in the labor market than Ukrainian refugees in the EU today, which affects their interaction with the native population and their ability and desire to integrate. Until recently, the German state treated ethnic Germans from abroad very differently than Turkish guest workers or other foreigners. Other examples abound. Such disparate treatment of individuals based on ethnicity, religion, or country of origin has downstream consequences for their interactions with the state and participation in the economy.

This discussion highlights the key role that state policy plays in facilitating forced migrants' economic integration. Beyond the moral imperative to assist people uprooted by violent conflicts and natural disasters, policymakers can act with the confidence that investing resources in supporting the newcomers and protecting their rights is likely to pay off in the long run. For one, mobilizing fiscal and administrative resources to assist forced migrants can strengthen subnational administrative capacity, making the state more resilient in the face of future crises. Moreover, the diverse skills and experience migrants bring can improve economic performance in the receiving communities, provided the newcomers have an opportunity to participate in the formal labor market. Providing integration assistance that enables forced migrants to obtain education and employment benefits the receiving economies.

Finally, the book questions the common belief that returning second- and third-generation refugees to their countries of origin will repair the harms of forced displacement. At the end of WWII, the Allies viewed postwar population transfers as a form of repatriation, with Poles and Germans coming back to their national homelands, where they supposedly belonged. Nationality took precedence over "the concrete realities" of "home" as a place (Long 2013, 47). Similar views remain prevalent and guide refugee policy today. One of three main solutions to the problem of mass displacement today, as articulated by the UNHCR, is refugees' "return in safety and dignity" (Zetter 2021). Repatriation is often championed not only by host countries that seek to reduce the number of refugees on their territories but also by international organizations that care about refugees' well-being.

My book shows, however, that repatriation may be incredibly traumatic for the refugees and may increase social tensions in the short run. Indeed, studies that examine the consequences of refugee return to their countries of origin in contemporary settings question the potential of repatriation to "undo" the consequences of displacement and instead show that repatriated refugees often end up uprooted for the second time (e.g., Schwartz 2019; Zetter 2021). This is a cautionary tale for the advocates of refugee repatriation as a solution to current refugee crises, particularly when some time has passed between forced migration and the refugees' return.

# Appendix A

## Additional Maps, Figures, and Tables

TABLE A.1 *Major migration episodes (over 500,000 people) used for Figure 1.*

| Start | End | Migration episode | Total affected | Region | Origin | Reference |
|---|---|---|---|---|---|---|
| 1914 | 1918 | WWI | 10,000,000 | Europe | European countries | 1 |
| 1915 | 1922 | Armenian Genocide and aftermath | 818,000 | Asia | Turkey | 2 |
| 1917 | 1923 | Russian Civil War | 1,500,000 | Europe | Russia | 3, 4 |
| 1923 | 1923 | Greece and Turkey population exchange | 1,550,000 | Asia | Greece and Turkey | 5 |
| 1936 | 1939 | Spanish Civil War | 3,724,000 | Europe | Spain | 6 |
| 1937 | 1945 | Japanese occupation of China | 20,000,000 | Asia | Japan-controlled China | 7 |
| 1937 | 1945 | WWII in Asia and war in China, not including Chinese displacement from Japanese occupation | 12,000,000 | Asia | Asia | 7 |
| 1939 | 1945 | WWII in Europe, not including Nazi deportations | 40,000,000 | Europe | European countries | 8 |

(*continued*)

TABLE A.1 *(continued)*

| Start | End | Migration episode | Total affected | Region | Origin | Reference |
|-------|-----|-------------------|----------------|--------|--------|-----------|
| 1939 | 1945 | Japanese occupation of Korea | 750,000 | Asia | Korea | 9 |
| 1941 | 1942 | Stalin's deportations | 2,293,000 | Europe, Asia | USSR | 10 |
| 1941 | 1943 | Nazi deportations to Chelmno, Belzec, Sobibor, and Treblinka | 1,733,300 | Europe | European countries | 11 |
| 1942 | 1944 | Nazi deportations to Auschwitz | 1,123,000 | Europe | European countries | 11 |
| 1945 | 1946 | Post-WWII population transfers | 19,580,000 | Europe | | 12 |
| 1947 | 1947 | Partition of India and Pakistan | 14,000,000 | Asia | British-controlled India/Pakistan | 8 |
| 1948 | 1950 | Fleeing communism | 1,000,000 | Europe | USSR | 8 |
| 1948 | 1950 | Establishment of Israel | 750,000 | Asia | New Israeli territory | 8 |
| 1950 | 1953 | Korean War | 7,000,000 | Asia | Korea | 13 |
| 1954 | 1956 | Establishment of communism in Vietnam | 1,000,000 | Asia | North Vietnam | 8 |
| 1954 | 1962 | Algerian War of Independence | 1,200,000 | Africa | Algeria | 8 |
| 1960 | 1969 | Internal displacement in South Vietnam | 10,000,000 | Asia | South Vietnam | 8 |
| 1965 | 1972 | South Vietnam emigration to North | 2,700,000 | Asia | South Vietnam | 8 |
| 1967 | 1967 | Biafran War | 2,000,000 | Africa | Nigeria | 8 |
| 1971 | 1971 | Bangladesh War of Independence | 10,000,000 | Asia | East Pakistan | 8 |

TABLE A.1 *(continued)*

| Start | End | Migration episode | Total affected | Region | Origin | Reference |
|---|---|---|---|---|---|---|
| 1974 | 1976 | Migration to Portugal after decolonization of African colonies | 800,000 | Europe, Africa | Mozambique, Angola | 14 |
| 1975 | 1995 | Vietnam War aftermath | 800,000 | Asia | Vietnam | 8 |
| 1976 | 1992 | Civil war in Mozambique | 5,700,000 | Africa | Mozambique | 8 |
| 1977 | 1979 | Somali invasion of Ethiopia | 620,000 | Africa | Ethiopia | 8 |
| 1978 | 1980 | Establishment of Communist government in Afghanistan and start of Soviet invasion | 1,780,000 | Asia | Afghanistan | 8 |
| 1980 | 1988 | Iran–Iraq War | 600,000 | Asia | Iraq | 8 |
| 1981 | 1989 | Remainder of Soviet-Afghan War | 4,520,000 | Asia | Afghanistan | 8 |
| 1981 | 1989 | Civil wars in Central America | 2,000,000 | Americas | Nicaragua, El Salvador, Guatemala | 8 |
| 1990 | 1990 | Fighting between Armenia and Azerbaijan over Nagorno-Karabakh | 800,000 | Asia | Nagorno-Karabakh | 8 |
| 1991 | 1991 | Iraqi suppression of rebel movement | 1,820,000 | Asia | Iraq | 8 |
| 1991 | 1991 | War of independence and subsequent ethnic cleansing in Croatia | 550,000 | Europe | Croatia | 8 |

*(continued)*

TABLE A.1  *(continued)*

| Start | End | Migration episode | Total affected | Region | Origin | Reference |
|---|---|---|---|---|---|---|
| 1991 | 1992 | Somali Civil War outbreak | 1,500,000 | Africa | Somalia | 15 |
| 1992 | 1992 | Civil war in Tajikistan | 600,000 | Asia | Tajikistan | 8 |
| 1994 | 1994 | Rwandan genocide | 3,500,000 | Africa | Rwanda | 8 |
| 1994 | 1995 | Conflict following breakup of Yugoslavia | 2,500,000 | Europe | Bosnia and Herzegovina | 8 |
| 1998 | 1999 | NATO airstrikes in response to Serbian oppression of Kosovar Albanians | 800,000 | Europe | Kosovo | 8 |
| 1998 | 2003 | Second Congo War | 3,600,000 | Africa | DR Congo | 16 |
| 1999 | 1999 | Indonesian suppression of East Timor | 540,000 | Asia | East Timor | 8 |
| 2000 | 2023 | Civil conflict in Colombia | 7,087,837 | Americas | Colombia | 17 |
| 2001 | 2021 | US invasion of Afghanistan | 6,100,000 | Asia | Afghanistan | 18 |
| 2001 | 2023 | US invasion of Pakistan and ongoing conflict | 3,724,396 | Asia | Pakistan | 19 |
| 2002 | 2023 | US intervention in Somalia | 4,300,000 | Africa | Somalia | 19 |
| 2002 | 2023 | Conflict in Philippines against Abu Sayyaf and other groups | 1,800,000 | Asia | Philippines | 19 |
| 2003 | 2023 | US invasion of Iraq and War against ISIS | 9,200,000 | Asia | Iraq | 19 |
| 2003 | 2023 | War in Darfur | 3,000,000 | Africa | Sudan | 20 |
| 2011 | 2023 | Syrian Civil War | 13,600,000 | Asia | Syria | 21 |

TABLE A.1 *(continued)*

| Start | End | Migration episode | Total affected | Region | Origin | Reference |
|---|---|---|---|---|---|---|
| 2011 | 2011 | Libyan Civil War | 1,200,000 | Africa | Libya | 19 |
| 2011 | 2023 | Conflict in Sahel region of Africa | 5,220,625 | Africa | Mali, Burkina Faso, Niger | 22 |
| 2012 | 2023 | Repression in Burma | 2,700,000 | Asia | Burma | 23 |
| 2013 | 2020 | South Sudanese Civil War | 4,540,000 | Africa | South Sudan | 24 |
| 2013 | 2023 | Conflict in Central African Republic | 1,900,000 | Africa | Central African Republic | 25 |
| 2014 | 2023 | Venezuelan refugee crisis | 7,130,000 | Americas | Venezuela | 26 |
| 2014 | 2022 | Yemeni Civil War | 4,595,173 | Asia | Yemen | 27 |
| 2017 | 2023 | DR Congo emergency | 6,800,000 | Africa | Democratic Republic of the Congo | 28 |
| 2020 | 2022 | Tigray Crisis in Ethiopia | 3,559,000 | Africa | Ethiopia | 29 |
| 2022 | 2023 | Russia-Ukraine war | 11,300,000 | Europe | Ukraine | 30, 31 |

REFERENCES FOR TABLE A.1

1. Gatrell, Peter. 2014. "Refugees." International Encyclopedia of the First World War. October 8, 2014. https://encyclopedia.1914-1918-online.net/article/refugees.
2. US Department of State. 1922. "Approximate Number of Armenians in the World, November 1922." https://upload.wikimedia.org/wikipedia/commons/6/66/US_State_Department_document_on_Armenian_Refugess_in_1921.jpg.
3. McElvanney, Katie. n.d. "The Russian Refugee Crisis of the 1920s." The British Library, European Studies Blog. https://blogs.bl.uk/european/2015/12/the-russian-refugee-crisis-of-the-1920s.html.
4. UNC Libraries. n.d. "Refugees." World on Fire: In Flames and Blood. https://exhibits.lib.unc.edu/exhibits/show/world-on-fire/refugees.

5. Gürsoy, Yaprak. 2008. "The Effects of the Population Exchange on the Greek and Turkish Political Regimes in the 1930s." *East European Quarterly* 42 (2): 95–128.

6. Rodrigo, Javier, and David Alegre Lorenz. 2022. "Before the Convention: The Spanish Civil War and Challenges for Research on Refugee History." *Refugee Survey Quarterly* 41 (2): 196–217. doi.org/10.1093/rsq/hdac005.

7. Oyen, Meredith. 2014. "The Right of Return: Chinese Displaced Persons and the International Refugee Organization, 1947–56." *Modern Asian Studies* 49 (2): 546–71. https://doi.org/10.1017/S0026749X14000420.

8. UNHCR. 2000. *The State of the World's Refugees 2000: Fifty Years of Humanitarian Action.* UNHCR. www.unhcr.org/publications/state-worlds-refugees-2000-fifty-years-humanitarian-action.

9. Moon, Rennie. 2010. "Koreans in Japan." Stanford Program on International and Cross-Cultural Education. http://spice.fsi.stanford.edu/docs/koreans_in_japan.

10. Aurélie, Campana. 2019. "The Soviet Massive Deportations: A Chronology." SciencesPo. April 18, 2019. www.sciencespo.fr/mass-violence-war-massacre-resistance/fr/document/soviet-massive-deportations-chronology.html.

11. United States Holocaust Memorial Museum. n.d. "Deportations to Killing Centers." Holocaust Encyclopedia. https://encyclopedia.ushmm.org/content/en/article/deportations-to-killing-centers.

12. Schechtman, Joseph B. 1953. "Postwar Population Transfers in Europe: A Survey." *The Review of Politics* 15 (2): 151–78.

13. Kim, Janice C. H. 2017. "Pusan at War: Refuge, Relief, and Resettlement in the Temporary Capital, 1950–1953." *The Journal of American-East Asian Relations* 24 (2/3): 103–27.

14. Smith, Andrea L. 2003. "Introduction: Europe's Invisible Migrants." In *Europe's Invisible Migrants*, edited by Andrea L. Smith, 9–32. Amsterdam University Press. www.jstor.org/stable/j.ctt46mxq8.4.

15. Prunier, Gérard. 1995. "Somalia: Civil War, Intervention and Withdrawal 1990–1995." Refworld. July 1, 1995. www.refworld.org/docid/3ae6a6c98.html.

16. Kreibaum, Merle. 2016. "Their Suffering, Our Burden? How Congolese Refugees affect the Ugandan Population." *World Development* 78 (February): 262–87. doi.org/10.1016/j.worlddev.2015.10.019.

17. UNHCR. n.d. "Refugee Statistics: Colombia." Refugee Data Finder. www.unhcr.org/refugee-statistics/.

18. UNHCR. n.d. "Afghanistan." UNHCR USA. www.unhcr.org/us/countries/afghanistan.

19. Vine, David, Cala Coffman, Katalina Khoury, Madison Lovasz, Helen Bush, Rachel Leduc, and Jennfier Walkup. 2021. "Creating Refugees:

Displacement Caused by the United States' Post 9/11 Wars." Costs of War. Watson Institute for International and Public Affairs, Brown University.

20. UNHCR. 2021. "Darfur Clashes Displace Thousands." UNHCR USA. December 7, 2021. www.unhcr.org/us/news/briefing-notes/darfur-clashes-displace-thousands.

21. Crawford, Neta. 2023. "Blood and Treasure: United States Budgetary Costs and Human Costs of 20 Years of War in Iraq and Syria, 2003–2023." Costs of War. Watson Institute for International and Public Affairs, Brown University.

22. UNHCR. n.d. "Situation: Sahel Crisis." UNHCR Operational Data Portal. https://data.unhcr.org/en/situations/sahelcrisis.

23. UNHCR. n.d. "Myanmar Situation." Global Focus. https://reporting.unhcr.org/operational/situations/myanmar-situation.

24. UNHCR. 2023. "South Sudan Refugee Crisis Explained." UNHCR USA. July 24, 2023. www.unrefugees.org/news/south-sudan-refugee-crisis-explained/.

25. UNHCR. n.d. "Central African Republic Refugee Crisis." UNHCR USA. www.unrefugees.org/emergencies/central-african-republic/.

26. UNHCR. n.d. "Emergency Appeal: Venezuela Situation." UNHCR. www.unhcr.org/emergencies/venezuela-situation.

27. UNHCR. n.d. "Refugee Statistics: Yemen." Refugee Data Finder. www.unhcr.org/refugee-statistics/.

28. UNHCR. 2023. "Emergency Appeal: DR Congo Emergency." UNHCR USA. February 2023. www.unhcr.org/us/emergencies/dr-congo-emergency.

29. UNHCR. n.d. "Ethiopia Refugee Crisis: Aid, Statistics and News." UNHCR USA. www.unrefugees.org/emergencies/ethiopia/.

30. UNHCR. n.d. "Ukraine Refugee Crisis: Aid, Statistics and News." UNHCR USA. www.unrefugees.org/emergencies/ukraine/.

31. UNHCR. n.d. "Situation: Ukraine." UNHCR Operational Data Portal. https://data.unhcr.org/en/situations/ukraine.

CHAPTER 2: EUROPE'S ZERO HOUR

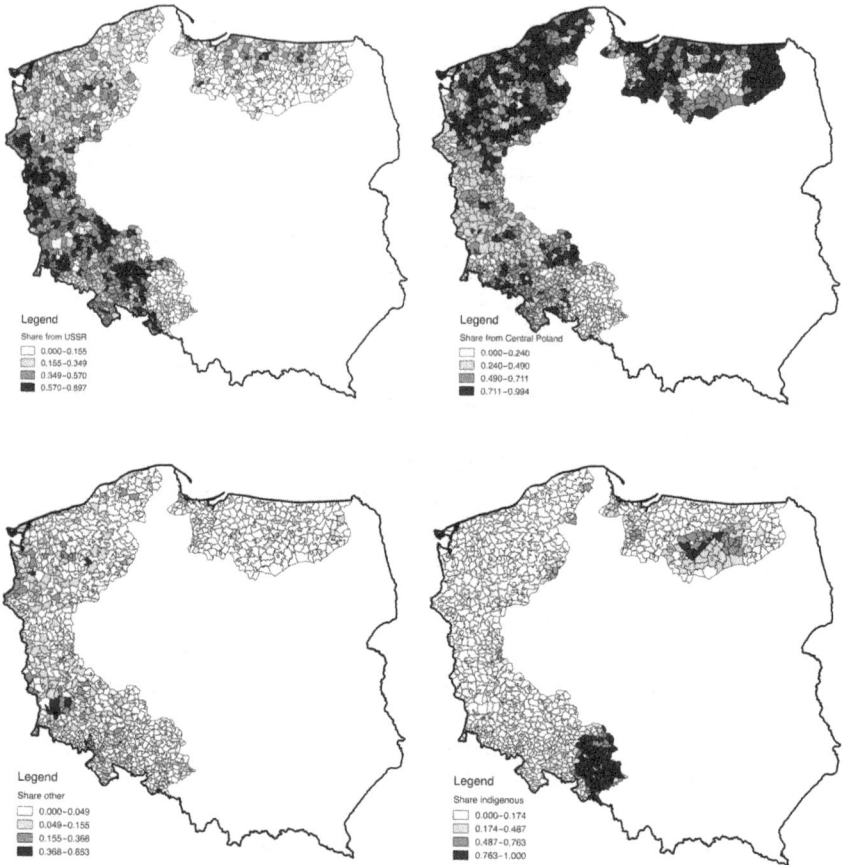

Map A.1 Distribution of main population groups in Polish municipalities. Groups plotted from left to right: repatriates from USSR; settlers from Central Poland; (3) reemigrants from Western Europe; (4) autochthonous population. Source: 1948 population census at the municipal level.

CHAPTER 3: COOPERATION IN HOMOGENEOUS AND
HETEROGENEOUS POLISH VILLAGES

TABLE A.2 *Migrant share, cultural diversity, and volunteer fire brigades in Opole villages.*

| | Dependent variable: OSP presence, yes==1 | | | |
|---|---|---|---|---|
| | (1) | (2) | (3) | (4) |
| Share migrants | −0.87*** | | | |
| | (0.21) | | | |
| Fractionalization index | | −1.11** | | |
| | | (0.54) | | |
| Type 1: heterogeneous | | | −1.16*** | |
| | | | (0.23) | |
| Type 1: homogeneous | | | −0.66*** | |
| | | | (0.24) | |
| Type 1: resettled as a whole | | | −0.68 | |
| | | | (0.43) | |
| Type 2: homogeneous | | | | −0.77** |
| | | | | (0.35) |
| Type 2: moderately heterogeneous | | | | −0.84*** |
| | | | | (0.23) |
| Type 2: resettled together | | | | −0.56 |
| | | | | (0.42) |
| Type 2: very heterogeneous | | | | −0.80*** |
| | | | | (0.26) |
| Share in agriculture | 2.27*** | 2.56*** | 2.66*** | 2.45*** |
| | (0.65) | (0.77) | (0.71) | (0.70) |
| Share farms over 20 ha | 1.15 | 0.37 | 1.30 | 1.14 |
| | (0.82) | (0.90) | (0.89) | (0.90) |
| Ln population | 1.81*** | 1.88*** | 1.90*** | 1.87*** |
| | (0.17) | (0.20) | (0.19) | (0.18) |
| Constant | −12.10*** | −13.01*** | −12.81*** | −12.61*** |
| | (1.30) | (1.61) | (1.44) | (1.41) |
| N | 825 | 586 | 712 | 726 |
| Log likelihood | −450.45 | −328.44 | −384.36 | −394.32 |
| Akaike inf. crit. | 910.90 | 666.87 | 782.73 | 804.63 |

*Note:* All models are logit. Reference category for village types in models 3 and 4 is the autochthonous village. Standard errors are included in parentheses. Significant at *p* < 0.10; **p* < 0.05; ***p* < 0.01.

CHAPTER 4: COOPERATION IN WEST GERMAN COMMUNITIES

TABLE A.3 *Descriptive statistics for Bavarian municipalities.*

| Statistic | N | Mean | St. Dev. | Min | Max |
|---|---|---|---|---|---|
| Share expellees (1950) | 2,052 | 0.25 | 0.07 | 0.04 | 0.71 |
| Share male (1950) | 2,052 | 0.25 | 0.07 | 0.04 | 0.71 |
| Landholding gini (1950) | 2,052 | 0.34 | 0.12 | 0.00 | 0.69 |
| Population (1939) | 2,052 | 3,452 | 21,977 | 107 | 840,586 |
| Distance to rail, km (1939) | 2,052 | 3.77 | 3.21 | 0.00 | 32.00 |
| Distance to Eastern border, km | 2,056 | 103.89 | 72.18 | 0.37 | 303.21 |
| Self-employed (1939) | 2,051 | 0.21 | 0.05 | 0.04 | 0.34 |
| Self-employed (1950) | 2,052 | 0.20 | 0.04 | 0.06 | 0.34 |
| Self-employed (1970) | 2,056 | 0.16 | 0.06 | 0.04 | 0.52 |
| Self-employed (1987) | 2,056 | 0.12 | 0.04 | 0.03 | 0.39 |
| Agriculture (1939) | 2,052 | 0.50 | 0.21 | 0.00 | 0.94 |
| Agriculture (1970) | 2,056 | 0.27 | 0.16 | 0.004 | 0.77 |
| Agriculture (1987) | 2,056 | 0.10 | 0.08 | 0.003 | 0.54 |
| Manufacturing (1970) | 2,056 | 0.45 | 0.12 | 0.08 | 0.84 |
| Manufacturing (1987) | 2,056 | 0.48 | 0.10 | 0.05 | 1.42 |
| Higher/vocational edu (1987) | 2,056 | 0.07 | 0.04 | 0.01 | 0.35 |

CHAPTER 5: STATE BUILDING IN THE POLISH WILD WEST

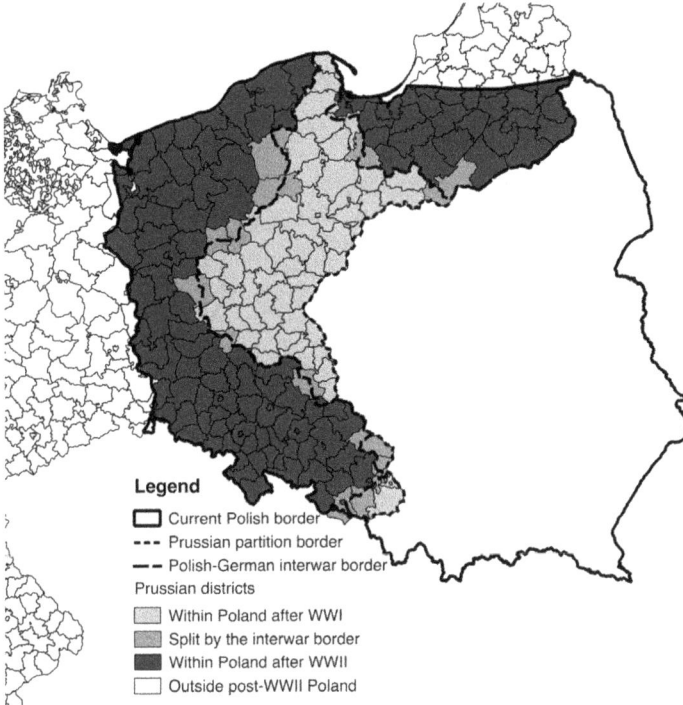

Map A.2 Prussian counties divided by the 1919 Polish–German border.

Map A.3 Differences in infrastructure between former imperial partitions of Poland. Railways were digitized by the author based on the map produced by the Cartography and Publishing Institute GLOB (*Instytut Kartogr. i Wydawniczy GLOB Jana Chodorowicza*).

TABLE A.4 *Pretreatment characteristics of counties divided by the 1919 border.*

| | Urban | In agriculture | In mining | Protestant | Catholic | Jewish | Farms over 100 ha |
|---|---|---|---|---|---|---|---|
| | (1) | (2) | (3) | (4) | (5) | (6) | (7) |
| Coefficient | −0.05 | 0 | 0.01 | −0.14 | 0.15 | −0.01 | 0.01 |
| Standard error (conv.) | 0.21 | 0.06 | 0.04 | 0.17 | 0.16 | 0.01 | 0.02 |
| Robust bias-corrected CI | [−0.55, 0.45] | [−0.16, 0.15] | [−0.07, 0.12] | [−0.53, 0.28] | [−0.28, 0.52] | [−0.03, 0.01] | [−0.04, 0.06] |
| Observations | 184 | 184 | 184 | 184 | 184 | 184 | 184 |
| Kernel type | Triangular | Triangular | Triangular | Triangular | Triangular | Triangular | Triangular |
| Polynomial | 1 | 1 | 1 | 1 | 1 | 1 | 1 |
| Bandwidth type | mserd | mserd | mserd | mserd | mserd | mserd | mserd |
| MSE-optimal bandwidth | 35.21 | 31.84 | 31.96 | 19.75 | 19.43 | 18.15 | 31.2 |
| Effective # untreated | 39 | 37 | 37 | 26 | 25 | 24 | 37 |
| Effective # treated | 34 | 33 | 33 | 22 | 21 | 32 | 34 |

*Notes:* Regression discontinuity analysis using MSE-optimal bandwidth from package *rdrobust* in R by Calonico et al. (2015). Forcing variable is the distance of each county centroid to the 1919 border between Poland and Germany. All dependent variables are shares based on the Prussian census in 1907–1910 compiled by Galloway (2007). Counties that were split by the border in half were excluded. I condition on the latitude and longitude and their interaction. None of the coefficients reach significance.

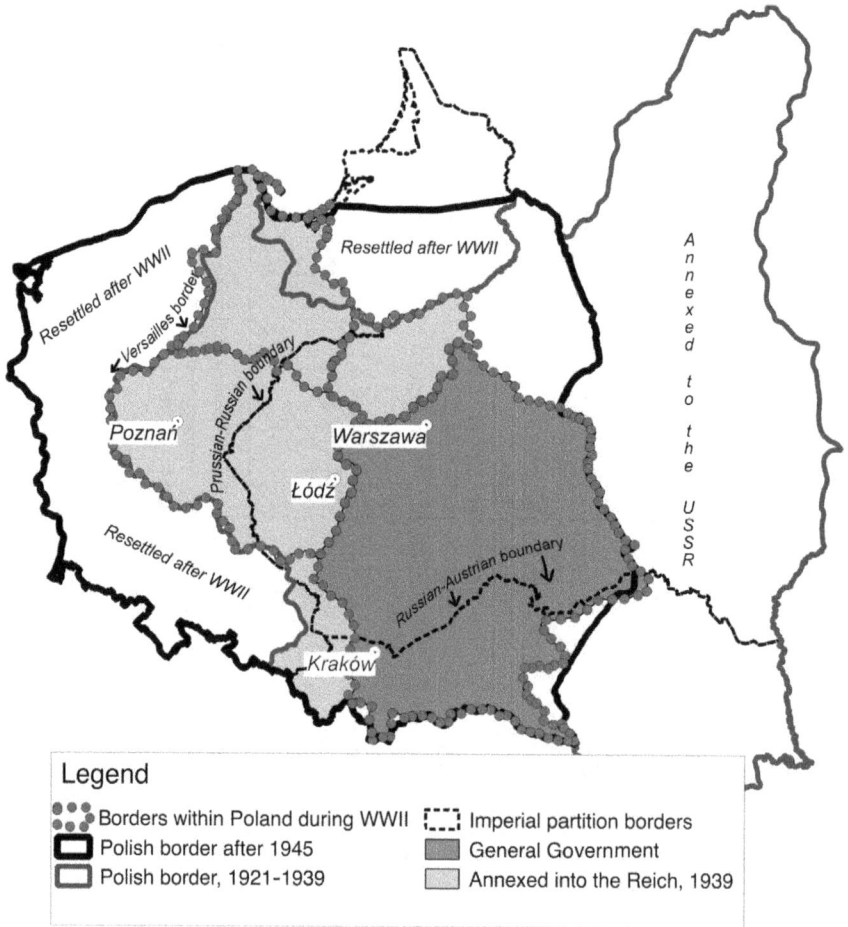

Map A.4 Divisions of Poland during and after WWII. The map is based on multiple sources, including MPIDR and CGG (2013) and the map produced by the Reich Office for State Recording (*Reichsamt für Landesaufnahme* – RfL).

TABLE A.5 *The effect of displacement on administrative capacity and placebo outcomes from the 1950 census.*

| | Officials | Municipal servants | Officials + municipal servants | Pop density | Outside agriculture |
|---|---|---|---|---|---|
| | (1) | (2) | (3) | (4) | (5) |
| *Results without covariates* | | | | | |
| Coefficient | 24.85** | 10.21** | 28.97* | −553.83 | −0.02 |
| Standard error | 12.39 | 4.45 | 14.84 | 757.61 | 0.19 |
| Observations | 32.00 | 17.00 | 40.00 | 89.00 | 34.00 |
| Bandwidth | 9.74 | 6.96 | 11.16 | 27.27 | 10.00 |
| *Results with covariates* | | | | | |
| Coefficient | 12.72*** | 7.41*** | 22.56*** | −237.48 | −0.09 |
| Standard error | 3.94 | 1.47 | 5.76 | 502.78 | 0.06 |
| Observations | 32.00 | 34.00 | 40.00 | 89.00 | 34.00 |
| Bandwidth | 9.74 | 10.00 | 11.16 | 27.27 | 10.00 |

*Notes:* Regression discontinuity analysis using Imbens–Kalyanaraman optimal bandwidth calculated in the RDD package in R. Forcing variable is the distance of each county centroid to the 1919 border between Poland and Germany. Covariates are city indicator, area, liberation month, and the latitude and longitude of each county. Significant at $*p < 0.10$; $**p < 0.05$; $***p < 0.01$.

TABLE A.6 *The effect of displacement on administrative capacity and placebo outcomes from the 1950 census: alternative specification.*

| | Officials | Municipal servants | Officials + municipal servants | Pop density | Outside agriculture |
|---|---|---|---|---|---|
| | (1) | (2) | (3) | (4) | (5) |
| Coefficient | 10.10* | 5.29*** | 15.43** | −0.56 | 0.06 |
| Standard error (conventional) | 5.22 | 1.78 | 6.35 | 0.78 | 0.04 |
| Robust bias-corrected CIs | [0.95, 24.75] | [2.43, 10.57] | [4.88, 33.83] | [−2.44, 1.34] | [−0.03, 0.15] |
| Covariates | ✓ | ✓ | ✓ | ✓ | ✓ |
| Observations | 198 | 198 | 198 | 198 | 198 |
| Kernel type | Triangular | Triangular | Triangular | Triangular | Triangular |
| Polynomial | 1 | 1 | 1 | 1 | 1 |
| Bandwidth type | mserd | mserd | mserd | mserd | mserd |
| MSE-optimal bandwidth | 19.86 | 16.25 | 18.5 | 25.92 | 27.07 |
| Effective # treated | 40 | 33 | 40 | 47 | 49 |
| Effective # untreated | 35 | 31 | 33 | 39 | 40 |

*Notes:* Regression discontinuity analysis using MSE-optimal bandwidth from package *rdrobust* in R by Calonico et al. (2015). Forcing variable is the distance of each county centroid to the 1919 border between Poland and Germany. Significant at $*p < 0.10$; $**p < 0.05$; $***p < 0.01$.

TABLE A.7 *Economic activity outside agriculture during the Stalinist period in resettled and non-resettled voivodeships.*

| Voivodeship | Industrial output (1955, in zł. per pers.) | | | | Private workshops (1957) |
| | Private | State | Total | State share | per 1,000 people |
| --- | --- | --- | --- | --- | --- |
| Warszawa (city) | 56.64 | 2303.40 | 3029.27 | 0.76 | 8.43 |
| Warszawskie | 13.24 | 507.17 | 622.24 | 0.82 | 5.51 |
| Bydgoskie | 5.51 | 1410.96 | 1604.70 | 0.88 | 6.37 |
| Poznańskie | 10.11 | 1390.54 | 1574.87 | 0.88 | 7.13 |
| Łódź (city) | 2.97 | 5289.32 | 5690.36 | 0.93 | 5.79 |
| Łódźkie | 9.70 | 1123.50 | 1300.00 | 0.86 | 4.79 |
| Kieleckie | 8.79 | 984.06 | 1106.98 | 0.89 | 2.76 |
| Lubelskie | 10.88 | 401.05 | 505.12 | 0.79 | 3.29 |
| Białostockie | 7.40 | 283.65 | 379.23 | 0.75 | 4.68 |
| Katowickie | 5.82 | 3492.86 | 3698.68 | 0.94 | 4.35 |
| Krakowskie | 9.62 | 1598.43 | 1844.26 | 0.87 | 4.18 |
| Rzeszowskie | 6.08 | 906.08 | 992.42 | 0.91 | 2.84 |
| Olsztyńskie* | 3.82 | 434.90 | 570.16 | 0.76 | 4.77 |
| Gdanskie* | 10.35 | 1534.38 | 1817.74 | 0.84 | 5.71 |
| Koszalińskie* | 1.27 | 482.91 | 630.38 | 0.77 | 3.85 |
| Szczecińskie* | 0.45 | 997.73 | 1168.84 | 0.85 | 3.90 |
| Zielonogórskie* | 0.29 | 1127.58 | 1271.24 | 0.89 | 4.21 |
| Wrocławskie* | 1.71 | 2190.58 | 2432.63 | 0.90 | 3.94 |
| Opolskie* | 5.30 | 1897.29 | 2069.45 | 0.92 | 5.06 |
| Resettled | 3.52 | 1451 | 1651.91 | 0.85 | 4.49 |
| Non-resettled | 10.91 | 1571 | 1767.64 | 0.86 | 4.88 |

*Notes:* The voivodeships located in the newly acquired territories are marked with an asterisk.
*Sources:* Statistical yearbook (*Rocznik Statystyczny*) (1956).

TABLE A.8 *Land ownership and agricultural employment by voivodeship.*

| Voivodeship | Land ownership (1955, %) | | Farm ownership (1955, %) | | | In agriculture (%) | |
|---|---|---|---|---|---|---|---|
| | Individual | State | Individual | Coop | State | 1950 | 1960 |
| Resettled in Prussian partition | | | | | | | |
| Olsztyńskie | 65.9 | 26.6 | 65.9 | 7.5 | 26.6 | 57.8 | 48.8 |
| Opolskie | 60.8 | 17.9 | 60.8 | 21.3 | 17.9 | 41.2 | 34.8 |
| Zielonogórskie | 57 | 26.8 | 57 | 16.2 | 26.8 | 47.9 | 34.9 |
| Koszalińskie | 51.8 | 36.5 | 51.8 | 11.7 | 36.5 | 58 | 44.2 |
| Wrocławskie | 46.5 | 22.8 | 46.5 | 30.7 | 22.8 | 40 | 30.9 |
| Szczecińskie | 32.1 | 41.8 | 32.1 | 26.1 | 41.8 | 40.9 | 31.8 |
| Gdańskie (partial) | 59.7 | 26.5 | 59.7 | 13.8 | 26.5 | 28.4 | 22.5 |
| Non-resettled in Prussian partition | | | | | | | |
| Bydgoskie | 71.2 | 14.7 | 71.2 | 14.1 | 14.7 | 45.2 | 38.6 |
| Poznańskie | 70.9 | 14.9 | 70.9 | 14.2 | 14.9 | 52.3 | 44.2 |
| Non-resettled in Austrian and Russian partitions | | | | | | | |
| Kieleckie | 97.7 | 1.3 | 97.7 | 1 | 1.3 | 68.5 | 57.5 |
| Krakowskie | 97 | 1.5 | 97 | 1.5 | 1.5 | 61.7 | 48.7 |
| Warszawskie | 95 | 3.1 | 95 | 1.9 | 3.1 | 61.4 | 52.9 |
| Łódzkie | 94 | 3.4 | 94 | 2.6 | 3.4 | 60.8 | 51.8 |
| Lubelskie | 93.4 | 3.4 | 93.4 | 3.2 | 3.4 | 76 | 67.3 |
| Katowickie | 90.7 | 7 | 90.7 | 2.3 | 7 | 13 | 9.6 |
| Białostockie | 90.2 | 6.5 | 90.2 | 3.3 | 6.5 | 72.8 | 62.5 |
| Rzeszowskie | 83.8 | 11.6 | 83.8 | 4.6 | 11.6 | 72.6 | 59.3 |
| Mean resettled | 53.4 | 28.4 | 53.4 | 18.2 | 28.4 | 44.9 | 35.4 |
| Mean non-resettled (Prussia) | 71.1 | 14.8 | 71.1 | 14.2 | 14.8 | 48.8 | 41.4 |
| Mean non-resettled (other) | 92.7 | 4.7 | 92.7 | 2.6 | 4.7 | 60.9 | 51.2 |

*Sources:* Statistical yearbook (*Rocznik Statystyczny*) (1956); Population census (1950).

TABLE A.9 *The effect of displacement on the authority of the Catholic Church.*

| | % Catholics in 1991 | | | |
| --- | --- | --- | --- | --- |
| | Attending Mass | | Receiving Holy Communion | |
| | (1) | (2) | (3) | (4) |
| Coefficient | $-15.49^{***}$ | $-15.69^{***}$ | $-7.27^{***}$ | $-7.29^{***}$ |
| Standard error (conventional) | 2.67 | 2.74 | 1.77 | 1.71 |
| Robust bias-corrected CIs | [−20.68, −8.47] | [−20.87, −8.47] | [−11.77, −3.3] | [−11.59, −3.4] |
| Covariates | | ✓ | | ✓ |
| Observations | 1,193 | 1,193 | 1,198 | 1,198 |
| Kernel type | Triangular | Triangular | Triangular | Triangular |
| Polynomial | 1 | 1 | 1 | 1 |
| Bandwidth type | mserd | mserd | mserd | mserd |
| MSE-optimal bandwidth | 31.13 | 29.62 | 26.47 | 27.75 |
| Effective # treated | 291 | 277 | 252 | 255 |
| Effective # untreated | 222 | 218 | 204 | 209 |

*Notes:* Regression discontinuity analysis using MSE-optimal bandwidth from package *rdrobust* in R by Calonico et al. (2015). Forcing variable is the distance of each municipality centroid to the 1919 border between Poland and Germany. Significant at $^{***}p < 0.01$.

TABLE A.10 *The effect of displacement on voting in 1990 and 1993 Sejm elections.*

| | Presidential election 1990 | | Parliamentary election 1991 | | Parliamentary election 1993 | |
| --- | --- | --- | --- | --- | --- | --- |
| | Walesa R1 | Walesa R2 | SLD 1991 | Solidarity 1991 | SLD 1993 | UD 1993 |
| | (1) | (2) | (3) | (4) | (5) | (6) |
| Coefficient | −3.92 | −7.70** | 2.35** | −2.58** | 3.68*** | 0.65 |
| Standard error (conventional) | 2.95 | 2.96 | 1 | 1.09 | 1.34 | 0.72 |
| Robust bias-corrected CIs | [−10, 4.29] | [−13.9, 0.46] | [−0.19, 4.62] | [−5.48, −0.44] | [0.26, 6.64] | [−0.91, 2.59] |
| Covariates | ✓ | ✓ | ✓ | ✓ | ✓ | ✓ |
| Observations | 816 | 816 | 831 | 789 | 831 | 831 |
| Kernel type | Triangular | Triangular | Triangular | Triangular | Triangular | Triangular |
| Polynomial | 1 | 1 | 1 | 1 | 1 | 1 |
| Bandwidth type | mserd | mserd | mserd | mserd | mserd | mserd |
| MSE-optimal bandwidth | 20.37 | 23.15 | 27.83 | 32.8 | 29.66 | 24.35 |
| Effective # treated | 110 | 126 | 142 | 166 | 155 | 129 |
| Effective # untreated | 126 | 143 | 164 | 166 | 172 | 157 |

*Notes:* Regression discontinuity analysis using MSE-optimal bandwidth from package *rdrobust* in R by Calonico et al. (2015). Forcing variable is the distance of each municipality centroid to the 1919 border between Poland and Germany. Significant at **$p < 0.05$; ***$p < 0.01$.

CHAPTER 6: EXPELLEES AND THE STATE IN WEST GERMANY

TABLE A.11 *Expellee share and voting in the 1949 federal election in Schleswig-Holstein municipalities.*

|  | Turnout 1949 | SPD 1949 | CDU 1949 |
|---|---|---|---|
|  | (1) | (2) | (3) |
| Share expellees (1946) | 0.08 | 0.12** | −0.14** |
|  | (0.09) | (0.05) | (0.06) |
| Share destroyed | 0.33 | −3.45 | 7.39** |
|  | (2.90) | (2.91) | (2.93) |
| Share Catholic (1950) | −0.22 | −0.01 | −0.27** |
|  | (0.19) | (0.14) | (0.11) |
| Share in agriculture (1950) | −0.05 | 0.02 | 0.07*** |
|  | (0.06) | (0.02) | (0.03) |
| Ln population (1939) | −0.01 | 0.01*** | −0.01** |
|  | (0.01) | (0.004) | (0.005) |
| Ln dist to Eastern border | −0.001 | −0.001** | −0.0002 |
|  | (0.0004) | (0.0003) | (0.0003) |
| County fixed effects | ✓ | ✓ | ✓ |
| Adjusted $R^2$ | 0.01 | 0.39 | 0.54 |
| N | 1,217 | 1,217 | 1,217 |

*Notes:* All models are OLS. Heteroskedasticity-robust standard errors in parentheses. Significant at **$p < 0.05$; ***$p < 0.01$.

TABLE A.12 *Expellee share in 1946 and administrative capacity in 1950. Alternative explanatory variable.*

| | Ln public employees per 1,000 | | Share expellees in public service | | Ln expellees in public service per 1,000 | |
|---|---|---|---|---|---|---|
| | (1) | (2) | (3) | (4) | (5) | (6) |
| Share expellees (1946) | 0.59 (0.37) | 0.44 (0.46) | 3.98*** (0.41) | 3.05*** (0.52) | 0.50*** (0.09) | 0.50*** (0.10) |
| Share destroyed | | −0.32* (0.17) | | −0.84*** (0.18) | | −0.04 (0.03) |
| Share in agriculture | | −0.89*** (0.21) | | −1.53*** (0.24) | | −0.17*** (0.06) |
| Ln dist to Eastern border | | 0.06** (0.03) | | −0.03 (0.02) | | −0.02 (0.02) |
| Ln population | | −0.04 (0.03) | | −0.11*** (0.04) | | −0.01 (0.01) |
| City-district | 0.77*** (0.06) | 0.62*** (0.08) | 0.63*** (0.06) | 0.41*** (0.08) | −0.03** (0.01) | −0.06** (0.02) |
| French zone | 0.34*** (0.10) | 0.26** (0.12) | 0.22* (0.12) | −0.02 (0.15) | −0.02 (0.02) | −0.01 (0.02) |
| State fixed effects | ✓ | ✓ | ✓ | ✓ | ✓ | ✓ |
| Adjusted $R^2$ | 0.40 | 0.42 | 0.47 | 0.55 | 0.17 | 0.18 |
| N | 409 | 407 | 409 | 407 | 409 | 407 |

*Notes:* All models are OLS. Heteroskedasticity-robust standard errors in parentheses. Significant at *$p < 0.10$; **$p < 0.05$; ***$p < 0.01$.

CHAPTER 7: ECONOMIC IMPLICATIONS OF DIVERSITY IN WESTERN POLAND

TABLE A.13 *Descriptive statistics for main variables at the level of Polish municipalities.*

| Variable | N | Mean | St. Dev. | Min | Max |
|---|---|---|---|---|---|
| Migrant diversity (1948) | 631 | 0.42 | 0.14 | 0.02 | 0.66 |
| Migrant share (1948) | 631 | 0.86 | 0.27 | 0.0 | 1.0 |
| Share of the largest group (1948) | 621 | 0.67 | 0.15 | 0.37 | 1.0 |
| Share from USSR (1948) | 631 | 0.28 | 0.20 | 0.0 | 0.88 |
| Share autochthonous (1948) | 631 | 0.14 | 0.28 | 0.0 | 1.0 |
| Share from Central Poland (1948) | 631 | 0.54 | 0.25 | 0.0 | 1.0 |
| Share from other countries (1948) | 631 | 0.05 | 0.07 | 0.0 | 0.64 |
| Share urban (1948) | 631 | 0.21 | 0.34 | 0.0 | 1.0 |
| Share men (1948) | 631 | 0.48 | 0.03 | 0.22 | 0.63 |
| Share in industry (1939) | 612 | 0.27 | 0.12 | 0.04 | 0.64 |
| Distance to border (km) | 631 | 59.895 | 45.38 | 0.74 | 186.13 |
| In private handicrafts per 1,000 (1982) | 615 | 10.95 | 7.33 | 0.00 | 61.59 |
| Shops per 1,000 (1982) | 606 | 6.96 | 2.29 | 3.09 | 41.67 |
| TVs per 1,000 (1982) | 589 | 210.90 | 36.48 | 68.00 | 364.00 |
| Phones per 1,000 (1982) | 612 | 31.86 | 20.29 | 4.50 | 139.10 |
| Libraries per 1,000 (1982) | 615 | 0.41 | 0.21 | 0.25 | 1.74 |
| Schools per 1,000 (1982) | 615 | 0.54 | 0.28 | 0.00 | 1.59 |
| Employed in collectivized agriculture per 1,000 (1982) | 615 | 79.54 | 61.80 | 0.00 | 318.00 |
| Employed in nationalized industry per 1,000 (1982) | 615 | 78.20 | 97.71 | 0.00 | 1081.00 |
| Share with secondary education (1978) | 631 | 0.16 | 0.08 | 0.00 | 0.58 |
| Share with secondary education (1988) | 631 | 0.15 | 0.06 | 0.07 | 0.49 |
| Share with secondary education (2002) | 632 | 0.25 | 0.08 | 0.12 | 0.59 |
| Personal income tax per capita, zł. (1995) | 632 | 101.40 | 21.70 | 8.52 | 154.80 |
| Personal income tax per capita, zł. (1998) | 632 | 169.50 | 64.91 | 13.60 | 656.70 |
| Personal income tax per capita, zł. (2000) | 632 | 143.59 | 48.89 | 67.99 | 343.68 |
| Private enterprises per 1,000 (1995) | 632 | 36.64 | 21.31 | 5.82 | 223.50 |
| Private enterprises per 1,000 (1998) | 632 | 54.66 | 27.25 | 13.10 | 312.70 |
| Private enterprises per 1,000 (2000) | 632 | 63.17 | 31.50 | 17.20 | 400.00 |

TABLE A.14 *Share and diversity of migrants and economic outcomes in a market economy in a sample without cities.*

| | Ln personal income tax | | | Ln private enterprises | | |
|---|---|---|---|---|---|---|
| | 1995 | 1998 | 2000 | 1995 | 1998 | 2000 |
| | (1) | (2) | (3) | (4) | (5) | (6) |
| Migrant diversity | 0.43*** | 0.39*** | 0.36*** | 0.55*** | 0.39*** | 0.35*** |
| | (0.07) | (0.07) | (0.07) | (0.15) | (0.12) | (0.11) |
| | [0.11] | [0.09] | [0.11] | [0.25] | [0.19] | [0.18] |
| Migrant share | −0.08** | −0.07*** | 0.05 | 0.19*** | 0.31*** | 0.27*** |
| | (0.03) | (0.03) | (0.03) | (0.06) | (0.05) | (0.05) |
| | [0.07] | [0.06] | [0.05] | [0.10] | [0.11] | [0.11] |
| Share urban | −0.03 | 0.21*** | 0.47*** | 0.59*** | 0.56*** | 0.60*** |
| | (0.04) | (0.04) | (0.05) | (0.09) | (0.07) | (0.07) |
| | [0.04] | [0.04] | [0.05] | [0.06] | [0.08] | [0.08] |
| Share in industry | −0.08 | 0.29*** | 0.85*** | 1.17*** | 0.99*** | 0.75*** |
| | (0.09) | (0.08) | (0.10) | (0.19) | (0.15) | (0.14) |
| | [0.10] | [0.11] | [0.10] | [0.23] | [0.17] | [0.16] |
| Share farms over 100 ha | 1.52*** | 1.16*** | −0.38 | −2.96*** | −3.51*** | −2.81*** |
| | (0.47) | (0.43) | (0.49) | (0.97) | (0.76) | (0.72) |
| | [0.93] | [0.63] | [0.46] | [1.12] | [0.89] | [0.81] |
| Ln population | 0.01 | 0.03** | 0.01 | −0.09*** | −0.09*** | −0.08*** |
| | (0.02) | (0.01) | (0.02) | (0.03) | (0.03) | (0.02) |
| | [0.02] | [0.03] | [0.02] | [0.04] | [0.05) | [0.05] |
| Distance to state | 0.00 | −0.00 | −0.00*** | −0.01*** | −0.01*** | −0.01*** |
| | (0.00) | (0.00) | (0.00) | (0.00) | (0.00) | (0.00) |
| | [0.00] | [0.00] | [0.00] | [0.00] | [0.00] | [0.00] |
| Distance to border | −0.00* | 0.00 | 0.00 | 0.00*** | 0.00 | 0.00 |
| | (0.00) | (0.00) | (0.00) | (0.00) | (0.00) | (0.00) |
| | [0.00] | [0.00] | [0.00] | [0.00] | [0.00] | [0.00] |
| Distance to railway | −0.01*** | −0.00*** | −0.00 | −0.01** | −0.00 | −0.00 |
| | (0.00) | (0.00) | (0.00) | (0.00) | (0.00) | (0.00) |
| | [0.00] | [0.00] | [0.00] | [0.00] | [0.00] | [0.00] |
| Province fixed effects | ✓ | ✓ | ✓ | ✓ | ✓ | ✓ |
| Adjusted $R^2$ | 0.20 | 0.31 | 0.50 | 0.31 | 0.37 | 0.37 |
| N | 549 | 549 | 549 | 549 | 549 | 549 |

*Notes:* All models are OLS. Personal income tax is measured per capita. Private enterprises are measured per 1,000 people. Heteroskedasticity-robust standard errors in parentheses. Conley errors in brackets. Significant at *$p < 0.10$; **$p < 0.05$; ***$p < 0.01$.

TABLE A.15 *Share of forced migrants and economic outcomes in a market economy.*

| | Ln personal income tax | | Ln private enterprises | | Share with higher education | |
|---|---|---|---|---|---|---|
| | 1995 | 1998 | 1995 | 1998 | 1988 | 2002 |
| | (1) | (2) | (3) | (4) | (5) | (6) |
| Share forced migrants | 0.11** | 0.11** | 0.07 | −0.01 | −0.01 | 0.01 |
| | (0.05) | (0.05) | (0.10) | (0.08) | (0.02) | (0.02) |
| Migrant share | −0.08** | −0.03 | 0.21*** | 0.32*** | 0.01 | 0.01** |
| | (0.04) | (0.04) | (0.06) | (0.05) | (0.01) | (0.01) |
| Share urban | −0.05 | 0.15*** | 0.60*** | 0.55*** | 0.17*** | 0.06*** |
| | (0.05) | (0.05) | (0.07) | (0.05) | (0.01) | (0.01) |
| Share in industry | 0.03 | 0.45*** | 1.04*** | 0.78*** | 0.05 | 0.02** |
| | (0.09) | (0.11) | (0.20) | (0.15) | (0.03) | (0.03) |
| Share farms over 100 ha | 1.43** | 0.79 | −2.77*** | −3.39*** | −0.14 | −0.08* |
| | (0.63) | (0.57) | (0.89) | (0.75) | (0.15) | (0.15) |
| Ln population | 0.02 | 0.11*** | −0.05 | −0.05* | 0.02** | 0.00* |
| | (0.02) | (0.03) | (0.04) | (0.03) | (0.01) | (0.01) |
| Distance to state | 0.00 | −0.00 | −0.01*** | −0.01*** | −0.00** | −0.00*** |
| | (0.00) | (0.00) | (0.00) | (0.00) | (0.00) | (0.00) |
| Distance to western border | −0.00*** | −0.00 | 0.00 | −0.00 | −0.00 | −0.00 |
| | (0.00) | (0.00) | (0.00) | (0.00) | (0.00) | (0.00) |
| Distance to railway | −0.01*** | −0.00*** | −0.01*** | −0.00 | 0.00 | −0.00 |
| | (0.00) | (0.00) | (0.00) | (0.00) | (0.00) | (0.00) |
| Province fixed effects | ✓ | ✓ | ✓ | ✓ | ✓ | ✓ |
| Adjusted $R^2$ | 0.13 | 0.31 | 0.41 | 0.46 | 0.54 | 0.59 |
| N | 611 | 611 | 611 | 611 | 611 | 610 |

*Notes:* All models are OLS. The share of forced migrants is measured in proportion to the total number of migrants. Migrant share is measured in proportion to the total population. Personal income tax is measured per capita. Private enterprises are measured per 1,000 people. Heteroskedasticity-robust standard errors in parentheses. Significant at $*p < 0.10$; $**p < 0.05$; $***p < 0.01$.

TABLE A.16 *Migrant diversity, fiscal capacity, and economic outcomes.*

| | Tax rate | Tax revenue | Ln capital spending | Ln income tax | Ln enterprises |
|---|---|---|---|---|---|
| | | Averaged for 1993–95 | | Measured in 2000 | |
| | (1) | (2) | (3) | (4) | (5) |
| Migrant diversity | 5.38 (4.91) | 0.72** (0.22) | | | |
| Migrant share | −1.81 (2.02) | 0.05 (0.11) | | | |
| Property tax revenue | | | 0.43** (0.07) | 0.16** (0.02) | 0.21** (0.03) |
| Covariates | ✓ | ✓ | ✓ | ✓ | ✓ |
| Province fixed effects | ✓ | ✓ | ✓ | ✓ | ✓ |
| Adjusted $R^2$ | 0.13 | 0.23 | 0.09 | 0.58 | 0.55 |
| N | 607 | 607 | 607 | 607 | 607 |

*Notes:* All models are OLS. Personal income tax is measured per capita. Private enterprises are measured per 1,000 people. Heteroskedasticity-robust standard errors in parentheses. Significant at **$p < 0.05$.

TABLE A.17 *Importance of specific groups for economic outcomes during the postcommunist period.*

| | Ln personal income tax | | | Ln private enterprises | | |
|---|---|---|---|---|---|---|
| | 1995 | 1998 | 2000 | 1995 | 1998 | 2000 |
| | (1) | (2) | (3) | (4) | (5) | (6) |
| Migrant diversity | 0.36*** (0.08) | 0.36*** (0.08) | 0.33*** (0.08) | 0.47*** (0.16) | 0.39*** (0.13) | 0.36*** (0.12) |
| Largest group: Central Poland | −0.06* (0.03) | −0.04 (0.03) | 0.02 (0.03) | 0.13** (0.06) | 0.21*** (0.05) | 0.18*** (0.05) |
| Largest group: abroad | −0.09* (0.05) | −0.22*** (0.08) | −0.18*** (0.06) | −0.19 (0.19) | −0.06 (0.11) | −0.17** (0.08) |
| Largest group: Kresy | −0.04 (0.03) | −0.03 (0.04) | 0.05 (0.04) | 0.14** (0.06) | 0.20*** (0.05) | 0.16*** (0.05) |
| Covariates | ✓ | ✓ | ✓ | ✓ | ✓ | ✓ |
| Province fixed effects | ✓ | ✓ | ✓ | ✓ | ✓ | ✓ |
| Adjusted $R^2$ | 0.15 | 0.32 | 0.52 | 0.42 | 0.46 | 0.47 |
| N | 611 | 611 | 611 | 611 | 611 | 611 |

*Notes:* All models are OLS. Personal income tax is measured per capita. Private enterprises are measured per 1,000 people. Reference category is Largest group: autochthones. Heteroskedasticity-robust standard errors in parentheses. Significant at *$p < 0.10$; **$p < 0.05$; ***$p < 0.01$.

TABLE A.18 *Share and diversity of migrants and human capital.*

| | Share w/ higher edu | | | Edu diversity |
|---|---|---|---|---|
| | 1978 | 1988 | 2002 | 1988 |
| | (1) | (2) | (3) | (4) |
| Migrant diversity | 0.00 | 0.00 | 0.02** | 0.15 |
| | (0.01) | (0.03) | (0.01) | (0.47) |
| Migrant share | 0.00 | 0.01 | 0.01* | 2.06*** |
| | (0.00) | (0.01) | (0.00) | (0.28) |
| Covariates | ✓ | ✓ | ✓ | ✓ |
| Province fixed effects | ✓ | ✓ | ✓ | ✓ |
| Adjusted $R^2$ | 0.48 | 0.54 | 0.59 | 0.42 |
| N | 576 | 611 | 610 | 611 |

*Notes:* All models are OLS. Education diversity is measured as an inverse Herfindahl index based on shares of population with different levels of education. Heteroskedasticity-robust standard errors in parentheses. Significant at $*p < 0.10$; $**p < 0.05$; $***p < 0.01$.

TABLE A.19 *Share and diversity of migrants and sorting after the resettlement.*

| | Share of the population | | | Economic outcomes in 1995 | |
|---|---|---|---|---|---|
| | not living from birth | | | Ln income tax | Ln enterprises |
| | (1) | (2) | (3) | (4) | (5) |
| Migrant diversity | 0.06** | 0.03*** | 0.04** | 0.37*** | 0.33** |
| | (0.03) | (0.01) | (0.02) | (0.08) | (0.16) |
| Migrant share | 0.17*** | 0.002 | −0.01 | −0.08** | 0.21*** |
| | (0.02) | (0.005) | (0.01) | (0.04) | (0.06) |
| Arrived 1980s | | | | 0.19 | 1.32*** |
| | | | | (0.16) | (0.33) |
| Arrived 1970s | | | | −0.31 | 1.35** |
| | | | | (0.31) | (0.68) |
| Covariates | ✓ | ✓ | ✓ | ✓ | ✓ |
| Province fixed effects | ✓ | ✓ | ✓ | ✓ | ✓ |
| Adjusted $R^2$ | 0.27 | 0.19 | 0.26 | 0.15 | 0.45 |
| N | 609 | 609 | 609 | 609 | 609 |

*Notes:* All models are OLS. The share of the population not living in a municipality from birth is measured in 1988. Models 4 and 5 include posttreatment migration measures to investigate the resulting change in the coefficient on main explanatory variables. Heteroskedasticity-robust standard errors in parentheses. Significant at $**p < 0.05$; $***p < 0.01$.

CHAPTER 8: ECONOMIC IMPLICATIONS OF DIVERSITY IN POLAND

TABLE A.20 *Share of expellees and changes in self-employment and agricultural employment in Bavarian municipalities.*

| | Self-employment | Agricultural employment | | |
|---|---|---|---|---|
| | (1) | (2) | (3) | (4) |
| Share expellees * Year 1950 | −0.10*** | −0.35*** | −0.35*** | −0.28*** |
| | (0.01) | (0.03) | (0.07) | (0.05) |
| Share expellees * Year 1970 | 0.09*** | 0.02 | −0.12 | 0.32*** |
| | (0.02) | (0.04) | (0.08) | (0.10) |
| Share expellees * Year 1987 | 0.05** | −0.24*** | −0.12 | 0.06 |
| | (0.02) | (0.07) | (0.14) | (0.14) |
| Ln dist to the Eastern border * Year 1950 | −0.00* | −0.01*** | −0.01*** | −0.01*** |
| | (0.00) | (0.00) | (0.00) | (0.00) |
| Ln dist to the Eastern border * Year 1970 | 0.00 | −0.01*** | −0.02*** | 0.00 |
| | (0.00) | (0.00) | (0.00) | (0.00) |
| Ln dist to the Eastern border * Year 1987 | 0.00*** | −0.00 | −0.03*** | 0.02** |
| | (0.00) | (0.00) | (0.01) | (0.01) |
| City * Year 1950 | 0.02*** | 0.02 | 0.14 | 0.00 |
| | (0.00) | (0.02) | (0.10) | (0.01) |
| City * Year 1970 | 0.03*** | 0.20*** | 0.19*** | 0.20*** |
| | (0.00) | (0.01) | (0.02) | (0.01) |
| City * Year 1987 | 0.06*** | 0.34*** | 0.37*** | 0.33*** |
| | (0.00) | (0.01) | (0.03) | (0.01) |
| Share Catholic | −0.05*** | 0.00 | −0.01 | −0.04 |
| | (0.01) | (0.03) | (0.04) | (0.06) |
| Share women | −0.02 | −0.38*** | −0.20 | −0.52*** |
| | (0.03) | (0.09) | (0.12) | (0.12) |
| Ln population | −0.02*** | −0.01 | −0.01 | −0.01 |
| | (0.00) | (0.01) | (0.01) | (0.02) |
| Share expellees | 0.65*** | 3.30*** | −2.32*** | 2.77*** |
| | (0.07) | (0.29) | (0.27) | (0.88) |
| Adjusted $R^2$ | 0.78 | 0.89 | 0.91 | 0.87 |
| N | 8207 | 8207 | 4104 | 4103 |

*Notes:* Change in each outcome is measured relative to the 1939 baseline. Model 3 subsets the data to municipalities with above the median share of expellees. Model 4 subsets the data to below the median share of expellees. Standard errors are clustered at the municipal level. Significant at $*p < 0.10$; $**p < 0.05$; $***p < 0.01$.

TABLE A.21 *Share and diversity of expellees and employment in agriculture in West German counties.*

| | Agriculture 1950 | Agriculture 1961 | Agriculture 1970 | Agriculture 1987 |
|---|---|---|---|---|
| | (1) | (2) | (3) | (4) |
| Share expellees | −0.06 | −0.01 | 0.09 | 0.05* |
| | (0.08) | (0.07) | (0.06) | (0.03) |
| | [0.09] | [0.05] | [0.03] | [0.02] |
| Expellee diversity | 0.02 | 0.04 | 0.07** | 0.02 |
| | (0.04) | (0.04) | (0.04) | (0.02) |
| | [0.02] | [0.02] | [0.02] | [0.02] |
| Share destroyed | 0.06** | 0.05 | 0.05** | 0.01* |
| | (0.03) | (0.03) | (0.02) | (0.01) |
| | [0.02] | [0.01] | [0.01] | [0.00] |
| Share Catholic | 0.002 | −0.01 | −0.01 | −0.005 |
| | (0.01) | (0.01) | (0.01) | (0.004) |
| | [0.00] | [0.00] | [0.00] | [0.00] |
| Share in agriculture | 0.80*** | 0.71*** | 0.48*** | 0.14*** |
| | (0.03) | (0.03) | (0.03) | (0.01) |
| | [0.05] | [0.05] | [0.04] | [0.01] |
| Ln dist to the Eastern border | 0.004 | 0.003 | 0.01** | 0.01*** |
| | (0.004) | (0.004) | (0.003) | (0.001) |
| | [0.00] | [0.01] | [0.00] | [0.00] |
| Pop density 1939 | −0.0000 | −0.0000 | 0.0000 | −0.0000 |
| | (0.0000) | (0.0000) | (0.0000) | (0.0000) |
| | [0.00] | [0.00] | [0.00] | [0.00] |
| Ln population 1950 | 0.01 | 0.01** | 0.01** | 0.004 |
| | (0.01) | (0.01) | (0.01) | (0.002) |
| | [0.01] | [0.01] | [0.00] | [0.00] |
| City-district | −0.01 | 0.03** | 0.04*** | 0.01** |
| | (0.01) | (0.02) | (0.01) | (0.005) |
| | [0.01] | [0.02] | [0.01] | [0.00] |
| French zone dummy | 0.04*** | 0.02** | 0.03*** | 0.005 |
| | (0.01) | (0.01) | (0.01) | (0.005) |
| | [0.01] | [0.00] | [0.00] | [0.00] |
| State fixed effects | ✓ | ✓ | ✓ | ✓ |
| Adjusted $R^2$ | 0.95 | 0.92 | 0.87 | 0.74 |
| N | 310 | 310 | 310 | 310 |

*Notes:* All models are OLS. Heteroskedasticity-robust standard errors in parentheses. Conley standard errors within a 500-km radius in brackets. Significant at *$p < 0.10$; **$p < 0.05$; ***$p < 0.01$.

TABLE A.22 *Share and diversity of expellees, entrepreneurship, and household income in West German counties.*

| | All companies | Freelance, science, tech | Information, communication | Admin. services | Education sector | Ln Household income |
|---|---|---|---|---|---|---|
| | (1) | (2) | (3) | (4) | (5) | (6) |
| Share expellees | 8.19 | 5.27** | 1.91** | 1.58** | 0.27 | 0.27** |
| | (9.84) | (2.22) | (0.82) | (0.72) | (0.28) | (0.12) |
| | [3.63] | [1.18] | [0.53] | [0.33] | [0.13] | [0.12] |
| Expellee diversity | 15.59** | 6.92*** | 2.67*** | 1.35** | 0.45** | 0.31*** |
| | (6.51) | (2.12) | (0.71) | (0.56) | (0.21) | (0.10) |
| | [5.77] | [1.75] | [0.71] | [0.78] | [0.12] | [0.05] |
| Share destroyed | −8.88** | −1.17 | −0.28 | −0.02 | −0.18* | −0.14*** |
| | (3.46) | (0.82) | (0.31) | (0.26) | (0.10) | (0.05) |
| | [2.26] | [0.53] | [0.20] | [0.14] | [0.08] | [0.04] |
| Share Catholic | 6.23*** | 1.38*** | 0.59*** | 0.43*** | 0.15*** | 0.01 |
| | (1.24) | (0.39) | (0.13) | (0.11) | (0.05) | (0.02) |
| | [1.30] | [0.18] | [0.08] | [0.08] | [0.03] | [0.01] |
| Share in agriculture | −19.92*** | −6.35*** | −2.32*** | −1.64*** | −0.29** | −0.37*** |
| | (4.00) | (1.16) | (0.46) | (0.34) | (0.12) | (0.06) |
| | [8.11] | [1.53] | [0.43] | [0.40] | [0.23] | [0.07] |
| Ln Dist to the Eastern border | 3.43*** | 0.88*** | 0.33*** | 0.27*** | 0.01 | 0.04*** |
| | (0.53) | (0.16) | (0.06) | (0.04) | (0.02) | (0.01) |
| | [0.44] | [0.19] | [0.08] | [0.04] | [0.01] | [0.01] |

| | | | | | |
|---|---|---|---|---|---|
| Pop density 1939 | −0.00 | −0.00 | 0.00 | 0.00 | −0.00** | −0.00 |
| | (0.00) | (0.00) | (0.00) | (0.00) | (0.00) | (0.00) |
| | [0.00] | [0.00] | [0.00] | [0.00] | [0.00] | [0.00] |
| Ln Population 1950 | 0.07 | 0.67* | 0.17 | 0.05 | 0.03 | −0.01 |
| | (1.20) | (0.39) | (0.13) | (0.10) | (0.03) | (0.02) |
| | [0.61] | [0.16] | [0.07] | [0.05] | [0.03] | [0.01] |
| City-district | 0.31 | 0.55 | −0.18 | −0.04 | 0.14* | −0.07* |
| | (2.33) | (0.69) | (0.26) | (0.19) | (0.07) | (0.04) |
| | [3.19] | [0.81] | [0.31] | [0.19] | [0.08] | [0.03] |
| French zone dummy | −0.55 | 0.16 | −0.02 | −0.13 | 0.08 | −0.01 |
| | (1.63) | (0.44) | (0.16) | (0.13) | (0.06) | (0.03) |
| | [0.44] | [0.17] | [0.09] | [0.05] | [0.02] | [0.01] |
| State fixed effects | ✓ | ✓ | ✓ | ✓ | ✓ | ✓ |
| Adjusted $R^2$ | 0.43 | 0.43 | 0.40 | 0.31 | 0.36 | 0.31 |
| N | 306 | 308 | 308 | 308 | 308 | 304 |

*Notes:* All models are OLS. Companies are measured in 2008. Household income is measured in 2000. Heteroskedasticity-robust standard errors in parentheses, Conley standard errors within a 500-km radius in brackets. Significant at *$p < 0.10$; **$p < 0.05$; ***$p < 0.01$.

TABLE A.23 *Share of expellees in 1961 and economic outcomes in West German counties.*

| | Self-employment rates | | | Education | |
|---|---|---|---|---|---|
| | 1961 | 1970 | 1987 | 1970 | 1987 |
| | (1) | (2) | (3) | (4) | (5) |
| Share expellees | −99.56*** | −42.84*** | −12.78 | 1.99* | 8.52*** |
| | (20.96) | (15.85) | (11.48) | (1.16) | (2.58) |
| | [9.99] | [6.55] | [6.17] | [0.67] | [1.64] |
| Expellee diversity | −2.19 | [14.40] | −2.92*** | [3.11] | −8.08*** |
| | (10.54) | 8.92] | (7.12) | [0.90] | (1.91) |
| | [6.55] | (3.35) | [3.75] | (0.90) | [2.14] |
| Share destroyed | −8.22 | [8.03*] | −9.24** | [−0.60] | −0.66 |
| | (5.46) | [4.62] | (3.90) | [0.48] | (0.94) |
| | [2.19] | (3.15) | [3.60] | (0.30) | [0.76] |
| Share Catholic | −4.90** | −2.91 | 1.44 | 0.80*** | [1.38***] |
| | (2.04) | (1.79) | [1.41] | (0.19) | (0.39) |
| | [1.26] | (1.06) | (1.04) | (0.13) | [0.36] |
| Share in agriculture | 91.58*** | 58.88*** | 19.66*** | −2.16*** | −5.17*** |
| | (6.78) | (6.15) | (4.64) | [0.54] | (1.11) |
| | [8.40] | (5.27) | (3.46) | (0.70) | [1.15] |
| Ln dist to the Eastern border | 2.26*** | 3.89*** | 4.55*** | 0.21*** | [0.74***] |
| | (0.70) | [0.63] | (0.57) | [0.07] | (0.15) |
| | [0.48] | (0.61) | (0.72) | [0.08] | [0.15] |
| Pop density 1939 | −0.00 | −0.00 | −0.00 | −0.00** | −0.00 |
| | (0.00) | (0.00) | (0.00) | (0.00) | (0.00) |
| | [0.00] | (0.00) | [0.00] | (0.00) | [0.00] |
| Ln population 1950 | 1.76 | 1.43 | 0.70 | [0.35**] | 0.67** |
| | (1.52) | [1.22] | (1.04) | [0.15] | (0.31) |
| | [1.18] | (0.88) | [0.27] | (0.11) | [0.21] |
| City-district | [5.06*] | 4.60* | −2.28 | [1.13***] | 0.65 |
| | (2.94) | [2.71] | (2.33) | [0.41] | (0.80) |
| | [1.93] | (2.41) | [2.85] | (0.54) | [0.87] |
| French zone dummy | −3.02 | −0.33 | −0.90 | [0.46] | [0.84] |
| | (2.55) | [2.51] | (1.91) | [0.34] | (0.65) |
| | [0.74] | (1.01) | [1.09] | (0.08) | [0.18] |
| State fixed effects | ✓ | ✓ | ✓ | ✓ | ✓ |
| Adjusted $R^2$ | 0.86 | 0.75 | 0.59 | 0.37 | 0.34 |
| N | 310 | 310 | 310 | 310 | 310 |

*Notes:* All models are OLS. Heteroskedasticity-robust standard errors in parentheses. Conley standard errors within a 500-km radius in brackets. Significant at $*p < 0.10$; $**p < 0.05$; $***p < 0.01$.

TABLE A.24 *Share of expellees in 1961 and entrepreneurship and household income in West German counties.*

| | All companies | Professional, science, tech | Information, communication | Administrative services | Education sector | Ln household income |
|---|---|---|---|---|---|---|
| | (1) | (2) | (3) | (4) | (5) | (6) |
| Share expellees 1961 | −2.95 | 6.18*** | 3.28*** | 1.55** | −0.17 | 0.62*** |
| | (9.20) | (2.13) | (0.77) | | (0.26) | (0.13) |
| Expellee diversity 1950 | 15.35** | 6.47*** | 2.47*** | 1.23** | 0.44** | 0.28*** |
| | (6.21) | (2.14) | (0.73) | (7.45) | (0.20) | (0.10) |
| Share destroyed | −10.25*** | −1.35* | −0.26 | −0.10 | −0.23** | −0.12** |
| | (3.36) | (0.81) | (0.29) | (3.80) | (0.10) | (0.05) |
| Share Catholic | 5.99*** | 1.39*** | 0.61*** | 0.42*** | 0.14*** | 0.02 |
| | (1.22) | (0.39) | (0.13) | (1.44) | (0.05) | (0.02) |
| Share in agriculture | −19.89*** | −5.40*** | −1.86*** | −1.39*** | −0.30** | −0.29*** |
| | (4.04) | (1.13) | (0.42) | (4.31) | (0.13) | (0.05) |
| Ln dist to the Eastern border | 3.38*** | 0.91*** | 0.35*** | 0.28*** | 0.003 | 0.04*** |
| | (0.52) | (0.16) | (0.05) | (0.58) | (0.02) | (0.01) |
| Pop density 1939 | −0.001 | −0.0000 | 0.0001 | 0.0000 | −0.0001** | −0.0000 |
| | (0.002) | (0.0005) | (0.0001) | (0.001) | (0.0000) | (0.0000) |
| Ln population 1950 | 0.06 | 0.75* | 0.21 | 0.07 | 0.03 | −0.004 |
| | (1.18) | (0.38) | (0.13) | (1.07) | (0.03) | (0.02) |
| City-district | 0.28 | 0.50 | −0.20 | −0.06 | 0.14* | −0.08*** |
| | (2.35) | (0.70) | (0.26) | (2.36) | (0.07) | (0.04) |
| French zone dummy | −1.58 | 0.15 | 0.06 | −0.15 | 0.04 | 0.02 |
| | (1.55) | (0.44) | (0.17) | (2.35) | (0.06) | (0.03) |
| State fixed effects | ✓ | ✓ | ✓ | ✓ | ✓ | ✓ |
| Adjusted $R^2$ | 0.43 | 0.43 | 0.43 | 0.32 | 0.36 | 0.37 |
| N | 306 | 308 | 308 | 308 | 308 | 304 |

*Notes:* All models are OLS. Heteroskedasticity-robust standard errors in parentheses. Significant at $*p < 0.10$; $**p < 0.05$; $***p < 0.01$.

TABLE A.25 *Origins of the dominant expellee group and economic outcomes in West German counties. Alternative specification.*

| | Self-employment rates | | | | Education | |
|---|---|---|---|---|---|---|
| | 1950 | 1961 | 1970 | 1987 | 1970 | 1987 |
| | (1) | (2) | (3) | (4) | (5) | (6) |
| Share expellees | −43.27** | −28.75* | 22.66 | 25.94** | 2.49** | 6.65*** |
| | (16.95) | (16.88) | (13.89) | (10.98) | (1.16) | (2.39) |
| Expellee diversity | 6.37 | 1.56 | 16.78* | 23.17*** | 3.18*** | 8.08*** |
| (origin) | (10.80) | (10.79) | (9.04) | (7.45) | (0.92) | (1.91) |
| Largest group: | −0.71 | −1.73 | −1.56 | −1.80 | 0.38* | 0.76* |
| Reichsdeutsche | (3.17) | (2.73) | (2.40) | (2.00) | (0.20) | (0.44) |
| Largest group: | −2.45 | −3.90 | −4.31 | −2.42 | 0.36 | 0.88 |
| Sudetendeutsche | (3.23) | (2.97) | (2.68) | (2.22) | (0.28) | (0.56) |
| Share destroyed | −0.10 | −2.95 | −1.99 | −5.36 | −0.32 | −0.29 |
| | (6.48) | (6.40) | (4.88) | (3.80) | (0.48) | (0.96) |
| Share Catholic | −3.64* | −3.48 | −1.45 | 2.39* | 0.79*** | 1.31*** |
| | (2.16) | (2.14) | (1.86) | (1.44) | (0.19) | (0.40) |
| Share in agriculture | 92.23*** | 101.38*** | 61.50*** | 19.32*** | −2.36*** | −6.05*** |
| | (6.85) | (7.51) | (5.84) | (4.31) | (0.54) | (1.13) |
| Ln dist to the | 3.26*** | 2.74*** | 4.34*** | 4.72*** | 0.22*** | 0.72*** |
| Eastern border | (0.92) | (0.91) | (0.71) | (0.58) | (0.08) | (0.16) |
| Pop density 1939 | −0.0003 | −0.001 | 0.0001 | 0.0001 | −0.0005** | −0.001* |
| | (0.002) | (0.002) | (0.002) | (0.001) | (0.0002) | (0.0004) |
| Ln population | 0.72 | 2.18 | 1.52 | 0.66 | 0.32** | 0.60* |
| | (1.79) | (1.59) | (1.27) | (1.07) | (0.15) | (0.32) |
| City-district | 2.17 | 4.02 | 4.24 | −2.39 | 1.17*** | 0.78 |
| | (3.54) | (3.89) | (2.98) | (2.36) | (0.41) | (0.79) |
| French zone dummy | 1.59 | 0.54 | 3.41 | 2.38 | 0.48 | 0.81 |
| | (3.39) | (3.05) | (2.94) | (2.35) | (0.44) | (0.79) |
| State fixed effects | ✓ | ✓ | ✓ | ✓ | ✓ | ✓ |
| Adjusted $R^2$ | 0.81 | 0.83 | 0.74 | 0.60 | 0.38 | 0.34 |
| N | 310 | 310 | 310 | 310 | 310 | 310 |

*Notes:* All models are OLS. Companies are measured in 2008. Household income is measured in 2000. Reference category is Largest group: Other. Heteroskedasticity-robust standard errors in parentheses. Significant at *$p < 0.10$; **$p < 0.05$; ***$p < 0.01$.

TABLE A.26 *Origins of the dominant expellee group, entrepreneurship, and household income in West German counties.*

| | All companies | Freelance, science, tech | Information, communication | Admin. services | Education | Ln household income |
|---|---|---|---|---|---|---|
| | (1) | (2) | (3) | (4) | (5) | (6) |
| Share expellees | 8.75 | 5.75*** | 1.98** | 1.81** | 0.27 | 0.26** |
| | (9.91) | (2.19) | (0.80) | (0.73) | (0.29) | (0.12) |
| Expellee diversity (origin) | 15.34** | 6.91*** | 2.73*** | 1.35** | 0.45** | 0.32*** |
| | (6.52) | (2.13) | (0.72) | (0.56) | (0.21) | (0.10) |
| Largest group: Reichsdeutsche | -0.20 | 0.29 | 0.20 | 0.15 | 0.01 | -0.0004 |
| | (1.79) | (0.42) | (0.15) | (0.13) | (0.06) | (0.02) |
| Largest group: Sudetendeutsche | -0.99 | -0.10 | 0.23 | -0.03 | 0.01 | 0.01 |
| | (2.02) | (0.52) | (0.19) | (0.15) | (0.06) | (0.03) |
| Share destroyed | -9.16** | -1.11 | -0.18 | 0.02 | -0.18 | -0.14** |
| | (3.73) | (0.90) | (0.33) | (0.27) | (0.11) | (0.05) |
| Share Catholic | 6.26*** | 1.37*** | 0.58*** | 0.42*** | 0.15*** | 0.01 |
| | (1.25) | (0.39) | (0.13) | (0.11) | (0.05) | (0.02) |
| Share in agriculture | -19.95*** | -6.29*** | -2.29*** | -1.61*** | -0.29** | -0.37*** |
| | (4.09) | (1.19) | (0.47) | (0.35) | (0.12) | (0.06) |
| Ln dist to the Eastern border | 3.49*** | 0.92*** | 0.33*** | 0.28*** | 0.01 | 0.04*** |
| | (0.52) | (0.16) | (0.06) | (0.04) | (0.02) | (0.01) |
| Pop density 1939 | -0.001 | -0.0001 | 0.0001 | 0.0000 | -0.0001** | -0.0000 |
| | (0.002) | (0.0005) | (0.0002) | (0.0001) | (0.0000) | (0.0000) |

(continued)

TABLE A.26 (*continued*)

| | All companies | Freelance, science, tech | Information, communication | Admin. services | Education | Ln household income |
|---|---|---|---|---|---|---|
| | (1) | (2) | (3) | (4) | (5) | (6) |
| Ln population | 0.09 | 0.67* | 0.16 | 0.05 | 0.03 | −0.01 |
| | (1.19) | (0.39) | (0.13) | (0.10) | (0.03) | (0.02) |
| City-district | 0.31 | 0.57 | −0.17 | −0.03 | 0.14* | −0.07* |
| | (2.35) | (0.70) | (0.26) | (0.19) | (0.08) | (0.04) |
| French zone dummy | −1.03 | −0.11 | −0.02 | −0.25 | 0.08 | 0.001 |
| | (1.88) | (0.53) | (0.19) | (0.15) | (0.07) | (0.03) |
| State fixed effects | ✓ | ✓ | ✓ | ✓ | ✓ | ✓ |
| Adjusted $R^2$ | 0.42 | 0.43 | 0.40 | 0.32 | 0.36 | 0.31 |
| N | 306 | 308 | 308 | 308 | 308 | 304 |

*Notes:* All models are OLS. Companies are measured in 2008. Household income is measured in 2000. Reference category is Largest group: Other. Heteroskedasticity-robust standard errors in parentheses. Significant at $*p < 0.10$; $**p < 0.05$; $***p < 0.01$.

# Appendix B

## Sources for Archival and Statistical Data

VILLAGE DATA ON THE COMPOSITION OF POPULATION
IN OPOLE REGION

The dataset was created by combining information about the origin of migrants from Central Poland and the USSR from Elżbieta Dworzak and Małgorzata Goc (2011) and information about the distribution of the indigenous population from Robert Rauziński and Kazimierz Szczygielski (2011).

Dworzak and Goc (2011) rely on two types of archival records from 1945 to 1946 to construct their dataset. The data on repatriates from the USSR are based on registration cards (*Karty ewidencyjne*) filled out at PUR offices and sent to regional inspectors and resettlement departments at the provincial level. Each card contains a field for noting when and where the repatriate came from (*Kiedy i skąd przybył*) as well as for when and where (s)he was settled (*Repatrianta osiedlono (dnia), (miejscowość)*). A second source is resettlement declarations (*Deklaracje przesiedlenia*) issued to migrants from Central Poland by representatives of the local Peasant Self-Help Union (*Związek Samopomocy Chłopskiej*) upon resettlement. These were temporary papers issued before the migrant received a title for the occupied property in the resettled territories from the state. These two sources could be verified against the registers of all migrants settled in each village (*Rejestry osiedlonych*) as well as against the protocols of property transfers issued by PUR (Dworzak and Goc 2011, 9).

The dataset is incomplete. As Dworzak and Goc (2011, 10–11) acknowledge, during the intensification of the settlement movement, the transfer of property took place in violation of the protocols and was not recorded. For some counties (Opole and Brzeg), property protocols were not preserved. The incompleteness of the data is evident from population size, which is much smaller than the pre-1939 census suggests. While the population of the resettled territories returned to its prewar levels only by the 1960s through national growth, low population numbers also indicate that many of the postwar residents went unrecorded until the 1948 census. The dataset excludes the indigenous population. To address this omission, I incorporated data on the presence of the indigenous population from Rauziński and Szczygielski (2011), verified against data in Opole State Archive (*Archiwum Państwowy Opole*). In the archive, data are organized by district-level office and varies in the level of detail and availability (*starostwa powiatowe*). The following records were used:

- Starostwo Powiatowe w Olesnie (No. 687)
- Starostwo Powiatowe w Grodkowie (No. 1260)
- Starostwo Powiatowe w Strzelcach Opolskich (No. 179)
- Starostwo Powiatowe w Opolu (No. 178)
- Starostwo Powiatowe w Kożlu (No. 587)
- Starostwo Powiatowe w Kluczborku (No. 686)
- Starostwo Powiatowe w Niemodlinie (No. 1549)
- Starostwo Powiatowe w Brzegu (No. 1265)
- Starostwo Powiatowe w Nysie (No. 1550)
- Starostwo Powiatowe w Głubczycach (no. 1774)
- Starostwo Powiatowe w Namysłowie (No. 1402)
- Starostwo Powiatowe w Prudniku (No. 1551)

MUNICIPAL DATA ON THE COMPOSITION OF POPULATION IN POLAND IN 1948

Archiwum Akt Nowych (AAN). Ministry for the Recovered Territories in Warsaw [1944] 1945–1949 (*Ministerstwo Ziem Odzyskanych w Warszawie [1944] 1945–1949*).

- MZO. 1515a Population of the Recovered Territories in 1948 – statistical tables (*Ludność na Ziemiach Odzyskanych w 1948 roku – tabele statystyczne*).
- MZO. 1515j Population Survey on Dec. 31, 1948 in counties Ełk, Goldap, Olecko – Białystok voivodeship (*Ankieta ludnościowa na 31 XII 1948 w Powiecie: Ełk, Gołdap, Olecko – województwo białostockie*).
- MZO. 1515k Population Survey on Dec. 31, 1948. Status of population in Gdańsk voivodeship (*Ankieta ludnościowa na 31 XII 1948. Stan zaludnienia w województwie gdańskim*).
- MZO. 1515l Population Survey on Dec. 31, 1948. Status of population in Olsztyn voivodeship (*Ankieta ludnościowa na 31 XII 1948. Ankieta ludnościowa na 31 XII 1948. Stan zaludnienia w województwie olsztyńskim*).
- MZO. 1515m Population Survey on Dec. 31, 1948. Status of population in Poznań voivodeship. (*Ankieta ludnościowa na 31 XII 1948. Stan zaludnienia w województwie poznańskim*).

- MZO. 1515n Population Survey on Dec. 31, 1948. Status of population in Szczecin voivodeship. (*Ankieta ludnościowa na 31 XII 1948. Stan zaludnienia w województwie szczecińskim*).
- MZO. 1515o Population Survey on Dec. 31, 1948. Status of population in Silesian voivodeship. (*Ankieta ludnościowa na 31 XII 1948. Stan zaludnienia w województwie śląskim*).
- MZO. 1515p Population Survey on Dec. 31, 1948. Status of population in Wrocław voivodeship. (*Ankieta ludnościowa na 31 XII 1948. Stan zaludnienia w województwie wrocławskim*).

STATISTICS ON MUNICIPALITIES IN BAVARIA

- *Bayerische Gemeinde- und Kreisstatistik. Heft 1: Oberbayern. 1942.* Band 132/1 der Beiträge zur Statistik Bayerns. München: Bayer. Statistisches Landesamt.
- *Bayerische Gemeinde- und Kreisstatistik. Heft 2: Niederbayern. 1942.* Band 132/1 der Beiträge zur Statistik Bayerns. München: Bayer. Statistisches Landesamt.
- *Bayerische Gemeinde- und Kreisstatistik. Heft 3: Oberpfalz. 1942.* Band 132/4 der Beiträge zur Statistik Bayerns. München: Bayer. Statistisches Landesamt.
- *Bayerische Gemeinde- und Kreisstatistik. Heft 4: Pfalz. 1942.* Band 132/4 der Beiträge zur Statistik Bayerns. München: Bayer. Statistisches Landesamt.
- *Bayerische Gemeinde- und Kreisstatistik. Heft 5: Oberfranken. 1943.* Band 132/5 der Beiträge zur Statistik Bayerns. München: Bayer. Statistisches Landesamt.
- *Bayerische Gemeinde- und Kreisstatistik. Heft 6: Mittelfranken. 1943.* Band 132/6 der Beiträge zur Statistik Bayerns. München: Bayer. Statistisches Landesamt.
- *Bayerische Gemeinde- und Kreisstatistik. Heft 7: Mainfranken. 1943.* Band 132/6 der Beiträge zur Statistik Bayerns. München: Bayer. Statistisches Landesamt.
- *Bayerische Gemeinde- und Kreisstatistik. Heft 8: Schwaben. 1943.* Band 132/6 der Beiträge zur Statistik Bayerns. München: Bayer. Statistisches Landesamt.
- *Amtliches Gemeindeverzeichnis für Bayern. Volkszählung am 13. September 1950. Heft 170 der Beiträge zur Statistik Bayerns. 1951.* München: Bayer. Statistisches Landesamt.
- *Amtliches Gemeinde- und Kreisstatistik. Band 1. Reg-Bez. Oberbayern. Heft 177 der Beiträge zur Statistik Bayerns. 1952.* München: Bayer. Statistisches Landesamt.

- *Bayerische Gemeindestatistik 1987. Band 8. Strukturdaten aus den Volkszählungen 1970 und 1987. Teil A und teil B. Heft 454a, 454b der Beiträge zur Statistik Bayerns.* 1990. München: Bayer. Statistisches Landesamt.
- *Bayerische Gemeindestatistik 1987. Band 1. Bevölkerung und Erwerbstätigkeit Ergebnisse der Volkszählung am 25. Mai. 1987. Heft 442a, 442b der Beiträge zur Statistik Bayerns.* 1990. München: Bayer. Statistisches Landesamt.

## STATISTICS ON MUNICIPALITIES IN SCHLESWIG-HOLSTEIN

- *Das Flüchtlingsgeschehen in Schleswig-Holstein infolge des 2. Weltkriegs im Spiegel der amtlichen Statistik.* 1952. Kiel: Statistisches Landesamt Schleswig-Holstein.
- *Gemeindestatistik von Schleswig-Holstein 1950.* 1952. Kiel: Statistisches Landesamt Schleswig-Holstein.

## RESULTS OF THE 1949 GERMAN ELECTION

- *Die erste Bundestagswahl in Bayern am 14 August 1949.* 1950. Heft 150 der Beiträge zur Statistik Bayerns. München: Bayerisches Statistisches Landesamt.
- *Die Wahl zum ersten Bundestag der Bundesrepublik Deutschland am 14 August 1949.* 1953. Band 10. Stuttgart: Statistisches Landesamt Baden-Württemberg.
- *Hessen wählt zum Bundestag. Das amtliche Ergebnis der Wahl zum ersten Bundestag in Hessen am 14 August 1949.* 1950. Nr. 29 der Beiträge zur Statistik Hessens. Hessisches Statistisches Landesamt.
- *Bundestagswahl 1953 in Niedersachsen.* Scanned pages provided by Landesamt für Statistik Niedersachsen via email.
- *Die Wahl zum ersten Bundestag in Schleswig-Holstein am 14 August 1949.* 1950. Sonderheft D. Kiel: Statistisches Landesamt Schleswig-Holstein.
- *Die Wahlen in Nordrhein-Westfalen in den Jahren seit 1948.* 1952. Düsseldorf: Statistisches Landesamt Nordrhein-Westfalen.

## ADDITIONAL SOURCES FOR STATISTICS ON WEST GERMANY

- Braun, S., Franke, R. 2021: A county-level database on expellees in West Germany, 1939–1961. Version: 1. *VSWG – Journal of Social and Economic History.* Dataset. https://doi.org/10.15456/vswg.2021067.075645
- *Statistisches Taschenbuch uber die Heimatvertriebenen.* 1953. Wiesbaden: Statistisches Bundesamt Wiesbaden.

- Schmitt, Karl, Hans Rattinger, and Dieter Oberndörfer. 1994. "Kreis-daten (Volkszählungen 1950–1987)." GESIS Datenarchiv, Köln. ZA2472 Datenfile Version 1.0.0.
- Economic Indicators for 2000s are from *Bundesinstitut für Bau-, Stadt- und Raumforschung*, www.bbsr.bund.de/BBSR/DE/ueber-uns/ bundesinstitut/_node.html.

# References

Acemoglu, Daron, and James A. Robinson. 2012. *Why Nations Fail: The Origins of Power, Prosperity, and Poverty*. New York: Crown Publishers.

Ahonen, Pertti. 2016. "The German Expellee Organizations: Unity, Division, and Function." In *Vertriebene and Pieds-Noirs in Postwar Germany and France: Comparative Perspectives*, ed. Manuel Borutta and Jan C. Jansen. Palgrave New York: Macmillan.

Ahonen, Pertti, Gustavo Corni, Jerzy Kochanowski, Rainer Schulze, Tamas Stark, and Barbara Stelzl-Marx. 2008. *People on the Move: Forced Population Movements in Europe in the Second World War and Its Aftermath*. Oxford and New York: Berg.

Albertus, Michael. 2021. *Property without Rights: Origins and Consequences of the Property Rights Gap*. Cambridge: Cambridge University Press.

Alesina, Alberto, and Edward Glaeser. 2004. *Fighting Poverty in the U.S. and in Europe: A World of Difference*. New York: Oxford University Press.

Alesina, Alberto, and Eliana La Ferrara. 2002. "Who Trusts Others?" *Journal of Public Economics* 85 (2): 207–234.

Alesina, Alberto, Elie Murard, and Hillel Rapoport. 2021. "Immigration and Preferences for Redistribution in Europe." *Journal of Economic Geography* 21 (6): 925–954.

Alesina, Alberto, Johahn Harnoss, and Hillel Rapoport. 2016. "Birthplace Diversity and Economic Prosperity." *Journal of Economic Growth* 21 (2): 101–138.

Alesina, Alberto, Reza Baqir, and William Easterly. 1999. "Public Goods and Ethnic Divisions." *The Quarterly Journal of Economics* 114 (4): 1243–1284.

Alfani, Guido, and Vincent Gourdon. 2012. "Entrepreneurs, Formalization of Social ties, and Trustbuilding in Europe (Fourteenth to Twentieth Centuries)." *Economic History Review* 65 (3): 1005–1028.

Algan, Yann, Camille Hémet, and David Laitin. 2016. "The Social Effects of Ethnic Diversity at the Local Level: A Natural Experiment with Exogenous Residential Allocation." *Journal of Political Economy* 124 (3): 696–733.

Ambrosius, Gerold. 1996. "Der Beitrag der Vertriebenen und Flüchtlinge zum Wachstum der westdeutschen Wirtschaft nach dem Zweiten Weltkrieg." *Jahrbuch für Wirtschaftsgeschuchte* 12 (2): 39–72.

*Amtliches Gemeindeverzeichnis für Bayern*. 1950. Volkszählung am 13. September 1950. Heft 170 der Beiträge zur Statistik Bayerns. München: Bayer. Statistisches Landesamt.

Andresen, Knud. 2013. "Der Schleswig-Holsteinische Heimatbund und die Entwicklung einer Deckerinnerung an den Nationalsozialismus." *Gedenkstätten-Rundbrief* 170: 3–12.

Anzelm, Gorywoda. 1970. *Z Problematyki Rozwoju Rzemiosła na Ziemiach Zachodnich i Północnych w Latach 1945–1965.* Opole: Instytut Slaski.

Apor, Balázs. 2004. "The Expulsion of the German Speaking Population from Hungary." In *The Expulsion of the 'German' Communities from Eastern Europe at the End of the Second World War*, ed. Steffen Prauser and Arfon Rees. San Domenico: EUI.

Arjona, Ana. 2016. *Rebelocracy: Social Order in the Colombian Civil War.* Cambridge: Cambridge University Press.

Bach, Stefan. 2011. "Lastenausgleich aus heutiger Sicht: Renaissance der allgemeinen Vermögensbesteuerung?" *Vierteljahrshefte zur Wirtschaftsforschung* 80 (4): 123–146.

Bade, Klaus J., Hans-Bernd Meier, Bernhard Parisius, and Ulrike Hindersmann, eds. 1997. *Zeitzeugen im Interview : Flüchtlinge und Vertriebene im Raum Osnabrück nach 1945.* Osnabrück: Rasch.

Baehr, Peter. 2005. "Social Extremity, Communities of Fate, and the Sociology of SARS." *European Journal of Sociology* 46 (2): 179–211.

Baldwin, Kate, and John D. Huber. 2010. "Economic versus Cultural Differences: Forms of Ethnic Diversity and Public Goods Provision." *American Political Science Review* 104 (4): 644–662.

Bałtowski, Maciej, and Szymon Żminda. 2005. "Sektor Nowych Prywatnych Przedsiębiorstw w Gospodarce Polskiej – Jego Geneza i Struktura." *Annales Universitatis Mariae Curie-Skłodowska* H (39): 55–67.

Banasiak, Stefan. 1965. "Settlement of the Polish Western Territories in 1945–1947." *Polish Western Affairs* 6 (1): 121–149.

Banerjee, Abhijit, Lakshmi Iyer, and Rohini Somanathan. 2005. "History, Social Divisions, and Public Goods in Rural India." *Journal of the European Economic Association* 3: 639–647.

Banik, Joanna, Wojciech Szwed, and Renata Kobylarz. 2009. *Dąbrowa. Zarys Monografii Gminy.* Opole: Gminny Ośrodek Kultury i Rekreacji.

Bansak, Kirk, Jens Hainmueller, and Dominik Hangartner. 2016. "How Economic, Humanitarian, and Religious Concerns Shape European Attitudes Toward Asylum Seekers." *Science* 354 (6309): 217–222.

Barth, Fredrik. 1969. *Ethnic Groups and Boundaries. The Social Organization of Culture Difference.* Oslo: Universitetsforlaget.

Bartkowski, Jerzy. 2003. *Tradycja i Polityka. Wpływ Tradycji Kulturowych Polskich Regionów na Współczesne Zachowania Społeczne i Polityczne.* Warszawa: Zak Academic Publishing House.

Bates, Robert. 1974. "Ethnic Competition and Modernization in Contemporary Africa." *Comparative Political Studies* 6 (4): 457–484.

Bauer, Thomas K., Sebastian Braun, and Michael Kvasnicka. 2013. "The Economic Integration of Forced Migrants: Evidence for Post-War Germany." *The Economic Journal* 123 (September): 998–1024.

Bazzi, Samuel, Martin Fiszbein, and Mesay Gebresilasse. 2017. "Frontier Culture: The Roots and Persistence of "Rugged Individualism" in the United States." Working Paper 23997.

Becker, Sascha, Irena Grosfeld, Pauline Grosjean, Nico Voigtländer, and Ekaterina Zhuravskaya. 2020. "Forced Migration and Human Capital: Evidence from Post-WWII Population Transfers." *American Economic Review* 110 (5): 1430–1463.

Beneš, Eduard. 1942. "The Organization of Postwar Europe." *Foreign Affairs* 20 (2): 226–242.

Beramendi, Pablo, and Melissa Rogers. 2018. "Disparate Geography and the Origins of Tax Capacity." *The Review of International Organizations* 16 (1): 213–237.

Bergen, Doris L. 1994. "The Nazi Concept of 'Volksdeutsche' and the Exacerbation of Anti-Semitism in Eastern Europe, 1939–45." *Journal of Contemporary History* 29 (4): 569–582.

Bernhard, Michael. 2005. "The Federal Republic of Germany: Learning from History." In *Institutions and the Fate of Democracy: Germany and Poland in the Twentieth Century*. Pittsburgh: University of Pittsburgh Press.

Besley, Timothy, and Torsten Persson. 2014. "The Causes and Consequences of Development Clusters: State Capacity, Peace, and Income." *Annual Economic Review* 6: 927–949.

Bharadwaj, Prashant, Asim Khwaja, and Atif Mian. 2008. "The Big March: Migratory Flows after the Partition of India." *Economic and Political Weekly* 43 (35): 39–49.

Bharadwaj, Prashant, and Rinchan Ali Mirza. 2019. "Displacement and Development: Long-Term Impacts of Population Transfer in India." *Explorations in Economic History* 73 (July): 101273.

Biddiscombe, A. 2007. *The Denazification of Germany*. Stroud: Tempus.

Bjork, James E. 2008. *Neither German nor Pole: Catholicism and National Indifference in a Central European Borderland*. Ann Arbor: University of Michigan Press.

Błąd, Marta. 2022. "Dismantling the State Farm System and Its Communities in Poland during the 1990s, and Its Social Consequences." *Family & Community History* 25 (1): 40–72.

Blanke, Richard. 2001. *Polish-Speaking Germans? Language and National Identity among the Masurians since 1871*. Cologne: Bohlau Verlag.

Blusiewicz, Tomasz. 2015. "How the West Was Won: Pioneers, Settlers and Communism in the Polish 'Ziemie Odzyskane,' 1945–1948." PIASA 73rd Annual Meeting.

Bodea, Cristina, and Adrienne LeBas. 2016. "The Origins of Voluntary Compliance: Attitudes toward Taxation in Urban Nigeria." *British Journal of Political Science* 46 (1): 215–238.

Bömelburg, Hans-Jürgen, Renate Stoessinger and Robert Traba, eds. 2000. *Vertreibung aus dem Osten: Deutsche und Polen erinnern sich*. Olsztyn: Borussia.

Boone, Catherine. 2003. *Political Topographies of the African State: Territorial Authority and Institutional Choice*. Cambridge: Cambridge University Press.

Borutta, Manuel and Jan C. Jansen, eds. 2016. *Vertriebene and Pieds-Noirs in Postwar Germany and France: Comparative Perspectives*. New York: Palgrave Macmillan.

Bösch, Frank. 2016. "The Political Integration of the Expellees in Postwar West Germany." In *Vertriebene and Pieds-Noirs in Postwar Germany and France: Comparative Perspectives*, ed. Manuel Borutta and Jan C. Jansen. New York: Palgrave Macmillan.

Bouscaren, Anthony T. 1963. *International Migrations since 1945*. New York: Praeger.

Bove, Vincenzo, and Leandro Elia. 2017. "Migration, Diversity, and Economic Growth." *World Development* 89: 227–239.

Bräu, Ramona. 2016. "The Economic Consequences of German Occupation Policy in Poland." In *Paying for Hitler's War: The Consequences of Nazi Hegemony for Europe*, ed. Jonas Scherner and Eugene N. White. Cambridge, UK: Cambridge University Press.

Braun, Sebastian, and Michael Kvasnicka. 2014. "Immigration and Structural Change: Evidence from Post-War Germany." *Journal of International Economics* 93: 253–269.

Braun, Sebastian, and Nadja Dwenger. 2020. "The Local Environment Shapes the Integration of Forced Migrants: Evidence from Post-War Germany." *Explorations in Economic History* 77.

Braun, Sebastian Till, and Richard Franke. 2021. "A County-Level Database on Expellees in West Germany, 1939–1961." https://doi.org/10.15456/vswg.2021067 .075645.

Brelie-Lewien, Doris von der. 1990. *'Und dann kamen die Flüchtlinge'. Der Wandel des Landkreises Fallingbostel vom Rüstungszentrum im "Dritten Reich" zur Flüchtlingshochburg nach dem Zweiten Weltkrieg.* Hildesheim: August Lax.

Broszat, Martin. 1961. *Nationalsozialistische Polenpolitik 1939–1945.* Stuttgart: Deutsche Verlags-Anstalt.

Brown, Kate. 2005. *Biography of No Place: From Ethnic Borderland to Soviet Heartland.* Cambridge: Harvard University Press.

Brubaker, Rogers. 1992. *Citizenship and Nationhood in France and Germany.* Cambridge: Harvard University Press.

Brubaker, Rogers. 2002. "Ethnicity without Groups." *European Journal of Sociology* XLIII (2): 163–189.

Brunow, Stephan, Michaela Trax, and Jens Suedekum. 2012. "Cultural Diversity and Plant-Level Productivity." IZA Working Paper No. 6845/2012.

Bukowski, Paweł. 2018. "How History Matters for Student Performance. Lessons from the Partitions of Poland." *Journal of Comparative Economics* 47 (1): 136–175.

Bulutgil, H. Zeynep. 2016. *The Roots of Ethnic Cleansing in Europe.* New York: Cambridge University Press.

Burchardi, Konrad B., and Tarek A. Hassan. 2013. "The Economic Impact of Social Ties: Evidence from German Reunification." *The Quarterly Journal of Economics* 128 (3): 1219–1271.

Burgoon, Brian, Ferry Koster, and Marcel van Egmond. 2012. "Support for Redistribution and the Paradox of Immigration." *Journal of European Social Policy* 22: 288–304.

Burszta, Józef. 1995. "Kategorie Społeczno-Kulturowe Ludności Ziem Zachodnich." *Przegląd Zachodni* (2): 79–100.

Cairns, Kelly Lynn. 2016. "Germany's Workshop: Expellee Craft and Postwar National Rebranding." Ph.D. diss. The University of British Columbia.

Calderón-Mejía, Valentina, and Ana María Ibáñez. 2016. "Labour Market Effects of Migration-Related Supply Shocks: Evidence from Internal Refugees in Colombia." *Journal of Economic Geography* 16 (3): 695–713.

Calonico, Sebastian, Matias D. Cattaneo, Max H. Farrell, and Rocío Titiunik. 2015. "Rdrobust: Software for Regression Discontinuity Designs." *Stata Journal* 17 (2): 372–404.

Capoccia, Giovanni, and Grigore Pop-Eleches. 2020. "Democracy and Retribution: Transitional Justice and Regime Support in Postwar West Germany." *Comparative Political Studies* 53 (3–4): 399–433.

Carey, Jane Perry Clark. 1951. "Political Organization of the Refugees and Expellees in West Germany." *Political Science Quarterly* 66: 191–215.

Carlin, Wendy. 1996. "West German Growth and Institutions, 1945–90." In *Economic Growth in Europe Since 1945*. Cambridge, UK: Cambridge University Press.

Caselli, Francesco, and Willbur John Coleman. 2012. "On the Theory of Ethnic Conflict." *Journal of the European Economic Association* 11 (S1): 161–192.

Cattaruza, Marina. 2010. "'Last Stop Expulsion' – The Minority Question and Forced Migration in East-Central Europe: 1918–49." *Nations and Nationalism* 16 (1): 108–126.

Central Office for National Measurements (*Główny Urząd Pomiarów Kraju*). 1949. "Polska Mapa administracyjna, stan z dnia 31.XII.1949 r." Obtained from the Institute of Geography and Spatial Organization (*Instytut Geografii i Przestrzennego Zagospodarowania PAN*).

Central Office for National Measurements (*Główny Urząd Pomiarów Kraju*). 1950. "Polska Mapa administracyjna, stan z dnia 31.XII.1950 r." Obtained from the Institute of Geography and Spatial Organization (*Instytut Geografii i Przestrzennego Zagospodarowania PAN*).

Chakravarty, Pallavi. 2014. *Post-Partition Rehabilitation of Refugees in India*. New Delhi: Nehru Memorial Museum and Library.

Chałaciński, Józef, ed. 1965. *Tu Jest mój Dom. Pamiętniki z Ziem Zachodnich i Północnych*. Warsaw: Ludowa Spółdzielnia Wydawnicza.

Chan, Kenneth Ka-Lok. 1995. "Poland at the Crossroads: The 1993 General Election." *Europe-Asia Studies* 47 (1): 123–145.

Charnysh, Volha. 2023. "Historical Political Economy of Migration." In *The Oxford Handbook of Historical Political Economy*, ed. Jeffery A. Jenkins and Jared Rubin. Oxford: Oxford University Press.

Charnysh, Volha, and Leonid Peisakhin. 2022. "The Role of Communities in the Transmission of Political Values: Evidence from Forced Population Transfers." *British Journal of Political Science* 52 (1): 238–258.

Chen, Jidong, Jennifer Pan, and Yiqing Xu. 2016. "Sources of Authoritarian Responsiveness: A Field Experiment in China." *American Journal of Political Science* 60 (2): 383–400.

Chevalier, Arnaud, Benjamin Elsner, Andreas Lichter, and Nico Pestel. 2018. "Immigrant Voters, Taxation and the Size of the Welfare State." UCD Centre for Economic Research Working Paper Series, No. 18/14.

Chmielewska, Bożenna. 1965. *Społeczne Przeobrażenia Środowisk Wiejskich na Ziemiach Zachodnich, na Przykładzie Pięciu Wsi w Województwie Zielonogórskim*. Poznań: Instytut Zachodni.

Chmielewski, Piotr, Antoni Kamiński, and Piotr Strazalkowski. 1990. "Entrepreneur and the State-Managed Economy under Socialism." *Entrepreneurship & Regional Development* 2 (4): 303–314.

Cho, Chansoo. 2003. "Manufacturing a German Model of Liberal Capitalism: The Political Economy of the German Cartel Law in the Early Postwar Period." *Journal of International and Area Studies* 10 (1): 41.

Christ, Oliver, Katharina Schmid, Simon Lolliot, Hermann Swart, Dietling Stolle, Nicole Tausch, Ananthi Al Ramiah, Ulrich Wagner, Steven Vertovec, and Miles Hewstone. 2014. "Contextual Effect of Positive Intergroup Contact on Outgroup Prejudice." *PNAS* 111 (11): 3996–4000.

Chuminski, Jedrzej. 1993. "Czynniki Destabilizujące Proces Osadnictwa we Wrocławiu (1945–1949)." *Acta Universitatis Wratislaviensis* 1512 (10): 55–78.

Churchill, Winston S. 1948. *The Second World War*. Boston: Houghton Mifflin.

Cichocka, Marta. 2013. "Działalność Prymasa Stefana Wyszyńskiego wobec Pomorza Zachodniego w Latach 1949–1953." In *Droga do Stabilizacji Administracji Kościelnej na Ziemiach Zachodnich*, ed. Wojciech Kucharski. Ośrodek "Pamięć i Przyszłość."

Ciesielski, Stanisław. 2000. *Przesiedlenie Ludności Polskiej z Kresów Wschodnich do Polski 1944–1947. Wybór Dokumentów*. Warszawa: Wydawnictwo Neriton.

Cleary, Matthew R. 2007. "Electoral Competition, Participation, and Government Responsiveness in Mexico." *American Journal of Political Science* 51 (2): 283–299.

Connor, Ian. 1989. "Die Integration der Flüchtlinge und Vertriebenen in den Arbeitsprozess nach 1945." *Jahrbuch für ostddeutsche Volkskunde* 32: 185–205.

Connor, Ian. 2006. "German Refugees and the SPD in Schleswig-Holstein, 1945–50." *European History Quarterly* 36 (2): 173–199.

Connor, Ian. 2007. *Refugees and Expellees in Post-War Germany*. Manchester and New York: Manchester University Press.

Connor, Ian D. 1986. "The Bavarian Government and the Refugee Problem 1945–50." *European History Quarterly* 16: 131–153.

Cook, Karen S., Russell Hardin, and Margaret Levi, eds. 2005. *Cooperation without Trust?* New York: Russel Sage Foundation.

Costa, Dora L., and Matthew E. Kahn. 2003. "Understanding the Decline in Social Capital, 1952–1998." *Kyklos* 56 (1): 17–46.

Curp, David. 2006. *A Clean Sweep: The Politics of Ethnic Cleansing in Western Poland, 1945–1960*. Rochester, NY: University of Rochester Press.

Czerniakiewicz, Jan. 1987. *Repatriacja Ludnosci Polskiej z ZSRR 1944–1948*. Warsaw: Państwowe Wydawnictwo Naukowe.

Dabrowski, Patrice M. 2011. "Uses and Abuses of the Polish Past by Józef Piłsudski and Roman Dmowski." *The Polish Review* 56 (1/2): 73–109.

Dancygier, Rafaela M. 2010. *Immigration and Conflict in Europe*. Cambridge: Cambridge University Press.

Darden, Keith, and Harris Mylonas. 2016. "Threats to Territorial Integrity, National Mass Schooling, and Linguistic Commonality." *Comparative Political Studies* 49 (11): 1446–1479.

Davies, Norman. 2005. *God's Playground. A History of Poland*. Vol. 2 New York: Columbia University Press.

Demshuk, Andrew. 2006. "Citizens in Name Only: The National Status of German Expellees, 1945–53." *Ethnopolitics* 5 (4): 383–397.

Demshuk, Andrew. 2014. "Godfather Cities: West German Patenschaften and the Lost German East." *German History* 32 (2): 224–255.

Dimmery, Drew. 2016. *rdd: Regression Discontinuity Estimation*. R package version 0.57.

Dinas, Elias, and Vasiliki Fouka. 2018. "Family History and Attitudes toward Outgroups: Evidence from the Syrian Refugee Crisis." Working Paper.

Dincecco, Mark. 2017. *State Capacity and Economic Development: Past and Present*. Elements in Political Economy. Cambridge, UK: Cambridge University Press.

Dinesen, Peter Thisted, and Kim Mannemar Sønderskov. 2015. "Ethnic Diversity and Social Trust: Evidence from the Micro-Context." *American Sociological Review* 80 (3): 550–573.

Distelhorst, Greg, and Yue Hou. 2017. "Constituency Service under Nondemocratic Rule: Evidence from China." *Journal of Politics* 79 (3): 1024–1040.

Dittrich, Erich. 1951. "Der Aufbau der Flüchtlingsindustrien in der Bundesrepublik." *Weltwirtschaftliches Archiv* 67 (2): 327–360.

Dobieszewski, Adolf. 1993. *Kolektywizacja Wsi Polskiej, 1948–1956 [Collectivization of the Polish Village, 1948–1956]*. Fundacja im. Kazimierza Kelles-Krauza.

Docquier, Frédéric, Riccardo Turati, Jérôme Valette, and Chrysovalantis Vasilakis. 2020. "Birthplace Diversity and Economic Growth: Evidence From the US States in the Post-World War II Period." *Journal of Economic Geography* 20 (2): 321–354.

Domke, Radosław. 2010. *Ziemie Zachodnie i Północne Polski w Propagandzie lat 1945–1948*. Zielona Góra: Uniwersytet Zielonogorski.

Dołowy-Rybińska, Nicole, and Claudia Soria. 2021. "Surveying the Ethnolinguistic Vitality of Two Contested Languages: The case of Kashubian and Piedmontese." In *Contested Languages: The Hidden Multilingualism of Europe*, ed. Marco Tamburelli and Mauro Tosco. Amsterdam: John Benjamins Publishing Company.

Douglas, Raymond M. 2012. *Orderly and Humane: The Expulsion of the Germans after the Second World War*. New Haven: Yale University Press.

Drury, John. 2018. "The Role of Social Identity Processes in Mass Emergency Behaviour: An Integrative Review." *British Journal of Social Psychology* 48: 487–506.

Dulczewski, Zygmunt, and Andrzej Kwilecki. 1963. *Pamiętniki Osadników Ziem Odzyskanych*. Poznan: Wydawnictwo Poznanskie.

Dulczewski, Zygmunt and Andrzej Kwilecki, eds. 1970. *Pamiętniki Osadników Ziem Odzyskanych*. Poznań: Wydawn. Poznańskie.

Dulewicz, Stanisław. 2016. "Burmistz Darłowa." In *Mój Dom nad Odrą: Pamiętniki Osadników Ziem Zachodnich po 1945 Roku*, ed. Beata Halicka. Kraków: TAiWPN Universitas.

Duwendag, Dieter. 1975. "The Postwar Economic System in Germany: Creation, Evolution, and Reappraisal." *Federal Reserve Bank of St. Louis* 57 (Oct): 16–22.

Dworzak, Elzbieta, and Malgorzata Goc. 2011. "Pochodzenie Terytorialne Ludności Napływowej i Geografia Powojennych Osiedleń na Wsi Opolskiej." *Opolski Rocznik Muzealny* 18 (2): 5–493.

Dzieniszewska-Naroska, Katarzyna. 2004. "Ochotnicze Straże Pożarne w Służbie Kultury Lokalnej – Wczoraj, Dziś i Jutro." *Kultura Współczesna* (4): 243–255.

Easter, Gerald. 2002. "Politics of Revenue Extraction in Post-Communist States: Poland and Russia Compared." *Politics and Society* 33 (4): 599–627.

Easter, Gerald. 2010. "Capacity, Consent, and Tax Collection in Post-Communist States." In *Taxation and State-Building in Developing Countries*, ed. Deborah Brätigam, Odd-Helge Fjeldstad, and Mick Moore. New York: Cambridge University Press.

Easterly, William. 2001. "Can Institutions Resolve Ethnic Conflict?" *Economic Development and Cultural Change* 49 (4): 687–706.

Edo, Anthony. 2019. "The Impact of Immigration on Wage Dynamics: Evidence from the Algerian Independence War." *Journal of the European Economic Association* 18 (6): 3210–3260.

Eisler, Cornelia. 2018. "'State-Supported History' at the Local Level: Ostdeutsche Heimatstuben and Expellee Museums in West Germany." In *The Palgrave Handbook of State-Sponsored History after 1945*, ed. Berber Bevernage and Nico Wouters. London: Palgrave Macmillian.

Ekiert, Grzegorz. 2003. "The State after State Socialism: Poland in Comparative Perspective." In *The Nation-State in Question*, ed. T. V. Paul, John G. Ikenberry, and John A Hall. Princeton, NJ: Princeton University Press.

Enos, Ryan D., and Noam Gidron. 2016. "Intergroup Behavioral Strategies as Contextually Determined: Experimental Evidence from Israel." *The Journal of Politics* 78 (3): 851–867.

Erhard, Ludwig. 1958. *Prosperity through Competition*. New York: Frederick A. Praeger.

Erker, Paul. 1988. *Vom Heimatvertriebenen zum Neubürger. Sozialgeschichte der Flüchtlinge in einer agrarischen Region Mittelfrankens, 1945–1955*. Wiesbaden Franz Steiner Verlag.

Erker, Paul. 1990. "Revolution des Dorfes? Ländliche Bevölkerung zwischen Flüchtlingszustrom und wirtschaftlichem Strukturwandel." In *Von Stalingrad zur Währungsreform zur Sozialgeschichte des Umbruchs in Deutschland*, ed. Martin Broszat, Klaus-Dietmar Henke, and Hans Woller. München: R. Oldenbourg Verlag.

Esipova, Neli, Julie Ray, and Anita Pugliese. 2020. "World Grows Less Accepting of Migrants." Gallup. September 23, 2020. https://news.gallup.com/poll/320678/world-grows-less-accepting-migrants.aspx.

Exner, Peter. 1999. "Integration oder Assimilation? Vertriebeneneinliederung und ländliche Gesellschaft - eine sozialgeschichtliche Mikrostudie am Beispiel westfälischer Landgemeinden." In *Geglückte Integration? Spezifika und Vergleichbarkeiten der Vertriebenen-Eingliederung in der SBZ/DDR*, ed. Dierk Hoffmann and Michael Schwartz. Berlin, Boston: Oldenbourg Wissenschaftsverlag.

Fafchamps, Marcel. 2004. *Market Institutions in Sub-Saharan Africa*. Cambridge: MIT Press.

Fahrmeir, Andreas K. 1997. "Nineteenth-Century German Citizenships: A Reconsideration." *The Historical Journal* 40 (3): 721–752.

Falck, Oliver, Stephan Heblich, and Susanne Link. 2012. "Forced Migration and the Effects of an Integration Policy in Post-WWII Germany." *The B.E. Journal of Economic Analysis & Policy* 12 (1): 1–27.

Fearon, James D., and David D. Laitin. 2011. "Sons of the Soil, Migrants, and Civil War." *World Development* 39 (2): 199–211.

Fiedler, Jerzy. 2005. *Ochrona Przeciwpożarowa w Powiecie Jeleniogórskim w Latach 1945–1950*. Warsaw: Komenda Główna Państwowej Straży Pożarnej.

Foa, Roberto Stefan, and Anna Nemirovskaya. 2016. "How State Capacity Varies within Frontier States: A Multicountry Subnational Analysis." *Governance: An International Journal of Policy, Administration, and Institutions* 29 (3): 411–432.

Frank, Matthew. 2017. *Making Minorities History: Population Transfer in Twentieth-Century Europe*. Oxford: Oxford University Press.

Freier, Ronny, Benny Geys, and Joshua Holm. 2013. "Religious Heterogeneity and Fiscal Policy: Evidence from German Reunification." DIW Discussion Papers, No. 1266.

Fritsch, Michael, Korneliusz Pylak, and Michael Wyrwich. 2021. "Historical Roots of Entrepreneurship in Different Regional Contexts – the Case of Poland." *Small Business Economics* 59 (1): 397–412.

Führer, Karl Christian. 2005. "Managing Scarcity: The German Housing Shortage and the Controlled Economy 1914–1990." *German History* 13 (3): 326–354.

Galloway, Patrick R. 2007. "Galloway Prussia Database 1861 to 1914." www.patrickrgalloway.com.

Gao, Eleanor. 2016. "Tribal Diversity, Fragmented Groups, and Public Goods Provision in Jordan." *Comparative Political Studies* 49 (10): 1372–1403.

Gareau, Frederick H. 1961. "Morgenthau's Plan for Industrial Disarmament in Germany." *The Western Political Quarterly* 14 (2): 516–534.

Garfias, Francisco. 2018. "Elite Competition and State Capacity Development: Theory and Evidence from Post-Revolutionary Mexico." *American Political Science Review* 112 (2): 339–357.

Gehlbach, Scott. 2008. "What Is a Big Bureaucracy? Reflections on Rebuilding Leviathan and Runaway State-Building." *Sociologický Časopis / Czech Sociological Review* 44 (6): 1189–1197.

*Gemeindestatistik von Schleswig-Holstein.* 1951. Kiel: Statistisches Landesamt Schleswig-Holstein.

GeoBasis-DE / BKG. 2011. "Shapefile of Administrative Boundaries (WGS84)." www.zensus2011.de/EN/Media/Background_material/Background_material_node.html.

Gerolimatos, George. 2014. "Structural Change and Democratization of Schleswig-Holstein's Agriculture, 1945–1973." Ph.D. diss. UNC Chapel Hill.

Gershman, Boris, and Diego Rivera. 2018. "Subnational Diversity in Sub-Saharan Africa: Insights from a New Dataset." *Journal of Development Economics* 133: 231–263.

GHDI, German History in Documents and Images. n.d. "The Ahlen Program of the CDU (February 1947)." https://bit.ly/3r1meoy.

Gieszczyński, Witold. 1999. *Państwowy Urząd Repatriacyjny w Osadnictwie na Warmii i Mazurach (1945–1950).* Olsztyn: Ośrodek Badań Naukowych.

Glassheim, Eagle. 2016. *Cleansing the Czechoslovak Borderlands: Migration, Environment, and Health in the Former Sudetenland.* Pittsburgh: University of Pittsburgh Press.

Glensk, Evelyn. 1994. *Die Aufnahme und Eingliederung der Vertriebenen und Flüchtlinge in Hamburg 1945–1953.* Hamburg: Verein für Hamburgische Geschichte.

Gorzelak, Grzegorz, and Bohdan Jałowiecki. 1996. "Koniunktura Gospodarcza i Mobilizacja Społeczna w Gminach '95." *Studia Regionalne i Lokalne* 16 (49): 1–160.

Gorzelak, Grzegorz, and Bohdan Jałowiecki. 1999. *Transformacja Systemowa z Perspektywy Dzierzgonia.* Warszawa: Wydawnictwo Naukowe "Scholar."

Grabowski, Tomasz. 2002. Breaking through to Individualism: Poland's Western Frontier, 1945–1995. Master's thesis, University of California, Berkeley.

Greenwald, Anthony G., and Thomas F. Pettigrew. 2014. "With Malice toward None and Charity for Some: Ingroup Favoritism Enables Discrimination." *American Psychologist* 69 (7): 669–684.

Greif, Avner. 1993. "Contract Enforceability and Economic Institutions in Early Trade: the Maghribi Traders' Coalition." *American Economic Review* 83 (3): 525–548.

Greif, Avner. 2006. *Institutions and the Path to the Modern Economy: Lessons from Medieval Trade*. Cambridge, UK: Cambridge University Press.

Grosfeld, Irena, and Ekaterina Zhuravskaya. 2015. "Cultural vs. Economic Legacies of Empires: Evidence from the Partition of Poland." *Journal of Comparative Economics* 43 (1): 55–75.

Gross, Jan. 1979. *Polish Society under German Occupation: The Generalgouvernement, 1939–1944*. Princeton, NJ: Princeton University Press.

Gross, Radosław. 2018. "Związek Samopomocy Chłopskiej na Olsztyńskiej Wsi (1945–1948). Początki 'Polityki Klasowej.'" *Echa Przeszłości* XIX: 203–214.

Grosser, Thomas. 1996. "Integrationshilfe vor Ort. Die Flüchtlingspolitik der amerikanischen Besatzungsmacht und ihre Auswirkungen in einem nordbadischen Landkreis." In *Die Flüchtlingsfrage in der deutschen Nachkriegsgesellschaft*, ed. Sylvia Schraut and Thomas Grosser. Mannheim: Palatium Verlag Mannheim.

Grottendieck, Michael. 1999. "Probleme der Eingliederung von Vertriebenen im münsterlandischen Greven sowie von 'antifaschistischen Umsiedlern' im mecklenburgischen Ludwigslust im Vergleich." In *Geglückte Integration? Spezifika und Vergleichbarkeiten der Vertriebenen-Eingliederung in der SBZ/DDR*, ed. Dierk Hoffmann and Michael Schwartz. Berlin, Boston: Oldenbourg Wissenschaftsverlag.

Grzymała-Busse, Anna. 2015. *Nations under God: How Churches Use Moral Authority to Influence Policy*. Princeton, NJ: Princeton University Press.

Guenbacher, Armin. 2004. "The Chancellor's Forgotten Blunder: Konrad Adenauer's Foundation for Refugees and Expellees." *German Politics* 13 (3): 481–498.

GUS. 1950. *Narodowy Spis Powszechny 1950*. Warsaw: Główny Urząd Statystyczny.

GUS. 1956. *Rocznik Statystyczny 1956*. Warsaw: Główny Urząd Statystyczny.

GUS. 1958. *Rocznik Statystyczny 1958*. Warsaw: Główny Urząd Statystyczny.

Habyarimana, James, M. Humphreys, D. Posner, and J. M. Weinstein. 2009. *Coethnicity: Diversity and the Dilemmas of Collective Action*. New York: Russell Sage Foundation.

Habyarimana, James, Macartan Humphreys, Daniel N. Posner, and Jeremy M. Weinstein. 2007. "Why Does Ethnic Diversity Undermine Public Goods Provision?" *The American Political Science Review* 101 (4): 709–725.

Halicka, Beata. 2011. "Kozaky und Pyrehne – zwei Dörfer, mehrere Nationalitäten." In *Polen, Deutsche und Ukrainer auf dem Erinnerungspfad erzwungener Migrationen*, ed. Beata Halicka and Bogusław Mykietów. Skórzyn: Wydawnictwo Instytutowe.

Halicka, Beata. 2013. *Polens Wilder Westen. Erzwungene Migration und die Kulturelle Aneignung des Oderraums 1945–1948*. Zürich: F. Schöningh.

Halicka, Beata, ed. 2016. *Mój Dom nad Odrą: Pamiętniki osadników Ziem Zachodnich po 1945 roku*. Kraków: TAiWPN Universitas.

Hangartner, Dominik, Elias Dinas, Moritz Marbach, Konstantinos Matakos, and Dimitrios Xefteris. 2019. "Does Exposure to the Refugee Crisis Make Natives More Hostile?" *American Political Science Review* 113 (2): 442–455.

Hanson, Jonathan K., and Rachel Sigman. 2020. "Leviathan's Latent Dimensions: Measuring State Capacity for Comparative Political Research." *Journal of Politics* 83 (4): 1495–1510.

Hauner, Milan. 2009. "'We Must Push Eastwards!' The Challenges and Dilemmas of President Beneš after Munich." *Journal of Contemporary History* 44 (4): 619–656.

Hayse, Michael R. 2003. *Recasting West German Elites: Higher Civil Servants, Business Leaders, and Physicians in Hesse between Nazism and Democracy, 1945–1955.* New York: Berghahn Books.

Herlemann, Hans-Heinrich. 1959. "Vertriebene Bauern in Strukturwandel der Landwirtschaft." In *Die Vertriebenen in Westdeutschland. Ihre Eingliederung und Ihr Einfluss auf Gesellschaft, Wirtschaft, Politik und Geistesleben*, ed. Eugen Lemberg and Friedrich Edding. Vol. II. Kiel: F. Hirt.

Hillenstedt, Ilka E. 2009. "'Meine goldene Judgendzeit endete mit neun Jahren.' Flüchtlingskinder in Schleswig-Holstein." In *Fremdes Zuhause. Flüchtlinge und Vertrieben in Schleswig-Holstein nach 1945*, ed. Hermann Heidrich and Ilka E. Hillenstedt. Neumünster: Wachholtz Verlag.

Hirschon, Renée. 1989. *Heirs of the Greek Catastrophe: The Social Life of Asia Minor Refugees in Piraeus.* Oxford and New York: Clarendon/Oxford University Press.

Hollenbach, Florian, and Thiago N. Silva. 2019. "Fiscal Capacity and Inequality: Evidence from Brazilian Municipalities." *Journal of Politics* 81 (4): 1434–1445.

Hołubecka-Zielnicowa, Aleksandra. 1970. "Proces Społecznej Adaptacji i Intergracji Ludności Napływowej na Dolnym Śląsku na Przykładzie Wsi Dziadowa Kłoda w Powiecie Sycowskim." *Prace i Materiały Etnograficzne* 20: 53–78.

Hughes, Michael L. 1999. *Shouldering the Burdens of Defeat: West Germany and Reconstruction of Social Justice.* Chapel Hill, NC: University of North Carolina Press.

Huntington, Samuel. 1968. *Political Order in Changing Societies.* New Haven: Yale University Press.

ICPSR, Inter-University Consortium for Political and Social Research. 1999. "German Weimar Republic Data, 1919–1933."

Instytut Kartogr. i Wydawniczy GLOB Jana Chodorowicza. 1945. "Rzeczpospolita Polska." Obtained from the Institute of Geography and Spatial Organization (*Instytut Geografii i Przestrzennego Zagospodarowania PAN*).

IOM Global Migration Data Analysis Centre. 2023. "Forced Migration or Displacement." Migration Data Portal. www.migrationdataportal.org/themes/forced-migration-or-displacementfootnote1_s7bqegl.

Isański, Jakub. 2017. "Pamiętnik Heleny Wróblewskiej, Mieszkanki Ziem Zachodnich." *Rocznik Ziem Zachodnich* 1: 573–596.

Jarecka-Kimlowska, Stanisława. 1968. *Ta Ziemia Jest Nasza.* Warsaw: Ludowa Spółdzielnia Wydawnicza.

Jarząbek, Marcin. 2009. "Separateness and National Identity – the Case of Upper Silesia in Interwar Poland." Ph.D. diss. Central European University.

Jedruszczak, Hanna. 1967. *Upaństwowienie i Odbudowa Przemysłu w Polsce 1944–1948. Materiały Żrodłowe.* Warsaw: Państwowe Wydawnictwo Naukowe.

Jha, Saumitra. 2013. "Trade, Institutions, and Ethnic Tolerance: Evidence from South Asia." *American Political Science Review* 107 (4): 806–832.

Johnson, Simon, and Gary Loveman. 1995. "Starting Over: Poland after Communism." *Harvard Business Review* 73 (2): 44–56.

Juzwenko, Adolf. 2011. "Zbawienie w Wagonie." In *Sami Swoi i Obcy. Z Kresów na Kresy*, ed. Mirosław Maciorowski. Warszawa: Agora S.A.

Kaasa, Anneli, Maaja Vadi, and Urmas Varblane. 2014. "Regional Cultural Differences within European Countries: Evidence from Multi-Country Surveys." *Management International Review* 54: 825–852.

Kaliński, Janusz. 2015. "Etatyzacja Gospodarki w Okresie Rządów Komunistycznych w Polsce." *Kwartalnik Kolegium Ekonomiczno-Społecznego Studia i Prace* 4: 177–201.

Kaliński, Janusz. 2019. "'Transformacja' do Gospodarki Centralnie Planowanej w Polsce (1944–1950)." *Optimum. Economic Studies* 1 (95): 32–45.

Kamusella, Tomasz. 2004. "The Expulsion of the Population Categorized as 'Germans' from the Post-1945 Poland." In *The Expulsion of the 'German' Communities from Eastern Europe at the End of the Second World War*, ed. Steffen Prauser and Arfon Rees. San Domenico, Italy: EUI.

Kamusella, Tomasz. 2012. "Poland and the Silesians: Minority Rights à la Carte?" *Journal of Ethnopolitics and Minority Issues in Europe* 11 (2): 42–74.

Kaufmann, Chaim D. 1998. "When All Else Fails: Ethnic Population Transfers and Partitions in the Twentieth Century." *International Security* 23 (2): 120–156.

Keil, Theo. 1967. *Die deutsche Schule in den Sudetenländern*. München: Schriften der Arbeitsgemeinschaft Sudetendeutscher Erzieher.

Kenney, Padraic. 1997. *Rebuilding Poland: Workers and Communists, 1945–1950*. Ithaca, NY: Cornell University Press.

Kern, Konrad. ND. "Geschichte der Freiwilligen Feuerwehr Waldkraiburg." Freiwilligen Feuerwehr Waldkraiburg.

Kersten, Krystyna. 1962. "U Podstaw Kształtowania się Nowej Struktury Agrarnej Ziem Zachodnich (1945–1947)." *Polska Ludowa, Materiały i Studia* 1: 37–84.

Kersten, Krystyna. 1965. "Poczatki Stabilizacji Zycia Społecznego w Środowisku Wiejskim na Pomorzu Zachodnim (1945–1947)." *Polska Ludowa* 6: 3–43.

Kersten, Krystyna. 1991. *The Establishment of Communist Rule in Poland, 1943–1948*. Berkeley: University of California Press.

Kersten, Krystyna. 2001. "Forced Migration and the Transformation of Polish Society in the Postwar Period." In *Redrawing Nations: Ethnic Cleansing in East-Central Europe, 1944–1948*, ed. Philipp Ther and Ana Siljak. Rowman & Littlefield.

Kertesz, Stephen. 1953. "The Expulsion of the Germans from Hungary: A Study in Postwar Diplomacy." *The Review of Politics* 15 (2): 179–208.

King, Gary, and Margaret Roberts. 2012. "EI: A(n R) Program for Ecological Inference." Working Paper.

Kittel, Manfred. 2020. *Stiefkinder des Wirtschaftswunders? Die deutschen Ostvertriebenen und die Politik des Lastenausgleichs (1952 bis 1975)*. Düsseldorf: Droste.

Kittel, Manfred, and Horst Möller. 2006. "Die Benes-Dekrete und die Vertreibung der Deutschen im europäischen Vergleich." *Vierteljahrshefte für Zeitgeschichte* 54 (4): 541–581.

Klon-Jawor. 2013. *Ochotnicze Straże Pożarne w Polsce*. Research Report. Stwaryszenie Klon-Jawor.

Knack, Stephen. 2002. "Social Capital, Growth and Poverty: A Survey of Cross-Country Evidence." In *The Role of Social Capital in Development: An Empirical Assessment*, ed. Thierry Van Bastelaer and Christiaan Grootaert. Cambridge, UK: Cambridge University Press.

Knack, Stephen, and Philip Keefer. 1997. "Does Social Capital Have an Economic Payoff? A Cross-Country Investigation." *Quarterly Journal of Economics* 112 (4): 1251–1288.

Knight, Jack. 1998. "The Bases of Cooperation: Social Norms and the Rule of Law." *Journal of Institutional and Theoretical Economics* 154: 754–763.

Knutsen, Carl Henrik, and Magnus Rasmussen. 2018. "The Autocratic Welfare State: Old-Age Pensions, Credible Commitments, and Regime Survival." *Comparative Political Studies* 51 (5): 659–695.

Kochanowski, Jerzy. 2001. "Gathering Poles into Poland." In *Redrawing Nations. Ethnic Cleansing in East-Central Europe, 1944–1948*, ed. Philip Ther and Ana Siljak. Boston: Roman & Littlefield.

Kochanowski, Jerzy. 2010. *Tylnymi Drzwiami: "Czarny Rynek" w Polsce 1944–1989*. Warsaw: Neriton.

Kochanski, Halik. 2012. *The Eagle Unbowed: Poland and the Poles in the Second World War*. Cambridge: Harvard University Press.

Kociszewski, Jerzy. 1993. "Problemy Badawcze i Efekty Integracji Gospodarczej Ziem Zachodnich i Północnych z Ziemiami Dawnymi Polski ze Szczególnym Uwzględnieniem Śląska." *Acta Universitatis Wratislaviensisratislaviensis* 1512: Socjologia 10: 31–54.

Kołodyńska, Stanisława. 1976. "Trzeba Walczyć o Zmiany na Lepsze...." In *Mój Dom nad Odrą [t.5]*, ed. Zygmunt Dulczewski. Zielona Góra: Lubuskie Towarzystwo Kultury.

Konopka, Hanna. 1997. *Religia w Szkołach Polski Ludowej: Sprawa Nauczania Religii w Polityce Państwa, 1944–1961*. Białystok: Wydawn. Uniwersytetu w Białymstoku.

Kontogiorgi, Elisabeth. 2003. "Economic Consequences following Refugee Settlement in Greek Macedonia, 1923–1932." In *Crossing the Aegean. An Appraisal of the 1923 Compulsory Population Exchange between Greece and Turkey*, ed. Renée Hirschon. New York and Oxford: Berghahn Books.

Kontogiorgi, Elisabeth. 2006. *Population Exchange in Greek Macedonia: The Rural Settlement of Refugees 1922–1930*. Oxford Historical Monographs. Oxford: Clarendon Press.

Kopstein, Jeffrey, and Jason Wittenberg. 2018. *Intimate Violence: Anti-Jewish Pogroms on the Eve of the Holocaust*. Ithaca: Cornell University Press.

Kornai, Janos. 1990. "The Affinity Between Ownership Forms and Coordination Mechanisms: The Common Experience of Reform in Socialist Countries." *Journal of Economic Perspectives* 4 (3): 131–147.

Kosinski, Leszek A. 1969. "Changes in the Ethnic Structure in East-Central Europe, 1930–1960." *Geographical Review* 59 (3): 388–402.

Kossert, Andreas. 2008. *Kalte Heimat: Die Geschichte der deutschen Vertriebenen nach 1945*. Munich: Siedler Verlag.

Kotlarska, Anna, ed. 1978. *Pamiętniki mieszkańców Dolnego Śląska*. Wrocław: Ossolineum.

Kowalczyk, Teresa, Janusz Marcinkowski, Krystyna Skośkiewicz, Jan Rutkowski, and Beata Chromik. 1970. *Mała Encyklopedia Powszechna PWN*. Warszawa: Wydawnictwo Naukowe PWN.

Kowalski, Mariuscz, and Przemysław Śleszyński. 2000. *Uwarunkowania Zachowań Wyborczych w Województwie Słupskim*. Vol. 21 of *Dokumentaca Geograficzna PAN IGiPZ*.

Krauss, Marita. 2000. "Das 'Wir' und das 'Ihr': Ausgrenzung, Abgrenzung, Identitätsstiftung bei Einheimischen und Flüchtlingen nach 1945." In *Vertriebene in Deutschland*, ed. Dierk Hoffman, Maritta Krauss, and Michael Schwartz. München: Oldenbourg Verlag.

Krauss, Marita. 2008. *Integrationen: Vertriebene in den deutschen Ländern nach 1945*. Göttingen: Vandenhoeck & Ruprecht.

Kreuzer, Marcus. 2009. "How Party Systems Form: Path Dependency and the Institutionalization of the Post-War German Party System." *British Journal of Political Science* 39 (4): 669–697.

Kruk, Genowefa. n.d. "Opowieść o życiu religijnym w Obertynie." Interview. Centrum Historii Zajezdnia. Świadkowe Historii. www.zajezdnia.org/swiadek-historia/genowefa-kruk.

Kubik, Jan. 1994. "The Role of Decentralization and Cultural Revival in Post-Communist Transformations: The Case of Cieszyn, Silesia, Poland." *Communist and Post-Communist Studies* 27 (4): 331–355.

Kučera, Jaroslav. 1992. "Die rechtliche und soziale Stellung der Deutschen in der Tschechoslowakei Ende der 40er Jahre und Anfang der 50er Jahre." *Bohemia* 33 (2): 322–337.

Kulczycki, John J. 2003. "'Repatriation': Bringing Poles from the Soviet Union Home after World War II." *Sprawy Narodowościowe* 23: 7–41.

Kulczycki, John J. 2016. *Belonging to the Nation: Inclusion and Exclusion in the Polish-German Borderlands, 1939–1951*. Cambridge, MA: Harvard University Press.

Kuran, Timur. 1998. "Ethnic Norms and Their Transformation Through Reputational Cascades." *The Journal of Legal Studies* 27 (S2): 623–659.

Kurowska, Hanna. 2022. "Niewykorzystany Potencjał – Przemysł Rolny, Handel i Rzemiosło w Gminach Wiejskich Powiatu Gubińskiego w Latach 1945–1949." *Zestyty Wiejskie* 28 (1): 71–101.

Kuta, Stanisław. 1987. *Ochotnicze Straże Pożarne w Polsce Ludowej 1944–1975*. Warsaw: Instytut Wydawniczy Związków Zadowodych.

Kyrieleis, Gisela. 1984. "Freiwillig im Verein und verpflichtet zur Wehr." In *Vereinsforschung*. Giessen: W. Schmitz.

Łach, Stanisław. 1978. *Przemiany Społeczno-Polityczne na Pomorzu Zachodnim 1945–1950*. Poznań: Wydawnictwo Poznanskie.

Łach, Stanisław. 1993. "Osadnictwo na Ziemiach Zachodnich i Północnych w Założeniach i Praktyce Osiedleńczej." *Słupskie Studia Historyczne* (3): 19–39.

Laitin, David. 1998. *Identity in Formation*. Ithaca, NY: Cornell University Press.

Lamont, Michèle, and Virág Molnár. 2002. "The Study of Boundaries in the Social Science." *Annual Review of Sociology* 28: 167–195.

Lassotta, Arnold. 2005. "Die Textilindustrie: '…der nächst Nahrung und Wohnung wichtigste Verbrauchsgüterzweig.'" In *Aufbau West: Neubeginn zwischen Vertreibung und Wirtschaftswunder; Ausstellungskatalog*. Essen: Dagmar Kift.

Lattimore, Bertram Gresh. 1974. *The Assimilation of German Expellees into the West German Polity and Society Since 1945: A Case Study of Eutin, Schleswig-Holstein*. The Hague: Martinus Nijhoff.

Lazzarini, Sergio G., Gary J. Miller, and Todd R. Zenger. 2004. "Order with Some Law: Complementarity versus Substitution of Formal and Informal Arrangements." *Journal of Law, Economics, & Organization* 20 (2): 261–298.

Lee, Alexander. 2017. "Ethnic Diversity and Ethnic Discrimination: Explaining Local Public Goods Provision." *Comparative Political Studies* 10 (51): 1351–1383.

Leisering, Lutz. 2001. "Germany – Reform from Within." In *International Social Policy: Welfare Regimes in the Developed World*, ed. Pete Alcock und Gary Craig. London: Palgrave.

Lewandowski, Paweł. 2013. "Wschód i Zachód Przemieszczone oraz Odtworzone. Powstanie Postmigracyjnego Społeczeństwa Polskich Ziem Zachodnich." *Kultura i Społeczeństwo* 3: 203–216.

Lieberman, Evan S., and Gwyneth C. McClendon. 2013. "The Ethnicity-Policy Preference Link in Sub-Saharan Africa." *Comparative Political Studies* 46 (5): 574–602.

Lippmann, Ingetraud. 2001. "Nach der Flucht aus Königsberg 1945." LeMO-Zeitzeugen, Lebendiges Museum Online. www.hdg.de/lemo/zeitzeugen/ingetraud-lippmann-nach-der-flucht-aus-koenigsberg.html.

Long, Katy. 2013. *The Point of No Return: Refugees, Rights, and Repatriation.* Oxford: Oxford University Press.

Lorenzen-Schmidt, Klaus-J. 2009. "Die integration der Flüchtlinge und Heimatvetriebenen in die Landwirtschaft." In *Fremdes Zuhause. Flüchtlinge und Vertrieben in Schleswig-Holstein nach 1945*, ed. Hermann Heidrich and Ilka E. Hillenstedt. Neumünster: Wachholtz Verlag.

Los, Maria. 1990. "Introduction." In *The Second Economy in Marxist States*, ed. Maria Los. New York: St. Martin's Press.

Lowe, Keith. 2012. *Savage Continent: Europe in the Aftermath of World War II.* New York: St. Martin's Press.

Lüttinger, Paul. 1989. *Integration der Vertriebenen. Eine empirische Analyse.* Frankfurt a.M., New York: Campus.

Luttmer, Erzo F. P. 2001. "Group Loyalty and the Taste for Redistribution." *Journal of Political Economy* 109 (3): 6–34.

Mach, Zdzisław. 1998. *Niechciane Miasta: Migracja i Tożsamość Społeczna.* Kraków: Universitas.

Machałek, Małgorzata. 2005. "Na Poniemieckiej Ziemi: Polityka Rolna Komunistycznych Władz na Pomorzu Zachodnim – 1945–1948." *Biuletyn IPN* 9-10 (September-October): 54–60.

Maciorowski, Mirosław. 2011. *Sami Swoi i Obcy. Z Kresów na Kresy.* Warszawa: Agora S.A.

Magierska, Anna. 1976. "Początki Szkolnictwa na Ziemiach Zachodnich i Północnych w Polsce Ludowej." *Rozprawy z Dziejów Oświaty* 19 (76): 201–222.

Majka, Józef. 1971. "Wpływ Kościoła na Integrację Kulturową na Ziemiach Zachodnich." In *Kościół na Ziemiach Zachodnich. Ćwierćwiecze Polskiej Organizacji Kościelnej*, ed. Jan Krucina. Wrocław: Wrocławska Księgarnia Archidiecezjalna.

Mann, Michael. 1984. "The Autonomous Power of the State: Its Origins, Mechanisms and Results." *European Journal of Sociology* 25 (2): 185–213.

Marcinkiewicz, Stefan M. 2017. "Trauma Dezintegracji i Integracji w Wymiarze Lokalnym na Przykładzie Powojennego Powiatu Ełckiego." *Opuscula Sociologica* 19 (1): 33–45.

Marshall, Barbara. 1988. *The Origins of Post-War German Politics.* London, New York, Sydney: Croom Helm.

McNamara, Paul. 2012. "Competing National and Regional Identities in Poland's Baltic 'Recovered Territories,' 1945–1956." *History of Communism in Europe* 3: 21–42.

McNamara, Paul. 2013. "The Sovietisation of Poland's Baltic 'Recovered Territories,' 1945–1956." Ph.D. diss. Department of History, National University of Ireland, Galway.

McNamee, Lachlan. 2018. "Mass Resettlement and Political Violence: Evidence from Rwanda." *World Politics* 70 (4): 595–644.

Melendy, Brenda. 2003. "Private and Public, Personal and Political: Exploring German Expellee Memory Tourism." *World History Review* 1 (1): 39–61.

Meltzer, Allan H., and Scott F. Richard. 1981. "A Rational Theory of the Size of Government." *Journal of Political Economy* 89 (5): 914–927.

Menon, Anil. 2022. "The Political Legacy of Forced Migration: Evidence from Post-WWII Germany." *Comparative Political Studies* 56 (9): 1398–1432.

Merritt, Anna J. and Richard L. Merritt, eds. 1970. *Public Opinion in Occupied Germany. The OMGUS Surveys, 1945–1949*. London, Urbana, Chicago: University of Illinois Press.

Michaloupoulos, Stellios. 2012. "The Origins of Ethnolinguistic Diversity." *American Economic Review* 102 (4): 1508–1539.

Migdal, Joel. 1989. "The Crystallization of the State and the Struggles over Rulemaking: Israel in a Comparative Perspective." In *The Israeli State and Society: Boundaries and Frontiers*, ed. Baruch Kimmerling. Albany: SUNY Press.

Migdal, Joel S. 1988. *Strong Societies and Weak States: State-Society Relations and State Capabilities in the Third World*. Princeton, NJ: Princeton University Press.

Migdal, Joel S. 2001. *State in Society: Studying How States and Societies Transform and Constitute One Another*. Cambridge, UK: Cambridge University Press.

Miguel, Edward. 2004. "Tribe or Nation? Nation Building and Public Goods in Kenya versus Tanzania." *World Politics* 56 (3): 327–362.

Miguel, Edward, and Mary Kay Gugerty. 2005. "Ethnic Diversity, Social Sanctions, and Public Goods in Kenya." *Journal of Public Economics* 89: 2325–2368.

Millard, Frances. 1992. "The Polish Parliamentary Elections of October 1991." *Soviet Studies* 44 (5): 837–855.

Misiag, Wojciech, ed. 2000. *Wspieranie Przedsiębiorczości przez Samorząd Terytorialny*. Warsaw: Polska Fundacja Promocji i Rozwoju Malych i Srednich Przedsiębiorstw.

Møller, Jørgen. 2020. "Reading History Forward." *PS: Political Science & Politics* 54 (2): 249–253.

Morales, Juan S. 2018. "The Impact of Internal Displacement on Destination Communities: Evidence from the Colombian Conflict." *Journal of Economic Development* 131: 132–150.

MPIDR, and CGG. 2011. "MPIDR Population History GIS Collection (Partly Based on Bundesamt für Kartographie und Geodäsie 2011)." Max Planck Institute for Demographic Research and Chair for Geodesy and Geoinformatics, University of Rostock.

MPIDR, and CGG. 2013. "MPIDR Population History GIS Collection – Europe (Partly Based on © EuroGeographics for the administrative boundaries)." Max Planck Institute for Demographic Research and Chair for Geodesy and Geoinformatics, University of Rostock.

Müller, Carl-Jochen. 1997. *Praxis und Probleme des Lastenausgleichs in Mannheim 1949–1959*. Mannheim: Südwestdeutsche Schriften.

Müller, Werner, and Heinz Simon. 1959. "Aufnahme und Unterbringung." In *Die Vertriebenen in Westdeutschland. Ihre Eingliederung und ihr Einfluss auf Gesellschaft,*

*Wirtschaft, Politik und Geistesleben*, ed. Eugen Lemberg and Friedrich Edding. Kiel: F. Hirt.

Murard, Elie, and Seyhun Orcan Sakalli. 2019. "Mass Refugee Inflow and Long-Run Prosperity: Lessons from the Greek Population Resettlement." Discussion Paper Series CDP 05/20.

Muszkiewicz, Marian. 2020. *Rzemieślnicy, Kupcy, Przemysłowcy na Dolnym Śląsku w Latach 1945–1950*. Wrocław: Wydawnictwo Uniwersytetu Ekonomicznego we Wrocławiu.

Nachum, Iris, and Sagi Schaefer. 2018. "The Semantics of Political Integration: Public Debates about the Term 'Expellees' in Post-War Western Germany." *Contemporary European History* 27 (1): 42–58.

Nahm, Peter Paul. 1971. *Doch das Leben ging weiter: Skizzen zur Lage, Haltung und Leistung der Vertriebenen, Flüchtlinge und Eingesessenen nach der Stunde Null*. Köln: Grote.

Naimark, Norman. 2001. *Fires of Hatred: Ethnic Cleansing in 20th Century Europe*. Cambridge, MA: Harvard University Press.

Nalepa, Monica, and Grigore Pop-Eleches. 2022. "Infiltration of Religious Organizations as a Strategy of Authoritarian Durability: Causes and Consequences." *Journal of Politics* 84 (2): 156–269.

Nicholls, Anthony James. 1994. *Freedom with Responsibility: The Social Market Economy in Germany 1918–1963*. Clarendon: Oxford.

Niethammer, Lutz. 1987. "Flucht ins Konventionelle? Einige Randglossen zu Forschungsproblemen der deutschen Nachkriegsmigration." In *Flüchtlinge und Vertriebene in der westdeutschen Nachkriegsgeschichte*, ed. Rainer Schulze und Doris von der Brelie-Lewien und Helga Grebing. Hildesheim: F. Steiner.

North, Douglas C. 1990. *Institutions, Institutional Change and Economic Performance*. Cambridge, MA: Cambridge University Press.

North, Douglass C, John Joseph Wallis, and Barry R. Weingast. 2006. "A Conceptual Framework for Interpreting Recorded Human History." NBER Working Paper No. 12795.

Nowakowski, Stefan. 1957. *Adaptacja Ludności na Śląsku Opolskim*. Ziemie Zachodnie. Studia i Materiały. Poznań: Instytut Zachodni.

Nowrasteh, Alex, and Benjamin Powell. 2021. *Wretched Refuse? The Political Economy of Immigration and Institutions*. Cambridge, UK: Cambridge University Press.

Ogilvie, Sheilagh, and André W. Carus. 2014. "Institutions and Economic Growth in Historical Perspective." In *Handbook of Economic Growth*, ed. Philippe Aghion and Steven N. Durlauf. Amsterdam: Elsevier.

Ortega, Francesc, and Giovanni Peri. 2014. "Openness and Income: The Roles of Trade and Migration." *Journal of International Economics* 92: 231–251.

Osa, Maryjane. 1989. "Resistance, Persistence, and Change: The Transformation of the Catholic Church in Poland." *East European Politics and Societies* 3 (2): 268–299.

Osękowski, Czesław 2001. "Ks. Prymas Stefan Wyszyński wobec Stosunków Polsko-Niemieckich." In *Stefan Kardynal Wyszyński wobec Ziem Zachodnich i Północnych oraz Stosunków Polsko-Niemieckich.*, eds. T. Dzwonkowski and C. Osękowski. Poznan: Garmond.

Osekowski, Czesław. 1994. *Społeczeństwo Polski Zachodniej i Północnej w Latach 1945–1956*. Zielona Góra: Wyższa Szkoła Pedagogiczna im. Tadeusza Kotarbińskiego.

O'Sullivan, Michael B. 2010. "The Greek Interwar Refugee Crisis as a Cause of the Greek Civil War, 1922–1949." *Historical Perspectives: Santa Clara University Undergraduate Journal of History, Series II* 15: 44–65.

Overy, Richard. 2012. *Why the Allies Won*. New York: W.W. Norton.

Owsińska, Stanisława. 1987. "Tworzy się Nowe." In *Wiosna na rumowisku i inne wspomnienia pionierów*, ed. Zdzisław Linkowski. Gorzów Wielkopolski: Gorzowskie Towarzystwo Kultury.

Özsu, Umut. 2015. *Formalizing Displacement: International Law and Population Transfers*. Oxford University Press.

Paczkowski, Andrzej. 1993. *Referendum z 30 czerwca 1946. Przebieg i Wyniki*. Warsaw: Instytut Studiow Politycznych PAN.

Pakulski, Jan. 2016. "State Violence and the Eliticide in Poland, 1935–49." In *Violence and the State*, ed. Jan Pakulski, Martin Killingsworth, and Matthew Sussex. Manchester: Manchester University Press.

Pellengahr, Astrid. 2002. *Vereinswesen als Integrationsfaktor. Eine volkskundliche Fallstudie zur kulturellen Integration der Vertriebenen und Flüchtlinge nach 1945 in Bayern*. München: Lucidium Verlag.

Pengl, Yannick I., Philip Roessler, and Valeria Rueda. 2021. "Cash Crops, Print Technologies, and the Politicization of Ethnicity in Africa." *American Political Science Review*: 1–9.

Peri, Giovanni. 2012. "The Effect of Immigration on Productivity: Evidence from US States." *Review of Economics and Statistics* 94 (1): 348–358.

Peters, Michael. 2022. "Market Size and Spatial Growth - Evidence from Germany's Post-War Population Expulsions." *Econometrica* 90 (5): 2357–2396.

Pfeil, Elisabeth. 1951. *Thema und Wege der deutschen Flüchtlingsforschung*. Mitteilungen aus dem Institut für Raumforschung; Heft 6. Bonn: Institut für Raumforschung.

Pietraszko, Aleksander. 1963. "Osadnik wojskowy." In *Pamiętniki Osadników Ziem Odzyskanych*, ed. Zygmunt Dulczewski and Andrzej Kwilecki. Poznań: Wydawnictwo Poznańskie.

Plotek, Marcin. 2011. *Trudne Poczatki. Okreg Mazurski 1945–1946*. Dąbrówno: Oficyna Retman.

Portes, Alejandro. 1998. "Social Capital: Its Origins and Applications in Modern Sociology." *Annual Review of Sociology* 24: 1–24.

Posner, Daniel N. 2004a. "Measuring Ethnic Fractionalization in Africa." *American Journal of Political Science* 48 (4): 849–863.

Posner, Daniel N. 2004b. "The Political Salience of Cultural Difference: Why Chewas and Tumbukas Are Allies in Zambia and Adversaries in Malawi." *American Political Science Review* 98 (4): 529–545.

Powell, G. Bingham. 2000. *Elections as Instruments of Democracy: Majoritarian and Proportional Visions*. New Haven and London: Yale University Press.

Prantl, Susanne, and Alexandra Spitz-Oener. 2020. "The Impact of Immigration on Competing Natives' Wages: Evidence from German Reunification." *The Review of Economics and Statistics* 102 (1): 79–97.

Pražmowska, Anita J. 2004. *Civil War in Poland 1942–1948*. Basingstoke and New York: Palgrave Macmillan.

Pryczkowski, Eugeniusz. 2019. "Discrimination against the Kashubians." *The Polish Review* 64 (2): 79–93.

Przybyla, Jan. 1958. "Private Enterprise in Poland under Gomulka." *The American Slavic and East European Review,* 17 (3): 316–331.

Putnam, Robert. 1995. "Bowling Alone: America's Declining Social Capital." *Journal of Democracy* 6 (1): 65–78.

Putnam, Robert D. 2007. "E Pluribus Unum: Diversity and Community in the Twenty-First Century. The 2006 Johan Skytte Prize Lecture." *Scandinavian Political Studies* 30 (2): 137–174.

Putnam, Robert D., Robert Leonardi, and Raffaella Y. Nanetti. 1993. *Making Democracy Work: Civic Traditions in Modern Italy.* Princeton, NJ: Princeton University Press.

Ramos, Miguel R., Matthew R. Bennett, Douglas S. Massey, and Miles Hewstone. 2019. "Humans Adapt to Social Diversity over Time." *PNAS* 116 (25): 12244–12249.

Rauziński, Robert, and Agata Zagórowska. 2007. *Przemiany struktury demograficznej i społecznej ludności Śląska 1946-2002-2030.* Opole: Politechnika Opolska.

Rauziński, Robert, and Kazimierz Szczygielski. 2011. "Przesiedleńcy z Dawnych Kresów Rzeczypospolitej w Strukturze Demograficznej i Społecznej Śląska Opolskiego 1945–2005." In *Wokół Ludzi i Zdarzeń. Przesiedleńcy z Dawnych Kresów Rzeczypospolitej w Strukturze Demograficznej i Społecznej Śląska Opolskiego w Sześćdziesięcioleciu 1945–2005,* ed. Robert Rauziński and Teresa Sołdra-Gwiżdż. Opole: Instytut Śląski w Opolu.

Report to H. Res. 238. 1950. "Expellees and Refugees of German Ethnic Origin." United States House of Representatives, Special Subcommittee of the Committee on the Judiciary. 81st Congress, Report No. 1841. Washington DC.

Rieber, Alfred J. 2000. *Forced Migration in Central and Eastern Europe, 1939–1950.* London: Frank Cass Publishers.

Rigoll, Dominik. 2018. "From Denazification to Renazification? West German Government Officials after 1945." In *Transforming Occupation in the Western Zones of Germany,* ed. Camilo Erlichman and Christopher Knowles. London, New York, Sydney, Oxford, New Delhi: Bloomsbury.

Robinson, Amanda Lea. 2016. "Internal Borders: Ethnic-Based Market Segmentation in Malawi." *World Development* 87: 371–384.

Rodríguez-Pose, Andrés, and Viola von Berlepsch. 2014. "When Migrants Rule: The Legacy of Mass Migration on Economic Development in the United States." *Annals of the Association of American Geographers* 104 (3): 628–651.

Rueda, David. 2018. "Food Comes First, Then Morals: Redistribution Preferences, Parochial Altruism, and Immigration in Western Europe." *Journal of Politics* 80 (1): 225–239.

Rüegger, Seraina. 2019. "Refugees, Ethnic Power Relations, and Civil Conflict in the Country of Asylum." *Journal of Peace Research* 56 (1): 42–57.

Sakson, Andrzej. 1998. *Stosunki Narodowościowe na Warmii i Mazurach 1945–1997.* Poznań: Instytut Zachodni.

Sakson, Andrzej. 2011. *Od Kłajpedy do Olsztyna : Współcześni Mieszkańcy Byłych Prus Wschodnich: Kraj Kłajpedzki, Obwód Kaliningradzki, Warmia i Mazury.* Poznań: Wydawnictwo Instytutu Zachodniego.

Sakson, Andrzej, ed. 2008. *Kaszubi, Mazurzy i Warmiacy – Między Polskością a Niemieckością.* Poznań: Wydawnictwo Instytutu Zachodniego.

Salehyan, Idean. 2008. "The Externalities of Civil Strife: Refugees as a Source of International Conflict." *American Journal of Political Science* 52 (4): 787–801.

Salehyan, Idean, and Kristian Skrede Gleditsch. 2006. "Refugee Flows and the Spread of Civil War." *International Organization* 60 (2): 335–366.

Sammartino, Annemarie H. 2010. *The Impossible Border: Germany.* Ithaca, NY: Cornell University Press.

Sauter, Wiesław. 2016. "Radości i Troski Szkolnego Inspektora." In *Mój Dom nad Odrą: Pamiętniki Osadników Ziem Zachodnich po 1945 Roku*, ed. Beata Halicka. Kraków: TAiWPN Universitas.

Schaub, Max, Johanna Gereke, and Delia Baldassarri. 2020. "Does Poverty Undermine Cooperation in Multiethnic Settings? Evidence from a Cooperative Investment Experiment." *Journal of Experimental Political Science* 7 (1): 27–40.

Schechtman, Joseph B. 1953. "Postwar Population Transfers in Europe: A Survey." *The Review of Politics* 15 (2): 151–178.

Schillinger, R. 1985. "Der Lastenausgleich." In *Die Vertreibung der Deutschen aus dem Osten*, ed. W. Benz. Frankfurt am Main: Fischer Taschenbuch Verlag.

Schioldo-Zürcher, Jan. 2016. "The Postcolonial Repatriations of the French of Algeria in 1962: An Emblematic Case of a Public Integration Policy." In *Vertriebene and Pieds-Noirs in Postwar Germany and France: Comparative Perspectives*, ed. Manuel Borutta. Palgrave Macmillan.

Schmitt, Karl, Hans Rattinger, and Dieter Oberndörfer. 1994. "Kreisdaten (Volkszählungen 1950–1987)." GESIS Datenarchiv, Köln. ZA2472 Datenfile Version 1.0.0.

Schneider, Petra. 2019. "Jubiläum am Samstag: Älter als Geretsried selbst." *Süddeutsche Zeitung.*

Schoenberg, Hans. 1970. *Germans from the East.* Springer Netherlands.

Schraut, Sylvia. 1995. *Flüchtlingsaufnahme in Württemberg-Baden 1945–1949. Amerikanische Besatzungsziele und demokratischer Wiederaufbau im Konflikt.* München: R. Oldenbourg Verlag.

Schraut, Sylvia. 2000. "'Make the Germans Do It': The Refugee Problem in the American Zone of Post-War Germany." *Journal of Communist Studies and Transition Politics* 16 (1–2): 115–124.

Schultz, Helga. 2002. "Self-Determination and Economic Interest: Border Drawing after the World Wars." In *National Borders and Economic Disintegration in Modern East Central Europe*, ed. Uwe Müller and Helga Schultz. Berlin: Berliner Wissenschafts Verlag.

Schulze, Rainer. 1989. "Growing Discontent: Relations between Native and Refugee Populations in a Rural District in Western Germany after the Second World War." *German History* 7 (3): 332–349.

Schulze, Rainer. 2002. "The Struggle of Past and Present in Individual Identities: The Case of German Refugees and Expellees from the East." In *Home to Germany? The Integration of Ethnic Germans from Central and Eastern Europe in the Federal Republic*, ed. David Rock and Stefan Wolff. New York: Berghahn Books.

Schumann, Abel. 2014. "Persistence of Population Shocks: Evidence from the Occupation of West Germany after World War II." *American Economic Journal: Applied Economics* 6 (3): 189–205.

Schwartz, Stephanie. 2019. "Home, Again. Refugee Return and Post-Conflict Violence in Burundi." *International Security* 44 (2): 110–145.

Scott, James C. 1977. *The Moral Economy of the Peasant: Rebellion and Subsistence in Southeast Asia*. Hew Haven, CT: Yale University Press.

Sequeira, Sandra, Nathan Nunn, and Nancy Qian. 2020. "Immigrants and the Making of America." *The Review of Economic Studies* 87 (1): 382–419.

Shah, Kristi M., and Shushant Sareen. 2019. "The Mohajir: Identity and Politics in Multiethnic Pakistan." Occasional Paper 222.

Singh, Prerna. 2015. *How Solidarity Works for Welfare: Subnationalism and Social Development in India*. New York: Cambridge University Press.

Singh, Prerna, and Matthias vom Hau. 2016. "Ethnicity in Time: Politics, History, and the Relationship between Ethnic Diversity and Public Goods Provision." *Comparative Political Studies* 49 (10): 1303–1340.

Skrzypkowski, Z. 1964. "Z Dolnośląska Ziemią Związani na Zawsze." *Strażak*: 12–13.

Slater, Dan. 2010. *Ordering Power: Contentious Politics and Authoritarian Leviathans in Southeast Asia*. Cambridge, New York: Cambridge University Press.

Smith, Eric Owen. 1893. *The West German Economy*. London and Canberra: Croom Helm.

Snyder, Timothy. 2003. *The Reconstruction of Nations. Poland, Ukraine, Lithuania, Belarus, 1569–1999*. New Haven: Yale University Press.

Soifer, Hillel. 2015. *State Building in Latin America*. Cambridge: Cambridge University Press.

Solinska, Irena and Janusz Koniusz, eds. 1961. *Mój Dom nad Odrą*. Zielona Góra: Lubuskie Towarzystwo Kultury.

Spicka, Mark E. 2002. "Selling the Economic Miracle. Public-Opinion Research, Economic Reconstruction, and Politics in West Germany, 1949–1957." *German Politics and Society* 20 (1) (62): 49–67.

Spiegel-Schmidt, Friedrich. 1959. "Religiöse Wandlungen und Probleme im evangelischen Bereich." In *Die Vertriebenen in Westdeutschland. Ihre Eingliederung und ihr Einfluss auf Gesellschaft, Wirtschaft, Politik und Geistesleben*, ed. Eugen Lemberg and Friedrich Edding. Vol. 3. Kiel: F. Hirt.

Stagnaro, Michael N., Antonio A. Arechar, and David G. Rand. 2017. "From Good Institutions to Generous Citizens: Top-Down Incentives to Cooperate Promote Subsequent Prosociality but Not Norm Enforcement." *Cognition* 167: 212–254.

Stasieniuk, Zaneta. 2011. "Wybrane Społeczno-Kulturowe Uwarunkowania Integracji Zbiorowości Ziem Zachodnich i Północnych Polski." In *Polskie Ziemie Zachodnie. Studia Socjologiczne*, ed. Andrzej Michalak, Andrzej Sakson, and Zaneta Stasieniuk. Poznań: Instytut Zachodni.

Statistisches Bundesamt Wiesbaden. *Statistisches Taschenbuch über die Heimatvertriebenen*. 1953. Wiesbaden: Statistisches Bundesamt Wiesbaden.

Stola, Dariusz. 2010. *Kraj bez Wyjścia? Migracje z Polski 1949–1989*. Warsaw: Instytut Studiów Politycznych PAN.

Stolle, Dietlind, Stuart Soroka, and Richard Johnston. 2008. "When Does Diversity Erode Trust? Neighborhood Diversity, Interpersonal Trust and the Mediating Effect of Social Interactions." *Political Studies* 56 (1): 57–75.

Sudziński, Ryszard. 1997. "Taktyka i Propaganda Władz Komunistycznych w Stosunku do Ziem Odzyskanych w Latach 1944-1949." In *Władze Komunistyczne wobec Ziem Odzyskanych po II Wojnie Światowej*, ed. Stanisław Łach. Słupsk: Wyższa Szkoła Pedagogiczna w Słupsku.

Sula, Dorota. 2002. *Dzialalność Przesiedlenczo-Repatriacyjna Państwowego Urzędu Repatriacyjnego w Latach 1944–1951*. Lublin: Redakcja Wydawnictw Katolickiego Uniwersytetu Lubelskiego.

Suryanarayan, Pavithra. 2016. "Hollowing out the State: Social Inequality and Fiscal Capacity in Colonial India." Ph.D. diss. Columbia University.

Suryanarayan, Pavithra, and Steven White. 2020. "Slavery, Reconstruction, and Bureaucratic Capacity in the American South." *American Political Science Review*: 1–17.

Süssner, Henning. 2004. "Still Yearning for the Lost Heimat? Ethnic German Expellees and the Politics of Belonging." *German Politics and Society* 22 (2): 1–26.

Swianiewicz, Paweł. 1996. *Zróżnicowanie Polityk Finansowych Władz Lokalnych*. Warsaw: Inst. Badań nad Gospodarką Rynkową.

Szaflik, Jozef Ryszard. 2005. *Dzieje Ochotniczych Straży Pożarnych w Polsce*. Warsaw: Fundacja Edukacja i Technika Ratownictwa.

Szarota, Tomasz. 1969. *Osadnictwo Miejskie na Dolnym Śląsku w Latach 1945–1948*. Wrocław: Ossolineum-PAN.

Szmeja, Maria, ed. 2000. *Niemcy? Polacy? Ślązacy! Rodzimi Mieszkańcy Opolszczyzny w Świetle Analiz Socjologicznych*. Kraków: Universitas.

Szydłowska-Szczecińska, Agnieszka. 2017. "Gmina Mściwojów." www.msciwojow.pl/nasz-region/historia-gminy/.

Tajima, Yuhki. 2014. *The Institutional Origins of Communal Violence. Indonesia's Transition from Authoritarian Rule*. New York: Cambridge University Press.

Techman, Ryszard. 2000. "Przejmowanie Portu Szczecińskiego przez Polskie Władze w Latach 1945–1947." *Zestyty Odrzanskie* 18–19: 117–145.

Ther, Philipp. 1996. "The Integration of Expellees in Germany and Poland after World War II: A Historical Reassessment." *Slavic Review* 55 (4): 776–805.

Ther, Philipp, and Ana Siljak. 2001. *Redrawing Nations: Ethnic Cleansing in East-Central Europe, 1944–1948*. Lanham, MD: Rowman & Littlefield.

Thum, Gregor. 2011. *How Breslau Became Wroclaw during the Century of Expulsions*. Princeton, NJ: Princeton University Press.

Tilly, Charles. 1990. *Coercion, Capital and European States: AD 990–1990*. Cambridge, MA: Basil Blackwell.

Troen, S. Ilan. 1999. "Frontier Myths and Their Applications in America and Israel: A Transnational Perspective." *The Journal of American History* 86 (3): 1209–1230.

Tsebelis, George. 1995. "Decision Making in Political Systems: Veto Players in Presidentialism, Parliamentarism, Multicameralism and Multipartyism." *British Journal of Political Science* 25 (3): 289–325.

Turnau, Irena. 1960. *Studia nad Strukturą Ludnościową Polskiego Wrocławia*. Poznań: Instytut Zachodni.

Turner, Frederick Jackson. 1920. *The Frontier in American History*. New York: Henry Holt.

Urban, Wincenty. 1965. "Archidiecezja Wrocławska w Latach, 1945–1965." *Nasza Przeszłość: Studia z Dziejów Kościoła i Kultury Katolickiej w Polsce* 22: 11–68.

Urbatsch, Robert. 2017. "Long-Term Effects of Ethnic Cleansing in the Former Polish-German Borderlands." *Political Geography* 58: 56–66.

Uslaner, Eric M. 2002. *The Moral Foundations of Trust*. New York: Cambridge University Press.

Varshney, Ashutosh. 2002. *Ethnic Conflict and Civic Life: Hindus and Muslims in India*. New Haven: Yale University Press.

Verme, Paolo, and Kirsten Schuettler. 2020. "Impact of Forced Displacement on Host Communities: A Review of the Empirical Literature in Economics." *Journal of Development Economics* 150: 1–21.

Vickers, Paul Andrew. 2014. "Peasants, Professors, Publishers and Censorship: Memoirs of Rural Inhabitants of Poland's Recovered Territories (1945–c.1970)." Ph.D. diss. School of Modern Languages and Cultures, University of Glasgow.

Vogler, Jan. 2019. "Imperial Rule, the Imposition of Bureaucratic Institutions, and Their Long-Term Legacies." *World Politics* 71 (4): 806–863.

Wang, Yuhua. 2022. "Blood Is Thicker Than Water: Elite Kinship Networks and State Building in Imperial China." *American Political Science Review* 116 (3): 896–910.

Wejman, Grzegorz. 2007. *Organizacja Kościoła Katolickiego na Pomorzu Zachodnim i Ziemi Lubuskiej w latach 1945–1972*. Szczecin: Uniwersytet Szczeciński.

Weldon, Steven A. 2006. "The Institutional Context of Tolerance for Ethnic Minorities: A Comparative, Multilevel Analysis of Western Europe." *American Journal of Political Science* 50 (2): 331–349.

Wendt, Stefan. 2009. "Ein Experiment mit Folgen. Die Ansiedlung der Gablonzer Glas und Schmuckwaren-Industrie im Ehemaligen Mairnesperrwaffen Arsenal Trappenkamp." In *Fremdes Zuhause. Flüchtlinge und Vertriebene in Schleswig-Holstein nach 1945*, ed. Hermann Heidrich and Ilka E. Hillenstedt. Neumünster: Wachholtz Verlag.

Wierzbicki, Marek. 2014. "Soviet Economic Policy in Annexed Eastern Poland, 1939–1941." In *Stalin and Europe: Imitation and Domination, 1928–1953*, ed. Timothy Snyder and Ray Brandon. Oxford: Oxford Academic.

Wierzbicki, Zbigniew Tadeusz. 1960. "Adaptacja Emigracji ze Wsi Żmiąca (Powiat Limanowski) na Ziemiach Zachodnich." *Przegląd Zachodni* 16 (1): 94–112.

Wiesemann, Falk. 1995. "Flüchtlingspolitik in Nordrhein-Westfalen." In *Die Vertreibung der Deutschen aus dem Osten: Ursachen, Ereignisse, Folgen*. Frankfurt am Main: Fischer Taschenbuch Verlag.

Wilkinson, Steven. 2004. *Votes and Violence: Electoral Competition and Ethnic Riots in India*. Cambridge: Cambridge University Press.

Williamson, Oliver. 1979. "Transaction-Cost Economics: The Governance of Contractual Relations." *Journal of Law & Economics* 22 (2): 233–261.

Wimmer, Andreas. 2012. *Waves of War: Nationalism, State Formation and Ethnic Exclusion in the Modern World*. New York: Cambridge University Press.

Wimmer, Andreas. 2013. *Ethnic Boundary Making: Institutions, Power, Networks*. Oxford: Oxford University Press.

Wimmer, Andreas. 2016. "Is Diversity Detrimental? Ethnic Fractionalization, Public Goods Provision, and the Historical Legacies of Stateness." *Comparative Political Studies* 49 (11): 1407–1445.

Wimmer, Andreas, Lars-Erik Cederman, and Brian Min. 2009. "Ethnic Politics and Armed Conflict: A Configurational Analysis of a New Global Data Set." *American Sociological Review* 74: 316–337.

Witkowska, Lilia. 2021. "Historia mówiona: Lilia Witkowska, interviewed by Dariusz Zuber." Museum Historyczne w Ełku, muzeum.elk.pl/historia/lidia-witkowska/.

Witnica, Gmina. n.d. "Pyrżany." www.witnica.pl/index.php.

Wittenberg, Jason. 2006. *Crucibles of Political Loyalty: Church Institutions and Electoral Continuity in Hungary*. New York: Cambridge University Press.

Wolf, Nicolaus. 2007. "Endowments vs. Market Potential: What Explains the Relocation of Industry after the Polish Reunification in 1918?" *Explorations in Economic History* 44: 22–42.

Wolfs, Stefan. 2003. *The German Question since 1919: An Analysis with Key Documents*. Westport: Greenwood Publishing Group.

Wurzbacher, Gerhard. 1954. *Das Dorf im Spannungsfeld industrieller Entwicklung*. Stuttgart: Unesco-Institut für Sozialwissenschaften, Bd. 1.

Zahra, Tara. 2008. "The 'Minority Problem' and National Classification in the French and Czechoslovak Borderlands." *Contemporary European History* 17 (2): 137–165.

Zahra, Tara. 2010. "Imagined Noncommunities: National Indifference as a Category of Analysis." *Slavic Review* 69 (1): 93–119.

Zaremba, Marcin. 2001. *Komunizm, Legitymizacja, Nacjonalizm. Nacjonalistyczna Legitymizacja Władzy Komunistycznej w Polsce*. Warszawa: Wydawnictwo TRIO.

Zaremba, Marcin. 2012. *Wielka Trwoga. Polska 1944–1947*. Warsaw: Znak, ISP PAN.

Zarycki, Tomasz. 1999. *The New Electoral Geography of Central Europe*. Budapest, Virtus, Prague: Research Support Scheme Electronic Library, Open Society Institute.

Zarycki, Tomasz. 2015. "The Electoral Geography of Poland: Between Stable Spatial Structures and Their Changing Interpretations." *Erdkunde* 69 (2): 107–124.

Zaryn, Jan. 1997. *Kościół a Władza w Polsce 1945–1950*. Warsaw: Wydawnictwo DiG.

Zetter, Roger. 2021. "Refugees and Their Return Home: Unsettling Matters." *Journal of Refugee Studies* 34 (1): 7–22.

Žmegač, Jasna Čapo. 2005. "Ethnically Privileged Migrants in Their New Homelands." *Journal of Refugee Studies* 18 (2): 199–215.

Żurek, Jacek. 2009. *Ruch "Księży Patriotów" w Województwie Katowickim w Latach 1949–1956*. Warszawa-Katowice: Instytut Pamięci Narodowej.

Zwingelberg, Edward. 2021. "Historia mówiona: Edward Zwingelberg, interviewed by Stefan Marcinkiewicz." Museum Historyczne w Ełku, muzeum.elk.pl/historia/edward-zwingelberg/.

# Index

Herbert Kitschelt, *The Transformation of European Social Democracy*

Herbert Kitschelt, Kirk A. Hawkins, Juan Pablo Luna, Guillermo Rosas, and Elizabeth J. Zechmeister, *Latin American Party Systems*

Herbert Kitschelt, Peter Lange, Gary Marks, and John D. Stephens, eds., *Continuity and Change in Contemporary Capitalism*

Herbert Kitschelt, Zdenka Mansfeldova, Radek Markowski, and Gabor Toka, *Post-Communist Party Systems*

David Knoke, Franz Urban Pappi, Jeffrey Broadbent, and Yutaka Tsujinaka, eds., *Comparing Policy Networks*

Ken Kollman, *Perils of Centralization: Lessons from Church, State, and Corporation*

Allan Kornberg and Harold D. Clarke, *Citizens and Community: Political Support in a Representative Democracy*

Amie Kreppel, *The European Parliament and the Supranational Party System*

David D. Laitin, *Language Repertoires and State Construction in Africa*

Egor Lazarev, *State-Building as Lawfare: Custom, Sharia, and State Law in Postwar Chechnya*

Fabrice E. Lehoucq and Ivan Molina, *Stuffing the Ballot Box: Fraud, Electoral Reform, and Democratization in Costa Rica*

Benjamin Lessing, *Making Peace in Drug Wars: Crackdowns and Cartels in Latin America*

Janet I. Lewis, *How Insurgency Begins: Rebel Group Formation in Uganda and Beyond*

Mark Irving Lichbach and Alan S. Zuckerman, eds., *Comparative Politics: Rationality, Culture, and Structure, 2nd edition*

Evan Lieberman, *Race and Regionalism in the Politics of Taxation in Brazil and South Africa*

Richard M. Locke, *The Promise and Limits of Private Power: Promoting Labor Standards in a Global Economy*

Julia Lynch, *Age in the Welfare State: The Origins of Social Spending on Pensioners, Workers, and Children*

Pauline Jones Luong, *Institutional Change and Political Continuity in Post-Soviet Central Asia*

Pauline Jones Luong and Erika Weinthal, *Oil is Not a Curse: Ownership Structure and Institutions in Soviet Successor States*

Doug McAdam, John McCarthy, and Mayer Zald, eds., *Comparative Perspectives on Social Movements*

Gwyneth H. McClendon and Rachel Beatty Riedl, *From Pews to Politics in Africa: Religious Sermons and Political Behavior*

Lauren M. MacLean, *Informal Institutions and Citizenship in Rural Africa: Risk and Reciprocity in Ghana and Côte d'Ivoire*

Beatriz Magaloni, *Voting for Autocracy: Hegemonic Party Survival and its Demise in Mexico*

James Mahoney, *Colonialism and Postcolonial Development: Spanish America in Comparative Perspective*

James Mahoney and Dietrich Rueschemeyer, eds., *Historical Analysis and the Social Sciences*

Scott Mainwaring and Matthew Soberg Shugart, eds., *Presidentialism and Democracy in Latin America*

Melanie Manion, *Information for Autocrats: Representation in Chinese Local Congresses*

Scott de Marchi and Michael Laver, *The Governance Cycle in Parliamentary Democracies: A Computational Social Science Approach*

Milton Keynes UK
Ingram Content Group UK Ltd.
UKHW031446041124
2582UKWH00050B/295